Francis William Bain

Body and Soul

The Method of Economy

Francis William Bain

Body and Soul
The Method of Economy

ISBN/EAN: 9783744644853

Printed in Europe, USA, Canada, Australia, Japan

Cover: Foto ©Suzi / pixelio.de

More available books at **www.hansebooks.com**

BODY AND SOUL.

'THEY that have no *Science* are in better and nobler condition with their
' naturall Prudence, than men that by misreasoning, or by trusting them
' that reason wrong, fall upon false and absurd generall rules. For ignorance
' of causes and of rules does not set men so farre out of their way, as relying
' on false rules, and taking for causes of what they aspire to, those that
' are not so, but rather causes of the contrary.'—HOBBES.

'So plain a matter could never have been rendered intricate and volumi-
' nous, if authority had not imposed on such as pretend to reason ; and
' if such as did attempt to reason had not been caught in the common snares
' of sophism and bewildered in the labyrinths of disputation. In this case,
' as in all those of great concernment, the shortest and the surest method
' of arriving at real knowledge is to unlearn the lessons we have been
' taught ; to remount to first principles, and take nobody's word about
' them.'—BOLINGBROKE.

'THE body, or, as some love to call it, our inferior nature, is wiser in its
' own plain way and attends its own business more directly than the mind
' with all its boasted subtilty. And it were infinitely better to remain
' possessed of the whole legion of vulgar mistakes, than to reject some,
' and, at the same time, to retain a fondness for others altogether as absurd
' and irrational.'—BURKE.

BODY AND SOUL,

OR

THE METHOD OF ECONOMY.

BY

F. W. BAIN, M.A.,

FELLOW OF ALL SOULS' COLLEGE, OXFORD.

' Agere constituit esse.'

JAMES PARKER AND CO.

6 SOUTHAMPTON-STREET, STRAND, LONDON;

AND 27 BROAD-STREET, OXFORD.

1894.

CUSTODI ET SOCIIS

———◆———

O Custos gregis optimæ decusque,
et vos, O Socii nimis beati,
inter pocula sæpius remotâ
cenâ salibus Atticis fruentes ;
me si fata miserrimum perosa
fugavere, ubi cæsii leones
errant viva vagantium sepulcra,
solesque insidias parant iniquas
sparguntque ætherios ubique morbos,
serpentesque periculosiores
mortem dente minantur et veneno ;
at desiderium domus relictæ
altum in pectore delitet fideli,
vestræ et totus amans amænitatis
dulcem semper imaginem recondo.
ipsi dum deus haud dabit redire,
hoc vobis opus en ! bonum malumve
magnam partem animæ meæ reportat.
sic si præda leonibus cadaver
hic vivum inveniet procul sepulcrum,
ludis nostram animam tuis tenete
præsentem, Socii pii, futura
inter pocula sæpe gaudeantes.

SYNOPSIS.

BOOK I.
NATURAL ECONOMY, OR THE SPECIES. THE PRINCIPLE OF CREATION, DYNAMICAL EVOLUTION, AND DEFINITION.

BOOK II.
POLITICAL ECONOMY, OR THE COMMODITY. THE PRINCIPLE WORKING IN THE COMMON OR SOCIAL SPHERE.

BOOK III.
ÆSTHETICS, OR THE WORK OF ART. THE PRINCIPLE WORKING IN THE PECULIAR OR PERSONAL SPHERE.

BOOK IV.
ETHICS AND POLITICS, OR THE COMMONWEALTH. THE PRINCIPLE WORKING IN THE MORAL AND POLITICAL SPHERE.

ANALYSIS.

x   *Contents.*

PREFACE.

THIS book, though second in the order of time, is in reality the first volume of a work entitled *The Principle of Wealth Creation*, which I published last year.

I showed in that book how the true definition of Wealth is the central idea, out of which flows naturally and spontaneously the whole complicated Science of Wealth-Creation: an idea which conciliates the contradictions of all previous systems of Political Economy: explains, and thus refutes, constructively, their various one-sided errors; provides a simple and convincing solution of the perplexing problems of Money and Credit; and stands, in fact, to Political Economy exactly as the Copernican idea stood to Astronomy; being the focus, the *fons et origo*, of the whole economical order. Indeed, without this central idea, even history is unintelligible. For history during the last few centuries is simply the record of the process by which society has changed its structure: it was formerly organised on a feudal and hierarchical, military and ecclesiastical basis, and is now organised mainly on a commercial basis: a basis which can only be understood by means of the idea explained on *The Principle of Wealth Creation;* for the economical organisation of the whole of society flows deductively from it. Society is nothing but the material embodiment of that central idea, which is its soul.

In that book, however, I confined myself strictly to the purely economical point of view. Here, I have shown Political Economy, regarded as the Science of the Production and Distribution of Wealth, to be simply a special case of the universal law, that *Structure is determined by Function.* The whole of this book is new, except that portion of it—Book II.—which covers the same ground as *The Principle of Wealth Creation.* The reader, however, will find that the one account is no mere repetition of the other. For though I did not think I could find a better expression for the essential matter than is contained in that first volume, yet here I have been able to explain some points more fully and analytically than there : and each account will gain by being regarded as complementary to the other. This volume stands to the other as a whole to its part : and *The Principle of Wealth Creation* will therefore be of primary importance to any one who only wants that one part. But each volume is incomplete without the other.

A few words are necessary on the subject of this book. The original cause of the chaotic confusion and anarchical internecine strife which now reigns in the domain of Political Economy is the absence of the real heir to the throne : a true economical method. Our methods were originated by men entirely destitute of the qualifications necessary to their task. The methods on which we vainly endeavour to base all our mental and moral, social and political theories have come down to us by direct hereditary succession from an age of dense physiological ignorance. But now, *nemo psychologus, nisi physiologus.* All sound and permanent economical philosophy must and can only be based upon the essential nature of man : a nature essentially not logical, but biological. Neither the abstractions of the meta-physico-rationalistic, nor the mathematical formulæ of the me-chanico-material, method, will avail us here. The man who begins with abstractions must end with them : it is impossible to start from abstractions and arrive at reality. We could never have discovered the line from the point : nor the surface from the line ; nor the solid from the surface : we cannot deduce the facts of mechanics from mathematics, nor those of chemistry from mechanics : nor those of biology from either. At each new point of departure, at every stage onwards in the progress of science, some new unknown, some x, is introduced from without ; and this could never have been deduced or discovered from the premises of the previous step, for they did not contain it. But though the later is not in the earlier, the earlier, on the contrary, is contained in the later stage. Each has all that went before it, but none that came after it. The elements actually exist in the composition, but not 'vice versâ.' Therefore it is, that the ANALYTICAL DISSECTION OF CONCRETE REALITIES, which begins with the complex whole and resolves it into its component parts, going ever backwards, is the ONLY METHOD by which we can be sure of leaving out nothing : and thus the only method of discovering truth and arriving at certain and adequate principles in human affairs. For only thus can we view everything in *all its relations*, the *sine quibus non:* without which it does not and cannot exist at all. Everything is *what* it is, because it is *when* it is and *where* it is and *as* it is. Abstracted from its constituent relations, a fact or thing is a non-entity. Thus the 'laws' of 'orthodox' Political Economy are at once *entities* and *non-entities*, but never *realities*. They are nought, because they are merely the abstract denizens of a ghostly unreal sphere. Orthodox Political Economy is, in fact, neither *Natural* nor *Political* Economy. It knows nothing of the first, and pays no attention to it; while as to the second, it is actually based on a theory which is the negation of the State. Its true name is not Natural and Political Economy, but Unnatural and Sophistical Economy. True Political Economy is neither abstract nor hypothetical : it is essentially an ANALYTIC OF REALITIES. That Economical method alone can be fruitful of solid results which is rooted in its true soil, the biological investigation of real growths and processes. ' The worship of theories,' says the man of the world, ' is the idolatry of the young : the real ' question when considering the merits of a system is, *how does* ' *it work ?*' That is the very thesis of this essay.

Orthodox Political Economy is a failure, because its originators knew nothing about Method, and never dreamed of consulting the Oracle. The truth is, that it is impossible, not only to get away from Aristotle, but to do without him. It is not merely that, as Renan says, the Bible and Aristotle being the two greatest authorities that have reigned over the world, all history is unintelligible without either. It is not merely the past which is unintelligible without Aristotle ; it is the present. I made, after a long comparison and criticism of systems of Political Economy, a discovery : I awoke suddenly to another discovery,—viz., that I was but repeating Aristotle's central thought. It is the old story. Harvey, Wolf, Pander make a great embryological discovery : Aristotle did it before them. Von Baer makes another : that too belongs to Aristotle. Darwin always attributes the law of economy to Goethe and St. Hilaire, never suspecting that Aristotle knew it well before either of them. Darwin's own law of correlated variation was perfectly well known to Aristotle. And so on. Moreover, what is to these men all is but a tiny fragment of Aristotle. Aristotle is omnilateral. Marx's ' Capital' is only the expansion, misunderstood, of the passage about *Chrematistic* in Aristotle's

Politics,—that astonishing book, in which the history of Europe is found sketched beforehand. Who has added a line of essential significance to his Logic, his Rhetoric, his Ethics? nay, who has risen to his level? The Critical Philosophy, says Schopenhauer, lies in embryo in Aristotle's writings. Yes, and more than the Critical Philosophy. Who ever dreamed of the true meaning of Aristotle's Psychology till the *Origin of Species* brought back to man the consciousness of his relation to animals? For the true commentary to Aristotle is not to be found in Simplicius or Philoponus, Themistius or even Averroes; it is the *Origin of Species*—as I have shown for the first time in this book. And when we come to look into the matter, we find that biology, which abolishes the dummy Aristotle, idolised by the schoolmen, and overturned by Bacon, replaces the true Aristotle on his proper pedestal, and hails him as the Master of the Wise; the one man in all history who knew how to define.

Poona, 1893.

ἐπὶ τάφῳ Ἀριστοτέλους ἑπταγώνῳ.

α.

πάντα Χάος, καὶ πάντ᾽ Ἀπάτη, καὶ πάντα Σόφισμα·
Νοῦς γὰρ ὁ πάντα λύων ᾤχετ᾽ Ἀριστοτέλης.

β.

Ἄιδη ἀδωροδοκητὸν Ἀριστοτέλης ὑπέδυσεν
πάντων ἐξειδὼς αἴτια, πλὴν θανάτου.

γ.

αὐτὴν βουλομένη καθορᾷν ὡς ἐστί, κατόπτρῳ
ἡ φύσις ὀφθάλμοις χρῆται Ἀριστοτέλους.

δ.

' οἶος πέπνυται· τοὶ δὲ σκιαὶ ἀΐσσουσιν·'
μάντις Ἀριστοτέλει φθέγξαθ᾽ Ὅμηρος ἔπος.

ε.

κεῖμαι ἐγὼ σκότιος· τὸ δ᾽ ἐμοῦ πλέον ἥμισυ παντὸς
ὡς Φάρος ἐν σκοτίοις φώσφορός ἐστι βροτοῖς.

ζ.

ψεῦδος ἐμοῦγε λόγος ψυχῆς πέρι; πῶς γ᾽; ἀπόδειξις
αὐτὸς, ἔνεργος ἐών οὐσίᾳ ἀΐδιος.

η.

βῶμον Ἀριστοτέλει, χρυσὸν Πάριόν τε παρειδὼς,
ἀντενεργετικῶν τόνδ᾽ ἀνέθηκα λόγων.

BOOK I.

ERRATA.

p. v. line 4, *for* salibus *read* noctibus

,, ,, ,, 21, *for* tenete *read* tenentes

,, ,, ,, 23, *for* gaudeantes *read* gaudeatis

p. xv. ,, 2, *for* λύων *read* λάων

,, ,, ,, 14, *for* ἀντενεργετικῶν *read* ἀντευεργετικῶν

p. 130 *n.* I owe an apology to Professor Ingram for having been led to allude to him as defunct. I had observed him so referred to in a recent economical work, which fell into my hands just as this book was going to press, and only discovered the error too late to correct it.

p. 375, last line but one, *for* θατέρου θάτερου *read* θατέρου θάτερου

B

BOOK I.

NATURAL ECONOMY, OR THE SPECIES. THE PRIN-
CIPLE OF CREATION, DYNAMICAL EVOLUTION,
AND DEFINITION.

τὰ γὰρ ὄργανα πρὸς τὸ ἔργον ἡ φύσις ποιεῖ, ἀλλ' οὐ
τὸ ἔργον πρὸς τὰ ὄργανα.

De Partibus Animalium, iv. 12.

B

BOOK I.

I. THAT nothing in Nature is isolated : that everything alike acts upon, and is acted upon by others : that all things accordingly reciprocally limit and determine one another : that thus each is as it is, in and through its relations to others : that one thing is for the sake of another, and consequently Correlation, or Co-adaptation, the first law of Natural Economy: that all things must necessarily adapt themselves to the place they fill, and the work they have to do, on pain of disappearing : that therefore function is the *raison d'être* and scientific explanation of structure, *as such* : that the shapes of all bodies, natural, political, or mechanical, from the fin of the shark to the Cabinet Government of England, are given to them and determined by the end they serve : that all institutions whatsoever take their form from the necessities that call them into being: that the constitution of all things organical, mechanical, moral, or social, religions, languages, political forms, traditions, customs, manners, laws, weapons, tools, instruments and what not, derives from the need for them, and answers strictly to special requirements, *on pain of death* : that all these things are but instruments and tools to perform certain definite

work : that everything truly is, only in so far as and
so long as it is able to do its appropriate work :
that, in short, *work* is the soul of everything in the
world, and the only principle of creation, definition,
and explanation : that we know what a thing is,
just in so far as we know what it is *for :* that the
reason for its existence, *as such*, and the cause of
its generation, *as such*, and the original why and
wherefore of its peculiar form, is just the special
work it has to do, and that, apart from its constituent relations, nothing is or can be ;—all these
are but different ways of expressing the same great
truth,—the truth κατ' ἐξόχην, the alpha and omega
of Natural Economy, the creative soul of Nature,
that *Function makes Structure.*

This truth was the central conception of the
philosophy of Aristotle, the superlative genius, who
coming at a time when all had still to be done,
nevertheless accumulated so vast a variety of facts,
and interpreted them with so piercing an insight,
that he was able to discover and complete, alone
and unassisted, the whole logic of science, carrying
it in many directions at a single bound to a height
to which even after two thousand years the world
has not yet attained. And now, when by the
united efforts of successive ages that mass of physiological data on which his scientific method rested
has once more been accumulated, Darwin has, by
his *Origin of Species*, once more established, im-
plicitly though not explicitly,—for Darwin was not
Aristotle,— that essential truth upon which all economical philosophy, whether natural or political,
must depend : and without which it must either fall
in ruins, or hang unsupported in the air, without

scientific justification. For it is nothing but the ignorance of this cardinal truth and its corollaries that has led astray the philosophy, mental and moral, social and political, of the last three hundred years ; during which, in an age of physiological darkness, men whose critical qualifications in comparison with those of Aristotle can only raise a smile have, in complete unconsciousness of their own inadequate equipment, founded rationalistic schools of all kinds, agreeing in nothing but their rejection, and even virulent abuse, of a man whose wisdom was all the time not beneath but above their comprehension : a man of whom we can but say that Nature seems to have made him in a moment of braggadocio, just to show what she could do. Nor is this all, for where error is only theoretical it is of less moment : but on the contrary, the failure to realise this truth lies at the bottom of those vicious political theories which have worked so disastrously in practice, and which have led historians radically to misconceive and misrepresent, in entire good faith, the history of the past, and give to all political moments and events a wholly false colour. Finally, in their ignorance of this very soul of economy, so-called Economists have put forth a chaotic jumble of one-sided and fragmentary abstractions, and baptized it the Science of Political Economy : whose preposterous assumptions and glaring inapplicability to the business of life have brought the whole subject into contempt and derision among people conversant and familiar with affairs. It is questionable, indeed if there has ever existed in the world any body of men whatever at once so arrogantly dogmatic and so totally mistaken, so dictatorial and so profoundly incompetent for their task, as the *quasi*-professors of orthodox Political Economy.

To explain, then, the exact significance of this truth, that Function makes Structure : to point out the cause of the erroneous methods by which men have attempted to investigate Natural, and *a fortiori* Political Economy : to show how the *Origin of Species* has restored the true point of view : and to illustrate by reference to the theory of Darwin and the philosophy of Aristotle the essential scheme of Natural Economy, and the necessarily resulting Principle of Scientific Explanation and Definition, which is and can be nothing but the mirrored image of the Principle of Creation, will be the aim of this first book. In the second, I shall show how this truth is the key to difficulties in Political Economy that have hitherto defied solution : how alike in the body natural or body politic, with the animal or the commodity, the same principle is at work, creating and destroying in answer to imperative necessity ; how things *are*, as they *do*, and handsome is as handsome does : how, in fact, the *operari* is the key to the *esse*, and the *esse* again to the *operari*. The third book deals with the æsthetic side of Wealth, which has been so entirely neglected by Economists that one might almost read their works all through without suspecting that the creations of music and sculpture, architecture and painting are Wealth at all. The last book will be devoted to an examination of the political significance and ethical tendency of the principle, where I shall show that nothing in political organisation or history is intelligible without it. And should the leisurely and impartial reader succeed in reaching the end of that book, he will be in a position to realise how much more accurately the words which Bacon applied to himself apply to Aristotle. Aristotle is the man who might with reason have exclaimed, *Equidem Organum præbui: materies vero a rebus ipsis petenda est.* For he did in very truth, old master wizard that he was, cunningly boil·down and extract in his great bronze Organon the hidden secrets of beasts and herbs, and press forth their quintessential virtues and properties into a golden phial that should last for ever. But we have got past Aristotle now? yes, quantitatively but not qualitatively. We know more facts, but do not understand them so well as he did. For facts are nothing; it is their interpretation which is all. Ours are the facts: but Aristotle supplied the organic method which is the key to their meaning, and their string of connection.

For philosophising without method may be accurately compared to sewing without thread: whatever pains and labour we may take, we shall accomplish nothing: we may pick up our arguments, like beads, one after another upon the needle of our wit, but having no string to hold them together we shall end with no chain, but the same old heap of isolated units we started to connect. And to vary the metaphor we may add, that just as method is the thread that gives to every link in a chain of reasoning its force and significance, so from another point of view is method the skein, the *filum labyrinthi*, the clue to the mazes of Natural and Political Economy, grasping which we may thread with sure step the dark ramifications and obscure windings of reality, losing our way in none of the intricate and involved side alleys of the subject, because we still hold fast our connection with the origin of all, and can accordingly return at will upon ourselves, or emerge into upper air. But on the contrary, those who have hitherto spoken with authority on Political Economy have been either without any method at all, or still worse, have trusted to the guidance of a wrong one, and hence, after much wandering about in the dark, they have finally gone entirely astray. And the cause of this is to be found in the philosophical systems to which they fell heirs.

II. The age in which Aristotelian Scholasticism flourished was an age of profound biological ignorance. The Schoolmen who worshipped Aristotle knew nothing of him, least of all on the biological side, which was just the heart of the matter. They were acquainted only with his superstructure, the logical upper story of his giant edifice, and used it or misused it with unfaltering intrepidity for their ends. They made of it, as all know, an *ancilla theologiæ*, but that was all: it was its logical and theological application that served their turn. But they could not either comprehend or appreciate it, in its totality. They galvanised it into a fictitious activity; they could do no more, for it was in their hands like a plant separated from its root, its biological soil. They were utterly destitute of that wide, and, indeed, for Aristotle's time really phenomenal knowledge of plants and animals, their varieties and their habits, their external and internal organisation, their biological generation and development, which astounds us even at this day, and on which he built up his whole logic of science. Without this basis, he is unintelligible. Knowing however, as they did, absolutely nothing of his foundations, but wielding his logic as a weapon in their theological disputations, their Aristotelianism of the Schools had the appearance of a fantastic and visionary unreality : it hung, so to speak, in the air, supported only by the prodigious intellectual gymnastics of Invincible and Angelic Doctors, who toiled on at their task like men under a spell. They toiled on, perpetually, endlessly combining and permutating hieroglyphics whose true meaning was hidden from them : just as men who should constantly be using such symbols as H_2O, or H_2SO_4, without understanding how they were arrived at.

Now when at the Reformation epoch the human mind began to throw off the chains that had kept it in bondage for a thousand years (Rabelais contains the real spirit of the period), this was the way in which Aristotelianism struck the philosophers who led the revolt against the scholastic method. Fine distinctions are not drawn by leaders of the public mind in an age of revolution, simply because an ignorant and bigoted public selects ignorant and bigoted leaders. All that belonged to the old order was bad : this was a principle on which the philosopher found himself at one with the religious and half-educated zealot. The philosophers who led this revolt were, it is to be carefully observed, in a physiological darkness quite as great as that of the Schoolmen whom they displaced. They were not one whit more able : nay, it is more than doubtful whether they were, in point of ability, on a level with the great scholastic hair-splitters whom they treated so cavalierly or so unmercifully abused. But as the whole science of these scholastic argumentators seemed to them to hang in the air and to be based on nothing, they tossed it impatiently aside. The deep wisdom which lurked, ' like gold in a dungheap,' in that scholastic logic was entirely hidden from the eyes of men who were bent—quite correctly, moreover,—upon returning to Nature. Here they were both right and wrong. Aristotle himself would have said to them : You are as certainly right in what you affirm, as you are wrong in what you deny. That fact and experience are the basis of all philosophy is beyond question : I know that better than you do. Here you are right : but you are wrong in condemning my logic of science, which you do not understand. That however is not perhaps your fault. To appreciate me, you must wait till you are as widely and closely familiar with the facts of natural history, biology, embryology, and development as I was. Then you will make amends and reparation to me. You owe me an apology, but I will wait. And indeed he could afford to be patient. *Patiens quia æternus.* He had ruled despotically over the human mind for ever so many hundred years ; and in the fulness of time when his facts had been rediscovered and his points of view regained, his imperial position would return. Till then he could lie still, like old Barbarossa, biding his time.

But this was for the future : in the meanwhile, the philosophers of that day erected their schools on the ruins of Scholasticism. They proceeded bravely on, building on no foundation, little knowing how impossible all attempts to establish a permanent philosophy of man and society must be, with no previous knowledge of organic nature, of which man is but a special case. *Gliscit intellectus humanus:* and if it has not the proper materials, the human mind will use anything ready to hand, so that only it may seem to be erecting something architecturally imposing. In rejecting Aristotle, they started philosophy on two entirely different lines. Descartes stands at the head of the one school : Bacon, at that of the other.

III. The method of Descartes was indeed widely different from that of Aristotle. Aristotle's philosophy started everywhere from the fact ; the objective fact to be explained : and always considered and contemplated all facts in their own peculiar relations, knowing well that out of these, a fact is not a fact at all. Descartes, on the contrary, began by denying all facts. He admitted nothing. He started from within himself, and having so started he never could get out, except to leap wildly in the dark, and go he knew not where. Across the bottomless gulf that now severed him from reality, he could not pass. But the cardinal error he made was his initial assumption : the subject or *ego.* The subject is, in reality, the precondition of knowledge, for it is the knower : *but it can only acquire a knowledge of itself by inference from objects.* The perceived fact is the first starting-point for the percipient subject. Only by inference can it know itself from objects, can it know its own existence. This is not only the rigorous, critical truth, but all history proves it. Early man in all ages and places begins naïvely and objectively : only by *re*flection, by

arguing from others to himself, can he become self-
conscious. Self-consciousness is not a starting-
point, but the attainment of a long series of ages.
To start, as Descartes did, from the self, is not
only a critical, but a historical blunder. It is
starting from a high stage in development; and
further, it is essentially nihilistic. Accordingly
Descartes, the philosopher who begins by radically
denying all history, tradition, and objectivity, not
only radically errs by founding philosophy on an
abstraction—the self removed from those conditions
which made it what it is, and in relation to which
alone it can exist—and thus annihilating it: but
also lays the fatal egg, from out of which proceed, in
which lurk embryonically, moral and political nihilism. Hume and Bakunin are but logical de-
velopments of Descartes. Abstract rationalistic
philosophy and politics spring from his *Cogito ergo
sum.* This, then, says Faust, when Mephistopheles
emerged from the poodle, was the poodle's kernel!
To the logical Cartesian what can the world be,
but a mere series of shadow-pictures, together or
in sequence? a mere dream? Such a philosopher,
exclaims Aristotle, annihilates the whole of Nature's
creation. To such a man, the very conception of
a dynamical evolution of Nature from protoplasm
to high organisation is a pure delusion. A magic-
lantern is the best philosophy, from the abstract
theoretical standpoint of Descartes. What is absent from his pictures is *power, force:* the chemical
energy of Nature: the wondrous dynamite that
drives Creation's wheel. Descartes is simply the
hypostasis of an abstract entity: a description after
the fact: a metaphysical scholasticism worse by

far than that which he dethroned. For that, though it had forgotten its origin, nevertheless *had* its origin in the analysis of realities ; but this was simply explaining *obscurum per obscurius.* And thus the philosophies which have been based on his foundation in later times, as those of Kant or Comte and their followers, have proved this only, that nothing can be based upon the rationalistic self, except nihilism. But if, now, there is one thing rather than another to which all history, fact, experience, and sentiment bear witness, it is this, that Nature is not rational, but real. These subjective philosophers would have been far wiser, if they had, —as in fact one and one only of all of them did— founded their philosophy not on the self of reason, but the self of feeling, not on the head but the heart, not the Self-Consciousness, but the Self-Will. For the Self-Will, with its passions, is deeper and more organic, more universal, more connective, than the Self of conscious ideas. Accordingly, it was well said of Schopenhauer, the solitary philosopher here referred to, that he was not a philosopher like the others, but a philosopher who had seen the world. For it is just this feeling of reality, of life, of work, of passion, of sympathy and energy, of doing and suffering, which is entirely absent from the lucubrations of the philosophers of the Cartesian school. But not one of these philosophers has succeeded in explaining anything. The self cannot be a principle of explanation : it requires itself to be explained. It is itself in Nature, acting and reacting. The soul, not, as from within, a self, but as from without, the total energetic activity of all the special organic functions of that body of which it is the

soul :—there is Aristotle ; how different from Descartes !—but for the present we pass over this contrast, only observing that all that is sound in
either the Cartesian or Critical philosophies is
thoroughly appreciated and fully expressed by
Aristotle himself.   As we proceed, the reader will
have ample opportunity of perceiving the deep
essential error lurking in the Cartesian position.
Yet it is not sufficient to confine ourselves here to
general indications, because these are vague, and
it is necessary to go into particulars.   Only in
this way can we hope to persuade the partisans of
a definite error that it *is* an error :   only thus can
we guard ourselves against the common counter-
charge of all irritated opponents, that the critic
has misunderstood what he denounces.   Nothing,
in fact, is easier, than to expose the logic of the
idealistic or sensational school.   Their thesis is
either a tautology, or a most miserable sophism.

Schopenhauer says, for example : ' Locke has
' completely and exhaustively proved that the feel-
' ings of our senses, even admitting them to be
' roused by external causes, cannot have any re-
' semblance whatever to the qualities of those causes.
' Sugar, for example, bears no resemblance at all to
' sweetness, nor a rose to redness ª.'   Now, what
does ' *sugar*,' or ' *rose* ' mean here ?   If ' sugar ' means
that which we see, who ever said it was like sweetness ?   If ' rose ' means that which we smell or
handle, who ever said it was like redness ?   But if,
on the other hand, by ' sugar ' or ' rose ' we mean,
that which lies behind the sensation of sweetness

ª *The Fourfold Root of the Principle of Sufficient Reason.   Eng.
Trans.*, p. 96.

or redness, then how in the world can we say that it is not like sweetness or redness ? *Ex hypothesi*, it is unknown ; and to compare two things, we must know them both. We cannot institute any comparison between two terms, only one of which we know. In this sense, to say, sugar is not like sweetness, or a rose, redness, has absolutely no meaning at all. It is nonsense. We have just as much right to say it is like, as that it is unlike. Just so J. S. Mill : 'an east wind is not like the feeling 'of cold.' Why, what on earth does he mean ? The truth is, all these 'thinkers' are the victims of their own over-subtilty. What they quarrel with is knowledge, for being what it is : for not being something else. When Kant tells us, e.g., that 'we know only appearances, never things in them- ' selves,' he appears very deep, but is really talking pure nonsense. To know = not to know, that is all he is saying : it is a mere quibble, a play upon the word know ; not nearly so amusing as many other plays upon words. The answer to Kant is simply, that things in themselves *are* appearances *on that side,*—i.e. to us. Knowledge *means* that. *Things in themselves,* forsooth ! things are not 'in themselves,' but in relations, of which knowledge is one. But Kant cries for the moon ; he wants to *know,* out of relation. Let us suppose, for example, that some deity were to appear, and grant to Kant a knowledge of things in themselves : he would immediately say, from that new stand- point, that he knew only appearances, not things in themselves. Let another deity appear, and again give him a knowledge of these : he would say the same : and so on to infinity. He quarrels

with knowledge for being what it is, and not something else. Because knowledge is a relation, therefore it is not knowledge, says Kant. These unfor-
tunate persons, in fact, all stand in sore need
of a little dose of Aristotle : he has refuted by
anticipation all their vagaries by pointing out the
distinction between the thing as actually visible,
and as potentially visible [b]. Of course, we never
can see the potentially visible, because, in the act of
vision, it becomes actually visible. ' Take away
' the thinking subject and the whole material world
' must vanish,' says Kant : 'because it is nothing
' but a phenomenon in the sensibility of our own
' subject and a certain class of its representations.'
Must vanish?—yes, *quá perceived.* Everybody
knew that : the knowledge must disappear with the
knower. But the known—does that disappear ?
Did Rome cease to exist when great Cæsar fell ?
The whole thing is a mere play upon the meaning
of the word ' world : ' world as being, and world as
known. Upon such a miserable quibble is the
Kantian philosophy founded.

But let us proceed. ' We know only our sensa-
' tions, or representations, never things in them-
' selves.' Now, let us ask the holder of this quibbling
thesis : Is there such a thing as error, illusion,
deception ? He must say No : deny the fact.
For suppose he says, Yes : then, how does he
know it ? The moment he admits that he knows,
at any given moment, or in any given illustration,
that he is being deceived, as, for example, when
looking at a stick which *appears* bent in water, yet
is not : or contemplating the *mirage* in the Arabian

[b] *De Animá*, iii. 2.

Desert, which *appears* to be water close at hand, yet is not : then he admits that he has, at one and the same moment, a sensation, and a knowledge of that which lies behind the sensation, and his thesis is destroyed^c. But if, on the other hand, he prefers to deny the fact, and say No : we can but leave him to revel in that error or illusion of which he denies the possibility. For the end of philosophy is to explain facts : and a philosophy which either begins or ends by denying the facts to be explained is simply nothing at all.

Or take an astronomical illustration. Astronomy is the grand stumbling-block for the philosophy of idealism, which starts from the *ego*. Astronomers tell us that the moon's face is always turned towards us, because it revolves around the earth in exactly the same time as it turns around on its axis : that is to say, that, relatively to the earth, it does not revolve. It acts just as though it were tied to the earth by an iron rod passing through it. Now, let the idealist take a plate, and lay it on the table. This plate, now, will act precisely like the moon. In twenty-four hours it will have revolved on its own axis, as the earth revolves. Let the idealist watch it steadily for the whole of that time, and then let us ask him, Has it revolved? He must say No ; denying the fact. For during the whole time, as far as he can see, it has lain absolutely still. If, on the contrary, he says Yes : then how does he know ? He is expressly assert-

^c So when we stand between two railway lines, and look up them, they *appear* to get closer together, the farther they go. But we *know* that they do not, otherwise the train could not run on them.

C

ing a knowledge respecting the plate which sensation not only cannot give him, but which it positively contradicts. Thus he is asserting a knowledge of the noumenon lying behind the sensation. On the other hand, if he prefers to deny the
fact, and say No: then doubtless the Astronomer
Royal would be glad to hear from him. The
scientific world would be interested in knowing his
grounds for denying the exploded Newtonian
theory. For, though no one has remarked it, (it
would have been very inconvenient), the idealist
must consistently deny that the earth moves round
the sun. For here appearances bear direct testimony to the reverse of what is the fact. If any
man holds the Newtonian theory of the universe,
he is directly asserting a knowledge of what lies
behind his sensations. For his senses tell him that
the earth is fixed, and that the sun moves round
it, with all the host of the stars. The heliocentric
theory of the solar system is a direct contradiction
to the anthropocentric Cartesian egoism.

In nothing does Kant more clearly show his
clumsy incapacity of thinking than in the terrible
pedantry with which he maps out the mind and
its Categories of the Understanding, Reason, and
what not. Psychologists ought to be absolutely
forbidden to use the words reason, understanding,
imagination, &c. These are only abstract general-
isations for special sorts of acts, and we ought
never to speak of them in the abstract, without
being on our guard. We may say, 'I judge,' 'I
imagine;' or 'the man judges, imagines,' and so
forth, with perfect propriety; but this merely states
a fact, and contains no abstract theorising or pre-

judice as to separate faculties, of which we know
nothing. But Kant carries this vicious procedure
to the very borders of absurdity. The whole of
his schematising, and indeed his whole philosophy,
save only the Transcendental Æsthetic, has been
pulverised by his greatest admirer, Schopenhauer.
Kant's only discovery, says the latter, is that Time,
Space, and Causality, are forms of intuition.
But this is but an empty truism. How is it
to assist us in understanding perception? The
difficulty lies not in the *general* temporal, spatial,
and causal relations of things, to which our mind
must necessarily conform, like other things, but in
the *special* temporal, spatial, and causal differences
of perceived bodies. Does the mind bestow upon
things their differences, forsooth? does it take to
itself an amorphous chunk of the *Ding-an-sich* and
turn it, now into boots, now a hat, now a stick?
But it is mere waste of time, exposing the shame-
less ineptitude of this bastard philosophy: ἀλλὰ
γὰρ εὔηθες τὸ τοὺς εὐήθεις τῶν λόγων λίαν ἐξετάζειν.

The curious thing, one of the strange aberrations
of the human mind, is that philosophers of *e.g.*, the
Kantian school, who assert that space is simply
the *form of intuition*, shriek with horror if you
suggest that the *ego is extended.* But here is a
dilemma. If the *ego* is not extended, then, as it
undoubtedly perceives spatially extended objects,
it perceives something not itself. Why not therefore real objects at once? If, on the contrary, the
ego is extended, then it must be in space. On either
horn the idealist will be compelled to admit the real
and absolute existence of space. Or we may, if we
choose, put it thus. I perceive the very objects

themselves, says the unsophisticated person. No, says the Kantian, you are mistaken : you perceive nothing of the sort : your visible object is merely the result of a very complicated physiological process in your brain. *Brain?* why, what do you mean ? How do I know that I have a brain ? *I cannot perceive my own brain:* then, pray, WHERE is it ? The fact is that the idealistic philosopher gets the knowledge of his brain by inference from objects, and then uses this inferential knowledge to base upon it a denial of objects : thus turning in a vicious circle. The evolutionist can easily sweep all these cobwebs away by a simple observation ; that our ideas and sensations do and must accurately correspond to the realities is proved by the fact that we are here : that is to say, have succeeded in adapting ourselves to our surroundings. Otherwise we should have gone out long ago.

But indeed, what point of community could there be between Kant, who laid it down that the form of things was given to them by our perception, and Aristotle, who knew that the forms of things are given to them by their function : between Kant, whose *dictum* is *esse* is *percipi*, and Aristotle, whose *dictum* might be expressed, *agere constituit esse:* between Kant, who held that we read teleology into Nature, and Aristotle, who knew that teleology was the soul of Nature : between Kant, who held that Time and Space are but forms of Intuition : and Aristotle, who knew that the intellect, like other things, has been developed from form to form in time and space : between Kant, who held that Causality was but the link imposed *a priori* by the intellect upon phenomena, and Aristotle, who knew that causality was the link that connected and accounted for the whole chain of creation? Or what point of community is there between Aristotle, who made such an analysis of causation as none but himself has ever done, and Hume, whose philosophy, apart from its bad psychology (i.e. the confusion of ideas, notions, and perceptions, with feelings and sensations) is based upon the vulgar confusion of the concepts *force* and *cause :* dynamical power, and antecedent conditions. A spark is applied to the gunpowder : result, an explosion. The cause is *patent,* = all the conditions ; but the *power,* or *force,* is *immanent* in them. Why, even Kit Marlowe could have taught Hume here. Faust says to Mephistopheles :

> ' Did not my conjuring raise thee ? speak ! '

and Mephistopheles answers :

> ' That was the cause : but yet *per accidens.*'

And his Satanic Majesty was quite right. Aha! *tu non pensavi ch' io loico fosse.* Because the eye cannot *see* force, *ergo,* we know none—there is Hume in a nutshell. A blow in the eye in a dark room is the true answer to this sort of philosophy. Moreover, it is ludicrous to note the complete un-consciousness of these philosophers of the existence of more kinds of causes than one[d]. The only

---

[d] There are four species of cause, material, formal, final, and efficient. Hume and his school are entirely unaware of all but the first. A glove fits the hand. Is there nothing, in the relation of the glove to the hand, but invariable antecedence? *Constancy forms the very essence of necessity,* says Hume (*Essays,* p. 366, *note*). *Very essence !* what an expression for Hume ! What, then, have things essences ? Is there no *reason why* the glove is so shaped ?

cause they know of is the *material* cause, interior power, or energy; and as they cannot see the necessary tie, they deny it. ' *All causation is nothing but invariable antecedence.*' Well, let us ask Hume this question : What is the cause of the form of a razor? *Must* not a razor, if it is to cut, be sharp? be, that is to say, of a definite and peculiar form such as will perform the function of cutting? Is there no necessity here? No necessity in Nature, forsooth? *Must* not animals feed, or die? *Must* not all organic beings adapt themselves to their conditions, or die? Is there no *necessity* in the struggle for existence? Why, necessity is the key to Natural Economy: structure is necessarily determined by function : all organic forms are shaped of necessity to and for the work they have to do : and disgrace has necessarily fallen upon philosophy, because a set of uncritical pedants have monopolised her, who hand on to one another the Cartesian error, conceived and begotten by a hermaphroditic and self-impregnated dreamer, in dense physiological ignorance, in total isolation from the world, and carefully nourished by book-worms, commentators, Germans and boobies during the last hundred years till it has sunk into a quibbling and imbecile senility. Just think, in connection with idealism, of even a hen's egg, out of which develops a chicken : consider the marvellous forces in that egg, and ask, is embryology consistent with Hume, with a world of *ideas* and *impressions, representations, sensations* and what not? But nature, says the Master, is not like a mere casual series of spectacular phenomena, without a plot : no mere disconnected show of coexistences and successions,

like a Transpontine melodrama, or J. S. Mill's
sensational philosophyᵉ.

IV. Such then is the one school which arose on
the ruins of Aristotelian Scholasticism: the philosophy which we may style the essentially Continental philosophy : which starting with an abstract
entity, seeks to evolve the whole economy of Nature
from its inner consciousness, and appears philosophically as absolute idealism in meditative Germany, politically as anarchy and nihilism in revolutionary France or mystic Russia. The other
school, the school of Bacon, Galileo, and Newton,
is a school of quite another kind. This school is
not, like the other, essentially visionary and abstract :
it is not essentially erroneous : it errs only relatively ; i.e. when it seeks to apply its own methods
to a sphere where they do not hold. Its method is,
in its own sphere, valid and excellent : but it errs
in attempting to extend its mechanical method to
the biological sphere. This is of extreme importance. The danger of this method lies just in the
argument, that because it is valid in its own sphere,
it must be so universally. Let us look into the
matter.

Bacon was not, like Descartes, a subjective philosopher : on the contrary. His philosophy, like
that of Aristotle, started from the fact. He might,
indeed, had he wished to have marked his starting-
point distinctively from that of Descartes, have

ᵉ οὐ γὰρ ἔοικεν ἡ φύσις ἐπεισοδιώδης οὖσα ἐκ τῶν φαινομένων, ὥσπερ
μοχθηρὰ τραγωδία. *Metaph.* xiii. 3. It is, as Professor Case says,
and has proved in his book on *Physical Realism,* 'the cognition
of the imperceptible' which annihilates idealistic and sensational
philosophy.

said, instead of *Cogito ergo sum : Percipio, ergo sunt.*
He condemned Aristotle, without entirely understanding him. He set aside the philosophy that
hung in the air, playing with vague notions hastily
abstracted from things, and not based upon solid
observation and experiment. But in this he was
both right and wrong. He was right, and Aristotle
would have been with him, against his own followers, in condemning a method of philosophising
not based upon natural facts. He was, further,
right in this respect also, that the strictly mechanical
side of Aristotle's philosophy was in truth its weak
side. But Aristotle was not to blame for this : it
could not have been otherwise. Aristotle had no
telescope or microscope : he could see neither the
big nor the little of existence : he could see only
that which lay in the middle, open to his own
piercing eye : he had no retort, no electrophorus, no
crucible : he did not start, like Newton, on the
shoulders of Galileo, Copernicus, and Kepler. He
knew, and could know nothing of the chemical,
material elements of material bodies. Bacon, then,
is so far right in condemning Aristotle's physics
proper. But he is, on the other hand, wrong, when
he condemns Aristotle's logic of science, and his organic method. He had not the requisite biological
knowledge to appreciate it. Nor can anything
show us more clearly, than a contrast between
Bacon and Aristotle, as to their fundamental ideas
and ends, the radical inapplicability and insufficiency
of the mechanical method in the sphere of organic
life : and the way in which one great man will
condemn another for faults which are in truth
virtues, and would be recognised as such, had the

critic only the knowledge that would enable him to appreciate them.

Bacon, as all the world knows, placed the great end and object of science in the discovery of forms, and condemned very strongly the Aristotelian teleology and logic, as opposed to the true spirit of scientific investigation. Final causes corrupt science: such was the dictum of Bacon. Now, Bacon here was quite right, *from his own point of view.* What he did not perceive was that the aim of Aristotle was something quite different from his own. He was, in fact, utterly at cross purposes with Aristotle. As far as Bacon went, Aristotle would entirely have agreed with him: but the latter had a deeper and higher insight, springing from his physiological knowledge, which Bacon entirely lacked: hence his misunderstanding[1]. The

---

[1] *Aristoteles, qui philosophiam naturalem dialecticâ suâ corrupit ; quum mundum ex categoriis effecerit: animæ humanæ, nobilissimæ substantiæ, genus ex vocibus secundæ intentionis tribuerit: negotium densi et rari, per quod corpora subeunt majores et minores dimensiones sive spatia, per frigidam distinctionem actus et potentiæ transegerit: motum singulis corporibus unicum et proprium, et si participent ex alio motu, id aliunde moveri, asseruerit; et innumera alia, pro arbitrio suo, naturæ rerum imposuerit: magis ubique sollicitus quomodo quis respondendo se explicet, et aliquid reddatur in verbis positivum, quam de internâ rerum veritate. Nov. Org.* i. 63.

All this, unfortunately, is pure nonsense, and only shows how immensely inferior the critic was to his subject. Observe, that Bacon expressly speaks, not of Aristotelianism, but Aristotle himself. He says he was worse than his followers, for they deserted experience altogether, whereas he took it captive, and forced it into harmony with its own arbitrary dogmas. Let the reader judge, after reading the account of Aristotle given below, how far this charge is true.

fact is, that Bacon was looking for that which was
common to things outwardly or apparently different : Aristotle was looking for a principle of
explanation of differences amongst things otherwise
the same.   Bacon was looking for *fundamental
identity* under *differences*, in the processes and
states of Nature: e.g. heat, light, and so forth,
which *identity* he called the law of pure action, the
latent process, or form, of heat.   Aristotle, on the
contrary, was attempting to explain the *differences*
or *varieties* of *structures* otherwise *identical*, which
differences he asserted to have their origin and
principle of existence in the difference of work or
function to be performed.   Bacon, in fact, is aiming
at gaining command over the processes and forces
of nature for mechanical ends by discovering the
nature of those processes; Aristotle is aiming at
nothing but the knowledge of Natural and Political
Economy.   Hence Bacon's Form is the mechanical
law of a process : Aristotle's Form, the shape or
structure of an organised body determined for a
special work.   Hence the two are totally different
things : and from this one may see the want of
insight in those who have compared the two, and
debated whether they were the same.   Further,
Aristotle was perfectly aware of the two methods.
He says expressly, 'the method of absolute mate-
' rial necessity, and that of structural or organic
' necessity, are two entirely different things [g],' and,
as I shall show, never had the slightest intention of
making one usurp the place of the other.˙ But he
devoted his attention principally to the second,

[g] ὁ τρόπος τῆς ἀποδείξεως καὶ τῆς ἀνάγκης ἕτερος.   *De Part. Anim.*
i. i.

because the Greeks, living in a warm climate, and requiring very little in the way of mechanical appliances or comforts to make their lives good, did not want to make Nature subserve their material ends so much as to understand her economy. Thus, though Bacon was quite right in looking for his own form, and in asserting that experiment and observation alone could discover it (for only by this means can the properties of matter *as such* be disclosed) ; he was, on the other hand, quite wrong, in condemning the logic of Aristotle, which was based on biology, and which aimed at an entirely different thing. Of this on a future page. It was entirely beside the mark to accuse Aristotle's philosophy of not leading to fruits, a charge which has been echoed by later writers after Bacon : all being entirely ignorant of the greatness of the man they were condemning. Hallam, *e.g.*, does but express the common criticism and the common ignorance when he says : ' The Aristotelian philosophy, *even in the hands of* ' *the master*, was like a barren tree that conceals its ' want of fruit by profusion of leaves[h].' There is more than mere Philistinism, there is dense ignorance in this sort of criticism. Where is the fruit in Newton's *Principia*, in Darwin's *Origin of Species* ? Whose bread will these great works butter ? Are we to scout the wonderful discoveries of Harvey and Von Baer (that is to say, of Aristotle), because they will not help us to make steam engines ? Is there any ' fruit ' in history—in Hallam's histories, for example ? And if so, if political wisdom be fruit, is there not more of it in Aristotle's

[h] Middle Ages.

Politics than in all the works of Hallam and his
whole generation? Is not light itself, fruit? Why,
what is fruit? Is there no utility in knowledge?
Or, even abandoning every reference to utility, is
not an avenue of elms or oaks as good as a field of
turnips? Such rubbish can men talk, when they
think they are judicial. As if, forsooth, we were
to abuse Cuvier, because he could not make us
a pair of boots!

Bacon, then, who was seeking to *discover identity*,
could not understand Aristotle, who was seeking to
account for variety. Bacon, who was thinking of
the ultimate states and chemical processes of matter
as such, could not comprehend Aristotle, who was
thinking of the formal structure of bodies *as such*.
Hence the *Novum Organum*, which all the same
Bacon derived from Aristotle, and the substitution
in the general mind of the mechanico-mathematical
for the organic method of scientific investigation.
The final cause, said Bacon, speaking of what he
did not understand, corrupts the sciences : and so,
indeed, it does, if it be employed and understood,
as Aristotle never either employed or understood
it : if it be intended to supplant the full material
and mechanical explanation of the facts. Aristotle
knew just as well as Bacon, that, regarded as the
explanation of material processes, the final cause is
not an explanation at all. But he knew a great
deal more than Bacon about causation, as I shall
presently show. In those sciences which investigate
matter and its properties, the mechanico-mathematical
sciences, the final cause is no use at all, and tells us
nothing : in physics proper, chemistry, mechanics,
astronomy, and so forth. Here ἀνάγκη reigns

supreme. And the Baconian condemnation of final causes, or teleology, was stamped and sealed into a dogma by the ever memorable achievement of the mathematical method in the *Principia* of Newton, and the development of experimental and analytical chemistry and physics. Nobody knew, till a very recent period indeed, anything whatever about biology. Nobody could accordingly perceive that there was no real antagonism between Aristotle's organic and Bacon's experimental method : for no one can understand logic apart from biology. Nobody perceived that the latter had no right to condemn the former, and was positively wrong when it attempted to force itself into a sphere where it was of no avail, the organic world. Nobody knew it then—and who knows it now ? Even the author of the *Origin of Species* was entirely unaware what the real significance of his book was, and wherein its true import lay. What that book really did was, to reinstate the Aristotelian philosophy throughout the whole domain of the organic world ; that is to say, in biology, embryology, physiology, natural history, logic, psychology, morals, politics, and political economy. In all these branches of science, the *Origin of Species* has simply proved that Aristotle was right, and all his detractors wrong : that it is not the abstract, hypothetical, ideal, nor the mechanico-mathematical, material, but the biological, analytical, evolutionary method, that can alone achieve solid and permanent results in the philosophy of the organic world. And, in fact, after condemning Aristotle's philosophy for three hundred years, we wake as it were from a long dream to find that the essentials in all these

Sciences were long ago anticipated by Aristotle, in whom alone we shall find organic truth: and indeed many a man has made in modern times a great reputation with a tiny chip of Aristotle's colossal block.

V. At the bottom of the scientific, i.e. mechanico-material condemnation of Aristotle's teleology lies the confusion between it and the Bridgewater Treatise conception of the universe. But the two have nothing in common. To confound them together is a vulgar error. People who look upon science with the eye of a Macaulay, the brilliant commonplace man, invariably argue in this way. Teleologist; *ergo*, Deist: this is the argument. But the *Origin of Species* has annihilated it, by showing that teleology, properly understood, is the true explanation of all structure : and is thus the verification of the whole Aristotelian philosophy, all the more valuable because completely unconscious, and drawn from the facts themselves.

What, in fact, is Darwin's result? What is the essence and sum of his teaching? This, that every detail of structure (except that which depends upon correlated variation) has become what it is from its function : that every organised body—plant or animal—and every part of that body, is constituted with reference to its peculiar end : that the countless and beautiful varieties of organisation are all merely the same fundamental type-form, or, as the Germans say, *Ur-Thier*, modified in accordance with different conditions: that the law of creation is co-adaptation of means to ends, and thus, by reason of the struggle for existence, constant victory of the forms best organised to achieve those ends : hence, that differentiation of structure to meet ever more various ends is the biological law of progress : every organised body, and part of such body, being strictly an *instrument* for the performance of work, which determines its structure : that accordingly, as a corollary from this view, the principle of explanation for all such bodies is their final cause : and thus the history of their development : that this is their true definition : the process of defining, scientific explanation, merely reflecting as in a mirror the actual process of defining, i.e. limiting or marking out the specific form by constant differentiation of the generic type : nature proceeding according to the great principle of gradation, gradual specialisation, by addition, of structure : that thus, as Lord Beaconsfield said, *all is race,* and that generation is the principle of identity and community, *conditions the principle of variety :* hence the meaning and significance of genus, species, difference, classification, and proof : the *what* or *essence* of a thing depending, alike in fact and knowledge, upon the *how* and *why :* the scientific understanding of *what a thing* is following upon, and only upon, the knowledge of *what it is for.*

I shall examine closely the theory in the *Origin of Species* on a future page : but this is the substance of Darwin's teaching. Now, what does Aristotle say ? The very same. Either Darwin or Aristotle might sign his name to the above passage. And in order to establish the truth of this assertion, I shall now proceed to give a short exposition of the biological basis of Aristotle's philosophy, no such thing, as far as I am aware,

existing in the English language. And as in a case
of this kind the reader is always apt, not without
reason, to suspect the writer of reading modern
views into ancient thoughts, I shall accordingly,
even at the risk of a little repetition, and a certain
stiffness, confine myself entirely to Aristotle's
ipsissima verba, translated with severe accuracy
from his own language, and set down in the order
in which they occur in his own writings, except
where occasionally a word or two of explanation
may be required. Further, to make assurance
doubly sure, I shall refer every passage to its
place in the original Greek. Nevertheless, I must,
preliminarily, beg the reader to remember that no
series of extracts can give a truly adequate idea
of Aristotle's genius ; that I am illustrating only the
basis, and not the superstructure of his philosophy ;
and finally that there never would have been so
general an ignorance of Aristotle's true meaning,
had his incorrigible commentators interpreted him
in his own light : had they begun by studying his
biological treatises as the key to his whole system :
and had they not wilfully forgotten, when dealing
with his Metaphysics, that in that work he was not
contemplating forms as originating, but as being
what they were, when they had originated : a very
different matter, which fully accounts for the apparent opposition between what he says there, and
what he says in every other part of his writings.

The problem of the natural philosopher is to
explain the world, as originating : to explain the
origin of things as they are. He starts from the
fact, and asks, What is it ? How is it ? Why is
it ? seeking for the causes of its generation. Now

we may look at anything in two ways : either we may ask, What is it when it is there ? or, How did it come to get there, to be as it is ? The former is the metaphysical and æsthetic point of view, and does not concern us here. The business of the natural philosopher is to account for how things come to be as they are. What Renan says of Averroes exactly paints Aristotle's conception of the natural philosopher : *le problème de l'origine des êtres est celui qui preoccupe le plus Ibn-Roschd : il y revient dans tous ses ecrits, et toujours avec une nouvelle instance* [i]. This is Aristotle : his own example strengthens all his laws. For the great fundamental fact in Nature is Change. Everything is constantly changing, and the *process of Change* in all its various forms and spheres is the object of scientific enquiry. Aristotle's treatise on *Physics* is not what we mean by ' Physics ' : it is a critical consideration of the process of change in general, and its conditions, Time, Space, and Causality [k] : the starting-point of his philosophy, the sketch or ground-plan subsequently to be filled in in all directions. Nothing in Nature is isolated. All things are in intricate correlation, in action and counter-action : everything is at once active and passive. Thus the only possible way to study anything from the scientific point of view is to study it in all its concrete relations : to study it in the abstract is superficial, and does not help us to any real knowledge of its nature : for all abstract treatment misses the point, viz., that everything is

[i] Renan, Averroes, p. 108.

[k] Compare Mr. A. R. Wallace's remarks on Change, in the first essay in his *Natural Selection.*

what it is, only because it is when it is, where it is,
and as it is[1]: in short, that 'everything's nothing
'except by position.' The philosopher who does not
understand this may be a good mathematician or
metaphysician, but will do no good as a scientific
or natural philosopher. The man who does not
understand motion is necessarily ignorant of everything in nature, says Aristotle. Now, there never
was any man who understood this point so well as
Aristotle; and just because he did so, he is the
greatest of all natural philosophers. Rightly does
M. Barthélemy S[te]. Hilaire praise his Physics : for
this is the starting-point. Let us hear some of the
things Aristotle has to say about people who did
not grasp this fundamental condition of all physical
investigation.   He speaks (*Metaph.* i. 5) of persons
'who made their investigations in too abstract and
'absolute a fashion ; thus defining things only super-
'ficially.' Elsewhere (*De Cælo*, vii. 7), 'It so hap-
'pens that what some persons say of the facts does
'not agree with the facts : the reason being that they
'have not correctly fixed their first principles : but
'seek to drag everything into harmony with certain
'definite dogmas.' (A description exactly fitting
orthodox economists.) Again (*De Gen. et Cor.* i. 2),
'The cause of the inability of certain persons to
'take a comprehensive view is a want of experience.
'For those who have been in the habit of investi-
'gating physical nature are better able to pitch on
'such principles as will connect the facts : whereas
'those who, versed in books and discussions, never

---

[1] This is the true doctrine of Relativity, of which the doctrine of Protagoras is only a special case. Mr. Grote, *e.g.* only
understands the superficial relativity.

'look at the facts of the case, are apt merely to cast
'a glance at a few instances, and so come to an easy
'conclusion. And from this we may learn what a
'difference there is between those who look deep
'into the concrete relations of things, and those who
'examine things merely in a rationalistic and dis-
'cursive manner.' Elsewhere, he says that the
reason why we cannot find out anything about the
movememt of the blood is the difficulty of observing
the facts : as dead animals are not living, and living
animals are closed up. (*Hist. Anim.* iii. 2.) Elsewhere he observes (*De Gen. Anim.* ii. 6) that 'some
'of the older scientific enquirers attempted to state
'the order in which each part of the animal comes
'into existence, without much observation of the
'special facts.' And again (*De Gen. Anim.* ii. 8),
'Possibly an *abstract* proof might seem to be more
'cogent than what has been advanced. By such
'a term I mean to imply that the more general
'a proof is, the further it is from the principles
'peculiar and appropriate to the case in point :'
and of this kind of argument he adds, 'this sort
'of argument is much too general and empty : for
'reasons not drawn from the peculiar principles of
'each kind of case are vague, and only seem to
'touch the matter, but do not really do so.' Again,
'of the generation of bees, he says (*De Gen. Anim.*
'iii. 10), 'Such seems to be the case with the
'generation of bees, as far as the reasoning goes,
'and the facts are known about them : but the
'facts have not yet been observed with sufficient
'accuracy : but should this ever be the case, then
'we must trust to observation rather than reasoning,
'and to the reasoning only in so far as it gives

'results in harmony with the facts.' Sir John Lubbock could say no more. Similarly, of certain opinions held concerning the soul, he says emphatic-ally (*De Anima*, i. 1), 'they are all mere vague and 'empty dialectical results.' And, discussing the views of certain predecessors as to the object of perception, he says (*De An.* iii. 2) that they erred, because they spoke absolutely and abstractly of things that are true only in certain relations. For, as he says (*De Soph. El.* c. 5), 'absolute existence, and existence in certain relations or conditions, are two very different things.' 'Those who speak in generalities,' he says in another connection (*Pol.* i. 13) 'only deceive them-'selves.' And, in regard to inquiries into the soul, he says (*De An.* ii. 3), 'It is ridiculous to seek for 'a definition common both to these cases and 'others: this would be the true definition of no 'real existence, nor one strictly appropriate to any 'peculiar and ultimate species (such a species being 'entirely left out of sight). For it is the same with 'souls as with figures: that which is earlier exists 'potentially in that which is later, both in the case 'of figures and of natural organisms: for example, 'the triangle exists in the square, and the nutritive 'in the percipient soul. We must accordingly seek 'in each case for the soul peculiar to it, as, e.g., the 'special soul of plants, of man or beast.' In this passage he strikes the keynote of his method. For just because each special class of objects is *sui generis*, and peculiarly determined and situated amid intricate special relations, it is impossible, according to Aristotle,—and unquestionably he is right,—to deduce the more from the less complex. Hence it is useless, and a mark of want of insight, to look for any grand universal principle from which the world should be deduced. In the sphere of nature, abstract deductions are useless : the only adequate and fruitful method is to go analytically backwards : to start from the complex and go back to the simple: to resolve the compound into its elements. Only thus can we obtain a really adequate and exhaustive knowledge of every particular subject, and make sure of omitting nothing : for the earlier is contained in the later, but not *vice versa :* in the state is the family : in the family, the man : but from the abstract individual, much less the *ego*, we could never discover either the man, the family, or the state. Nor are Aristotle's precepts, as is often the case with philosophers, at variance with his practice. He is the most concrete of all philosophers. Before his eyes he has ever the limitations of time, places and circumstances which qualify his statements : on every page you find him distinguishing between the absolute or unqualified, and the relative statement : the ἁπλῶς and the κατά τι. His mind was 'immersed in matter' more than ever Bacon's was, and he understood reality better than Bacon or any other philosopher that ever lived.

But to return. All things being in such close and intricate relations and correlations, everything being equally active and passive: acting upon others, and itself reacted upon by them ; only a close and intimate analysis of things *in their relations* can furnish us with their explanation. Our success in discovering the *what* and the *why*, the nature and causes of things, will essentially depend upon a close attention to the *when, where* and *how*.

We see in the universe an infinite multitude and variety of Shapes constantly changing, constantly arising and passing away. It is a sea of matter in perpetual agitation. Out of matter all the Shapes of things arise, and into it they all fall back again. What, now, are the causes of all these transformations? Certainly, all are made of material, and so far determined by their material. But this is not enough. For from the point of view of matter, all things are identical : there is no difference between them. Matter is the principle of identity and indistinguishable indifference. The differences lie, not in the matter, but in the Shapes and Structures, combinations and compositions of things. It is the differences, and not the resemblances, which are the important matter for us. It is in respect of its Form that everything is peculiar and distinctive. Therefore, although the material element is one side, and an altogether indispensable side of the explanation of the universe, it is yet neither exhaustive nor sufficient. We may have a full and complete material explanation of any Form or Shape, yet this is not enough : it is, in reality, thoroughly inadequate. For *why* should matter combine to produce just this Shape! Things are not matter only : matter never appears, as it is in itself, but always as determined in a special Shape. If, then, matter furnishes the stuff out of which all these Shapes arise, and of which they consist, we have still to ask *why* this happens just as it does. What is the instigating cause, and the *raison d'être* of each form ? What strange shapes they all are ! Consider then in the abstract, how anomalous, how capricious, how unintelligible they appear ! yet in their proper place, how natural! What is the principle which determines Shapes, which makes them just what they are? It cannot be the matter in them : this is obviously insufficient to account for them, since it remains the same in different Shapes. We must, therefore, seek some further explanation, some further principle ; this alone being insufficient (οὐκ ἱκανον). (It was from this that Leibnitz derived his *raison suffisante*[m].) The material elements of which the Shape is composed cannot explain, or furnish the *reason why* of the composition : the composition, the synthesis, is something more than its elements. The elements are perfectly happy, perfectly natural, when existing out of combination, as elements. It is not the matter, *as such*, but the particular state or condition of matter, which we want to explain. What, then, can this principle be ? It is obvious that the *raison d'être* of the Shape, Structure, or Constitution of any body compounded of elements cannot be found in itself, in its material elements. Where then ? *In the conditions which surround it*, and in which it exists, to which it responds, on which it acts, and by which it is acted upon. *The special conditions of each Form contains its secret, its raison d'être, its creative principle.* Every body, in fact, every Form and Shape of body, is an adaptation to the work it

[m] And Wolf elaborated Leibnitz' Sufficient Reason into the triple principle : *Principium Fiendi: Principium Essendi: Principium Cognoscendi.* But this is taken straight out of Aristotle (Met. iv. 1), πασῶν δὲ κοινόν ἐστι τῶν ἀρχῶν τὸ πρῶτον εἶναι ὅθεν ἢ ἔστιν, ἢ γίνεται, ἢ γιγνώσκεται. Schopenhauer, in his little treatise on the Principle, adds to these three a fourth, which is a delusion : like the fourth figure in Logic, merely an instance of the way in which men think they are improving upon Aristotle, when they are adding to him only what is nonsensical.

has to do. Everything, in this intricate web of related things, exists for the sake of the others. Its true principle of explanation does not lie in itself, but in others. It exists, to fit its place : to do its appropriate work. An isolated thing could have no Shape : for why should it be this rather than another ? The principle of form would be gone. For everything *quâ* its Form, is to be explained not *from* its constituent elements, but *to* its constituting conditions. Its Shape is originally determined not *from* its original interior stuff, but *towards* what is in front of and outside it. The principle of explanation of Shape and Form lies, not in what it is made *of*, but what it is made *for*: not in the necessary properties of its matter, but in the necessities of the conditions which it has to meet. This is the meaning of Aristotle's final cause, his τέλος and his οὗ ἕνεκα : which, after being misunderstood for two thousand years, will now, thanks to the *Origin of Species*, receive its due recognition.

No sooner is the truth perceived, than it becomes obvious that all true explanation of the origin of Shapes, Forms, Structures and Species is double. There are two necessary sides to all scientific explanation : each is valid only on the assumption of the other obtaining : both are in reality indispensable. Aristotle calls them respectively absolute (material, innate and original) necessity, and conditional necessity : *N*ecessity and *Need*cessity, to borrow an expressive Scottish colloquialism, which exactly hits the truth. Matter, *quâ* matter, obeys the law of its own nature. But no portion of matter finds itself alone in the universe : on the contrary, it finds itself in a jostling crowd. Hence it cannot have entirely its own uncontrolled way, but must adapt and adjust itself to other natures. Its first law is its own material *ne*cessity : its second, conditional *need*cessity (ἡ ἀνάγκη τοῦ πῶς ἕκαστον γίγνεσθαι πέφυκε, καὶ ἡ τοῦ διὰ τί ἀνάγκη). Matter, *as such*, obeys first its own law : but all organised bodies must pay, *as such*, as organised bodies, first regard to the second, the conditional necessity, *if they are to continue.* The first is subordinate to the second, for them. For example, it is, from a purely material point of view, all the same whether a wolf lives or dies : exists as a whole living wolf, or cut into two or more pieces. But from the wolf's point of view, it is not the same. *If* he is to exist as a wolf, and not merely as his elements, he must obey the laws of his organic nature first, and make his material elements subordinate to these. He must eat, he must run, he must find prey, and avoid enemies, or conquer them, and his organs must be such as to enable him to do this. In other words, the Principle of Creation, Scientific Explanation, and Definition, for organised beings, is primarily the final cause, the principle of adaptation of means to ends : and only secondarily their material cause. The principle of explanation for *Structure is Function.* It is the work it has to do that makes every being what it is, and it lives, just as it is capable of performing its work. *The soul and creative principle of every organic being is thus the work it has to do : i.e. the harmonious and proper performance of its function by its structure.* This is Aristotle's definition of the soul : this is the meaning of his saying, τὸ γὰρ αἴτιον τοῦ εἶναι πᾶσιν ἡ

οὐσία. The body, i.e. the Structure, is, for the sake
of the soul, the Function. For the soul of all organised beings is nothing but their proper function or
work. All things are defined by their work : for
those things that can best perform their work most
truly are. For nature suits her tools to the work,
and not the work to the tools : these being constructed, indeed, of materials necessarily and definitely endowed with properties ; nevertheless, the
structure is not determined by the material elements, but the end they must serve. And there
being thus two principles of explanation, the natural
philosopher might give both : but, beyond all, the
function. For the special business of the scientific
enquirer into Nature's Economy is to investigate
the souls of things.

Having now placed the Aristotelian philosophy
in its true light from a general point of view, I shall
show by a copious citation of important passages
from his principal scientific writings, how fully he
realised the scientific meaning of his own philosophy ; to what a depth he had sounded the ocean
of organic existence : how comprehensive was his
survey of the field, how piercing his scrutiny into
the forms, of the vegetable and animal world.

The *History of Animals* is a vast mass of facts
accumulated as the material wherein to discover his
philosophy of the Animal, which he gives us in his
treatise on the *Parts of Animals*, on the *Generation
of Animals*, and on the *Soul:* and on which he
bases the whole of his higher philosophical structure, logical, moral, and political. How any one
with these treatises lying before him could accuse
Aristotle of not appreciating the importance of

facts as the basis of science and philosophy, I do not know : but we find calumny generally in the company of ignorance and prejudice. There are more facts in Aristotle's works than in the works of all the other philosophers put together. He had indeed a kind of genius for facts : the marvel is that he should have been able in so short a life to bring such a vast variety on all sorts of subjects together. He had to be his own Encyclopædia.

If then, we think of things by their appropriate names, we shall easily realise the organic connection running through the whole Aristotelian philosophy. Thus beginning with Change in general he goes on to consider it in detail, meteorological and geological change, formation, generation and decay ; next he arrives at biological change, and investigates living beings (plants and animals), then their structure and parts, their generation, their life (soul) and kindred subjects : then rising to the highest animal, man, he considers his manners, customs, character, and morals, habits of life and society ; (Ethics and Politics ;) his thinking and reasoning power ; (Logic or Analytic ;) his speech and rhetoric ; and his productive activity ; (Economics and Poetics). The whole is simply an ascending series based upon a biological conception derived from a close study of life in all its forms. Living beings, their structure, their functions, their life, (spirit or soul,) habits, and doings :— this is the Aristotelian philosophy. It is essentially, through and through, evolutionary. A basis of deep generic unity, rising by successive differentiations, adapted to ever more complex ($\pi o\lambda v\tau\epsilon\lambda\acute{\epsilon}\sigma\tau\epsilon\rho a$) functions, to essential dif-

ferences : this is the scheme.   The central word in
Aristotle's whole philosophy is *difference* (διαφόρα)
just as in that of Darwin it is *variety*.

  'The parts of animals differ in degree, among
'those of the same kind.'   (*Hist. Anim.* i. 1.)
'Animals differ in respect of their lives, their ac-
'tions, their characters, and their parts.' (*Ib.*) 'But
'some animals have parts which are the same
'neither in kind nor in degree, but *analogically*:
'thus the feather is to the bird what the scale is to
'the fish.' (*Ib.*) The problem is to explain the
reason why of these differences on a basis of resemblance.   The way to attack the problem is to
accumulate facts, 'we must first get at the existing
'differences, and the facts of each case, and after
'this attempt to discover their causes : for this is
'the natural method of proceeding, having first ac-
'cumulated the material facts in each case.' (*Ib.*)
'Now, all animals have some parts in common :
'viz., that wherewith they receive food, and that
'whereinto they receive it ; (the mouth and the
'stomach ;) and these parts are the same and yet
'different in the way we have already mentioned :
'that is to say, either in kind, or degree, or in
'position,' and these parts he calls the 'necessary
parts' (ἀναγκαιότατα μόρια). (*Ib.*) 'People,' he
says, 'know the external parts of man better than
'those of animals, just as they know the coins of
'their own country best : but the reverse is the
'case with the internal parts.' We see here how
hampered he was by the prejudices of his day
against human anatomy, and this will account for
many of his curious blunders : yet in spite of this
what did he not achieve ? He constantly refers for

evidence to his anatomical works ; (according to Diogenes Laertius he wrote eight books of Anatomy ;) but we gather from his expressions that he did not dissect man.

'All animals have some parts in common, and ' some peculiar each to its kind. Those parts which ' are the same are also different from each other, in ' the way we have often mentioned before. For as ' a general rule animals different in kind have most ' of their parts different in kind : and those which ' are only analogically the same are generically dif- ' ferent : some, again, are generically the same, but ' specifically different : others again some animals ' have and others have not.' (*H. A.* ii. 1.) 'Ani- ' mals with four legs use their forelegs as hands in ' many ways.' (*Ib.*) ' The same species often has two ' different kinds of the same part.' (*H. A.* ii. 11.) ' In all animals which have bones the spine is the ' radical or original principle.' (*H. A.* iii. 7.) He complains of the difficulty of examining the blood and the veins, quoting, where observation fails, the opinions of various doctors, Syennesis, Diogenes, and Polybus. (*H. A.* iii. 2.) 'All insects, with ' certain exceptions, live when cut in two.' (*H. A.* iv. 7.) He believes in spontaneous generation, ' some animals are spontaneously generated when ' their original principle, whatever it be, is formed ' by chance.' (*H. A.* v. 1.) He is fully aware of the close and gradual progress from lower to higher organisation running through all nature : ' so grad- ' ually does nature mount up little by little from ' inanimate to animate beings, that the border- ' land eludes our observation, by reason of her ' continuity, and we cannot tell to which it belongs.

'For after inanimate things, next in order come
'plants : and these differ one from the other in the
'degree in which they share in life, as it seems : and
'in general, plants, as compared with bodies below
'them in the scale, seem as it were alive : as com-
'pared, on the contrary, with animals, dead : but
'the ascent from them to animals is, as I said, con-
'tinuous ; and indeed, as to some things in the sea,
'it is doubtful whether they are animals or plants :
'for they grow fixed to their spot, and many of
'them perish, if torn away from it.   And the sponge
'is almost exactly like a plant,' (*i.e.* Aristotle held
it to be an animal) : 'and thus proceeding gradu-
'ally by imperceptible differences, one thing after
'another seems to acquire more and more life and
'motion.' (*H. A.* viii. 1.)   Darwin had no clearer
conception of the 'great principle of gradation,' as
he calls it, than Aristotle.

He notices how 'animals differ in respect of the
'places they frequent, and in which they are found,'
and discusses, in fact, their distribution : meagrely,
indeed,— how could it have been otherwise ?
nevertheless, he perceives its bearing on the problem. (*H. A.* viii. 27.)   'There are many kinds
'of food, and consequently many different lives
'both of men and animals.   For it is impossible to
'live without food : consequently the differences
'in food have produced differences in animals.
'For some beasts live in flocks, and some by
'themselves, according to whichever way best fits
'them (ὁποτέρως συμφέρει) for obtaining their food :
'and their manner of life is such as necessity com-
'pelled them to make it.' (Pol. i. 8.)   Just so, 'the
'difference of their *habitat* makes their characters

' differ.' (*H. A.* viii. 28.) The whole Ninth Book of the *History of Animals* is devoted to the characters of animals. For, as he says—and only since Darwin has the world begun to return to his point of view, ' in most other animals we perceive ' traces of the soul's ways.' (*H. A.* viii. 1.) ' The ' traces of all these moral characteristics are, as ' it were, in all animals, but they become even ' plainer in proportion as the animal acquires more ' character : plainest of all in man.' (*H. A.* ix. 3.) He notes the ' mimicries of human life ' which we see in other animals. (*H. A.* ix. 8.) He is perfectly alive to the struggle for existence, and, as we shall see presently, explains the structures of animals always with regard to their need for defence (πρὸς βοήθειαν, ἄλκην, σωτηρίαν, φύγην). ' There is war among animals between themselves : ' in the case of all animals which occupy the same ' places, and support their life on the same food : if ' food be in scarcity, even animals of the same ' species will fight for it.' (*H. A.* ix. 2.) He has, however, no perception of ¡the high ratio of increase, the Malthusian element in Darwin's theory, in its evolutionary bearing : although in the purely political sphere the Malthusian argument, that too many children ruin the state, was familiar to him and other Greek thinkers.

In proceeding, now, after accumulating the facts, (it is only by perusing the *History of Animals* that the reader will appreciate Aristotle's insatiate industry)—in proceeding to ascertain the philosophy of organic life, to find, that is to say, its cause or principle, ' the first cause or principle is obviously ' that which we call the principle of adaptation.

' For this is the account or definition of the thing :
' alike in natural or artificial combination.' (*De Part.
Anim.* i. 1.) ' The principle of necessity does
' not apply to all natural objects in the same way,
' *although nearly everybody tries to base his defin-
' itions or scientific explanations on a reference to one
' sort of necessity only*, not distinguishing the differ-
' ent meanings of the term necessity. Absolute
' necessity belongs only to eternal things, (Aristotle
is thinking of the heavenly bodies, of which he
knew of course nothing,) ' but conditional necessity
' is the first law for all things that come into being'
(i.e. have a passing or temporary form), ' just as it
' is for the productions of art, as a house or any
' similar object.' (*D.P.A. Ib.*) Matter, that is to
say, *as such*, obeys the laws of its own necessary
nature, but matter, *as organised in form* must obey
first the laws of the organisation, *as such:* i.e. Aristotle's οὗ ἕνεκα, or final cause, the adaptation. If
this is not done, the organisation cannot originally
arise, and will disappear, even when arisen. If the
animal is to live, it must eat, and so forth : if it
is to do such and such work, it must be thus or
thus. Death represents the final triumph of matter
over form : the conditional necessity is broken,
and consequently the organisation disappears, having existed only as long as it obeyed it. For all
organisation is adaptation to an end, and the law of
adaptation or coadaptation is the supreme law of
Natural Economy :—there is the Aristotelian philosophy in a nutshell. To mistake or overlook this
distinction of double necessity is to philosophise
absolutely and abstractly, and not *concretely: i.e.*
with regard to the special relations of the thing :

it is the πρῶτον ψεῦδος of all philosophies such as Plato's, on the one hand, or one-sided material necessitarians on the other. For ' the method of ' scientific proof and investigation, and the method ' of absolute necessity, are two entirely different ' things,' says Aristotle (*D. P. A.* i. 1), refuting by anticipation Bacon's imaginary refutation of himself. The one, that is, material absolute necessity, starts from the original and necessary elements of things as they are : the other, biological proof, conditional necessity, starts not from what things are elementarily, but what they are going to be : ' the ' principle of the one is what is, of the other, what ' is going to be ' (*D. P. A.* i. 1), i.e. absolute necessity is the principle of identity amidst differences : discovered inductively : conditional necessity is the principle of the *raison d'être* of difference among things at bottom identical : which follows deductively : this is the true distinction between Bacon and Aristotle. Fire burns, because it is its nature so to do : but the structure of the animal follows from the work it has to do. The one method starts with its eye on matter *as such :* the other with its eye on matter, *as definitely shaped towards an end.* As matter *is,* so it *does : operari sequitur esse,* says Bacon : as structure *does,* so it *is : esse sequitur operari,* says Aristotle. And though Aristotle understood Bacon's method, Bacon entirely failed to understand Aristotle's : he knew nothing about organic forms or biology : whereas Aristotle's Logic of Science is based on his biological knowledge : and in biological matters, said Aristotle, the fundamental principle is not the nature of the elements as such, but the structure of

E

the whole as such. Upon this adaptive or conditional necessity; this necessity of structure to conform to and accord with function, depends the whole creation : and of course, as science is nothing but the mirror of nature, the principle of scientific explanation, definition, and proof. For the cause of a thing's existence, and the definition of its nature, are the same : τὸ γὰρ αἴτιον τοῦ εἶναι πᾶσιν ἡ οὐσία, καὶ ὁ λόγος τῆς οὐσίας (*De Anim.* ii. 4), i.e. the need for cutting is the cause of the saw, gives its peculiar form to the saw : and the definition of the saw is an instrument for cutting : the need for flying gives its form to the wing, and the definition of the wing is an instrument for flying. *Esse sequitur operari.*

Therefore our scientific salvation depends upon our making and attending to this distinction between the necessities of matter *as such,* and the necessity of the structural organisation. This is what Aristotle means when he says, 'we must not forget to ask, 'whether it is better to account for a thing, as the 'older philosophers did, by reference to its own 'original material constituents, or by reference to its 'organised form : for it makes all the difference.' (*D. P. A.* i. 1.) 'The structural explanation is by far 'the most important : for the process of its genesis 'is determined by the final structure : and not *vice* '*versâ.*' (*Ib.*) 'For to give its material elements 'is not a sufficient explanation of the organic being' (*Ib.*), i.e. the web feet of the goose are not adequately explained from the merely material side : but from their function : the necessities of their conditions. 'So much more influential is the structural than the 'material side of the animal organisation :' for the material has to grow to, shape itself to, its conditions. (*Ib.*) ' Now the soul of animals is just their function : ' their reality in accordance with the definition : ' this is the cause of their structural organisation ' and their essence.' (*Metaph.* vi. 10.) ' The soul ' is the actual working of the form : the body ' is only the material possibility of the same.' (*Metaph.* vi. 11.) ' Democritus was wrong in ' asserting that the Shape and Form only was the ' animal : it is not so ; the truth is, that it is function ' which makes Shape or Structure real : for a dead ' man has the same Shape as a living man, yet is ' not a man : the essential is gone : *he can no longer* ' *do his work.*' (*D. P. A.* i. 1.) ' Therefore to say ' that the reality of a body lies in its Shape is to ' speak *abstractly*, not *concretely.*' (*Ib.*) For by thus speaking, we miss the heart of reality. The explanation and reality of shape or structure lie in its *action*. *Agere constituit esse.*

From all this it follows that ' the special business ' of the natural philosopher is to account for and ' know the souls of things.' (*Ib.*) ' As we saw, ' nature has a double meaning corresponding to the ' double sides of the existence of organic bodies : ' which are on the one side matter, and on the ' other structure organised to perform work.' (*Ib.*) ' There are accordingly these two sides of all ex- ' planation, and two causes ; that of material ne- ' cessity, and that of organic necessity, or adapta- ' tion.' (*Ib.*) ' We say that food is necessary, not ' meaning necessity in the absolute sense, but mean- ' ing that it is impossible to live without it ; that is ' to say, the necessity is conditional : for just as, if ' the axe is to cut, it must be hard ; and if hard, of

' brass or iron or what not : so too, since the organic
' body is an instrument (for each part of it, as well
' as the whole, is adapted to an end), it is necessary,
' if it is to do its work, that it should be thus or
' thus, and made of this or that material. Plainly,
' then, there are two species of cause, and scientific
' explanation must give both : or at any rate, must
' try to : and all who do not do this miss the point
' in their attempts to explain nature : for the organic
' structure is far more the essential principle than
' the material element.' (*Ib.*) And he expressly
says ' the reason why my predecessors never
' arrived at this method, was that they knew no-
' thing of the formative cause, and the definition of
' the essential organic nature.' (*Ib.*) He says
again, ' Necessity sometimes means, that if a
' certain end is to be obtained, this or that are
' necessary as means : sometimes, it means, that
' things are thus or thus in their original elementary
' nature.' (*Ib.*) ' Now since every instrument is
' adapted to an end, and each part of the body
' likewise, and the end to which each is adapted is
' some action, it is manifest that the whole body is
' constituted to perform a certain complete action :
' thus the body too is for the sake of the soul, and
' each part for the sake of the work which it is
' constituted to perform.' (*D. P. A.* i. 5.) ' But now
' the instruments of all actions that aim at an end
' will differ among themselves as variously as the
' actions do.' (*Ib.*) ' Since then the actions and
' movements of animals are very various, both as
' wholes, and in their parts, their constituent ele-
' ments must necessarily be of different capacities.'
(*D. P. A.* ii. 1.)   ' But the organic necessities do

'not determine the original material potentialities
'*as such*, these were originally so from the begin-
'ning' (*D. P. A.* ii. 1); the organic necessity only
determines the form in which the potentialities of
matter shall reveal themselves.   'All the differ-
'ences displayed to us by the parts of animals are
'determined by the principle of the better adapta-
'tion.'   (*D. P. A.* ii. 2.)   'The animal that has but
'few functions, requires but few organs: on the
'other hand, those that in addition to bare life,
'possess also perception, have a much more
'variously formed structure.'   (*D. P. A.* ii. 10.)
'In all animals that are not imperfect the two abso-
'lutely essential parts are that whereby it receives its
'food, and that whereby it gets rid of what is
'superfluous, for without food it is impossible either
'to grow or to exist.'   (*D. P. A.* ii. 10.)   (Aristotle
does not mention the stomach here, as in the
passage previously quoted from the *History of
Animals*, because he is thinking of the stomach as
the basis of the animal, and the mouth and vent as
its instruments.)   Over and over again he uses
and enforces, as the reader will see, that law of
economy, which Darwin ascribes to Geoffrey
S^{te}. Hilaire, and Goethe.   'In the case of the
'elephant, as the legs owing to their structure are
'not available for certain functions, nature, as we
'said, makes use of the trunk to compensate the
'animal for the assistance (βοήθεια) which it would
'have derived from the legs.' (*D. P. A.* ii. 16.)
'For nature's peculiar and original way of working
'is, as we said, to employ the parts which are com-
'mon to all animals so as to obtain special and
'peculiar ends : as for example, in the case of the

' mouth : all animals use it to receive their food,
' but only some use it as a weapon of attack and
' defence : others, again, use it for speech.   Nor do
' all animals use it for breathing.   But nature has
' crammed all these functions into one instrument,
' making it differ according to its different require-
' ments.   Some animals, accordingly, have small,
' some large mouths.   Those that use the mouth
' for food, breathing, and speech have small mouths :
' those that use it as a weapon and a means of
' security have great jaws and teeth.   For as they
' find their safety in biting, it is serviceable for
' them to have the opening of their mouth large.
' And the wider their mouth can open, the better
' can they bite.   And such fish as bite or are car-
' nivorous have just such a mouth : those that are
' not carnivorous, again, have little mouths : for
' these are useful to them, whereas the big mouth
' would be of no service to them.   Birds again have
' what we call the beak for a mouth : for this is
' to them what the lips and teeth are to other
' animals.   Now this beak differs just in accordance
' with its different functions and the different
' methods of preservation (βοήθειας) of the bird
' owning it.'   (*D. P. A.* iii. 1.)   Similarly of the
horns he says :   ' As to the horns, these, in the
' animals which have them, are placed on the head.
' Only viviparous animals have them.   But certain
' others are metaphorically said to have horns,
' owing to a certain resemblance of their organs to
' horns : *but they are not horns, because none of them*
' *perform the work of the horn, properly so called.*
' For viviparous animals have them for their pre-
' servation and defence ;   and this is not the case

' with any of those other animals which are said to
' have horns, for none of them use their " horns "
' either in defence or attack : which are the func-
' tions that strength is given to meet. No animal
' that has digits has horns. And the reason is that
' the horn is a weapon of defence, whereas the
' *digitalia* have other means of defence than horns :
' for nature has furnished some with claws, some
' with teeth, and others with other parts sufficient
' to secure their preservation. But many cloven-
' footed animals have horns as weapons of defence :
' as well as some solid-hoofed animals : others have
' them for attack. But those to whom nature has
' not given them, have other means of safety : as
' swiftness, which is the horse's weapon, or size,
' which is that of the camel : for a superiority of
' size is sufficient to keep off the destruction arising
' from other animals, and this is the case with
' camels and still more with elephants. Tusked
' animals, as well as all kinds of pig or boar, are
' cloven-hoofed. But all animals whose immense
' excess of horn renders it useless to them are
' furnished by nature with another weapon : stags,
' for example, with speed : for the size and branch-
' ing of their antlers is rather injurious than other-
' wise to them. So, too, with antelopes and ga-
' zelles. It is true that against some animals they
' offer to resist and defend themselves with their
' horns, but against fierce and savage animals they
' take to flight. But a certain kind of wild ox
' (whose horns grow together inwards) has as its
' weapon the discharge of its superfluity : for thus
' it defends itself, when frightened ; and this means
' of defence is employed also by other animals : but

' nature never gives to the same animal more than
' one adequate and sufficient weapon of defence.'
(*D. P. A.* iii. 2.)   It is here that Aristotle declares
' that the man who studies nature must take a wide
' and comprehensive survey of facts, for it is what
' happens in all or most cases which is to be called
' natural.'   So much alive was he to the paramount
importance of exhaustive induction.   He states
the law of organic differences thus : ' Let us now
' consider ' (he is still considering horns) ' how the
' absolutely essential and necessary material of the
' generic organic nature, in those that have it to
' start with, is employed by the specially determined
' and defined nature [n] and adapted to various ends.
' The superfluous excess of material existing in
' such a body is used by nature for the preservation
' and advantage of the animal, now for horns, now
' tusks, and so on.   But not both at once.   For
' nature is niggardly.   She takes from one part to
' add to another : and the nutriment that would be
' given to tusks is expended (ἀναλίσκεται) in the
' increase of the horns.'   (*D. P. A.* iii. 2.)   Thus
Aristotle, like Darwin, makes the Principle of
Utility the basis of all explanation.   How near he

---

[n] Dr. Andrew Wilson, in his admirable little book, *Chapters on
Evolution*, p. 122, was not thinking of Aristotle when he wrote,
' By modification or adaptation we mean to indicate that potent
' power, or factor, which seizing the common type moulds the
' structure,—limb or body,—to the special way of life in which
' the being ultimately comes to walk : ' yet he is using Aristotle's
very words.   That is exactly what Aristotle means by Nature,
or φύσις.   I recommend the reader who really wishes to appreciate Aristotle to read *Chapters on Evolution.*   Without thinking
of it, Dr. Andrew Wilson has exactly illustrated, even to the
very words, Aristotle's biological method, in every page.

comes, in this place, to the very core of Darwin's
theory.

Of the neck he says, ' not all animals have this
' part, but only those influenced by the needs to
' answer which the neck exists.' (*D. P. A.* iii. 3.)
The closeness of his biological observation is proved
by his remark, 'as soon as any animal that has
' blood is composed, and while it is still a mere
' pigmy, the heart can be seen. For it appears
' sometimes in eggs, only three days old, as big as
' a point, and also very small in certain embryos.
' And just as the external parts are not used in the
' same way by all animals, but each animal has its
' own peculiar form of organ adapted to its life and
' its movements, so too are the inward parts adapted
' differently to different uses.' (*D. P. A.* iii. 2.) 'The
' limbs,' he says, 'are different in different cases,
' and not (like the heart) absolutely, but only rela-
' tively, necessary to life : therefore, even when they
' are removed, the animal lives.' (*D. P. A.* iii. 4.)
Again, ' in embryos, the heart is immediately per-
' ceived moving, alone of the parts, as if it were
' alive : as though to indicate that it is the principle
' of life and their nature, in animals that have blood.'
(*Ib.*) ' Nature,' he says again, ' makes use of super-
' fluous matter sometimes for the benefit of the
' animal ; nevertheless we must not expect, on this
' account, to be able to explain all the parts of
' animals on the principle of adaptation ; but in
' some cases, some parts being so adapted, other
' things will follow of necessity from the adapted
' parts being as they are.' (*D. P. A.* iv. 2.) This
is exactly Darwin's ' correlated variation,' of which
principle he makes so much use ; and Aristotle fully

understood the principle °, as he often employs it :
the reader will find other examples given below.
Of the cuttlefish he says, 'it has what we call its ink
' as a weapon of preservation and defence : for when
' it is alarmed and frightened it makes its inky dis-
' charge so as to shield its body.' (*D. P. A.* iv. 5.)
Of oysters he observes : ' they differ in their nature
' very little from plants, yet seem to have more of
' life than sponges : for these have an altogether
' plant-like capacity. For nature ascends by gradual
' steps continuously from inanimate objects to ani-
' mals, through those things that are animate, in-
' deed, but are not yet animals : so that one thing
' seems to differ almost nothing from the next, by
' reason of her continuity. The sponge, as we said,
' is almost like a plant, in that it can only live
' growing to a spot, but dies when pulled off. But
' holothurians, and certain zoophytes, and other
' such things in the sea, differ just a little from
' this, in that they live when pulled off. None of
' them have senses, but they live as it were like

 ° G. H. Lewes in his *Aristotle* (p. 318), (the only book I know
of in which any attempt is made to estimate Aristotle's biological
value) remarks on this passage : ' This important passage should
' be a set off against the many formal declarations of teleology
' to be met with in his writings. It shows that he had a glimmer-
' ing of the philosophic conception, and that, like the modern
' advocates of teleology, he was only disposed to employ final
' causes where proximate causes were hidden from him.'
    Thus does Lewes presume to criticise Aristotle, while all the
time it is not Aristotle, but *himself*, who is at fault: knowing
nothing of evolution, or correlated variation. This is a sample
of Lewes' book : the most superlatively contemptible effort that
ever was made by a Comtist pigmy to pat an evolutionary giant
on the back. Two thousand years, apparently, will not level
a small man with a great one.

' detached plants. And among land plants there
' are some such as live and are generated, some in
' other plants, others when detached; as, for ex-
' ample, that which comes from Parnassus, and is
' called Epipetron (the Rocky), for this will live
' a long time hanging on a peg. And oysters, and
' other kinds similar to these, only resemble plants
' in that they grow fixed to a spot, but in having
' a fleshy nature would seem to have some spark of
' sensation. We cannot tell how to class them.' (*Ib.*)
And of another marine creature, apparently the sea-
nettle, he says, 'it seems to partake both of animal
' and plant nature. For in that it can detach itself
' and fall in with its food, it resembles an animal, and
' also in that it perceives things that come across it.
' Further, it uses the roughness of its body as a
' weapon; yet in that it is imperfect, and easily
' grows to rocks, it resembles a plant: and it has
' no vent, but only a mouth.' (*Ib.*) So, of other
similar organisms, he says, that 'like plants, they
' can live when cut in two.' (*Ib.*)

' Wherever two organs can be used for two
' functions, and this is not hindered by some other
' impediment, nature never produces any dirty little
' cheap-jack instrument of all trades: but where
' this is impossible, she employs the same organ for
' many functions.' (*D. P. A.* iv. 6.) 'The organs of
' motion in animals are necessarily very various,
' because their actions are so: for animals that move
' about most variously require the most various
' organs.' (*D. P. A.* iv. 7.) 'It is with a view to their
' safety that nature has encompassed the shell-fish
' with their hard shell.' (*Ib.*) 'All such creatures,
' like plants, have their heads turned downwards:

' because they draw their nutriment from below :
' like plants with their roots : thus they have their
' upper parts below, and their lower above.' (*Ib.*)
' Shrimps differ from crabs in having a tail : from
' another sort of crab, in not having claws : which
' they have not, because they have many feet : for
' their increase has been taken from the claws and
' expended on feet.' (*D. P. A.* iv. 8.) [The crab,
it may be noticed here, has a tail during development, which it loses.] ' The *astakoi* (a kind of
' crab) are the only crabs which have either the
' right or left claw larger than the other (the others
' always the right), whichever it happens to be
' which they have, both males and females.   The
' reason why they have claws at all is that they are
' in the genus which has claws.   But they are
' anomalously constituted in that they exhibit them
' in a rudimentary condition (πεπήρωνται), and do
' not use them for their true purpose, but to walk
' with.'   (*D. P. A.* iv. 8.) ' One sort of cuttlefish
' has a big body, and another a small one : so that
' nature has in the former case taken from the body
' to give length of feeler, and in the other con-
' versely.'   (*D. P. A.* iv. 9.) ' All animals have
' a dwarfish appearance as compared with man.'
(*D. P. A.* iv. 10.) ' The plant comes into existence
' upside down—with its head below.' (*Ib.*) ' Na-
' ture always makes the best thing possible under
' the circumstances.'   (*Ib.*)   This is a favourite
axiom of Aristotle's : Darwin has proved that it is
true.   ' The hand is not one tool, but many : it
' is, as it were, the tool of tools.   All other animals
' have but one tool, one weapon of defence, and
' they cannot change it for another : the animal

' has, as if it were bound, to sleep with it, do all
' with it, nor ever lay aside its constant watchfulness
' for its bodily care, nor change the one weapon
' it chances to possess. But man has a variety
' of means of preservation, and he can always
' change them : further, he has what weapon he
' chooses, and whensoever he chooses ; for the
' hand is both nail and claw, and horn, at will, and
' spear and sword, and any other tool or weapon
' whatever.' (*D. P. A.* iv. 10.) ' The parts we
' call tails differ widely, and nature uses many, not
' merely to protect and shield the seat, but also for
' the benefit and utility of those who possess them.'
' (*Ib.*) ' Man cannot without inconvenience remain
' long standing up, but the body requires rest and
' must sit down.' (*Ib.*) A most acute observation
in this connection : as Evolution shows. ' Nature's
' works are never supererogatory.' (This does not
mean that nothing in nature is wasted : but that
all the formed productions of nature have a reason
for their existence.) Speaking of the facility with
which snakes turn their heads he says : ' this follows
' from the mechanical necessity of their structure,
' but it is also determined by the principle of the
' best : to guard against enemies attacking it from
' behind.' (*Ib.*) ' The bodies of the *raptores*, apart
' from the wings, are small : because their nutri-
' ment has been expended in these, as weapons
' of attack and defence.' (*D. P. A.* iv. 12.) Speaking of the *raptores* and their claws, talons, and
beaks, he; says : ' nature does not develop the bird
' in all directions at once : for, if it were split up and
' divided among many parts at once, the superfluity
' of material would be weak and of no effect.' (*Ib.*)

             Body and Soul.

'Some birds have long legs because they live
' in marshes. For Nature suits her tools to the
' work, and not her work to the tools.' (*Ib.*)
' These birds,' he says again, ' have had the matter
' which might have gone to make tail expended in
' the legs. And in fact, when flying, they use their
' legs as a tail.' (*Ib.*)

And we may sum up the whole treatise *On the
Parts of Animals* by saying, that it explains the
whole structure of animals, on the principle of
adaptation or utility, except those parts that are due
to correlated variation, which follow necessarily from
the others.

He commences his treatise *On the Generation of
Animals* thus : 'Since we have spoken about the
' Parts of Animals, both in general, and concerning
' each kind in particular, stating how each arises
' owing to this cause : by which I mean, the adap-
' tation to function : for there are four causes, the
' principle of adaptation, or end, and the definition
' of the form of the thing : these we must regard as
' one : the third and fourth are the matter and the
' beginning of motion : we have spoken of the rest :
' for the formal and final cause are the same, and
' the matter, in animals, is their parts,' (the beginning
of motion is the parent). This passage clearly
shows how Aristotle really conceived his formal
and final cause : the two are identical, the first is
the structure, the second the function, and the
latter is the *raison d'être* of the former. He now
proceeds to consider generation. ' The male differs
' from the female, according to their definition, in
' that each has a different function : according to per-
' ception, in certain parts.' (*De Gen. An.* i. 2.)

' Now since all things are defined by their capaci-
' ties and their work or function : and since tools
' are required to perform all work, and the tools for
' the functions are the parts of the body, it is
' necessary that there should be parts for generation
' and copulation, and these differing from each
' other, as male from female.' (*D. G. A.* i. 2.) ' We
' should carefully observe that a very small change
' in a principle is wont to bring with it changes in
' those things that depend on the principle. And
' this is plain in the case of castrated animals, for
' the generative part alone having been destroyed,
' the whole form changes to such an extent, as to
' seem almost female, or but little removed from it :
' as though to indicate that the animal is male or
' female not in virtue of any chance fact or any
' chance capacity in it. Obviously, then, the male
' or female principle is an original and radical prin-
' ciple : at least, any change in the animal, *quâ*
' male or female, brings much change in its train,
' as though to show that a fundamental principle is
' gone.' (*Ib.*) (Readers of the *Origin of Species*
know how emphatically Darwin's testimony cor-
roborates this.) ' Nature does all, either by
' necessity, or as well as possible under given cir-
' cumstances.' (*D. G. A.* i. 4.) Speaking of certain molluscs, he says, ' the egg they produce is at
' first undifferentiated (ἀδιάφορον) : then it differ-
' entiates and becomes many,' or as moderns say,
segmentates. This is the cardinal fact in embryological development. (*D. G. A.* i. 15.) ' Not
' just anything can come from each germ, but the
' special thing from the special germ ; nor again can
' just any germ come from any body : the germ,

'then, is the original and creative principle of that
'of which it is the germ,' (*D. P. A.* i. 1), and this
argument he uses against Empedocles : both here
and elsewhere.   Things cannot be generated by
chance, he says, because 'it is necessary that the
'germ should pre-exist, having within it a definite
'capacity for development.' (*D. P. A.* i. 1.) (In the
celebrated passage which is quoted in the Introduction to the *Origin of Species* from Aristotle's
Physics, Darwin never understood that Aristotle
was here denying chance from a point of view
from which both Darwin himself and Herbert
Spencer have denied it, and all must deny it.) 'The
Germ is simply the hand, or face, or whole animal
'in an undifferentiated state : and just what each
'of these is in final actuality that is the germ
'potentially.' (*D. G. A.* i. 19.) 'Woman is, as it
'were, a man without seed.' (*D. G. A.* i. 20.) 'In
'all animals that move about, the male is differ-
'entiated from the female : the female being one
'animal, and the male another : but both of the
'same species : both, for example, man. But in
'plants, these faculties are still mixed up, and the
'female is not yet severed from the male.   Therefore
'they generate from themselves, and do not emit
'seed, but have an offshoot,—what we call "seed."
'And Empedocles was quite right in speaking of the
'eggs of olive trees. For the egg is a sort of offshoot,
'and from a certain egg arises the animal : the rest is
'nutriment : so too from part of the seed arises the
'vegetable growth : and the rest is nutriment,
'coming to the little sprout and the early root.
'Now in a kind of way this takes place with those
'animals which have the sexes separated.   For

' when it is necessary to generate, they conjoin,
' becoming as plants : and their nature wishes to
' become one, which is shown, in that one animal
' results from the mixture and conjunction of the
' two. And some, which emit no seed, remain
' conjoined a long time, till the germ be consti-
' tuted, as, for example, those insects which copu-
' late : others only till they have imported some
' part which shall constitute the germ in a longer
' time, as animals that have blood. In short,
' animals are just like plants that have been differ-
' entiated : as though a man should tear plants
' apart, and separate them into the sexes immanent
' in them.' And he goes on to explain that animals
have as it were risen in the scale of existence, and
yet when they wish to propagate their kind, they
have to fall back as it were on their fundamental
and lower nature, and become one, like the plant.
But hard-shelled animals, holding a middle place
between plants and animals, being as it were in both
departments, perform the function of neither. For,
as being plants, they are not differentiated into male
and female, and one does not generate into its
opposite : but on being animals, they do not bear
fruit like plants, but are constituted and generated
from some moist and earthy composition. (*D. G. A.*
i. 23.) Now though this passage shows that Aristotle was not as well informed about the facts of
plants and their generation as we are, yet how
completely he understood the fundamental corollary
of evolution, that sex and individuality are the
product of the evolutionary process : both being
absent in the lower forms of organic life.

As regards generation ' there is much com-

F

' plication between different kinds of animals. For
' not all bipeds are viviparous (since birds are ovi-
' parous); nor are they all oviparous (for man is
' viviparous); nor are all quadrupeds oviparous
' (since the horse, the ox, and innumerable others
' are viviparous); nor are they all viviparous (for
' alligators and crocodiles and many others are
' oviparous). Nor does the difference lie in having
' or not having feet : for animals without feet are
' viviparous, such as vipers, and cartilaginous fish :
' but some are oviparous, as fish in general and
' other snakes. Also animals that have feet are
' both viviparous and oviparous, as the quadrupeds
' mentioned above : and both animals with feet,
' as man, and without feet, as the whale and dol-
' phin, are viviparous within themselves. There-
' fore it is impossible to make a division in this
' respect : nor does the *cause of the difference* lie in
' any of the organs of locomotion : but those animals
' are viviparous which are biologically more highly
' developed, and have a more distinctly differ-
' entiated principle (καθαρωτέρας ἀρχῆς); for no
' animal is viviparous within itself, which does not
' inhale and exhale air.' (*D. G. A.* ii. 1.) Whoever will reflect upon this passage will understand Aristotle's logical method, and realise that
Bacon's inductive Methods were no news to Aristotle.

' Insects at first are vermiparous : then as it
' goes on the worm becomes egglike, for what
' we call the chrysalis has the capacity of an
' egg : then out of this comes the animal attaining
' the end of its generation in the third change.'
(*Ib.*) It is here that he discusses and maintains

that biological view known as Epigenesis[P],
which he discovered long before Harvey. 'Con-
' cerning the which there is much difficulty, as
' to how the plant or animal, whatever it be,
' arises out of the germ. No part can exist to start
' with. But the parts lie potentially in the germ;
' and the process of its evolution is started by an
' impulse given from without by the parents : the
' effect remaining after this preliminary touch has
' been given: just as in automata, in a certain way
' the external impulse moves them; not being now
' any longer in contact with any part, but having
' been in such contact before : so too the parent
' from whom comes the germ, or that which makes
' it, having formerly been in contact with it, but no
' longer being so, is the originating cause of the
' productive process: in another way the cause is
' the inward motion so originally set going, just as
' the house is built by the process of house-building.'
(*Ib.*) This truly prophetic passage shows how
little those critics understand Aristotle, who suppose that his final cause was intended to obviate
the necessity for a full material mechanical explanation. *Both* are indispensable, says Aristotle.
E. g., at the beginning of this second Book, he expressly asserts that after having stated what is the one
cause, on the principle of the best possible adaptation, we must then seek a full material explanation.
(*D. G. A.* ii. i.) Again, 'heat and cold and so forth
' will make the stuff of the parts, but not the law of
' combination, nor the essential nature : that comes

[P] Yet in historical accounts of the doctrine, as, e.g., that in
a recent text book on Embryology by Hertwig (translated by
Mark), Wolf, Pander, and Harvey, are credited with the discovery, and *Aristotle is not even mentioned.*

' from the instigation of the begetter, who is in
' actuality what the germ is only potentially, and
' out of which it arises.'   And again, ' as to whether
' the germ has a soul, or not, that is a question
' essentially connected with the account of the parts.
' For no soul can possibly exist except in that of
' which it is the soul; nor can any part be a
' part, not partaking of the soul : except meta-
' phorically : the dead eye is not an eye.'   (*Ib.*)
No mere extract will, however, adequately convey
to the reader the depth of Aristotle's insight into
embryology.   ' None of the principles which give
' to bodily activity its existence, and which it ex-
' emplifies, can possibly exist apart from the body :
' there is no walking without feet.'   (*D. G. A.* ii. 3.)
' Some of the older physiologists attempted to
' state the order in which the parts succeed one
' another, but failed owing to want of observa-
' tion of the parts.'   (*D. G. A.* ii. 6.)   ' The
' parts about the head and eyes are observed to
' be the largest at the beginning in embryos : but
' the parts below the navel, as the limbs, small.'
(*Ib.*)   And of certain investigators he says, ' They
' do not say well, nor do they point out the
' *necessity of the reason why* in their statement.'   (*Ib.*)
' Cold,' he says, ' is simply the absence or negation
' of heat, and nature makes use of both, having
' necessarily certain potentialities or capacities, so
' as to make now one thing, now another : the
' principle of inner material necessity, and outward
' structural adaptation, combining to form the parts[q].'

---

[q] Aristotle's material *potentialities* correspond exactly to Darwin's *variation* : the factor contributed by the irregular spontaneity of nature's material.

(*Ib.*) '*All these things we must account for partly*
'*on the principle of inner material necessity, partly*
'*not so, but on the principle of adaptation to an end.*'
(*Ib.*) From an embryological point of view, he says
that 'all things are first definitely sketched out, and
' at a later stage get their colours, and hardness
' and softness : nature going to work exactly like
' a painter, for painters sketch the outline first and
' then fill in the animal with colours.' (*Ib.*) (This
is just Aristotle's own invariable method : cf.
Ethics I.) He knows how the embryo acquires
its characteristics only gradually. 'Not at once
' does the horse become a horse, or a man, a man.'
(*Ib.*) 'Nature like a good economist is not wont
' to throw away anything out of which anything
' good can be made.' (*Ib.*) In a subsequent chapter he discusses the question of mules and hybrids :
finishing much as Darwin does, with uncertainty.
' Animals naturally breed with their own kind :
' nevertheless they do so also with other animals
' closely akin to them, but not specifically identical,
' if their sizes be about on a par and their periods
' of gestation equal.' (*D. G. A.* ii. 7.) 'What
' nature takes from one part, she adds to another.'
(*D. G. A.* iii. 1.) 'If one part of any importance
' changes, the whole structure of the animal be-
' comes specifically very different.' (*D. G. A.* iv. 1.)
This is *the* important principle from an evolutionary
point of view, and Aristotle shows how close he
was to the Darwinian theory by the way he applies
it to politics. 'For just as the organic body
' consists of parts, and must increase propor-
' tionally all round, if its harmony is to be pre-
' served ; otherwise it will perish : and some-

' times it would change into the form of a wholly
' different animal, if one part were to change dis-
' proportionately not merely quantitatively, but
' qualitatively: so is it with states.' (*Pol.* v. 3.)
This is the very core of evolution. Speaking of the
resemblance of progeny to their parents, he says:
' Yet when we come to think of it, the child that
' does not resemble its parents is already in a sense
' a miracle.' (*D. G. A.* iv. 3.) ' It is impossible for
' anything to be born except in its own proper
' period.' (*Ib.*) He develops here the principle of
correlated variation, as Darwin calls it, at more
length. ' Concerning these and all similar things, we
' must no longer think of their cause in the same
' way. For such things as are not organic forma-
' tions, whether they be common to all, or peculiar
' to some species, are not instances of adaptation,
' nor formed on that principle. The eye, for ex-
' ample, is an adaptation, but its blueness is not,
' except where this colour is an essential peculiarity
' of the species.' (Compare Darwin on the blue
eyes of deaf white cats.) ' In some cases, then,
' it will come within the definition of the essential
' nature of the animal, but in general we must refer
' it, as happening by correlative necessity, to the
' properties of matter and the efficient cause. For
' as we said when treating of principles (in the first
' book of the treatise *On the Parts of Animals*) in
' the case of well-defined and regular works of
' nature, a thing is not what it is, owing to its innate
' original material potentialities, but on the contrary,
' because it has to adapt itself, and become specially
' coadapted thus or thus, so must its material be
' determined. For the process of generation is

' conditioned by the nature of the fully formed
' structure, and is adapted to this, but not *vice versa*.
' But the old physiologists thought the contrary.
' The reason for this was, that they did not perceive
' that the causes were many, but took note only of
' the material and efficient cause, and even these
' only vaguely, but had no perception of the bio-
' logical definition, and the principle of adaptation
' to an end. Each thing then is an adaptation to
' an end, and comes into being in general from this
' cause, and is determined by its peculiar demands
' in each case. But of those things that are not
' adaptations, which nevertheless come into exis-
' tence in this way, the cause must be sought in the
' material motion, and the process of generative
' growth, as being things that derive their distinctive
' differences from the very nature of the organic
' composition. The eye, for example, in the case
' of an animal that has one, must necessarily be
' there (on the animal's account) ; but any par-
' ticular kind of eye (blue or green, e.g.) is also
' necessary indeed, but not in the same sense of the
' word (it might, as far as the animal is concerned,
' be otherwise) : but the material necessities of the
' composition of the animal make it what it is.'
(*D. G. A.* v. 1.)

' Small changes,' he again says, ' may be causes
' of great results, not in themselves, but because it
' so happens that they change the principle. For
' principles are insignificant in size, but all important
' in their potential results.' (*D. G. A.* v. 7.) And
he is never tired of reiterating this : as e.g. in the
treatise *On the Locomotion of Animals* (c. 7), 'it is
' obvious that a slight change in an original principle

' may cause many and great differences at a distant
' point.' And if philosophers of history had remembered this, they would not have written such
volumes of rubbish about the ' great universal laws '
that determine historical moments. For the very
law of history and politics is, that a stitch in time
saves nine.

Coming now to the treatise *On the Soul :* a work
that both for its intrinsic doctrine and for its historical influence must be pronounced the most important book that ever was written, except the
Bible, we shall find that it presents no difficulty to
those who approach it in its natural order after the
treatises *On the Parts* and *the Generation of Animals,*
being in fact nothing but the summation and corollary of those treatises ; though apart from them, and
taken only in connection with the Metaphysics, it
can only be unintelligible and the cause of perpetual
quibbling. 'The soul is as it were the original
' principle of the body.' (*De An.* i. 1.) The soul
is, in fact, simply the function of the structure. 'At
' present those who investigate the soul apparently
' confine their attention to the human soul only.'
(*Ib.*) Aristotle knew—how different from Descartes !—the impossibility of studying the human
soul except as viewed as the apex of soul in general.
He refers to the 'empty dialectical babbling' of
people who talk about things without knowing any
of the special facts of the case. ' Plants live when
' cut in two, as do also some insects, as though to
' indicate that the parts have the same soul speci-
' fically, though not numerically, as the whole. At
' any rate each part has perception and moves about
' for some time. That they do not continue to do

' so, is no wonder : for they have not (as the whole
' had) organs wherewith to preserve their nature
' (σώζειν τὴν φύσιν). None the less on that account
' are all the parts of the soul in each part so
' severed : and they are specifically similar to each
' other and to the whole : and the principle of life
' in plants seems to be a kind of soul, shared
' equally by plants and animals.' (*De An.* i. 5.)

'The soul is the actual working reality of the
' natural organic body, which has the capacity of
' such work in it,' (*D. An.* ii. 1), explaining his meaning accurately and admirably by the addition : ' if
' the eye were an animal, sight would be its soul :
' for this is just what it is to be an eye, according
' to the definition. The eye is simply the material
' organ of sight ; which failing it is no longer an
' eye, except by playing on the word.' (*Ib.*) ' The
' soul is thus the cause and creative principle of the
' living body. For the cause of every organic being
' is its essence ' (i. e. the function it performs).
(*De An.* ii. 4.) ' The animal must have perception,
' if every product of nature be an adaptation to an
' end. For every natural body is such an adapta-
' tion, or else a necessary corollary of such adap-
' tation : unless, then, all bodies that move about
' had perception, they would perish, and never
' attain that end, or perform that function which is
' the business of their nature : for how could they
' keep themselves alive ? Stationary animals find
' their nutriment where they are born.' (*D. An.* iii.
12.) ' Further, the animal which is to preserve its
' life must not only perceive when in contiguity with
' the perceived object, but also at a distance. (*Ib.*)
' The head of the animal is analogous to the root

' of the plant: if it be the function of organs which
' we refer to, in pronouncing any organ the same or
' different,' (*D. An.* ii. 4.) He makes a very deep
remark when he says, 'since it is from its end that
' we ought to define everything, and the really
' universal end of the organic body be, as it seems
' to be, to produce another like itself, the lowest
' and most radical form of soul would be the gen-
' erative principle.' (*D. An.* ii. 4.) Lastly, we may
notice his remark, that ' the activities and actions
' with which the definition of soul is concerned are
' prior to the capacities that have to perform them:
' and prior again to the former are the objects of
' the activity, which accordingly we ought to study
' first.' (*D. An.* ii. 4.)

The above extracts will give a fair idea of the
biological basis of the Aristotelian philosophy, nor
can any one competent to form an opinion reflect
upon it without being struck with astonishment. He
had to wait two thousand years to be understood.
For his philosophy is throughout evolutionary and
biological : he is all along, as it were, on the brink
of that evolutionary theory, descent with modification, which he could not, however, arrive at,
because the preconditions of the discovery were not
in existence. Nevertheless, the further step taken
by Darwin does not overthrow, but confirms and
substantiates his explanation : it supplies, as it were,
the missing key, the light to that which is still
dark in him. Aristotle's whole doctrine of science
is simply a corollary from evolution. Let us consider, for example, what is his conception of definition, as indicated in the above extracts. ' The
' definition,' he says, 'is a knowledge of the essence:

'a declaring of what a thing essentially is. All
'things are defined by their function and their
'capacity : for those things most truly are which
'can do their work. Everything is thus a com-
'pound : it is on the one side material, and as such
'requires full material explanation : it is, on the
'other, form, that is to say, a structure organised
'for a function, an instrument to perform work,
'material adapted to an end. This end, then,
'this function, this work, is the cause of the exist-
'ence of the thing, and the principle of its definition
'and scientific explanation. The adaptation, how-
'ever, is less and less obvious in things, according
'as we get less and less form. There is more
'adaptation in exact proportion as there is more
'form : and less adaptation exactly as there is more
'and more matter'. The higher, then, the organ-
'ism, the more definite it be, the better can it be
'defined. To define, then, is to give the common
'genus or class of the object, the material of which
'it is a species, and add on all the differences
'essential till we arrive at the ultimate differentiated
'form, which it is our problem to define. In other
'words, the definition of any organic structure is
'simply the logical account of its life history; an
'enumeration of the causes that have made it.
'Animals are constructed on a fundamentally iden-
'tical type ; the differentiations, according to Aris-

' ' Domestic races often have a somewhat monstrous character.'
Origin of Species, p. 16. So Wallace : ' Domestic animals are
'abnormal, irregular, artificial.' *Natural Selection*, p. 31. Because,
Aristotle would say, matter, or the superfluity, gets the upper
hand over form : since they are lifted out of the conditions that
kept their form true.

' totle, are due to the differences of function,
' habitat and conditions, to which the animal has
' to conform itself. *The animal is made to an-
' swer to special conditions.*' Darwin adds to this
but a single word : *gradually*, or in the course
of ages.

VI. The teleology of Aristotle has nothing
whatever in common with what we may call
the Bridgewater Treatise conception of the universe. His final cause has no connection with
' final causes ' in the sense in which that expression
is commonly understood. But Bacon, and those
who since Bacon's day have tossed aside Aristotle
as an obsolete teleologist were quite unable to
understand any teleology other than that of final
causes implying conscious design and a Providential
scheme : they accordingly accused Aristotle of
corrupting natural philosophy with his logic, and
introducing final causes—in the sense in which they
understood them—into Nature : just because they
could not conceive how an organism could be an
adaptation to an end, how structure could correspond
with function, except by an agency similar to that
by which man makes his tools, manufactures his
productions : according to design. But observe,
how the whirligig of time brings about his revenges.
Aristotle, though he was accused of doing so, did
not argue from τέχνη to φύσις, from art to nature,
from manufactures to creatures. He placed them
both on the same level. He looked at nature on
her own ground, and pronounced the natural body
to be just as much an instrument formed to accomplish certain ends as the mechanical body was—and
he was right. He asserted that function was the

raison d'être and explanation of structure, just as much in the natural as in the artificial body, and Darwin has proved that he was right. Nevertheless it is undeniable, that the weak point in Aristotle's philosophy lies here. He said, indeed, that structure was determined by function, but he did not explain the process by which the thing was effected, and here Darwin differs from him. Aristotle stated the *why*, but not the *how*. He based his whole philosophy on the principle that coadaptation was the law of Natural Economy : he accounted for structure by function, and the forms of bodies by the work they did. Looking straight at the facts without prejudice or theory, he divined the truth that all bodies are instruments or tools to perform work, and determined by that work. But he did not explain *how* this came about. Darwin's theory is an attempt to supply the answer to this *how*. But not to mention the age in which Aristotle lived; not to dwell upon the fact that the three causes which led Darwin to his *Origin of Species*, viz. the 'ever memorable theory,' as Darwin calls it, of Malthus, the great development and suggestive facts of cattle-breeding, and the geographical and geological distribution and succession of plants and animals in time and space—these three conditions without which Darwin could no more have arrived at his *Origin of Species* than Newton at his *Principia* without Copernicus, Galileo, and Kepler ;—not to mention, I say, that these three suggestive and significant preconditions were non-existent as yet for Aristotle, the truth is that Darwin himself, on the one hand, has done just what his critics object to Aristotle,—he *has* argued

illegitimately from art to nature ; and on the other,
he has *not* given us a valid solution of this *how*
of structural adaptation.   He agrees with Aristotle
in his result, that all structure is adaptation, and
to be explained primarily on the principle of Utility :
he differs and passes beyond Aristotle, in attempting
to solve the problem of the way in which it came
about : in furnishing a theory of how things came
to be so.   That theory, I make bold to say, is the
most palpable fallacy that ever was offered to
the world as a truth : an assertion which I proceed
to justify.   I hope, however, that the reader will
not misunderstand me—the question here is not as
to the fact of evolution.   A man who does not
now-a-days believe in evolution ; that is, in the
theory that all organised bodies have descended
from earlier, simpler, progenitors by successive
steps of modification ; proves only that he is not
acquainted with the main facts of embryology and
biology, which alone are sufficient, as Darwin says,
to place the fact of evolution beyond all doubt.
But it does not follow, because a man accepts
evolution, that he must also accept Darwin's theory :
nor because he rejects the latter that he is not an
evolutionist : that he believes in special creation.
There are, in fact, not two, but three alternatives.
There is the theory of special creation, which is
only a dogma : a survival from an age of black
scientific darkness, the child of misunderstood
oriental metaphors : the mere statement of the facts
in other words : the creed of ignorance.   This,
however, was the prejudice which Darwin found
in possession of the field.   Hence he constantly
argues, especially in the later chapters of his book,

as if there were but two alternatives; as if the rejection of the special creation hypothesis were the establishment of his own.   And much of the reasoning, towards the end of his book, if regarded as contributing to the support of his own theory, is of no force whatever, because it only negatively throws discredit upon special creation, without adding any strength to his own theory.   The theory of descent with modification, however, or evolutionary differentiation, by no means stands or falls with Darwin's theory of the *modus operandi*.   Embryology leaves no doubt as to the first : reason discredits the second.

VII. We must distinguish, in the *Origin of Species*, between what is and what is not peculiar to Darwin.   To give to Darwin the credit of evolution, in a biological sense, is enough to make Lamarck and Aristotle turn in their graves : though Darwin will always retain the honour of having done, partly by genius and partly by fortune, and ' occasion fitting virtue,' more than any one to bring evolution into public notice and esteem.   But what is peculiar to Darwin is his theory as to how it was done.   Beyond all question, his theory is an entire failure.   It is not only not proven : it is, as can be shown, logically impossible even on his own principles.

The argument from art to nature is the keystone of the Darwinian arch. He derived his theory of Natural Selection from a careful investigation of human selection, as even the name implies.   Under the breeder's bands, he says [*], the animal organisa-

* The quotations from the *Origin of Species* are from the fifth edition.

tion seems to become plastic.   Breeders ' habitually
' speak of an animal's organisation as something
' quite plastic, which they can model almost as they
' please.'   Selection, according to Youatt, was the
magician's wand, by means of which he could sum-
mon into life whatever form and mould he pleased.
Lord Somerville, speaking of what breeders had
done for sheep, said, ' It would seem as if they had
' chalked out upon a wall a form perfect in itself, and
' then had given it existence.'   The key to these
wonders is ' man's power of accumulative selection.
' Nature gives successive variations : man adds
' them up in certain directions useful to him.'
(*O. S.* p. 33.)   ' We see in our domesticated races
adaptation, not indeed to the animal's or plant's
' own good, but to man's use or fancy.'   (*O. S.* pp.
41, 32.)   Observe that ' any variation which is not
' inherited is unimportant for us.'   (*O. S.* p. 13.)
' The importance of selection consists in the accu-
' mulation in one direction during successive genera-
' tions of differences absolutely inappreciable by an
' uneducated eye : differences which I for one have
' vainly attempted to appreciate.   Not one man in
' a thousand has accuracy of eye and judgment
' sufficient to become an eminent breeder.'   (*O. S.*
p. 34.)   ' Hence unless the closest attention is paid
' nothing can be effected.'   Hence too ' facility in
' preventing crosses is an important element of suc-
' cess.'   (*O. S.* p. 44.)
　　Now this being so, these being the conditions of
human selection and the production of new forms,
Darwin obtains his theory of Natural Selection by
extending the argument to Nature : ' applies the
' principles arrived at in the last chapter to organic

' beings in a state of nature.' (*O. S.* pp. 4, 48.) ' As
' there is between all organic beings a very keen
' struggle for existence, many more being born than
' can possibly survive, it follows that any being,
' if it vary in any manner profitable to itself, will
' have a better chance of surviving, and thus be
' Naturally Selected. From the strong principle
' of inheritance any selected variety will tend to
' propagate its new and modified form.' (*O. S.*
pp. 4, 72.) ' There is no obvious reason why the
' principles which have acted so efficiently under
' domestication should not act under nature.' (*O. S.*
p. 554.) ' If man can by patience select variations
' useful to him, why, under changing and complex
' conditions of life, should not variations, useful to
' nature's living products, often arise, and be pre-
'served or selected ?' (*O. S.* p. 556.) ' The theory
' of Natural Selection is grounded on the belief that
' each new variety and ultimately each new species
' (for a variety is on the theory only an incipient
' species) is produced and maintained by having
' some advantage over those with which it comes into
' competition.' (*O. S.* p. 393.) ' Natural Selection
' acts only by taking advantage of slight successive
' variations.' (*O. S.* p. 239.) ' Natural Selection
' acts solely by the preservation of profitable modi-
' fications.' (*O. S.* p. 208.) ' It would be an extra-
' ordinary fact if no variations ever occurred useful
' to each being's own welfare in the same manner
' as so many variations have occurred useful to
' man.' (160.) ' Only those variations which are
' in some way profitable will be preserved or
' naturally selected.' (133, 125, 110.) ' Natural
' Selection can act only through and for the good

'of each being.' (97.) 'This preservation of
'favourable variations, and the destruction of in-
'jurious variations, I call Natural Selection or the
'Survival of the Fittest. *Variations neither useful*
'*nor injurious* COULD NOT BE affected by Natural
'Selection.' (92.)

Now, that any man should fail to see the gross
and palpable fallacy in this reasoning is unaccountable. Let the reader observe, that with human
selection, *first*, the variations are so slight as to be
almost imperceptible, even to an eye like Darwin's :
second, that they are useful, not to the animal itself,
but the fancy of man : third, that they are of no
account unless preserved and inherited : 'free inter-
'crossing will stop the breeder's work.' (117.)
In all these points, man can exercise influence :
he can select for his own fancy : he can select
variations imperceptibly small : and he can ensure
inheritance. He performs his miracles by these
three means. Now, any one of these three points
would render the argument from Art to Nature
absurd and fallacious : all together, they absolutely
annihilate it.

First, the variations selected under domestication
are of a totally different *kind* from those selected, *ex
hypothesi*, under Nature. The ambiguous word
useful covers the fallacy. Useful, in the first sense,
means whatever suits man's aims, or hits his fancy :
the useful, in the second, must favour, profit, or
preserve the organism itself. 'Nature cares nothing
'for appearances except in so far as they are useful
'to any being . . . man selects for his own good ;
'Nature only for that of the being which she tends.'
(95.) Darwin contrasts the power of Nature with

the weakness of man. 'Natural Selection is as
' immeasurably superior to man's feeble efforts, as
' the works of Nature are to those of Art.' (73, 124.)
No doubt : but he fails to observe that, feeble as he
is, *man is potent precisely where Nature is impotent*,
according to Darwin himself : he can select any sort
of variation, however slight in degree, of whatever
kind, that hits his fancy ; whereas she cannot select
any variation at all, except it be in kind and degree
sufficient to profit the organism. This is the very
crucial point. How, then, can the argument from
Selection under domestication to selection under
Nature possibly hold water? How can Natural
Selection be inferred from Human Selection? The
variations which under human selection have produced such astonishing results are different in *kind*
from those which alone Nature could select. She
cannot select any but those which profit the organisation varying. And yet further. Not only is the
kind distinct, but the degree. The variations are
infinitely slight. This is Darwin's cardinal principle. He guards himself repeatedly here. If they
were not slight his theory would be open to objection from another side, as we shall see. Accordingly, when it is objected to him that the production
of *e.g.* the eye or instincts of certain kinds would
imply simultaneous variations accurately adjusted to
each other, he says, 'the force of this objection rests
' entirely on the assumption that the changes in both
' instinct and structure are abrupt.' (288.) '*Natura
' non facit saltum* must on my theory be strictly
' true.' (253.) 'Natural Selection acts only by taking
' advantage of *slight successive* variations : she can
' never take a sudden leap.' (239.) (Yet how about

G 2

the Ancon sheep?)   'It is not necessary to suppose
'all the modifications were simultaneous, if they
'were extremely slight and gradual' (225); 'if any
'organic being varies *ever so little*, and thus gains
'an advantage' (222), and many more passages to
the same effect[1].   Now, note, that putting out of
consideration the fallacy of arguing from man's selection of variations profitable to himself, *i.e.* pleasing
to himself, to natural selection of variations profitable to the organism—the variations are then infinitely slight.   Yet we are asked to suppose that
this infinitely slight variation, when arisen in a single
individual, is decisively to determine throughout life,
on all occasions, the existence of its possessor, in
every case of struggle, in spite of innumerable other
circumstances, whether of organisation, luck, or external conditions ; and that then, handed down to
its progeny, it is again to determine their lives similarly, which are to vary in the same direction, and
increase the variation in amount !   Here comes in
the third condition, inheritance. (117.) The breeder
can not only select variations infinitely slight, suiting
his fancy or taste : but he can ensure inheritance by
preventing intercrossing.   But how could an organism varying infinitely slightly under nature possibly
be prevented from intercrossing, either itself or its
progeny ?

[1] ' Natural Selection follows from the struggle for existence.'
Descent of Man, p. 142.   It does nothing of the kind, *unless*
the variations are, what Darwin has not proved, capable in *degree*
of deciding the victory, when profitable in *kind*, and necessarily
inherited, by the prevention of intercrossing.   Just so, Mr. Wallace attempts to prove the theory *apodeictically*, in set syllogistic
form, on p. 166 of *Natural Selection :* not observing the fallacy
in one step of the argument—viz. *heredity with variation.*

Yet further. Is this slight variation to occur in one being only, or in a whole multitude at once? If the latter, then it is not variation at all : but the definite result of conditions common to the organisms in question: i.e. it is not natural selection, but the definite and direct action of conditions that determine the change in structure : since it is clearly ridiculous to assume the spontaneous variation (Darwin's own phrase) in a number of cases at once in the same direction. But if on the contrary the variation only occurs in one organism at a time (and it must do so, or it would not be variation : see below), then it is absolutely impossible, on his own principles, that it should be preserved, for intercrossing would instantly destroy it, even if luck did not. This is Darwin's own principle. ' Rare species will be less ' quickly modified or improved within a given ' period, and will consequently be beaten in the race ' for life.' (126.) 'Any form represented by few ' individuals will during fluctuations in the seasons ' or the number of its enemies run a good chance of ' being exterminated.' (123.) Compare also p. 104.

Let the impartial reader observe that this criticism is not captious, not directed against non-essential doctrines, but the very core of the Darwinian hypothesis : and let him judge, whether it does not utterly wreck the argument from human to Natural Selection. The kind, the degree, of man's selection are such as Nature cannot act upon, and even if she could, intercrossing would instantly obliterate her attempt. Yet Darwin never seems to be conscious of the extraordinary sophistry of his reasoning. This curious unconsciousness, however, does not arise from any undue partiality for his

own theory such as might have blinded him to
its faults. On the contrary, he is candid to an
unusual degree; perhaps no author was ever
more so. He discovers many objections to his
theory, of which more anon : but the cardinal
error, the fallacious analogy between human and
natural selection, never seems to have entered his
head. Had it done so, he would never have written
his book, which is entirely based on that argument.
The whole of his laborious investigation into the
subject of Variation under Domestication is an
ignoratio elenchi. And here it is convenient to
notice another point. It might be argued, and with
justice, that even though we grant the palpable
fallacy of arguing from domesticated to natural
organisms ; even though, as has been shown, no
amount of evidence as to the former can be adduced
as evidence bearing on the latter, yet that putting
the accumulated evidence drawn from variation
under domestication entirely on one side, his theory
might hold. There might be sufficient evidence,
under nature, without having recourse to domestication at all. But now, the truly remarkable thing
is, that Darwin has *not a single fact,* NOT ONE,
within the sphere of Natural Selection to prove
his theory. This is just why he had to turn to
Human Selection to help him out. And there is
a very good reason why he could not bring a single
fact : it is, that, first, as has been shown, his theory
is impossible, and hence there are no facts : and
secondly, even if there were, from the very nature
of the case it would be impossible either to know
them, or bring them forward. For *ex hypothesi*
the process is too slight in kind and degree to be

observed; too slow, requiring æons for its accomplishment, for any eye to mark it; and essentially untraceable; for catch, *e.g.* your hare, how can you compare it with its forerunners or descendants, or contemporaries? *The process necessarily eludes observation, assuming it to be real.* What then does Darwin do? Mark the absurdity. He apparently brings forward evidence, but it is all supposition: all imaginary: and he invariably falls back in reality upon two props: one, variation under domestication; the other, the necessary consequence (which is a truism) that *if* profitable variations occur, they will be selected. They must. Every page of the *Origin of Species* furnishes illustrations of this method: *e.g.*: on p. 103 he illustrates the action of Natural Selection by one or two imaginary examples. ' Let us take the case of a wolf, which ' preys on various animals, securing some by craft, ' some by strength, and some by fleetness: and let ' us *suppose* that the fleetest prey, a deer, for in- ' stance, had from any change in the country in- ' creased in numbers, or that other prey had ' decreased in numbers, during that season of the ' year when the wolf was hardest pressed for food. ' Under such circumstances the swiftest and slim- ' mest wolves *would have* the best chance of sur- ' viving, and so be preserved or selected,—*provided* ' *always* that they retained strength to master their ' prey at this or some other period of the year when ' they *might be* compelled to prey on other animals. ' *I can see no more reason to doubt this, than that* ' *man can improve the fleetness of his greyhounds* ' *by careful and methodical selection,*' &c. Now this exactly illustrates the essential weakness of his argument. His natural facts are *always*, not facts, but suppositions, and he always has to fall back on a reference to domestication, which, as has been here proved, does not hold, and on the obvious truth, that the fittest will survive in the struggle : obvious, because we cannot tell which was the fittest, except after the struggle is over : we know *a priori* that that one which survives will have been the fittest. It is in fact just the extremely obvious nature of this argument which gives a specious appearance to the whole reasoning. But the point is not there. The point is not, whether, in a struggle, that will survive which is fittest to survive under the circumstances. That is certain. But even excluding, which is manifestly absurd, all circumstances from the problem but that of the variation of the organism, the point is, the *degree* and *kind* of the variation : and this is precisely the point in which the whole theory fails, and in support of which no fact can possibly be adduced. On p. 106 he gives us another illustration, drawn from plants : and we find '*let us suppose that,*'—'insects *would get* dusted with the pollen, ' and *would certainly* transport it '—' the flowers of ' two species *would thus* get crossed : and the act of ' crossing, *as we have good reason to believe, would* ' produce vigorous seedlings, which *would conse-* ' *quently have the best chance of flourishing and* ' *surviving.* Those plants which produced flowers ' with the largest glands or nectaries, *would* oftenest ' be visited, and *would* oftenest be crossed, and so ' in the long run *would* gain the upper hand.' And so on. This is merely a sample of his procedure all through the book. He cannot help himself.

Not being able to produce a single fact in evidence, he has, willy-nilly, to fall back on the two arguments given above. In fact, Darwin's hypothesis is one to which I defy any one to produce a parallel in the history of the world. It is an hypothesis, supported, A. by facts drawn from one sphere and applied to another where they do not hold : and B. by conjectures. The facts are inapplicable, and the conjectures are not facts.

As was stated above, any one can see at a glance— for it is a truism—that in any struggle that being will survive which is fittest to survive, under the circumstances. To attempt to prove this is simply otiose, and a mark of want of understanding : we might as well go about to prove that two and two are four. And it is from this that uncritical people are apt to conclude, hastily, that Darwin's case is proved. But it is nothing of the sort. Nobody denies, or ever thought of denying, this proposition : and if they did, it makes no difference : for it is a necessary truth. After any struggle, that thing which has survived, is, *ipso facto*, that one which was fittest to survive. All circumstances whatever must be taken into the account, or the thing is false. But it does not follow in the least that *infinitely slight variations in the structure of the organism* will determine the result. To establish his theory Darwin ought to have proved, or at any rate, attempted to prove, bring evidence tending to prove, 1. that infinitely slight variations are profitable to the organism, can be selected, and do in fact determine the survival of the organism in question. 2. That intercrossing will not destroy the variation, or that such infinitely slight variation will tend to be

inherited. 3. That these things being so, there is
every reason to believe that *during the life of the
organisms in question* additional variation in the
same direction will occur so as to enable Natural
Selection to accumulate them, or add them up.
4. That such insignificant variations, even assuming,
what is manifestly impossible, the other three
conditions, could all along preponderatingly decide,
amidst all the complex accidents and conditions
of life, survival in the struggle. He has not brought
a particle of evidence to establish any one of them.

Any one can see that *other conditions being
carefully eliminated*, in any struggle preponderance
in one required quality will give victory: as, for
example, in races, swiftness; in single combat,
strength : and this metaphor is one of the illustrations
that Darwin most commonly uses, and which
impresses uncritical people. But in Nature, *other
conditions are not eliminated.* No one has proved this
more indisputably than Darwin himself. The race
is not to the swift, nor the battle to the strong.
No, some one might object, but generally speaking
it will be so. Yes, but this misses the point. The
point is that a *single variation*, infinitely slight,
having occurred, it should give the decisive turn,
and observe, not once only, but continuously, for
many lives, at all times, and many generations :
other influences and conditions powerless before it.
For variation begins, and as its very name implies,
as the very essence of the idea of variation shows,
with individuals : each varies from each : if all vary
simultaneously it is not variation, but the definite
result of a common cause. Therefore a single
variation infinitely slight, is Darwin's starting-point.

And yet, even assuming it to be capable of being selected, this miserable variation is to outweigh the countless host of surrounding circumstances all bringing to bear. The life of the variation, we are asked to believe, must be as safe as that of a hero of romance, passing unscathed through every perilous combination of circumstances. Should it succeed in so doing, it must be endowed with eyes of the sharpest, so as to choose for its bride, with unerring instinct, a variety similar to itself, and so hand on to its posterity the precious charge, uncontaminated by mixture with plebeian ordinaries.

But this is not all. The truth is that the *Origin of Species* is a misnomer. It is the second title which accurately describes Darwin's book: *The Preservation of Favoured Races in the Struggle for Life*. Natural Selection, or to employ the more scientific and accurate term, the Survival, under keen competition, of the Fittest, is not an explanation of the origin of species at all. It is the cause and principle, not of the progress of organisation from lower to higher, but of the perpetuity and maintenance of organisation essentially as it is: it tells us, not how a form came to be what it is, but how it is kept as it is. It does not raise from one step to another, but prevents degeneration. It keeps structure up to the mark, but does not explain how it passes beyond it: nay, it does not permit it. It is no explanation of the change of forms, but of their immutability. It acts, in fact, exactly in the opposite way, does exactly the opposite of what Darwin conceived it to do. For observe, that, under keen competition, which is the hypothesis, every organism must live by its organs:

i.e. find in the weapons with which it is furnished
its safety. Consequently, it cannot possibly vary
out of its own line. In so far as its preservation
depends upon itself it has nothing but its own style
of self-preservation to trust to. Now it lives and
must live from hand to mouth constantly on the
watch to find prey or escape itself from being prey
to others : hence, it is true, competition will keep
all its faculties keen, polish them to the utmost,
eliminate inferior specimens, and so on : but on the
other hand, it will absolutely prevent it from varying
or even so much as attempting to develop along any
line but its own. It has no time to develop new
methods of preying or escaping. Long before it
could trust to any newly arisen—very slight—variation *differing in tendency in kind :* i.e. tending to
transform it and requiring ages for its full realisation,
it must have perished. It must stick to its old form
and find therein its life : and hence, though doubtless varying slightly in unessential points, just as
it does under domestication, none of these variations
can be selected, because they are of no value or
account under nature. Competition keeps it rigor-
ously to its own organs, and absolutely prevents
it from varying away from its shape, on pain of
death. Darwin most unaccountably overlooks the
fact that if, in a race for prey, as *e.g.* in his own
illustration of wolves, quoted above, the victory lies
with the swiftest (putting out of sight the consideration that, unless deer were the *only* food, the beaten
wolf might otherwise feed), yet this natural selection
does not and cannot alter the form, for it assumes
the species wolf, with its organs, already there.
[And how are we to conceive the possibility of such

cases as this tending to permanently change the wolf into a subsequent form : except by the exclusion of all circumstances save the fleetness of its prey? But is, forsooth, this all?] For Natural Selection to act upon organs, they must be already there. Rigid competition may keep the animal from degenerating, but then on the other hand it ties it down to its conditions. Let the conditions alter, so as to render the animal's weapons either of attack or defence useless, unfit, then it must cease to exist. For it cannot change within the period of its life. It is better to be a high organisation than a low one, provided that you can live in your appropriate conditions : otherwise the case is altered. The more definite a thing is, the less is its capacity of alteration.

But some one might say : this is just where Natural Selection comes in. It is true, that a sudden change in conditions would destroy the organism. But let the change be slow and constant : this will slowly and constantly change the organism. No doubt it will (or else destroy it) : but the point is not, whether the change will occur : but *how* it will occur. Beyond all question, and this is what is not peculiar to Darwin, changing conditions will either destroy or change the organism : that is the essence of the truth, that function makes structure. But will this change be effected by the Natural Selection of one insignificant variation, by the constant adding up of an infinitely slight, inherited variation, or by the action of the conditions upon all the members of the species? That is the question for the Darwinian, and that is exactly what we are now discussing. The point is exactly there : Darwin gives us a theory of the *how* of the change : and on the contrary, reason shows that the principle he invokes to account for the change would on the contrary account, not for the change, but the fixity. Natural Selection, as presented by Darwin, is powerless to effect alteration. In the sea of chopping circumstances, his variation must be lost.

And this shows us, on the one hand, how little Darwin comprehended his own principle, and how he confused together two things essentially distinct : the one, the law, that changing conditions change the organism, which is not his : and the other, the theory, as to how this is to be explained, which is his, and which, as we have seen, is erroneous. And it shows us, on the other hand, how we may solve some difficulties that puzzled him, with his aid. He denies (15) the statement of naturalists that domestic varieties, if run wild, gradually but invariably revert in character to their aboriginal stocks. Were this true, he admits, that we could deduce nothing from domestic varieties in regard to species : but he says that there is not a shadow of evidence for it[x]. Now, on the contrary, reason shows that it must be so. It follows from Darwin's own principle of Natural Selection. The constitution acquired by any organisation under domestication, does not depend any longer, as it did once, on the necessity of preserving its life (for, as Aristotle says, domestic animals derive advantage from their position : they are in safety), but on the accidents

---

[x] He goes on to say, significantly, '*As has always been my 'practice*, I have sought light on this head from our domestic 'productions.'

of matter and the whim of man   It may therefore become, and generally does become, as Darwin and Wallace both say, somewhat monstrous. (Monstrosities, says Aristotle, are cases where matter conquers the adaptive organisation.) Therefore, all that artificial formation, enveloping, as it were, and disguising the original organisation, 'must fall off and away from it, if it is dropped back into the struggle for existence, and the state of war : leaving only those organs of self-preservation with which it started. It must, as it were, again strip for the contest. For each specific form is determined by the way it has to keep itself alive, as was long ago pointed out by Aristotle : hence however much luxury and security may have transmogrified it under domestication, it must, if turned loose, lose all those clothes which clog it and fetter its action, unless it is to perish : it must get its living, just as it did before ; it must be thrown again into Nature's crucible : be born again : i.e. it must revert, and lose its acquired character.

All this, now, while it throws into strong relief the wide and essential distinction between the results of variation under domestication, and variation under nature, solves for us other problems that Darwin did not succeed in solving : the limits of variation : the definition of a species : and the apparent paradox that though, according to his view, species were mutable, yet there is no evidence for it, and a good deal against it [y].

[y] It is an error to say, as is often done, that 'change is the 'law' or that 'nature puts a premium upon variation'—without qualification. Change is the law, only in so far as the conditions do not require fixity. The more definite, the less

It is most curious to see, what an amount of difficulty has been imported into the essentially simple question, what are the limits of variation. It would be easy, but invidious, to adduce passages from many well-known authors, showing how curiously they misunderstand a thing on Darwin's own principles easily accounted for. No two things in Nature are exactly alike : that is the whole and complete meaning of variation : a fact proved by inspection, as universal as gravitation. This is the whole material on which breeders go to work, infinitely slight as the variations are : and it would also be the whole material on which Natural Selection must work, according to Darwin. *If by varia-tion is meant anything more than this, then it is simply a gratuitous assumption, for which there is no warrant.* For Darwin expressly excludes the notion of sudden unexplained leaps of Nature. But now, though this is the whole meaning of variation : viz. that things vary : it should seem, that no sooner does a theory get based upon the fact, and Variation acquire a big V, than it thereby acquires a sort of mystical significance. Observe, that the question here is not of the chemical *causes* of variation : those are as mysterious as all chemistry : but the organic limits of it. Obviously, and from the very meaning of it, it has, intrinsically, no limit : no two

---

capable of change is any structure : *e. g.*, Darwin says, p. 156 : ' a structure which has been developed through long continued ' selection, when it ceases to be of service to the species, will ' generally become variable, as we see with rudimentary organs : ' for it will no longer be regulated by this same power of ' selection.' This, though he does not see it, is antagonistic to his theory of progress by means of selection.

things are ever quite the same. But on the other hand, relatively, its limits are given to us by the theory of Natural Selection itself. As shown above, no organic form, insignificantly as it may vary from its like, can vary from its essential, i.e. its specific, form. What, then, is its specific form? What is a species? Here we come upon a knotty problem indeed. But though he does not answer the question, he has yet, I think, shown us how to answer it.

' No one definition has as yet satisfied all natu- 'ralists : yet every naturalist knows vaguely what 'he means when he speaks of a species.' (48.) It is most striking to compare this utterance of Darwin's with J. S. Mill's similar statement as to wealth : 'every one knows vaguely what he means 'by wealth.' Nothing can be more singular, or more ominous, than these two declarations. For a species is to Natural, precisely what a commodity is to Political Economy : and the vagueness and indeterminate uncertainty proves in each case that the question is still unsolved. To undervalue, as J. S. Mill did, ' metaphysical nicety of expression,' is merely a mark of inferior thinking power : for it is certain that the definitions of *species* and *wealth* respectively contain the key to Natural and Political Economy : and the fact that the definitions are still wanted proves that the appropriate method of study is not pursued. I have shown this to be the case with Wealth in my *Principle of Wealth Creation,* and shall deal with the question anew in the following book : here we are concerned with the definition of species.

Darwin does not attempt the definition. He looks upon species as a name arbitrarily given for

H

the sake of convenience to a set of individuals closely
resembling each other, and holds that it does not
essentially differ from the term variety, which is
given to less distinct and more fluctuating forms.
(63.) From this, as we shall see, it is clear that
Darwin did not fully grasp the bearing and corollaries
of his own principle.   Further, he was not anxious
to mark any essential difference between *species*
and *variety:* for his theory would fail, were this the
case.   He was thinking here of the ordinary applications of the terms ' species' and 'variety' as
given by naturalists in the epoch before the *Origin
of Species* had made popular and public the idea of
evolution.   We must never forget, as is admitted
by all authorities now-a-days, that our catalogues
of species and varieties had been drawn up by men
who had no principle of classification to guide them,
nothing but arbitrary accidental or numerical considerations : and that until the *Origin of Species*
appeared ' natural history science was a mere collec-
' tion of descriptions of species.   It was a science
' in which the search after new species, merely for
' the sake of adding to the number of known forms,
' was the paramount aim of the zoologist and botanist.
' Classifications grew apace, but the relations of one
' species to another, of group to group, or the general
' plan upon which the animal world was constructed
' and organised, were either undreamt of, as subjects
' of study, or were cursorily dismissed from scientific
' view.   We have but to open a volume of natural
' history lore of the past decade of zoology, to
' realise the truth of this statement.   We may readily
' perceive that attention to outside characters and
' to the construction of artificial systems of classifica-

' tion represented the chief labours of the biologists
' of past years[1].' Nothing can show the futility of
the method better than the criticisms of G. H. Lewes
on Aristotle's *History of Animals*. He condemns
it, as though from a higher plane, for not proceeding
in this exploded style, and attempting to establish
some nonsensical artificial classification. He never
perceives that Aristotle's book is, in truth, a mass
of facts collected for the purpose of comparing their
differences with a view to discovering the *reason
why* and *plan* of organic structure in general. It
has taken the world as usual two thousand years
to get back to Aristotle : in the meanwhile, those
who could not understand, could at least abuse him.

Seeing, then, that all organised beings are instruments, both the whole and the parts, we see also
that a species is simply *a definite grade of form or
structure strictly organised for the preservation of
life and the propagation of the same in a definite and
peculiar way*, or if we like, *under a definite and
peculiar set of conditions*[2]. The necessary or generic
part of the animal, for example, that which is common to all, is, as Aristotle correctly says, the
stomach, mouth and vent, so that the material out
of which the species of animals are formed or derived, the *Ur-Thier*, might be roughly defined as
a portable sack, for the consumption of food. All
species of animals are simply complicated variations

---

[1] *Chapters on Evolution*, p. 31. Compare Darwin, p. 58 : 'to
' discuss whether they ought to be called species or varieties
' before any definition of these terms has been generally ac-
' cepted is vainly to beat the air.'

[2] Flourens, De Candolle, Quatrefages, and to some extent
Cuvier, include descent in their essential notion of species.

on this theme. The process of evolution has simply
endowed them with different organs, weapons of
attack or defence, according to the different demands made upon the organic structure by its conditions : food, habitat, enemies, and so forth. Putting aside the consideration as to the *how* of the
process, and attending only to the result, it is important to observe that the lower any organism be
in the scale, the more indefinite its structure, the
more capable will it be of adapting itself to new
conditions : i.e. the Hydræ may be turned inside
out, and the exterior surface will then digest, and
the stomach respire (*O. S.* 227), whereas the higher
and more definite it be, the less will it be able to
alter. Just as in the outset of life, a man may be
lawyer or doctor, this or that, but the longer he
specialises the less will he be able to start again :
for to determine, is to end, in all directions but one :
so will it be with the organism which has once entered upon a definite direction of development.
· Once let it trust to legs for safety, it must give up
all thought of wings : if it depend upon speed, it
cannot, after a while, pause to change its weapon
for that of strength. It must go on. As it made
its bed, so must it lie upon it. Now the reader who
will reflect upon this and grasp its full significance,
will be able to correct what appears to me to be an
important error in the *Origin of Species.* Instead of
concluding with Darwin that evolution, descent with
modification, essentially involves the idea of the
mutability of species (a point which Darwin enforces
again and again, as though evolution and the mutability of species were convertible terms), he will see
that the *immutability* of species is an essential

corollary of the gradual formation of species. This will explain difficulties that will puzzle the Darwinian. It explains why many naturalists, in spite of much evidence in favour of evolution, could yet never bring themselves to believe that species were mutable. It explains why we have no indication of change in species within historic times. It explains why species do not change within huge geological epochs. It explains why Darwin, who was primarily a botanist, a student of vegetable life, should be strongly impressed with mutability; just as Lamarck, who was the same, maintained evolution against Cuvier, who, being concerned particularly with higher animals, and big organic forms, stoutly defended immutability. It explains again why every one who knows anything of biology inevitably arrives at the conclusion that natural organic structures have been formed by degrees, while on the other hand the uneducated man is apt obstinately to .maintain the fixity of species. And indeed, when we consider the perfect adaptation, and the original and peculiar character of animals, the sober, imperturbable ox, the generous, high-spirited horse, the sly and crafty fox, the idiotic sheep, the noble lion, the merciless spider, the voracious crayfish, the hypocritical, demure cat, the gentle dove, the unwearied, industrious ant or bee, the joyous, bustling, chattering jay, the familiar friendly robin, the grotesque, waggish bear, the vain, self-important cock, the wilful, self-opinionated, unmanageable pig, and a hundred others, it is difficult indeed to believe that such definite, strongly marked, idiosyncratic characters, recurring with such inevitable unerring truth in every specimen, are not absolute : can once not have been, but have step by step arisen. And this difficulty rests indeed on a mystical perception of a truth which is deeper than reason : namely, that they have become thus definite, in course of time, and having so become, must so remain : that in short the days of their generation are over : that they are, to borrow the expression of the school-men, mutable *a parte ante*, but immutable *a parte post*. Time was, when they were not : but now, they must be as they are, or die. For the exigencies of their conditions, the need of self-preservation, a bottomless pit their continual exertions can never fill, keep them rigidly to their own weapons : keep them true to their specific form. Only when and if they are delivered from their exigent condition can they change their shapes : when they escape from the GRINDSTONE OF NECESSITY : but these are then not battle shapes, but peace shapes, given to them not by the stern pruning-knife of a competition which makes each beast find its life in its organisation, but the caprices of matter or man.

And hence it is obvious that the specific characteristics might quite accurately be described as those of *vital* importance : for as Darwin says, Natural Selection acts by life and death. The animal lives by its form, and for its form : according to Aristotle's admirable expression, its aim is to preserve its nature (σώζειν τὴν φύσιν). It has as it were the usufruct of its form : a life interest only in it. It must hand it on to posterity. It is the deep perception of this that makes Aristotle say that every living being strives to produce another like itself in order to share in the eternal and divine (ἵνα τοῦ ἀεὶ καὶ τοῦ θείου μετέχωσι). For it is only the specific element in the organisation that is divine; i.e. produced by the supreme and universal law of co-adaptation of structure to function. In every organisation a large element exists which is not essential, not so constructed : but has arisen merely incidentally, by the material peculiarities of the individual. The specific form, owing to the irregularities of matter, in which it is expressed ; matter, which at bottom prefers its own laws to those of the organic form it composes, and insubordinately breaks out on its own account wherever it can ; the specific form, I say, is never found naked and pure ; it is always enveloped in non-essential clothing. Here we come upon the relation of *species* and *variety.* Beings that have the specific form may vary infinitely in non-essential particulars. Accordingly, there will always be, potentially, though not actually, an indefinite number of varieties of the species : though how many is determined by the accidents of life. To call one form, simply because it is numerically the largest, the species, and other varieties, is essentially arbitrary and unscientific [b]. All are equally varie-

---

[b] 'All naturalists have learned by dearly-bought experience 'how rash it is to attempt to define species by the aid of in- 'constant characters . . . every naturalist who has had the mis- 'fortune to undertake the description of a group of highly varying 'organisms . . . if of a cautious nature, *will end by uniting all the* '*forms which graduate into each other under a single species,* for he 'will say to himself that *he has no right to give names to objects* '*which he cannot define.*' Darwin, *Descent of Man,* 2nd Ed., p. 174.

This is just what I say: naturalists do not know what they mean by species. But now, how can Darwin reconcile this view with his theory that *varieties are incipient species?* Let the

ties of the species. That one is numerically larger than the other is of no moment at all ; it matters, philosophically speaking, not the least, whether there be one lion or a million.

According to Darwin, varieties are incipient species, species in course of formation : and species, varieties that have arrived. This is essential to his view. According to the view explained here, this misses the heart of the question. All varieties, including that to which naturalists arbitrarily give the name of species, are equally varieties of the species. All are but different expressions of the same fundamental root : but so many variations on a single theme, which is the species. Varieties do not lead to the species but away from it. They are not prior to the species, but later : modifications of it. But some one might urge, this is precisely Darwin's view : what he seeks to show is just this, that in course of time these varieties go far enough to constitute new species. But here comes in the essential difference between species and varieties. No amount of variation will ever specifically change the organisation, for varieties do not and cannot differ in points of *vital importance*, of *specific value*. The specific organisation is deep ; the variation shallow and superficial : just as all swords are swords, though there may be infinite varieties of them. No one has expressed the essential dis-

reader judge : is it *unity* or *variety* which conditions tend to produce ? Will not one species diverge into varieties ? and is it likely that innumerable varieties will tend to one species ?—in the Darwinian sense of that word. Is it not clear that varieties vary not *to* but *from* the species ?

tinction between species and varieties more strongly than Darwin himself : he speaks of ' the almost ' universal sterility of species when first crossed, ' which forms so remarkable a contrast with the ' almost universal fertility of varieties when crossed.' (546.) ' The fertility of varieties, that is, of the ' forms known or believed to have descended from ' common parents when intercrossed ; and likewise ' the fertility of this mongrel offspring is with re- ' ference to my theory of equal importance with ' the sterility of species : for it seems to make ' a broad and clear distinction between varieties ' and species.' (300.) ' Varieties, even strongly ' marked ones, though having somewhat of the ' character of species—as is shown by the hopeless ' doubts in many cases how to rank them—yet ' certainly differ from each other far less than do ' good and distinct species. Nevertheless according ' to my view, varieties are species in the process ' of formation, or as I have called them incipient ' species. How then does the lesser difference ' between varieties become augmented into the ' greater difference between species ? ' [This is certainly the knotty point.] ' That this does ' habitually happen, *we must infer* ' [that is to say, *if my theory is true :* if it does *not* happen, the theory is false] ' from most of the innumerable ' species throughout nature presenting well-marked ' differences : whereas varieties, the supposed proto- ' types and parents of future well-marked species, ' present slight and ill defined differences.' (127.) Thus, to support his theory, Darwin bridges the gulf between varieties and species by an *arbitrary assumption.*

We see, in this reference, how Darwin has to admit that facts are against him : but he endeavours to explain them away. He tries, in a most elaborate manner, to get round the facts. But the slightest critical sifting of his arguments will show us that he has completely failed. He endeavours to make out how, by *artificial* means carefully devised to that end, *some* fertility may be forced to appear between crossed species. But here, as usual, in arguing from art to nature he misses the point and begs the question. He cannot show that Nature could do what man may just possibly, by far-fetched devices, do : for the point is, does the thing in question take place in Nature? ' The real diffi- ' culty,' he truly says, ' is not, as it appears to me, ' why *domestic* varieties have not become mutually ' infertile when crossed, but why this has so gene- ' rally occurred with natural varieties, *as soon as they* ' *have been modified in a sufficient and permanent* ' *degree to take rank as species.*' (334.) These last words in italics (mine) are of course merely his assumption expressed as a fact : viz. that varieties *are* incipient species. But now, this difficulty only arises from his theory, that varieties turn into species : and moreover, it is one which, pending any evidence to establish the fact, absolutely an- nihilates it. He has not shown, nor could he pos- sibly show, how, on his theory, varieties should somehow or other cease to be fertile : for on the theory of Natural Selection, fertility would be the greatest of all conceivable advantages to any species. He has therefore to take refuge in ignorance : ' we are far from precisely knowing the ' cause : nor is this surprising, considering how

' profoundly ignorant we are, &c. : ' and he continues with conjectures : ' must have been '—' this
' may well make a difference '—' would probably in
' like manner be '—and so on.   But this is utterly
preposterous.   Here we have a theoretical hypothesis, flatly contradicted by facts, in its very heart,
and we are asked to take it, *because* we are ignorant : i.e. on the strength of another hypothesis,
that there may conceivably be some way or other
of reconciliation.   Hypothesis based upon ignorance : this is certainly a new scientific method !
The fact is, that in this chapter on Sterility, as
well as in that wonderful chapter on Instinct, the
most extraordinary amalgam of ' may be,' conjecture, theory-stretching, question begging, and
airy nothings, that ever was offered in support of
a halting theory to a credulous and illogical world,
Darwin is struggling with impossibility.   Having
somehow or other established an *apparent* basis
for his theory by analogies drawn from human
selection, which, as we have seen, are entirely fallacious, he finds himself obliged to face portentous
difficulties that refuse to be explained, and accordingly performs intellectual gymnastics of the
strangest kind to try and lay their spirits.   He
was drawn on by the truth in his book, descent
with modification ; and never perceived the astounding fallacy in that part which was unsound.
The miserable folly, ignorance and prejudice of
many of the objections that were brought against
him created a revulsion in his favour, and did him
good service, by leading people to suppose, later
on, that nothing but prejudice could dictate any
objections at all.   Yet, though he considers many

objections, the most serious of all never so much as presented themselves to his mind [c].

The fact is simply that this fertility of varieties and sterility of species is fatal to his view (otherwise untenable), that varieties are but incipient species: (unless of course we apply the name species arbitrarily to the variety numerically largest, in which case variety and species do not essentially differ, are simply convertible terms, and the whole question is stripped of its meaning and becomes futile). But the whole of this discussion shows us, that this is an inversion of the truth, and only plays upon the surface of the mysterious origin of species. All varieties are merely the specific form in different clothes. They all get it, by generation. Descent, as Darwin says, is the hidden bond revealed to us by our classifications. Unity of species is really unity of origin; implies common origin. Thus generation is the principle of identity: conditions, the principle of difference. As the specific form is handed down from form to form the conditions clothe it differently: but they cannot radically alter it: for keen competition, i.e. Natural Selection, keeps its nose to the GRINDSTONE OF NECESSITY: keeps it constantly de-

[c] Yet in the *Descent of Man*, p. 172, he takes his theory as proved. 'I may here remind the reader that the sterility of ' species when crossed is not a specially acquired quality, but, ' like the incapacity of certain trees to be grafted together, is ' incidental on other acquired differences. *The nature of these* ' *differences is unknown.*' He sees that it could not have been acquired by Natural Selection, so he denies that it is a specially acquired quality: but he has not succeeded in showing it to be ' incidental.' It is merely the necessary assumption, if his theory is to be true.

pendent on its essential organs for life. When we remember how short is the individual life, we can easily see, that the specific form can never change under a stern competitive régime. It would not have time. For the change would have to occur in a single life. The form is permanent only through the succession of individuals. Therefore, however much the individual may and does vary, the variation can never be considerable relatively to its essential organs, or it would go out. The very meaning of the term 'to vary' shows us this. Each individual varies infinitesimally from each, but they intercross freely, and hence there cannot possibly be that *accumulation of one very slight variation in a definite direction* which is the postulate and the essential condition of Darwin's theory of Natural Selection. There is no breeder here with a plan in his head to watch for, preserve and accumulate some infinitesimal distinction, and carefully isolate it by preventing crosses. It re-quires but a few days of starvation, and the indi-vidual, and with it the species, is dead and gone. Let the reader bring this home to his mind. Let him contemplate some organic form ; let him watch a few crows, or sea-gulls, as they fly about and settle together, and observe how one will differ— but the word is too strong—just a little from an-other, yet let him wake himself up, as it were, to see, feel and realise how identical at bottom each is with each, in respect of its life : how this crow and that crow are after all *the* crow : how each *is*, ac-cording as it *works :* lives by its organs. We speak loosely of the crow having wings, of the horse having legs, yet this really includes a fallacy : the

crow *is* its wings : the animal is but the sum total
of its essential organs : we might, indeed, speak of
a crow *having* a white spot on it, with less in-
accuracy ; but properly speaking, to say that it *has*
wings is to make a metaphysical entity of the crow,
apart from its shape. The sum total of the animal's
organs, working correctly : that is the crow, and
that is Aristotle's definition of the soul, the life.
As, then, its life depends on, and is in fact nothing
but its organs working, how can the animal possibly
vary in any essential organ [d] ? and how if it vary in
any non-essential organ, if it vary only in particulars
both in kind and degree relatively to its nature
insignificant, can these be so accumulated by Natural
Selection so as to produce an essential change in
its form ?   How can it vary away from its form ?

No one has brought home to us the intricate
relations of all organic beings in nature, the extraordinary complexity and tangled balance of forces,
more clearly than Darwin himself. Each being
is just *what* it is, because it is *when* it is and
where it is : such is the sum total of his teaching ; such was the root idea of Aristotle.   In the

[d] Darwin says (*O. S.* p. 50), that he can give instances of
variation in important organs (though he gives none), but he
does not say he can give instances of essential variation in
essential organs.

He says again (p. 106) : ' It may be objected by those who
' have not attended to Natural History that the long continued
' accumulation of individual differences could not rise to parts
' or organs which seem to us and are often called new.'   Let
the reader observe, that the question is not whether the long
continued accumulation of individual differences could do this :
the question is, whether Darwin's theory of Natural Selection
could effect this long continued accumulation.

competitive struggle, ' a grain in the balance will
' determine the result.' (554.) 'Under nature,
' the slightest differences of structure or con-
' stitution may well turn the nicely balanced scale
' in the struggle for life and so be preserved.'
(96.) But is it not astonishing to see how totally
Darwin misses the point. Most true it is, that
the slightest circumstance may determine the result,
but just for that reason is his theory impossible.
He always assumes in the most unaccountable·
way, that *the* circumstance determining the result
(which is the life of the individual,) will be just
this insignificant variation of his, in the one individual in which it arises. For observe, though
he talks loosely about a 'variety having been
' formed ' by his process, it must begin with the
individual variation ᵉ. But now, a thousand cir-

ᵉ *Origin of Species*, p. 47. 'In order that a great amount
' of modification in any part should be effected, *a variety* when
' once formed must again, *perhaps after a long interval of time,*
' vary or present individual differences of the same favourable
' nature, and these must again be preserved, and so onwards
' step by step.'
    Observe the fallacy here: a variety is not a variation. The
question is how is a variety to be formed? Darwin says, by
individual variation. Yes, but how is the variation to be preserved? If we assume the formation of a variety on Darwin's
principles, we may as well assume the formation of a species
at once. Variation begins with the individual, and even supposing it to favour the individual, and even supposing it to
descend to his posterity, how is this slight variation to be
preserved during a long interval of time? amid the myriad
other determining factors, till another of the same kind arises?
Or are all the individuals to vary together? then it is not
variation, but the definite result of the same conditions.

cumstances come into play to determine the existence of this individual, and after it, of all its
progeny.   Imagination plays us a trick here, and
gives to Darwin's theory its specious appearance.
When he speaks of a 'profitable variation de-
'termining survival,' we feel of course that it must
be so, because we unconsciously picture this profitable variation as something big enough to give
decisive advantage throughout life.   But this is
just what, as the facts of experience and Darwin's
hypothesis both require, it could never be.   As
usual, the error lies not in the major premiss
but the minor.   Nobody denies or could deny the
obvious and necessary truth, that a variation profitable to or giving advantage to the organism in the
struggle for life would preserve it, and this is what
gives to Darwin's hypothesis its apparent solidity.
But this does not touch the point, *unless it can
be shown* that variations profitable *in kind and
degree* could occur, or having occurred, could
be perpetuated by generation.   The variation
that we know is quite insignificant, quite impotent
both in kind and degree, to produce any bene-
ficial effect whatever.   Darwin's theory breaks
down entirely, just because the three essential
points, the nature, amount, and inheritance of
variation under domestication are such as could
do nothing at all under nature.   The variations
are so slight, that they could not be profitable ; and even if they were, they could not be
accumulated, by reason of the mixture and crossing
of different individuals.   The resultant of the intricate play of forces in the competitive struggle
must necessarily be determined by the whole of

them. Of all these forces, the very slightest is just the insignificant, isolated, casual variation on which Darwin builds his theory [f].

He says with a truth that touches him nearly : ' Nothing is easier than to admit in words the truth ' of the universal struggle for life, or more difficult— ' *at least I have found it so*—than constantly to bear ' this conclusion in mind. Yet unless it be thoroughly ' ingrained in the mind, *the whole economy of nature,* ' with every fact bearing on distribution, rarity, ' abundance, extinction *and variation* will be dimly ' seen or quite misunderstood.' (73.) Again : ' here ' we see that cattle absolutely determine the existence ' of the Scotch fir.' (83.) (Then, let the reader note, how could any slight variation in the organisation

[f] Mr. Wallace, in his excellent and most unselfish statement of Darwinism, has seen most fully the paramount importance of establishing this point of variation in nature, but in his chapter on that subject he has only succeeded in proving what I have stated in the text, that great variation is only found in low forms, largest in marine organisms and plants, and least in higher organic forms : i.e. that the more special the organic form, the less essential is its variation. As to important specific organs, he leaves the question just where he found it. '*We can well understand,*' he says, on p. 130, ' how after the first step was taken, every variation tending to ' more complete vision would be preserved till we reach the ' perfect eye of birds and mammals.' Mr. Wallace may, but I for one understand not at all how variations, not very large and simultaneous, could produce the eye of the swan, owl, or eagle, adapted respectively for seeing under water, in the dark, and at long ranges. The point is not, whether accumulation could produce them : the point is, how *slight* variation ultimately tending to issue in them could decisively influence the survival of the organisms over all other influences.

As to how the variations could be perpetuated by inheritance, Mr. Wallace leaves us in the dark.

I

of the Scotch fir get over this preponderating factor
in the struggle for its existence.) Again he shows
how cats determine the existence of flowers (85) : of
what use then slight variations in the organisation
of flowers? Again in his imaginary illustration
as to how bees acquired their cell-making instinct,
he has a sort of perception of the point here enforced,
for he says : 'saving of time *must be* an important
'.element of success to any family of bees. *Of course
'the success of the species may be'* (he might have
said, *must be*) '*dependent on the number of its
'enemies, or parasites, or on quite distinct causes,
'and so be altogether independent of the quantity of
'honey which the bees could collect.* But let us
'suppose, that this latter circumstance determined,
'as it *probably often* has determined, whether a bee
'could exist, &c.' (286.) Certainly, suppositions will
prove anything. 'Much virtue in if,' says Touchstone, and would doubtless have repeated the
remark, with emphasis, on perusing the *Origin of
Species.* Again 'a corollary of the highest import-
'ance may be deduced from the foregoing remarks,
'namely, that THE STRUCTURE OF EVERY ORGANIC
'BEING IS RELATED, IN THE MOST ESSENTIAL YET
'OFTEN HIDDEN MANNER, TO THAT OF ALL THE OTHER
'ORGANIC BEINGS WITH WHICH IT COMES INTO COMPE-
'TITION for food or residence, and from which it has
'to escape, or on which it preys.' (88.) And similar
passages could be quoted in numbers to the same
effect. Thus he most emphatically expresses to us,
how decisively that equilibrium of forces in the
competition and play and battle within battle,
depends upon the energetic operation of each
being's essential organs ; or, to express it in other

words, the existence of every being is determined
and conditioned by the structures of a thousand
others; and yet he never perceives that since this
is so, the very least factor in determining the
existence of any being is some trifling variation
in a non-essential point. He never perceives that
this very war to the death on which he lays stress
in proof of his theory is precisely that which
annihilates it. The insignificant and trifling and
temporary variation (for it appears with and disappears with the individual) is but a vanishing atom
in the presence of immensity : just because it is
merely individual and peculiar and not typical,
it can never influence the result. It is not the
peculiar and varying and inconstant, but the common
and typical qualities of the individual that give it
its place in the economy of nature : because
a permanent position in such economy can only
be won by permanent qualities. Take, for example,
his own illustration (85) : the existence of red clover
depends on humble-bees, of humble-bees on field-
mice. Here we have a chain—red clover,—humble-
bees,—field-mice. But observe that thus the clover
depends on the mice, not *quâ* their non-essential
differences, but *quâ* their essential resemblances—
not on this mouse or that mouse, but *the* mouse.
The equilibrium depends not on the inconstant, but
the constant element in the mouse. The variations,
just because they *are* variations, *cannot* affect the
result or come into play, or produce equilibrium.
Nature shows her power *through* the individual,
but only because he is so numerous : not *quâ* his
individuality. Individuality, as such, is impotent.
It is of course, in every case, *a* particular mouse

which acts : yet for all that it is not the particular
mouse, but the universal mouse, the mouse *quâ*
mouse, and not *quâ* what is peculiar to him as
an individual, that really influences the economy.
Hence I say that the deadly competition to which
Darwin appeals, the intricate web of relations which
he adduces, in support of his theory that variations
determine the survival of the animal, really destroys it ; and it shows that he did not fully
grasp the full significance of his own theory.

And I could show by a detailed critical examination of the *Origin of Species*, that Darwin did
not understand his own principle in many other
points of view, but I shall content myself with only
one—Sexual Selection.   Darwin speaks of this as
if it were something different from Natural Selection.   He says that its action is less rigorous than
that of Natural Selection, and depends not on
a struggle for existence, but on a struggle of the
males from the females. (100.)   From this it is
quite plain to me that he did not understand
Natural Selection.   Natural Selection means nothing at all, unless it comprehends every circumstance that could possibly influence, or go to
determine, survival in the struggle.   If it does not
mean this, it is simply an abstraction, an entity,
an unwarranted sophism.   And sexual selection
is simply a special case of it; one of the factors
which go to determine survival.   How could Darwin say that it did not involve existence? it involves inheritance, progeny, which, for his principle, is the same thing?   It is true, that a male
rejected by one female may subsequently find
another.   So may a wolf which has proved slower

than a competing wolf in the pursuit of a deer, find another deer. Sexual Selection stands exactly on the same ground as any other factor in Natural Selection influencing the survival of a particular variation. It is no more possible to make a separate item of Sexual Selection in the account than of selection by speed, selection by cunning, strength, size, or anything else. All are but cases of Natural Selection, and that Darwin should not have seen it is conclusive proof that he did not fully appreciate the bearings of his own theory. Further, it may be incidentally remarked, that sexual selection will by no means explain facts to which Darwin attempts to apply it. Many brilliant butterflies could not possibly have been formed by the selection of the female, partly because the colours are so placed as to be out of her sight: and partly, as has been shown by entomological authorities, because in many cases the female does in fact actually exercise no selection, but plays a perfectly passive part, being impregnated without resistance by the first male that finds her. If then we find colouring of the most gorgeous description in cases, as e.g. that of the Emperor moth, where sexual selection *could* not act, why need we have recourse to it in others ?

The reader will observe that throughout this criticism, it is not with side-issues, but the very core of the Darwinian theory that we have been dealing. We have met the theory, negatively, on its own ground. But it would be additionally easy to bring arguments of a very positive nature against it. 'If it could be shown,' says Darwin (227), 'that any complex organ existed, which

'could not possibly be formed by numerous, *suc-*
'*cessive*, slight modifications, my theory would
'absolutely break down. But I can find no such
'case.' Now, I have shown above that, *in general*,
numerous successive slight modifications could not
accumulate by Natural Selection, so as to produce
by addition a large positive specific difference. But
to pass over this for a moment, it is obvious, that
this assertion is a most novel and preposterous
method of gaining credit for a hypothesis. It
is not for us to accept any incredible hypothesis,
unless we can positively show that it is wrong.
It might be quite impossible to prove that any
particular theory as to the formation of a structure
was unsound, yet it by no means follows that
it must therefore be true. Such a challenge is
at once unmeaning, and a gratuitous *ignoratio
elenchi*. The *onus probandi* lies upon the man
who maintains a dogmatic thesis : not upon his
audience. Darwin's business is to prove that the
theory *can* explain the facts : it is not ours to prove
that it cannot. And yet it does so happen that we
can accept his challenge. For there is, as it seems
to me, an element in *complex* organs which utterly
destroys his theory. This I have noted by under-
lining, in the above quotation, the word *successive*.
For the effective action of a complex organ depends upon a complicated *co-adaptation* of frequently
very numerous component parts, parts constructed
upon a highly differentiated and surprising plan :
which in order to be of any use at all (and this
is the *sine quá non* for Darwin) involve not a
successive but a *simultaneous* adjustment and variation. For example, the human eye, the human

ear,—one of the most miraculous pieces of mechanism in nature—the eagle's eye, the method
of nutrition in the kangaroo, and similar organisa-
tions ; or still better, the interdependent and highly
artificial co-adaptations of two or more different
beings. Here is a hard nut for the Darwinian
to crack. Darwin does not attempt to disguise
it. But it is no defence to say, as he does, that
' it is not necessary to suppose that all the modifi-
' cations were simultaneous, *if they were extremely*
' *slight and gradual'* (225), or that ' the force of this
' objection rests entirely on the assumption that
' the changes in both instinct and structure are
' abrupt.' Apart from the fact that he here comes
under the criticism as to the slight and gradual
process which has been given above, who does
not see that no amount of *simple* variation can
ever account for *complex* co-adaptation ? no amount
of *sequence* can explain *co-existence ?* for one part
cannot exist, so as to be useful, before the other.
It is a logical impossibility. It is not in point to
appeal here, as he does, to the series of gradations
arising by unequal and often abrupt leaps from low
to high structure. The point here is not the fact
of evolution, but the way it is done[g]. And till the

---

[g] 'He who will go thus far, ought not to hesitate to go
' a step farther, if he finds on finishing this volume that large
' bodies of facts otherwise inexplicable can be explained by
' the theory of *descent with modification :* he ought to admit
' that a structure even so perfect as an eagle's eye might be
' formed by *natural selection*, although in this case he does
' not know the transitional states.' (225.) He ought to do
nothing of the kind. Darwin here, as I have said above, confounds his theory of Natural Selection with the fact of evolution :

Darwinian can show how slight and gradual successive variations could ever, on the hypothesis
of utility, become simultaneous complicated co-
adaptations, his theory is simply out of court.
Darwin's own way of solving this portentous difficulty is simply the appeal to ignorance : we must
not say it could not happen, because we do not
know how.   But with his permission, he must not
say it could happen, because he does not know
how : or until he can show how.   Why, on this
method, I must believe anything.   It is not scientific
explanation ; it is faith. The soul, I am told, is
immortal : I must believe, for I do not know *how*.
Why, if these are your methods, should I not believe in special arbitrary creation at once : for it
would save me a great deal of trouble, and rests on
precisely the same evidence as your own theory
of Natural Selection : viz. that I cannot prove that
it did not happen, and I do not know how it
was done.   Why not believe that the moon is made
of cream-cheese, or that the walls of Jericho fell
down at the blast of the trumpets of the children
of Israel ?   Of all remarkable scientific methods,
this *hypothesis based on ignorance* is the strangest.
Deduction we know, and induction we know : nay,
even dogma we know, but what in Creation is this ?

   Yet again there is a difficulty which, as far as I
am aware, has never yet been adduced against the
theory of Natural Selection, which is certainly
never considered by Darwin or Wallace, and which
nevertheless seems to me to be of all difficulties

as if the two were the same, and there was no alternative :
as if who accepted the latter necessarily and *ipso facto* accepted
the other.

one of the most striking and obvious—the question
of *size*. I believe, says Darwin, that all animals
have descended from at most four or five progenitors, and plants even less. Well, we may
believe anything. But what is there to justify the
belief that this could have come about by Natural
Selection? Consider and contrast the giant structures with the infinitesimal specks of Nature: compare the mammoth, the elephant, the whale, the
megatherium, the pterodactyl, the albatross, the giant
trees of California and the tropical forests, with the
ant, the humming-bird, the gnat, the microscopic
infusoria and mosses. How are we to account for
these extraordinary differences? Size is, indeed,
from one point of view, nothing: but from the
point of view of existence, it is everything. How
can we conceive the possibility of forms, so intensely
and definitely organised, yet so marvellously dis-
parate in size, arising from the same progenitors?
Is there not here suggested to us the suspicion that
there must have been an *original* difference: that
to prove community of origin, between such infinitely disproportionate structures, we need more
than a mere survival in a struggle for existence?
It is no explanation to say, as some might say, that
the larger the variation, the better the individual
would survive. For if that were true, why do small
things remain small? Obviously because they fit
their conditions in the struggle. Then how can we
explain the origin of the big monsters? Are we to
assume with Lucretius and Empedocles, that vast
shapeless lumps, huge conglomerations of undetermined and chaotic matter, struggled for existence
in the primeval age of the world? For if there is

one thing rather than another which Natural Selection cannot explain, it is the proportionate and
all-round increase in size of a structure in its
totality.   For every organised structure must be
proportionate; and disproportionate increase in one
point would, as Aristotle says, tend to turn it into
a different sort of structure altogether : but that
every point of any structure should simultaneously
and continuously vary in size, is contrary alike to
reason and experience : not to mention that increase in size would be just as likely to injure as to
benefit the organisation.   What has Natural Selection to say to this?   If we reflect upon it, we
shall, I think, see that Darwin's *Origin of Species*
is no theory of the origin of species at all.   Natural
Selection, indeed, may be a perfectly valid explanation of the preservation of favoured races in
the struggle for life : it may be perfectly true that
the best specimens of every form have the best
chance, *ceteris paribus*, of surviving : but the longer
we examine this idea, the more plainly shall we
discern, that this principle can do no more than
improve within specific limits : *i.e.*, that it will
grind like a whetstone, and keep all the organic
weapons, or specific organs, keen and sharp, but
that it will not and cannot explain the origin
of species, or the transmutation of one species
into another.

The reader would very much misunderstand the
import of this discussion, if he were to gather from
it that it tended in any way to depreciate Darwin.
Much otherwise.   We must not allow our respect for
the character of the author of the *Origin of Species*
to turn us aside from the main point, or bias our

judgment[h]. The first qualification of a critic is to be no respecter of persons. That is mere puerility. We pay a far greater compliment to, and mark our respect for an author in a far more deep and genuine manner by closely and inquisitively thumbing his classic work and sifting his views, even though we should differ *in toto* from him, than by helping to swell the chorus of worthless and insignificant adulation, which Diogenes long ago correctly estimated, by calling it 'the noise of madmen.' Nor could there possibly be a greater mistake to suppose that, if his theory is unsound, his book is of no value. I consider the *Origin of Species* to be, after the principal works of Aristotle and the *Novum Organum*, the most valuable book from the point of view of scientific method that ever was written. It is true that Darwin's intellect was imaginative and sympathetic rather than deeply critical and analytic. We look in vain, in the *Origin of Species*, for the close, never failing, sleepless, critical, limitative thinking of Aristotle, always awake to the qualifying influence of circumstances, and the special conditions in which his thought is moving, so that he is constantly taking his bearings, as it were. Yet where indeed shall we look for it? Darwin, on the contrary, had as it seems to me an essentially religious mind. Yet, though the doctrine of evolution was not originated by him, but Lamarck, nevertheless he did more than any man to bring the fact of evolution home

[h] Nothing could give us a better idea of Darwin's character than the *trait* which appears in what he said himself of the human eye, 'the thought of which even to the very last gave 'me a cold shiver.'

to the world, and by refounding the doctrine that function makes structure (however in the natural world it may subsequently be explained) he has reconstituted unintentionally for us the biological, organic, dynamic and evolutionary scientific method which was the soul of Aristotle's whole philosophy, and which, as will appear presently, is the key to Political no less than Natural Economy.

VIII. But let me take this opportunity of presenting this parallelism from another point of view, by means of some extracts from Darwin.

He speaks of 'the perfection of structure and 'co-adaptation' of specific forms. (3.)   Again : 'we 'see these beautiful co-adaptations most plainly 'in the woodpecker and the mistletoe; and only 'a little less plainly in the humblest parasite which 'clings to the hairs of a quadruped or the feathers 'of a bird : in the structure of the beetle which 'dives through the water : in the plumed seed 'which is wafted by the gentlest breeze : in short, 'we see beautiful adaptations everywhere and in 'every part of the organic world.' (71.)   Again : 'the 'chief *use* in the nutriment in the seed is to favour 'the growth of the young seedling.' (89.)   Again : 'in Lobelia fulgens, there is a really beautiful and 'elaborate *contrivance*, &c.,' and a little above, 'a special contrivance for self-fertilisation.' (113.) 'I believe this objection to be valid, but that *nature* '*has largely provided against it*, by giving to trees 'a strong tendency to bear flowers with separate 'sexes.' (115.)   'No one will maintain that we as 'yet know the uses of all the parts of any one plant, 'or the functions of each cell in any one organ.' (151.) 'We must suppose that there is a power

' represented by Natural Selection or the Survival
' of the Fittest, always intently watching each slight
' alteration and carefully preserving each, &c.'
(226.) ' The common rule throughout Nature is that
' the same end is gained by the most diversified
' means.' ' How differently constructed is the
' feathered wing of a bird and the membrane
' covered wing of a bat with all its digits largely
' developed : and still more so the four wings of
' a butterfly, the two wings of a fly, and the two
' wings of a beetle together with the elytra. Bivalve
' shells are made to open and shut, but on what
' a number of patterns is the hinge constructed,
' from the long row of neatly interlocking teeth
' in a Nucula to the simple ligament of a Mussel.
' Seeds are disseminated by their minuteness ; by
' their capsule being converted into a light balloon-
' like envelope,—by being imbedded in pulp or
' flesh, formed of the most diverse parts, and
' rendered nutritious as well as conspicuously
' coloured, *so as to* attract and be devoured by
' birds—by having hooks and grapnels of many
' kinds *so as to* adhere to the fur of quadrupeds—
' and by being furnished with wings and plumes as
' different in shape as elegant in structure, *so as to*
' be wafted by every breeze.' (235.) A little lower,
he speaks of the simple *plan* by which fallen grains
' are blown on to the stigma of a flower;' then again :
' from this simple stage we may pass through an
' inexhaustible number. of *contrivances*, all for the
' same *purpose* and effected in essentially the same
' manner, but entailing changes in every part of the
' flower.' Of the coryanthus orchid, he says, after
describing it : ' now at last we see the full *use*

'of every part of the flower, of the water secreting
'horns, of the bucket half full of water, which
'prevents the bees from flying away and forces them
'to crawl out through the spout, and rub against the
'properly *placed* viscid fallen masses, and viscid
'stigma.'   'Flowers rank among the most beautiful
'productions of nature, and they have become
'through Natural Selection beautiful, or rather
'conspicuous in contrast with the green leaves *that*
'*they might easily be* observed and visited by insects
'*so that* their fertilisation *might be favoured:*' 'the
'scarlet leaves of the holly serve merely as a guide
'to birds and beasts *that* the fruit *may* be devoured
'and the manured seeds thus disseminated.'   (245.)
Again : 'the elaboration of dense clouds of pollen
'by our fir trees *so that* a few granules may be
'wafted by a chance breeze on to the ovules.'
(249.) And he constantly speaks of Nature working
'for the *good* of each being: or *improving* their
'structure.'

Truly did Aristotle say, 'the nature of a thing
'is its final cause'—ἡ φύσις τέλος ἐστὶν—'nature
'suits her tools to their work, and not the work
'to the tools.'   Let me appeal to the impartial
reader, and ask him whether if these extracts
were given him as coming from Aristotle, or
quoted, say, two thousand years hence to some
one who had never heard of Darwin, he would
not be apt to dismiss them as old exploded teleological views: which Science since Bacon's day
has entirely condemned and flung aside, as *mere*
popularia.   Well, that is what is done with Aristotle.   People who know nothing of him, or who
know of him only this, that he was an obsolete

teleologist, judge him by isolated and mistranslated fragments, and never suspect that his teleology is just that which Darwin has reinstated. For Darwin's result and Aristotle's result coincide: they both say that a thing is what it is, is defined both in fact and thought, gets its structure or form from its final cause, i.e. its function, the work it has to do, its adaptive necessity. True it is, that Darwin has given an explanation of the *how*, while Aristotle gave none. But apart from the fact that this 'how' of Darwin's is fallacious, we may well ask, could Darwin have given it, unless he had lived just when he did? The geological succession of beings in time, the geographical distribution of organic forms in space, the Malthusian doctrine, and the general practice and peculiar results of cattle breeding—these were the essential preconditions of Darwin's theory, and Aristotle knew nothing of them. The astonishing thing is that without them he should have risen, alone and unaided, by the sheer force of his miraculous genius, to his matchless scheme of a dynamical evolution from potential to actual, from matter to form ; to his marvellous all-embracing doctrine that structure is explained by function, and that development proceeds by consecutive and gradual differentiations from the simple and homogeneous to the complex and unhomogeneous, which is the essence of that view popularly accredited to Von Baer and Herbert Spencer, and which holds within it the secret of Natural and Political Economy.

But let us look into this teleology a little more closely. Let us concede for a moment that Darwin has proved his point, and that Natural Selection is sound and sufficient : yet I say that Aristotle has a point of view still further than this, and it is one which is most curiously and conveniently ignored by modern mechanical philosophers.

Here is a wood-pigeon's egg, or the germ of e.g. a pig. Now, says Aristotle, this egg or this germ contains potentially the wood-pigeon or the pig that is to arise out of it by differentiation and growth. Not just any germ or egg will develop into just anything : but a wood-pigeon's egg will only become a wood-pigeon, and a pig germ nothing but a pig. Now, is not this a fact? How can we escape teleology here? Grant, if you please, that Darwin has given us a full and satisfactory explanation of the origin, the development *in time* of the wood-pigeon or the pig—its phylogeny, as the Germans say : (which, as the argument has shown, is not the case : but grant it :) how does that enable us to get out of the fact that looking at the individual specimen before us, at the ontogeny, or growth and development not of the race, but the individual, the full-formed animal is contained potentially in the germ : or that the germ's development is definitely determined by its *final* result? Is not that the case? and can we explain how it is done? We can explain nothing : we have not the dimmest of dim conceptions how it is done. The more closely we examine modern biology, the more do we discern that to increase and multiply terminology is not therefore to account for facts. *Post hoc* is not *propter hoc.* How, then, do we fail to see that Aristotle's teleology, so far from being metaphysics[i], is only a simple

[i] Metaphysics, a meaningless word never used by Aristotle,

expression of the fact. The evolution of the individual germ and embryo is determined by its final cause : *i.e.* as Aristotle says, ' that which a thing is, ' when the process of its generation is completed ' is what we call its nature, as, *e.g.*, a man, horse, ' or a house.' And again, ' the generation is for ' the sake of the essential nature, and not *vice versâ.*' Is it not so ? Can any man who knows anything of Embryology deny it ? Then what becomes of all the ignorant abuse of Aristotle all these three hundred years ? And how, in this regard, is Dar win in advance of Aristotle ; in the essential particular of the development of the individual animal from its germ to its full and predetermined form ? But Aristotle has not given us any chemical explanation of the process ? No : but who said he had, or who has ? Does that invalidate his exposition of the fact ? Is there any book in modern embryological literature which has laid its finger on the essential more clearly and firmly than his treatise *On the Generation of Animals?* The microscope has indeed told us a little more, in extent : but has it told us anything radically deeper than what Aristotle saw with his own unassisted piercing eye ?

Long consideration of this point has convinced me that the misapprehension of Aristotle's meaning

means in the mouths of nineteen people out of twenty, only something unintelligible to them. In the mouths of Comtists, it means *realistic* philosophy, philosophy that discovers *causes*— for causation is synonymous with reality. No causation, no reality. But modern evolution and embryology have vindicated Aristotle from the superficial rationalistic criticism of Positivism, which emasculates Nature by denying dynamical causation.

K

here is simply due to the want of critical subtlety in
the Teutonic mind.   People unconsciously suppose
that by final cause Aristotle meant a sort of other
mechanical and material cause of a mysterious and
mystical kind.   But he did no such thing.   By final
cause he meant adaptation to conditions; nor did
he ever imagine for a moment that by assigning
this, the most essential of all the causes of structure,
there was any the less necessity for a full material
and mechanical explanation as well.   Over and
over again, as I have shown in the account given
on a preceding page, he insists on the double nature
of all true and thorough-going explanation.   I shall
endeavour to make this, however, still clearer by an
illustration.   Here is heated water in a boiler.   To
the idealist, it is just a sensation, *et præterca nihil*:
to the mechanico-mathematical philosopher, it is
H_2O, and the heat is, say, 212°: but is this all?
No; we still do not know the causes of that hot
water: the cause still needed is, that it is heated,
so as to drive the engine, and the causes of this
again ramify out into untold branches: it is to
put money into the pockets of shareholders: to
carry ever so many people rapidly to their destina-
tions, and so on.   Or take a natural illustration.
Here is a green butterfly.   What is this green
colour?   To the idealist, a sensation [k] (poor, thin,

[k] The late Prof. Ingram says (*Hist. of Pol. Econ.*, 61), 'the
'subjection of the phenomena of the social, and in particular
'the economic, world, to fixed relations of co-existence and
'succession.   This is the positive doctrine which lies at the
'bottom of all true science.'
   It may be the positive doctrine, but there is no science in
it at all.   It only says, that a thing does occur; never *why it*

incorrigible idealist) : to the mathematical philosopher, a certain quantitative vibration : let us suppose that he can give it exactly : has he explained
it fully? No : we still require a further answer:
the reason why, *raison d'être* of the green is to
enable the butterfly, by mimicking other species, to
escape destruction. The green is materialised imposture. And so on. In every case of composition, of organic structure, the mechanical explanation is inadequate : it is only half the truth : just
so, the final or adaptive explanation is inadequate.
Neither is wholly adequate. We may have a full
mechanical explanation, yet still remain ignorant of
the reason why of the fact : so, contrariwise, may
we have the final adaptive, functional explanation,
yet still remain ignorant of the mechanical explanation of the fact. The one does not exclude,
but is complementary of the other. To know the
one, does not in the least do away with the necessity for knowing the other : *e.g.* we may know that
the cause of A's death was that B struck him, yet
ignore the reason why : so we may, conversely,
know that the reason why a plant is thus or thus
constructed is that it must be visited by bees ; but
we may ignore the mechanical explanation. Both
are essential to complete knowledge. *The Principle
of Scientific Explanation and Definition comprises*
BOTH. But according to the end we wish to arrive
at, now one, now the other, is the more important.

must. The social and economic world is determined by relations, not of co-existence and succession, but cause and effect:
thus, *e.g.*, if this state is to survive, an army *must* be raised,
and so on. Not the material, but the conditional necessity,
is the social and political and economical principle.

And just because the mechanical philosophy has monopolised attention, no progress has been made in Political Economy, because that has always neglected the one thing essential in that sphere— the final cause : the function which gives to structure its shape, its meaning, and its significance.

Let me illustrate still further by a crucial instance the cardinal superficiality of modern mechanical philosophy. In his Address to the British Association at Norwich in 1868, Professor Tyndall described the formation of salt pyramids, as precisely resembling Egyptian pyramids, but produced by mechanical spontaneity : from these he went on to apply the mechanical method and argument to organic life—grain : then he says, ' Given the grain ' and its environments, an intellect the same in kind ' as our own, but sufficiently expanded, might trace ' out *a priori* every step of the process, *and by the* ' *application of purely mechanical principles* would ' be able to demonstrate that the cycle of actions ' must end as it is seen to end in the reproduction ' of forms like that with which the operation began. ' *A similar necessity rules here to that which rules* ' *the planets in their circuits round the sun.* . . . *The* ' *formation of a crystal, a plant, or an animal* is in ' the eye of many scientific thinkers a purely ' mechanical problem, *which differs from the prob-* ' *lems of ordinary mechanics* in the smallness of the ' masses and the complexity of the processes in- ' volved.'

Here we see just what I wish to point out : the illegitimate extension of the mechanico-mathematical method to the organic sphere. It shows, as I have said above, that modern science which

fondly supposes itself superior to and beyond
Aristotle, stands in sore need of a little of his
criticism. Organic forms can *not* be explained
on purely mechanical principles : nor again does
a similar necessity rule in the organic world to
that which rules in the inorganic or mechanical.
Darwin has taught us just this. Purely mechanical
principles will never tell us just the essential
thing in the organic world. Take, for example,
the owl's eye. Mechanical principles will explain
exactly the mechanical adjustment and operation
of the eye : but they will not explain *why* it is
so :—to see at night. Purely mechanical principles
will explain (assuming they are full enough) the
proboscis of the moth, and its mechanism ; but
they will not give us the cause of the proboscis :
which is to extract food from a well. Purely
mechanical principles will explain the arrival of the
carriage and horses : yet the cause *why* it is there is
still wanting. In fact, any one can, I think, now see
the wisdom in Aristotle's distinction between the
absolute or material necessity of the inorganic, and
the conditional necessity of the organic world. A
lump of inorganic matter must obey its own nature :
the laws of its material constitution. But the necessity in the organic world is not of this kind. There
is no absolute necessity that A should exist : but
there is necessity that, *if* he is to exist, he should
eat. There is no necessity for this bird to live :
it may die : but if it is to live, it must have wings.
The necessity that rules the organic world is not
like that ruling the inorganic, absolute : but
hypothetical or conditional. It is conditional on
a required or assumed end. If the knife is to cut,

it must be sharp. If the state is to survive, it must do so and so. In other words, necessity is two-fold. There is the absolute necessity of the material constituent elements : they cannot act otherwise than as they are : and there is the conditional necessity of the organic bodily structure. Living or dead, the body must always and everywhere obey the laws of its material : but from the organic point of view the case is altered : for it only obeys the organic law on certain conditions. To retain and perpetuate a certain form or shape, it *must* act thus or thus. Or, to put it in other words, when the material elements are so united as to form an organic body, it is not *quâ* its elements, but *quâ* its totality that it must act. The elements are now elements *plus* something else : their special arrangement[1]. Accordingly the good of the organic body is not determined by the laws of its elements, but the laws of its organisation. That is to say that the mechanical explanation of its elements cannot give us the explanation of its organic constitution. That can only be found in its function. We might conceivably, though we probably never shall arrive at the exact numerical expression of the chemical and molecular constitution of the hand. Yet this does not tell us the true reason why a hand is just as it is. We require the function : *what it is for*. It is an instrument for grasping. All things organic must be defined by their func-

---

[1] In nothing is this more obvious than in the case of Protoplasm. It eludes all attempts at discovering its secret. The very approach to analysis kills it—and then the secret has flown away.

tion. It is this which is their raison d'être. The
material elements are subordinate to this, which
adapts them to itself. Just as a gun or an oar
gets its shape and its constituent elements from
the work it has to do : so are all things in the
organic world constituted as they are, built to
perform a peculiar function.

As our whole philosophical salvation hangs on
this distinction, the reader will forgive me for
trying to make my meaning still plainer, even at
the risk of a little repetition. Truism though it
may seem, nothing is less understood than this,
that the difference between organic and inorganic
bodies lies in the fact that the former are organic.
It is just the failure to understand this distinction,
and the nature of organic bodies, that has caused the
ignorant abuse of Aristotelian teleology during three
hundred years [m]. The differences between inorganic
bodies lie in their material and their masses : stuff
or degree : but organic bodies may be identical in
these particulars, yet differ entirely—in form and
function. Inorganic masses are lumps or heaps or
accumulations : you may put two or three together
and form one lump of them : they will coalesce :
but you cannot put two or three organic bodies
together and form a unity : you cannot do away
with their limits, unless you destroy them. Look
up at the stars, where Professor Tyndall's necessity,
the Greek ἀνάγκη, rules with absolute sway : now
quâ this necessity they are nothing but lumps of
inorganic mechanical material. Or conversely, all

[m] Take, as an example, the way in which Glanvil in his
Scepsis Scientifica handles the Aristotelian definition of the soul.
It reminds us of a monkey with a violin.

the organic bodies, plants and animals, which swarm on our own earth, count, when viewed astronomically, only as lumps : it is only their material which makes any difference. If, with certain philosophers, we suppose that the earth is an animal : or if, what is the same thing, we were to imagine an animal, a colossal elephant or mammoth, the size of our earth, revolving round the sun in its orbit, its organic nature would not, relatively to its astronomical position, count : it would, in that regard, be merely so much matter, obeying the laws of its material constitution.   It is, to put the same theory from another point of view, a matter of total indifference to the sun whether the race of men, or elephants, or trees keep their organic forms, or simply lie in lifeless heaps : alive or dead, it is only their material he cares about : but from their own point of view it makes all the difference in the world.   This is precisely the point in Talleyrand's remark to the man who said *Il faut vivre*. *Monsieur*, said Talleyrand, *je n'en vois pas la necessité*. But if Talleyrand did not, the man did : and this *mot* contains the whole of organic philosophy.   Absolute necessity rules organic bodies, *quâ* material lumps : but *quâ* their organic structure, a conditional necessity only.   A butterfly may either live or die : but *if* it is to live, it must follow the laws not merely of its material, but additionally and primarily of its organic nature.   If a butterfly goes into the fire, it will thereupon cease to be a butterfly : but it will nevertheless obey strictly the laws of its material elements.   For these are what they are.   And it was just because Bacon was thinking only of the material point of view that he superficially con-

demned Aristotle's Logic of Science, which he
could not understand. But the Aristotelian Organon laughs at such criticism : laughs, that is to
say, in the long run : for he laughs best who laughs
last. Barbarians may misunderstand me : what
then ? Is it the fault of the Belvedere Apollo if
an orang-utang takes no interest in it ? Are we to
blame Shakspeare if a Hanoverian King of England
thinks him ' sad stuff ?' Does not the ass prefer
thistles, as Heraclitus the Dark said long ago ? Is
it the fault of Disraeli if a House of Commons
rejects his wisdom for the nostrum of a Cobden or
a Peel ? Patience ! patience ! yet a little while, and
the same stone which Bacon rejected will become
the headstone in the economical corner. I bide
my time [n]. Rationalistic systems have their little
bustling day : they run to and fro, in an age of
hurry, shouting, gesticulating, and writing their
names, like American globe-trotters, on the colossal
legs of Egyptian Pharaohs, which wait the while,
silent and imperturbable, their hands reposing
on their knees and pointing downwards, their
eyes on the horizon of the past and future, and
on their thick lips the stony smile of smiles,
the sneer of sneers, as who should say : *Qui vivra,
verra.*

Aye, Time is the eternal ally, the constant prince,
the incorruptible auxiliary of genius, but he comes
everlastingly too late. O bitter irony of Fate, what
fiend inspired those old Egyptian sculptors to seize

[n] ' Being asked, What hope was, he replied, the dream of
' a waking man.' *Diog. Laert. in Vita Aristotelis.* (Bacon took
this as he took much else from Aristotle without acknowledg-
ment.)

with such intuitive accuracy and express with
such poignant and unfaltering fidelity the hidden
secret of which all history is but a revelation :
that the gift of imagination is a Nessus shirt : that
genius is a martyrdom, and that though the work may
win its way, at last, to immortality and a niche in
the Pantheon, the crown of glory is awarded to its
author only too often long ages after the fell troop
of Furies, Obscurity, Poverty, Ignorance, Prejudice, Stupidity, Derision, Bigotry, Malice, Envy,
Plagiarism, and Hatred and all Uncharitableness
have hounded him to his lonely, disregarded
grave.

And now after all this, if the reader has gone
with me through the exposition of this difficult
point, and supplemented the gaps and deficiencies
in the argument with a sympathetic understanding,
he will suddenly awake, like one who has forced
his way through a dark and impervious thicket, to
the fundamental identity between Darwin and
Aristotle. For whereas in the inorganic world °
the great law of Nature is, Structure makes Function, and *operari sequitur esse*, i.e. matter acts after
its nature : contrariwise in the organic world, the
truth is that Function makes Structure, and *esse
sequitur operari:* the thing acquires its nature
from its acts, and gets its form from the work it
has to do : keeping that as long as it can do this.
This is, as Aristotle saw, and Bacon did not see,
the universal law of organic formation, from the
dawn of life in the lowest rung of the biological
ladder up to the fully developed moral and political

° This is just why Bacon's philosophy strikes us as being
so jéjune and unsatisfactory on the moral side.

constitution and action of man. In this thought
lies the key to all ethics and politics. Not without
reason did the Jesuits, the greatest educators that
the world has ever seen, pin their faith to the
philosopher who saw all sides of the moral question : who declared virtue to be a habit, and understood, alone of all moralists, that if the spirit or
intention of the actor determines the nature of the
act, so the nature of the actor springs from the
constant repetition of his acts. 'Tis in ourselves
that we are thus or thus, says the greatest of the
barbarians : but who is responsible for our becoming so? The acts and the persons who educated us, says Aristotle, and he is right. In
Education lies the secret of the universe. It is
not Natural Selection that explains the origin of
species, the creation of shape, it is *Constant Repetition*. Work is the Soul of Creation. Habit is
second nature ; and the work they do makes things
what they are. And it is with the world just as
it is with the individual : it is when he is young
that he is plastic : old forms cannot change. To
become actual is to cease to be potential : that
which is DEFINED has lost the *power* of choosing,
of being other than it is. In this world it is, like
as it was with the steps to the lion's den in the
fable : there is no step back. 'Who chooseth me
' must give and hazard all he hath.' Form is the
riddle of Portia, which he who adventures to win
must take with all its risks. For the organism,
once having chosen, there is no divorce nor putting
asunder of matter and form, till death them do
part.

But some one may say : it is not enough to say

that *Constant Repetition* is the true secret of structure : this is mere vague assertion : it requires to be
proved. The answer to that is, first, it is the universal fact, which appeals to everybody with a force
which is deeper than reason : and secondly, that
it never can be proved. Why? Because in the first
place we are so entirely ignorant of the material
of life even in its simplest forms, that it is, when
properly considered, pure presumption, and a mark
of want of logical insight, to suppose that, as yet,
without holding the truth of the facts, we can *explain.* No man is in a position to explain, till he
has evidence drawn from the nature of the case,
says Aristotle : it is vain to suppose that speculation,
imaginative or hypothetical, is knowledge. It will
be time enough to begin speculating on the material
how of the Origin of Species then, when we have
acquired some intimate knowledge of the chemical
process of life. And in the second place, it should
never be forgotten that it is vain to attempt to
explain the origin of things, unless we are thoroughly
acquainted with the *conditions.* Now these, in the
case of the origin of species, we do not know and
never can know. Indeed, it is probable that the
conditions were so different in primeval times that
a simple account of the true state of the case, even
if it were somehow or other discovered, would seem
so improbable and unnatural as not only to obtain
no credence, but even appear ridiculous. Of this
much, at least, we can feel certain, that as all
progress is from the vague and confused and homogeneous, to the distinct and separate and different,
it is probable that in the beginning of things land,
sea, and atmosphere were not definitely differen-

tiated, but that they existed mixed up together in
a thick and soupy homogeneity : that the original
forms, however they did in fact originate, were of
a gelatinous and fishy nature, floating about in ooze
and slime; that as by the mere mechanical action
of this protoplasmic solution, the lighter and heavier
part tended to rise or settle, gradually in course of
time some of these more or less amorphous beings
came to live on solid matter, some to rise, little
by little, and find their being in a rarer fluid, the
atmosphere, and some again remained in the intermediate and original fluid; these latter would be
the parents of fish, representing the old and aboriginal form, while animals and birds, which must
have begun in a fishy state, would develop from
the other two. The very gradual solidification of
land and rarefaction of air would admit of slow
adaptation to those elements : just as we may look
forward to a time when the process will have still
further advanced, and all atmosphere and liquid
having disappeared, nothing will remain but desert
and rock : like the present position of the moon.
However we may endeavour to account for the
variety in the sizes of animals, there seems to be no
reason to doubt that, in a semi-fluid viscous material, original and protoplasmic bodies of indefinite
potentialities might have arisen of all sizes, and by
action and interaction, the rationale of which we
cannot explain, gradually grown more definite and
hard in various directions, giving rise to innumerable animals 'in the rough,' which time would lick
into shape. If this seems to be somewhat fanciful
and visionary, the reader should remember that
embryology itself indicates nearly all of it. I do

not believe we shall ever know more of the origin
of species than embryology hints to us. Now, if,
as everybody admits, embryology really gives us
an epitome of the past development of the animal,
then it must have been of this kind. For all animals pass through a fish-like stage : and before that,
they are mere amorphous and indeterminate masses
of a soft pulpy nature. The beginning of organic
life, as we see it in the embryo, is a sort of pul-
sation and agitation in a mass of protoplasm which
gradually spreads from the centre outwards, beginning with a streak and constantly subdividing :
now it seems to me that we may boldly throw
this back into the past, and, little as we understand
the chemistry or mechanics of the process, conclude
that in primeval times such exactly was the origin
of life and species. To watch an embryo develop
is to follow the history of creation. But we ought
never to forget that after all it is a vain effort to
attempt to discover the indiscoverable. It is not
the past, but the present that is our affair. It is
the understanding of the present which is our
business ; dabbling in the past is only a luxury.
For as time is eternal, we are really just as much
at the beginning now as it was in the dawn of
creation. The essence of wisdom is, to remember
that creation is a constant process, not an act that
began long ago : that creation is beginning now,
just as much as ever : that this very moment forms
just as good a starting-point as the imaginary
starting-point we postulate in our cosmogonies.
The fact that things do not all begin and end
together deceives us. But every fifty years or so,
the whole of organic nature is entirely renewed : it

is but a short while ago, at any moment we like to take, since everything now existing was merely seed, or non-existent.

Whatever defects there may be in Darwin's theory of the *how* of evolution, nevertheless in result he coincides with Aristotle : that things come to be, by reason of what they have to do. He has done for us exactly what Aristotle did in his day. He has annihilated the old statical absolute view of structure. He has abolished the old system of looking to *forms* for explanation of effects : by showing that form, structure, shape, requires itself to be explained and interpreted by function. Form cannot be explained from matter : this is what the philosophers of the school of Kant and Hume never understood. The only sense in which it is true to say that causation cannot be known is that of material potentiality. You cannot, said Aristotle, know matter in itself : this is the whole truth in the Critical Philosophy. But Aristotle knew what modern philosophers do not know, that there is another side to causation which can be and is known and is necessary : the causation of form : i.e. function. Is there no necessary reason, no *raison d'être*, for the shapes of, e.g. swords, billiard-balls, pens, chairs, carriages? Must not things that are to perform certain work have a shape necessarily thereby determined? The truth is that Darwin has reinstated the Aristotelian philosophy, the essence of which is that forms are not, as Plato said [p], entities, but *accommodations.* The key to forms

[p] It is the fashion now-a-days to try and save Plato, Ricardo, and other miserable quibblers by frigid explanations and distinctions. Plato meant by his Ideas, ' laws of nature,' we are

lies not in the metaphysical and statical, still less
in the mathematical, but in the dynamical method.
Nature is on the one hand the dynamical power
that makes, and on the other the structures
dynamically made : but it is the process not the
result that we must look at : the working, not the
work.   Nature in fact, makes her works make
themselves by working : as they work, so they are.
So far from *esse* being *percipi* (a poor human
sophism, invented to buttress a special dogma, which
mistakes description for explanation) *esse* is *agere*.
AGERE CONSTITUIT ESSE.   Function makes structure,
and work is the soul of the world.   Instead of
Cogito ergo sum: the superficial epigram of an
ignorant dreamer, Darwin and Aristotle proclaim
aloud the secret of everything in Nature to be *Sum*,
quia ago. I work, therefore I am.   I LIVE, TO WORK.
Actuality, reality, *wirklichkeit*, the true metaphysic
lies in language itself : what do the words tell us
but that to be real is to work, act?   To be is to
do one's work : to stop working is to die, cease to
exist.   And this is Aristotle's definition of the soul,
the life, the biological essence :   the active operation of the structure proper to any organic body :
the dynamical condition of structure.

When Darwin tells us that flowers are beautiful
to attract insects : when Mr. Wallace tells us, that
such and such a butterfly looks like a leaf, to
escape its enemies :   what are they doing but
giving illustrations of the Aristotelian aphorism

now told.   I, too, have sat at the feet of the great Polymyth,
and consulted his Oracle, and I am sure that he meant nothing
of the sort.   People are unwilling to admit in the case of Plato
and Ricardo that they took, like Caliban, 'a drunkard for a god.'

that nature suits her tools to their work. Look
at the pink mantis of India, 'which is so formed
' and coloured as to resemble a pink orchis, or
' some other fantastic flower. The whole insect
' is of a bright pink colour, the large and oval
' abdomen looking like the labellum of an orchid.
' On each side the two posterior legs have im-
' mensely dilated and flattened thighs, which re-
' present the petals of a flower, while the neck and
' forelegs imitate the upper sepal and column of
' an orchid. The insect rests motionless in this
' symmetrical attitude, among bright green foliage,
' being of course very conspicuous, but so exactly
' resembling a flower that butterflies and other
' insects settle upon it and are instantly captured.
' It is a living trap, baited in the most alluring
' manner to catch the unwary flower-hunting in-
' sects.' Can the rationalistic idealist, who tells
us that form and design are put into Nature by
our intellect, or the mechanico-mathematical man
of science, explain the *cause*, the *raison d'être* of
this structure? No indeed, something else is required: Darwin's answer or Aristotle's answer;
the most essential cause of all, the final cause or
adaptation: it is so—*in order to trap insects*[q].

And now the reader will perceive the full significance of that criticism of the Darwinian theory
and explanation of Natural Economy which has
been given here. Darwin's solution is in fact half
right and half wrong. In opposition to the me-

[q] Wallace (*Darwinism*, 212). Note, in this case, the de-
pendence of such a structure as this mantis on the existence
of such orchids (which again depend on insects) as it
mimics.

chanical school, he has shown that a mechanical explanation cannot touch the heart of the matter : on the other hand, we find that neither is his principle of explanation exhaustive or adequate : it requires to be supplemented, or complemented, by the mechanical explanation. Not till both are fully given have we the truth in its totality. This is that which was spoken of Aristotle the prophet : we must account for the origin of all these things partly on the principle of material necessity, partly on the principle of adaptive necessity [r]. And here lies the true solution and laying of that antagonism existing between men of science, as they are called, and their opponents. Both are right in what they affirm, wrong in what they deny.. The former are right in maintaining that a full material explanation of the facts must be required ; yet they are wrong in supposing and asserting that this explanation exhausts the problem. The latter are right in asserting that the material explanation never touches the heart of the matter, and in calling for an ' *im-material*' principle of explanation : for though they entirely misconceive what they mean by this term, and drag in under cover of this phrase puerilities of all kinds, yet beneath their misconception lies the dim presentiment of the truth, that only the function of a thing can explain, as it alone can originate, its form. They feel what they cannot express ; namely, that a principle non-material

---

[r] *De Gen. Anim.* II. 6, and elsewhere. Compare the quotation from Naudin in the Historical Introduction to the *Origin of Species*, on the *puissance mysterieuse* of the principle of finality, and the '*fonction*,' which is for each organism its *raison d'être*. This is the very point of Aristotle.

lies at the bottom of the shapes of things, that their explanation must be sought in another direction, and they are right. And in denying this, the mechanical materialistic philosophers have gone beyond their last, and displayed a superficial dogmatism that springs from a want of critical insight into Nature, and an insufficient preparation in analytical method (δι' ἀπαιδευσίαν τῶν ἀναλυτικῶν). Yet on the other hand, we have no right whatever to suppose that this teleological, dynamical Aristotelian principle does away with the necessity of a full material, mechanical, chemical Baconian explanation. We have no right to use it as a cloak for our ignorance. We have said much when we have said that *e.g.* the caterpillar is green in order to elude his enemies, and secure his existence ; but this no more does away with the need of a full material explanation in addition, than the possession of a ship and sails does away with the need of wind and water. For Why is one thing, and How is another : and one can no more replace the other than the outside of a circle can replace the inside, or male replace female.

The old mystic poet of Silesia, Johann Scheffler, or as he called himself, Angelus Silesius, wrote a number of apophthegms on the thesis *Ohne Warum*, that is to say, *Without a Wherefore*, without a *raison d'être* [1]. For example, 'the rose,' he

---

[1] *Vide* Metcalfe's *History of German Literature* and the companion volume of extracts by Max Müller. People who have not penetrated into Aristotle's philosophy, and who do not understand that in his Metaphysics he is expressly considering existence not as to how it comes to be what it is but as what it is, when it is, absurdly identify this mystical

says, 'is without a wherefore. It blooms because
' it does bloom : it thinks not of itself : does not
'ask whether people see it.' Now this is a very
poetical and attractive point of view, and possesses
invincible fascination for such an author as Schopenhauer, who expresses exactly the same thing
in his theory of the Self-Will. The rose is, according to him, only a definite grade of the Will,
objectified. And now, we can see exactly where
Darwin and Aristotle come in. They say, that
the rose is *not* without a wherefore : that on the
contrary it is essentially just what its *raison d'être*
makes it. True, it thinks not of itself, and does
not ask whether people see it. But the Beautiful
must make itself Useful, *if it is to exist.* The beauty
of the rose is not put there on our account : we
can do nothing for it : but it courts the insect eye.
Its colour is a bait for these. *Ohne Warum* is not
the law of its existence : not the law of Life,
but of Death.

For what is life and what is death? Aristotle
tells us. Life is the proper performance of function,
and death, the cessation of that performance. Let

doctrine of Scheffler's with Aristotle's. But though the pro-
fessors may make a fool of him (see Grant's *Ethics*, Introduction
on the End-in-itself, and Stewart, *Notes on the Ethics*, p. 4,
and elsewhere) Aristotle was not a fool. He never said
anything so ridiculous as that a thing could be its own final
cause. That is not Aristotle, but professorial twaddle. What
Aristotle does say is that the soul is the cause of the body :
function makes structure : a very different thing. But Aristotle's
commentators are incorrigible ἀκόλαστοι : instead of testing and
interpreting him by the fruitful realities of life and biology,
they are busy with musty Greek or German pedantry, perverting
and obscuring his meaning by Kantian comparisons or Platonic
parallels.

any organic body cease to be capable of performing its function ; or from the other side, let the need for the performance of that function cease, and the form must die. Life and death, according to Aristotle, have meaning only in relation to functions and the structures that perform them. And is not this just the last grade of evolutionary wisdom ? Death is a product of evolution. Death is nothing but the stoppage or cessation of organic structure to perform its function. But Death is mere negation : nothing positive. It has no meaning in relation to matters inorganic. Form rises up into being and passes away, but that of which it is the form, the material, changes only in respect of its form, and not in respect of its own nature : it is as Carlyle said, in his own inimitable fashion, ' born ' forward through the bottomless, shoreless flood of ' action and lives through perpetual metamorphoses.'

How could it be otherwise ? Let the reader pause for a moment, and divesting his mind of all its customary prejudices, and the deadening effect of habitual familiarity, look hard at these forms, these SHAPES that hedge him in on every side. Only consider the oddness, the irregularity, the anomalous and grotesque nature of these shapes, if we can but forget for a moment what the things are. A book,—a watch,—a hatchet,— a guitar,—a rifle,—an orchid,—a squirrel,—a fish, —an omnibus,—a sheep,—a court of justice,—a porcupine,—a special religious service—what you will : *what* are these shapes, what *can* they be, but just what the work they have to do requires them to be ? How *can* shape receive any other explanation of its origin and existence than function ? Apart from its function, any shape is a monstrous, an absurd and unaccountable *lusus naturæ*. And herein lies the quaint and always bizarre effect of any thing—organic or artificial, antique or unfamiliar foreign body—of which we do not know and cannot readily see the use. It springs exactly from the fact that the shapes of things only cease to be meaningless or absurd, when considered in relation to their function. There, on the contrary, they appear 'natural,' and so much so, that we feel quite unable to conceive that they could be otherwise than they are. This is what, as Schopenhauer tells us, Goethe felt, ' when ' contemplating whelks and crabs at Venice : ' he exclaimed : ' How delightful, how glorious ' is a living thing ! how well adapted for its ' condition ! how true, how real '.' For Goethe had a mind of essentially the same realistic analytical kind as Aristotle himself : and in this as many other of his ejaculations (the ejaculation always springs from reality, from something *striking*) we see the true critical spirit.

And now at last the reader will perceive why no progress was possible for Political Economy, as long as Political Economists attempted to define and explain organic or social structures on principles purely mechanical or mathematical : being entirely destitute of the knowledge of the analytical and biological method, and vainly attempting to get at the truth in politico-economical matters, which are only the highest form of biological organisation, by a laborious and empty shuffling and rearrangement of mathematical, mechanical, hypothetical,

' Schopenhauer, *Will in Nature. Eng. Tr.*, p. 277.

statical, partial conceptions. Not one single economist has had the faintest conception of the truth,
that a thing is and can only be explained, or defined, by its function : that this is the *original cause*
of all structure. Hence the futile absurdity of economical investigations into Wealth, Money, Credit
and so on : hence the chimerical delusions of Socialism, which is nothing but Political Economy
turned inside out.

Let me give an illustration to show how vain is
the attempt to comprehend Political Economy along
abstract lines : how absolutely essentially necessary
is the Aristotelian analytic, and the knowledge of
the truth he expressed aphoristically by saying :
One thing is, for the sake of another : i.e. co-adaptation is the secret of nature, and the key to economy.
There is a ship sailing, say, an ocean steamer, crossing the Bay of Bengal. Now try to explain that
fact. You perceive a material fact : so much wood,
iron, and so forth, passing along in a definite direction on the sea. But its causes? How does
it go? Who sent it? Where and why is it going?
How is it made? Why is it made? Who made it?
Who and what does it carry? Just think of this,
an ordinary social fact. Just think where the
answer will take you. The ship, its builders, of
all kinds : its docks : its engines : the skill and
science and workmen that made it : its sailors and
officers : the people and things it carries : its charts
and chronometers : commerce : trade : Indian civil-
ians and soldiers : the shipping company and the
East India Company : the post office and the mails :
politics and the British Empire : England and
India : husbands and wives, fathers and sons : the

rupee and the gold pound : the stars and Sir Isaac
Newton:—and then comes Political Economy and
tells you that Labour is the sole cause of Wealth.
And do we really suppose that Political Economy
can investigate such a problem as this, merely a
single and common case of Wealth, on any method
but the analysis of reality ? Place, in connection
with such a fact as this, the frigid miserable abstractions of Ricardo, and refrain, if you can, from
a sneer or a smile.

Certainly, Proudhon is right : there is more in
Economics than Newton ever dreamed of. The
depth of the heavens is not as the depth of the
human mind, as exhibited in life and realised in
society. Society is the material embodiment of the
human soul. Mathematics, abstraction, are at one
end of the ladder of Nature : they deal with nothing
but the material form of things. As we rise from
grade to grade, from pure mathematics and geo-
metry, through mechanics, phoronomy, chemistry,
physics, geology, embryology, biology, psychology,
logic, ethics, politics and political economy ; the
further we go, the more we lose sight of exact
mathematical symbolism : the more insoluble to
mathematics become the complicated inextricable
mazes of reality. The rational has become lost in
the real. How then can we possibly treat that
economical correlation by anticipations, abstractions,
mathematical and theoretical formulæ ? It is not
the simple and absolute qualities of matter as such,
nor any deductive juggling with the mere abstract
forms of bodies, as material, but the complex
dynamical correlation, co-adaptation, action and interaction of organic bodies as such, that we have

to deal with. Of the two sides of all explanation
with which we have been dealing during the whole
of this discussion, the material side of absolute
necessity, in such a sphere as this, utterly disappears; and the other side, the side of conditional
necessity, the principle of adaptation, the depend-
ence of all structure on special, causative, originating,
instigating conditions becomes the supreme law.
The principle of explanation for all bodies, facts,
processes, and institutions in the sphere of Political
Economy lies *not in themselves, but in others:* those
others, in which they live and move and have their
being, and *minus* which they are non-existent.
This is the opposite pole of all previous systems of
Political Economy. A fine Political Economy, to
be sure, whose axioms lead directly to a denial of
that of which it is the economy: the State! If
there is and ought to be no such thing as a State,
but only 'individuals,' then there is and can be no
such thing as Political Economy. For just as the
end of Natural Economy is the good of organic
beings: so is the end of Political Economy the
good of the State, and through it, of its component
men and women. And the good of each thing, as
Aristotle said long before Darwin, is not that which
destroys it, but that which preserves and per-
fects it.

Sir Isaac Newton was a great, and also a lucky
man. Every time we stand under the canopy of
heaven, and look up at the starry dome, with
thoughts for which we can find no adequate expression, we are ready to exalt his sublime genius,
and fall in with the ordinary meaningless adulation
of his 'lone icy grandeur' and similar commonplace

cant. But imagination deludes us here as elsewhere. The stars were not the essence but the
accident of the matter to Newton. His problem
was simply a mechanical mathematical problem,
motion of the very simplest, purest kind, and
the ethical reference which is so impressive,
and which we cannot help mixing up with it,
had nothing whatever to do with it. The
ethical sublime was no more concerned in the
matter than it is in the algebraical formula
$(x+y)(x-y) = x^2-y^2$, or in the sine, cosine, or
tangent of θ. There is nothing here of that feeling
which the astonishing genius of Pascal so admirably
expressed when he said, *Le silence eternel de ces
espaces infinis m'effraye.* When Kant, not without
reminiscences of Pascal, said: Two things fill me
with awe: the starry heavens, and the sense of moral
responsibility in the soul of man : he was really
talking not of two things at all, but one. Viewed
mechanically, there is no more of depth or sublimity
in the stars than there is in half a dozen balls
rolling in a box. The sublime comes from the
mind that puts into them its own wonderful deeps
and profundities. They are not in the stars, and
they were not in Newton's problem. The enigma
in his case was purely formal and algebraic. *There*
was neither the depth of chemistry nor the intricacy
of biology. For Chemistry is to Economy what
the abyss is to the height, the Nadir to the Zenith.
The mysterious Protean tranformations of matter
in its chemical constitution defy us by their minuteness, their depth, their impenetrable abysmal darkness : and on the other hand when we rise through
every gradation to the biological realities of Eco-

nomics, these again present to us a problem equally inscrutable, though in a different way, for their inextricable mazes and tortuous inter-relations, their circles within circles, of ever-increasing complexity. But in comparison with these, the Newtonian problem was relatively simple and clear as glass. It was such a problem as is solved by a Bidder, a prodigious calculating boy : and reminds us of Mr. Babbage and his calculating machines. Given the elliptical form of motion, find the force of *pull* required between body and body so as to keep them just as they are. In addition to mere mathematics, nothing is taken in here but a single abstracted quality, weight, gravity, or better, attraction ; which is itself an assumption. Mass and motion—nothing more. But what is such a problem as this to the chemical or biological, that is, economical riddle ? Its very completeness, its apparently masterly comprehensive sweep, its architectonic simplicity and apodeictic certainty, arise precisely from the fact that all the essentially incomprehensible and enigmatic side of nature is left out of account. How infinitely the reverse of sublime Sir Isaac Newton's mind really was is seen when he attempts to deal with moral instead of mechanical relations in the Book of Revelation. Anything more fatuous and imbecile it is impossible to conceive. And this is quite common with mathematical minds. There seems to be some inner connection between extraordinary deficiency in understanding and mathematical talent, as though to indicate that mathematical power of calculation is a mere peculiar trick: a quality capable of existing in perfection in minds perfectly foolish

and uneducated in all other respects. But the
stars in their courses create a prejudice which we
cannot overcome, when we think of Newton: and
we attribute to him that mysterious sublimity which
we ourselves lend to the stars. It is not Newton,
it is Copernicus, who founded the sublime heliocentric conception; if indeed there is anything
sublime about the matter. A spider making and
using its web, or a dragon-fly hovering on a stream,
are to me infinitely more deep and wonderful than
all the countless host of stars. And this is why
Astronomy, *as long as we do not study it*, seems
to be so fascinating and attractive, whereas, when
we do approach it, we find with a kind of disgust,
that we are deceived, and instead of revelling in
sublimities, we are only wearisomely juggling with
x and y, ellipses and parabolas. The study of
Astronomy is exactly like the Arabian mirage. It
seems, from afar off, so unspeakably beautiful: but
we come up into it only to break the spell, and toil
on through dusty desert, lifeless, unvarying, and
unspeakably unprofitable.

But Aristotle—who shall estimate the sublimity
of his mind? How shall we adequately appreciate
the man who could read and interpret, not the
merely formal abstract relations of a handful of
bodies in space, but the play of innumerable myriads
of forces in organic nature, who could sound the
never-before sounded abysses of the human mind
and Nature's economy, and introduce order and
everlasting light into the chaos, separating and constructing logic and psychology, embryology and
biology, ethics and politics: who had penetrated
into the *adyta* of Science, mastered the scheme of

organisation, and grasped in its totality the whole of life in all its manifestations, as no man before his time or since his time had or has ever done. Put all the philosophers of all the ages, biological or logical, ethical, metaphysical, or political into a bag : shake them up and roll them about : braze them in a mortar and extract their quintessence ; and then you will not have all that Aristotle will give you. They have nothing essential to add to his work : they fall short of it in innumerable particulars of chief importance. For Aristotle reached the summit of human possibility : he is in every department, save only and inevitably that of pure physics, matter and its qualities, supreme : full to the fullest, and yet short to the shortest. In ethics, politics, and their corollaries, he is not only the greatest, but the only master : and he has fixed for ever in his Organon the essential working of the human mind. Science, thy name is Aristotle. And when the world has awoken from its middle-age nightmare, the miserable little rationalistic, sophistical systems that have presumptuously aimed at replacing his giant evolutionary realism will stiffen into stony death, like Polydectes and his guests before the head of the Gorgon, or vanish like a troop of goblins, spectres, and night terrors, flying at cockcrow before the morning light.

BOOK II.

POLITICAL ECONOMY, OR THE COMMODITY. THE
PRINCIPLE WORKING IN THE COMMON OR SOCIAL
SPHERE.

ἐνεργείᾳ δὴ ὁ ποιήσας τὸ ἔργον ἐστί πως.

Eth. Nicom., ix. 7.

BOOK II.

I. MAN being physically dependent for his existence upon external nature and his fellows, naturally endeavours to better his condition, or make his existence as good as possible under the circumstances in which he finds himself : and to this end he tries as far as he can to make Nature subserve his needs ; twists the material with which she furnishes him into shapes and forms that answer to his wants and purposes. And here then we come, beginning at the beginning, upon the definition of Wealth. Wealth was accurately defined by Aristotle, and by him alone, as an accumulation of instruments, private and public, serviceable to existence. Language enshrines the true philosophy of the subject. Wealth is simply that which tends to the weal of man. The same thing is expressed in the term 'commodities' : *i.e.* accommodations, or adaptations of material to perform a special function, subserve a particular use, or demand, of the human will. These commodities, again, are synonymous with the word 'goods' : a good being that which answers to a particular end : and again, these are called also 'wares,' which term expresses the notion of wealth

M

regarded as exchangeable or transferable : a point of view which is not fundamental or original to wealth, but which in course of time has become so inseparably associated with the idea of wealth that it has been confounded with the essential and original idea. But to this we shall return at a subsequent stage.

Under wealth, considered as an accumulation of instruments of existence, would come of course political institutions, language, situation, climate, health and similar things : unquestionably forming part of the wealth of man : what, for example, could be of greater value to man than language ? But the term wealth is by ordinary usage commonly restricted to material objects : and as I shall in a subsequent Book deal with the political and ethical side of the subject, we may for the present neglect what we might call the immaterial and inalienable wealth of man and confine ourselves in this Book to the investigation of Political Economy proper : considered, that is, as the science dealing with the production of the material instruments to which we habitually refer when we speak of wealth.

If, then, we look closely into wealth, considered as an accumulation of the material instruments of life, we observe that every commodity, or unit of wealth, is, in ultimate analysis, just a piece of matter, wrought or worked up, after a design, to answer to a particular need. want, or demand. Each is, in fact, a structure, fitted and contrived to perform a definite function. Obviously the function it discharges is, as it were, the soul or *raison d'être* of every commodity. This was that which gave it its existence, called it into being, bestowed upon it its peculiar form. What could be stranger than the infinitely various shapes of those things that constitute wealth. What could have suggested or dictated those queer forms, but the work each had to do? How could *e.g.* a corkscrew or a theatre ever have acquired its peculiar structure? how could we understand such a strangely constituted object, apart from its work? And, on the other hand, how natural, satisfactory, and appropriate each form, however anomalous, appears, as soon as we understand for what it is intended! How little we are accustomed to wonder at or pause over forms in themselves most extraordinary, just because familiarity deadens us to their essential strangeness! how strange, on the contrary, seem to us instruments with which we have no acquaintance! The truth is, of course, that all structure is strange, odd: nay, even absurd and ridiculous considered apart from its function, or the work it has to do: and yet again, considered in close connection with that work, it seems not only not absurd, but even curiously natural: so much so, indeed, that we fancy it could hardly have been other than it is. Indeed, it requires no small degree of imagination to innovate in this connection: to design new structures better fitted than the old to perform any particular work. The analogy in this respect between natural organisms and commodities is exact: each strike us as being admirably constructed, and fill us with pleasure, just in proportion as they are specially determined to a particular work.

Obviously, then, if we examine any commodity,

we may consider it as the embodiment of four causes : we may view it from four aspects. It is, to begin with, so much matter : *e.g.* a hat, on one side, is nothing but a definite amount of material. Again, this material is definitely shaped thus or thus : it may be, for example, a lady's bonnet, a man's tall hat, a cricket cap, a helmet, a sun hat, a cardinal's hat, a broad brim, or a mitre : and again, these various shapes are all determined by the functions each has to perform. Lastly, these shapes are not produced by nature : no one finds helmets or mitres growing on trees : human labour is necessary to effect the transformation, and produce the required shape. Or to sum up, every commodity presents itself, when closely analysed, under four essentially different aspects : its material, its form, its function, and the labour necessary to produce it[a]. Briefly, every commodity is, according as we regard it, *Matter, Form, Labour,* and *Use.*

This result we also obtain by considering not the commodity but its creator, man. We can see the fact, not only by examining and analysing, inductively, every commodity : but also, by examining the nature of man, we can show deductively, not only that every commodity is, but that every commodity must be, of this four-sided nature. This, says Aristotle, is scientific knowledge, when we

---

[a] The reader must carefully guard against confounding the *work that makes the saw,* meaning the *labour* which makes it, with the work that makes it, meaning, the work or function the saw itself does and performs. Both are causes of the saw, but the *work which the saw performs* is the soul, or original cause of the saw.

know the proximate necessary and original causes
of any fact, and that it cannot be other than it is.
There is reciprocal and exact correspondence between men and their commodities. That which on
the side of the commodity is Use or Function, is
on the side of the man, Need, Want, or Value.
Man's wants determine his wealth. He must eat,
drink, be warm, beget children, travel, fight on
occasion, play : he must still be up to all kinds of
mischief, or the reverse : and so on. Thus he
needs,—and produces,—instruments, to serve his
will : imparts to matter the form in which it will be
useful to him. But in order to do this, he must
know, and he must *work*. Thus it follows, from
a merely cursory inspection of the nature of man,
that his creatures, his commodities, his wealth, his
goods, the instruments he presses into his service,
must of necessity be foursquare in their essential
nature. They must be useful, correspond to a
definite need : they must, accordingly, be designed
or shaped to that end : they must be the product of
labour: and lastly, they must consist of material,
such as will best achieve the required end or
function. And we express the same thing by
scientific limitation. Not all material, not all sub-
stances, are wealth : but only some : *i.e.*, those upon
which man sets his seal, selects, fashions, and
stamps with his approval. Thus if definition be, as
Aristotle says, a making known of the essence of
a thing, and if this is nothing but enumerating the
causes, or the life history, or evolution, of the
thing, the genus and specific differences that mark
it out and limit it, Wealth is most accurately defined, always and everywhere, as Material, so

Shaped and Wrought as to serve a definite End or Function, Want, Use, or Need.

This definition of a Commodity corresponds exactly with the definition of a natural specific form. Commodities are in the kingdom of man precisely what species are in the kingdom of nature. Both are formed, acquire their structure, on precisely the same principle. The soul of an animal is exactly analogous to the function of a commodity. All bodies, as Aristotle said long ago, natural or artificial, are nothing but instruments : and the cause of their generation is their essence or soul ; viz. the work they have to perform. To define a body is to give its essence, its *raison d'être ;* to state the ground of its being, its *ratio essendi.* And the difficulties which have played such havoc with Political Economy up till now all arise from the simple fact that those who have hitherto laid down the law upon the subject have one and all been quite unaware of what it is to define. How could men who use the word substance as a synonym of the word essence, who seem to imagine that the essence of a thing is a sort of something material existing inside it and underneath its visible qualities, a sort of second self, a metaphysical entity, ever comprehend the abstruse problem ? The essence of a thing, as, for example, of a hat or pen, is simply its function. And this is not something material existing behind or in addition to its material, but lies in the action of its constituent parts as arranged in a structural whole. Crush a pen to powder ; its matter will still be there ; but its function, *i. e.* its essence, that which made it a pen, its capacity of writing, is destroyed. It can now no longer perform the work of a pen. This was what gave it its existence in that shape. And if we wish to define a pen, we must give this function : it is an instrument for writing. Writing is the soul or essence of a pen. Just so, the performance of function is in general the creative soul of wealth. The body is subordinate to the soul : for it is for the sake of the soul, for the performance of peculiar work, that all commodities come into existence. ' Let it then,' says Dante, ' be un-' derstood, that God and Nature make nothing to ' be idle. Whatever comes into being, exists for ' some operation or working [b].'

This shows us at once that of all the four causes of wealth, the final cause, or the function it serves, is in a sense the most important. All the others are determined by this. The wood of a bow, the steel of a sword, and so on, are chosen and determined for and by the work they have to do. If the knife is to cut, it must be sharp : hence it must consist of a material that will take and keep its appropriate shape ; fitting it to cut. And therefore, we see at once that the material constituents of wealth are throughout determined by the functions it serves. Wealth must be as various in structure as are the needs or functions of mankind. Wealth is but the shadow of the life of man : the flower of which he is the root. As men are, so is wealth. To every desire, purpose, or action of men correspond the bits of wealth that answer and minister to it. *Quot homines, tot commoda vitæ. Qualis homo, tale opus. Operari sequitur esse.* It

[b] Dante, *De Monarchiâ.*

is man's own nature that determines his production ; and this again determines the nature of his business. The whole business of the world gets its structure, in order to minister to the pleasure and life, the action of the world.

For the activity of man may be perfectly correctly divided into two species : he is always either *actor* or *maker :* his action is always either practical or productive. He produces in order to act : investigates in order to know how to produce and to act. Hence all Wealth naturally consists and must consist either of *instruments of action,* or *instruments of production.* Here we get at once the essential idea of Capital. By this term is meant, originally and essentially, every instrument of production. It is this which makes any part of Wealth Capital. The same individual commodity may or may not be Capital, according as it is, or is not, employed in producing. To this we shall return : only in this place it is worth notice, how large an element of the confusion prevailing in Economics springs from a total haze surrounding the ill-defined and completely misunderstood term Capital. Instead of following the natural and pregnant division, already laid down by Aristotle, of instruments into *productive* and *practical,* economists went astray after Adam Smith's miserable distinction of *productive* and *unproductive* labour. Whatever of use and worth and validity lay in this negative term '*unproductive*' is more accurately expressed by the term *practical :* on the other hand, by branding all labour, not directly productive, as unproductive, in a positive sense, Adam Smith and his successors, as I have shown elsewhere, fundamentally misunderstood the part played by ' unproductive ' labour in the production of wealth. Why, production exists only to minister to 'unproductive,' *i.e.* practical action ; and this ' unproductive,' that is, practical action is nothing whatever but the final cause of all the production. Yet the economists, after Adam Smith, would seek to persuade us that production would go on just the same, nay, better, if there was none of this unproductive labour at all. The idea! As if any one would produce e.g. guns, if there were no sportsmen to use them ? As if there could be production at all, in any direction, unless action, *i.e.* 'unproductive' consumption, called for it ! As Aristotle says, life itself is not production but action. These philosophical economists, incredible as it may seem, in condemning ' unproductive ' labour, are really condemning life itself. Did they ever ask themselves, *why production exists ?*

The fourfold definition of Wealth, which I have elsewhere called the Quadruple Principle of Wealth Creation, explains accurately and clearly what hitherto has never been explained ; the reason why society has assumed the structure it now displays [c]. Let us consider briefly the natural course of its evolution.

Of commodities, some are of course more vitally necessary than others : in Aristotelian language, some are necessary, others useful or pleasant. In early stages of society, in the primitive and protoplasmic, as yet undifferentiated state of production,

[c] The reader will find these points admirably illustrated in Cunningham's *Growth of English Industry and Commerce,* which has now happily been completed.

existence and action, each man, or (for we must not perhaps go back so far as a theoretical and impossible unit) each small family group, hamlet, village community, or tribe of men must be self-supporting and self-producing. One man will unite many trades : just like the emigrant, or backwoodsman, pioneering in new countries, each must be Jack of all trades : soldier, sailor, tinker, tailor. But as gradually the advantage of combination and separation impressed itself upon the mind, arose the *division of labour.* The early man produces his own wealth (as do indeed creatures lower in the scale than man), scantily and with hard labour adapting nature's niggard materials to poor and unimaginative needs and uses. But time passes on : one man comes to do one thing and one another, combining for a common object (the principal instrument enabling this to be effected being language and reason) : and then men come to perceive that things are done best when not one man does many things but each has one definite work. And this is true not only of men, but things. Both men and things now come to be instruments in a common work : and as the work grows out in all directions, so does the structure to accomplish it. Differentiation begins. This is the principle of biological evolution, first discovered by Aristotle ; continuous and gradual differentiation of originally simple structure to meet ever new and more complicated functions. The principle and the limit of this differentiation is the nature of the work to be done. We have seen that all commodities, i.e. products, consist of four elements :—matter : form : labour : and use. Well, this fourfold structure of the work to be

done, the wealth to be made, gradually splits society
up, or combines it (for the two are but different
aspects of the same process) in that form. Society
gradually becomes, from an economical point of
view, sectionally arranged : dances, as it were, into
order to the tune of the Quadruple Principle : it
comes to consist of classes which answer to these
functions : classes of practical agents ; (many of
whom are otherwise necessary to society, as soldiers,
sailors, legislators, lawyers, &c.) workers ; designers ;
discoverers ; holders of property in land or things,
real or personal. The whole structure of society becomes essentially determined on the lines of production, and the more so, in proportion as wealth-creation
becomes more exclusively the function of the society[d].

But at this point it becomes necessary to take the
subject up anew, and notice a further consequence of
the division of labour.

II. When people begin to subdivide and combine
their employments, and also to mix more freely with
others, there arises a phenomenon destined to exercise important influence over the whole economic
development : *Exchange.* Some people would gladly
have something they do not possess, and cannot
procure for themselves : they hit upon the expedient
of exchanging what they have for what they have
not. Now, the question arises, what is the principle upon which these exchanges will be conducted ?
What constitutes the basis of exchange ? Upon what

[d] There is a peculiar species of Wealth, which has been utterly
neglected by Economists, either not at all or only very slightly
susceptible of Division of Labour, and which stands in many
ways in opposition to ordinary Wealth : I mean Works of Art.
They will be considered in the Third Book.

considerations and qualities does *Value* depend?
Here is the fundamental question of Economics.
For all the categories of distribution are simply cases
of Value, and to misunderstand the essential cause
of Value is to shut yourself off from all possibility
of ever understanding any part of Economics whatever.   Yet this is just what economists have done.
There is not a single economist from Adam Smith
down to this day, who has the dimmest conception of
the truth as to value, or even the way to arrive at
the truth.   No one has ever ANALYSED THE RELATION.

If, says Aristotle, people would only look at
things in their growth and origin, in this as in
other matters, they would best gain insight into
the truth.   A gives B, we will say, an apple for
a fish : now what determines the exchange ?   What
are the constituent elements and the essential notion of value ?   This is the *pons asinorum* of Political
Economy.   This is a question on which solutions
that seem quite obvious are really quite wrong ;
and as every future step depends on the correct
solution, we must either make sure of the ground,
or give up Political Economy.   I do not know of
any work in the whole field of Political Economy,
which contains an analysis of this notion of value
worth the paper it is written on.   This was where
Adam Smith went so entirely astray.   What is the
essence, cause, *raison d'être*, of Value ?   I shall
show that the fundamental error in orthodox
Economics and ordinary statements of the question
lies in this, that economists have considered commodities *out of relation to the men who exchange
them :* and thus, by substituting a mathematico-
mechanical, for the true biological analytical method,

have effectually cut themselves off from all possibility of arriving at a true solution of the question.

Two leading solutions have been given. One is the Smith-Ricardian-Marxian solution, to give it the name of its best known exponents. This asserts that the *cost of production* of every commodity is what essentially determines its value. The other, which we may designate from the name of its ablest exponent, the Macleodian or Exchange Value solution, asserts that when one commodity exchanges for another, the one *is* the value of the other : or, the value of any thing is any other thing for which it can be exchanged.

I shall now show, first, negatively, by a critical examination of these views, and then positively, by an exposition of the truth, that both these views contain a small element of the truth, but that both are erroneous. And erroneous science, it should always be remembered, is infinitely worse than no science at all.

The element of truth in the first solution may be thus explained. Under a system of keen competition, so keen as to render social relations very fluid, and to admit of the rapid and reciprocal influence of one part of the productive system upon another, (observe that this, to begin with, at once destroys the generality of the truth, because such a competitive system only exists, if at all, to some extent, in special periods, and in special places, and where it does not exist the law does not hold) : the value of *some* commodities only will tend to approximate to their cost of production. Suppose, for example, that I customarily give £1 for a pair of boots : then if some one undersells the bootmaker, supplying the *same* boot for 10*s.*, the value will go down to that sum. But does the value depend *solely* upon the cost of production here? Not in the least. It depends upon the cost of production taken in connection with the other elements, i.e. the material, make or shape of the boots, and the customer's desire for them. All this is assumed in the solution. But suppose, that at the moment the *cost of production* fell to 10*s.* the need of the customer doubled : then the value would not sink. And in fact, this solution confines itself to a mere fragment : attends solely to one element in the problem. It arbitrarily leaves out all the factors determining the problem except one.

Thus even in the case of those commodities in which this solution contains a grain of truth, it is really a fragmentary and accidental explanation. But further, it will hold, even in this partial extent, only of those common commodities which can easily be replaced, and which therefore specially depend upon their *cost of production.* Even under its own competitive régime, this miserable solution halts and limps. For take instances : Is it *cost of production* that determines the value of a Stradivarius violin, or a picture by Raphael ? Two plays cost the same to produce : will their value, on that score, be equal ? Why one may be damned on the first night, and the other run for years. Does *cost of production* determine the value of a house or a ground rent ? Bad or good weather may ruin a crop : does its value, therefore, depend on *cost of production ?* Why, it is perfectly obvious that it does nothing of the kind. A thing may cost what you please to produce : it will not *on that account* necessarily have any value at all : and on the other hand it may cost next to nothing to produce, yet have enormous value.

Hence it is clear that merely from a critical inspection this solution of value is radically false and insufficient[e]. It assumes, first, a special set of conditions which never yet existed in any country or any time, in the degree that would be required to make Ricardo's theory true : which has only existed to a limited extent in certain cases, and which is often entirely absent. Next, even under these conditions, it only provides a fragmentary and to a large extent futile solution, in a double sense : for to the great mass of commodities it is entirely inapplicable, and even where it does apply it fails to account for more than one side of the facts. And I shall show further on that it rests on a fundamentally erroneous basis. Exchange is not and never can be based solely on equal costs of production, for the very simple reason that such a thing is a delusion and an absolute impossibility. These economists have presented a special and exceptional case as the rule and essence of value.

So much then for the first : what then as to the second, the *exchange value* solution? The value of one thing is any other thing for which it will exchange, say these Economists. It is valuable because it will exchange : the essence of wealth lies in its *exchange value.*

[e] Of course, even *when* value = cost of production : it is not the same thing. Value is one thing : cost another. This is what Malthus objected to Ricardo. That illustrious economist never even saw the point. See his *Works*, p. 30, n.

This, an entirely mathematical and mechanical solution, altogether misses the heart of the question. It has fallen into an error somewhat similar to the first : it assumes as essential something merely accidental and by no means essential to wealth. It reverses the truth. Commodities are not, as it asserts, Wealth, not valuable, because they will exchange : on the contrary, they will exchange, because they are valuable. Their value does not come from the fact of their exchanging, but exists quite independently of that. Could a thing have no value, forsooth, because it did not exchange ? Why, obviously, the fact that a man will give such or such a thing for another, is not the cause, but merely the indication of the value of this other. It is no more the *cause* of value than light is the cause of the sun. And if a thing were valuable *because* it would exchange, why do people who have ac-quired a fictitious object, or sham, object to it ? Simply because it is not the fact of exchange, but the qualities of the thing that give it its value. It is not exchange, it is that which lies behind ex-change, the demand of the person exchanging, that bestows its value upon a commodity. To call A the value of B, because two people exchange one for the other, is an abuse of language. *It leaves out the men standing behind the things :* CHANGE THE MEN, *and A will no longer be the value of B.*

Here, for example, is, say, a box of cigars, for which £3 have been given. Now, the *cost of production* says : these two are of the same value because their cost of production is equal : which is manifestly ridiculous. The *exchange value* theory says : their values are equal, because they have exchanged. This is either an otiose tautology, an empty truism, or radically erroneous. For observe. On the *cost of production* theory, the cigars and the money are of equal value. On the exchange value theory, they are also of equal value. But THE FACT IS, NOT SO. For the fact is, that even though they exchange for one another, *in a particular case*, their values are nevertheless not equal, because *in another case* they will not so exchange. One man will give £3 for the cigars : another will not. That is to say that with the £3 you can always get the cigars : but with the cigars you cannot always get the £3. Consequently, paradoxical though it may seem, the £3 are yet really more valuable than the cigars, even though these 'exchange' at that price : because the demand for the £3 is more general than the demand for the cigars.

Let us make this still clearer.

A gives B a fish for an apple. Now, this does not take place *because* the costs of production of fish and apple are equal : that would afford no reason why they should exchange. Nor is it because the exchange values are equal. The very contrary. A gives B a fish, and B gives A an apple, *because, and only because, each party to the transaction values the thing he has not MORE than the thing he has.* If it were not so, no exchange could take place. If A valued or esteemed his fish as much as the apple, he would keep it : so would B his apple. It is quite false, and it misses the very core of the problem to say in this case, that the fish is of the same value as the apple. To begin with, were that so, no exchange could be

N

effected. For each would keep what he had. Accordingly, those who base their notions of wealth on 'exchange value' are, curiously enough, basing their Economics on a view which, if it held, would make exchange impossible. No exchange could ever take place if, in that exchange, things were of equal value. It is just because they are *not* so, that the exchange takes place. It is just because each places a *higher* value on what he has not, that the exchange comes about. Or to put it in another way, the fish is of the same value as the apple *only in this exact particular case*, because the owners are A and B. Let them be C and D, and the fish will then no longer be the same in value as the apple, because C may prefer his fish to an apple, and D his apple to a fish. In other words, it is impossible to solve the problem of value apart from the valuers. It is quite false to assert that because two things exchange for one another they are of the same value. The truth is the very opposite. The truth is, that because they are exchanged, each is of *more* value than the other in the eyes of the man who gets it, and of *less* value than the other in the eyes of the man who parts with it. Change the men exchanging, and the exchange value theory will not hold. For value is always and everywhere determined by the relation of the thing valued to the valuer : by the degree in which structure answers to function. It is *not* determined by *cost of production*, nor by *exchange value*, a meaningless expression that seems to mean much, but which only means what is wrong, in so far as it means anything at all.

In every case of value there are two terms, the

valuing mind and the thing valued. In every case of exchange there are four terms, two valuing minds, and two things valued. Just because the two theories I have been considering eliminate two elements,—the two valuers,—the theories are mere abstractions and perfectly worthless. Everything they say with regard to two things valued tacitly assumes two valuers, and if these are changed, what they conclude will be wrong. For nobody will ever find out the truth in human affairs who views things abstracted from their concrete relations, in which alone they have any existence and validity. And it is because the economists from Smith and Ricardo to Macleod and Marx have all without exception philosophised absolutely, without regard to special relations, that they have none of them ever been able to understand money. The true understanding of money depends upon the right appreciation of value.

Value expresses a relation between a person and a thing. On the side of the thing, its value depends upon its material, its cost of production, its workmanship or form, and its use : the four causes which gave it its existence. On the side of the person, its value depends upon all these, together with the greater or less need or demand he may have for it, *and the greater or less value of what he has to give for it.* He will not give £1 for it, if he can get another in the next street for 10*s.*, *and knows this :* he will again not give £1 for it, if at the moment other causes make other things, which he can get with the money, relatively more valuable to him. All these elements are essential elements of value : and it is mere puerility to suppose that we have settled the question of value, by laying down such thin and frigid abstractions as that value depends upon cost of production, or upon supply and demand.   Supply and demand! —We might as well say that a man is not as tall as the moon, nor as short as a hat.   For the phrase is purely vague and general : the difficulty lies in the details.   It is no explanation of a man's death to say he died because he was at Jerusalem : the cause is not specified.

Just because they deemed these miserable abstractions sufficient, economists have most radically misunderstood the nature and function of money, with consequences so disastrous in practice to the world.   The paradox of money is just this, that it is both more and less valuable than anything it will buy.   And the explanation of this paradox can only be discovered on the lines of a true theory of value.   Let us see whether we can arrive at it.

III.   In those early stages of production which succeed to the period of barbaric self-sufficiency, during which each makes what he can for himself, every man his own universal provider :—in the stage when people begin to exchange one thing for another, the era of barter, there would be of course great clumsiness and difficulty in exchange.   People would haggle with one another over their goods, and find it very hard to come to an agreement as to what each might consider a satisfactory equivalent for his own produce.   This at least we may confidently assert, that the very last thing that would ever weigh with a man in estimating another's commodity would be the amount of labour it might have cost. That would be a matter on which he never bestowed a thought. The question in his own mind would simply be, the extent of his own want or desire of the article in question, *in relation to what he had to give for it.* And they would no doubt find much difficulty in coming to an arrangement : sometimes that would be next door to impossible : how could they measure or compare each other's need or demand for the several articles ? It is this difficulty which, as Aristotle rightly said, money has *necessarily* arisen to solve. It is impossible of course, in the absence of all facts bearing on the question, to trace the exact steps, historically, by which money acquired its position. For we should never forget that no enquiries can reach back to the historical origin of anything. At first, no doubt, even money would be but a sorry makeshift. For in a rude and un-certain age, where very little could be had for money, exchange of goods for money must have been precarious, more or less arbitrary, and con-stantly changing.

The qualities which would lead people to fix upon metal, or whatever it might be, to function as the measure of value, or degree of need, would doubtless be that it was itself originally a com-modity among commodities, but more permanent more portable, more divisible, small in bulk, gene-rally acceptable, easily concealed. Before it was money, it would be, of course, a mere metal, valued for its uses as such, ornamental as well as utilitarian. But the point for us is this, that no sooner, however we may explain it, had it got definitely recognised and established as the universal go-between, than

it acquired thereby a position which differentiated
it in many ways from every other thing.   Hence
its paradoxical nature.   In order to make this clear,
let us consider the essential nature of wealth in
general, from a point somewhat further back.

Every commodity, says Aristotle, rather loosely,
has two uses : its direct use, or special function,
and its indirect or derivative use, as enabling its
possessor to get something else for it.   We may
wear a shoe, or give it away and get something
else for it.   Of course, these two uses are not
really two, from the point of view of the commodity : they are only two, from the point of view
of the owner.   The secondary use, exchange power,
is merely the first use viewed in relation to another
owner, who wants to satisfy his demand.   Exchange value is simply use value, viewed from
the standpoint of someone who as yet does not
possess the commodity.   Now, on the side of
their special function, all commodities differ :   a
hat is one thing, a boot another, and so on.   But
on the side of their capacity of acquiring another
thing in exchange for them, they are all exactly
alike, indistinguishable.   It makes all the difference
to the man who wants boots, whether he has boots
or a hat : but if he can get the same thing for
either boots or a hat, wanting himself neither,
it makes no difference to him which he has.   To
the special want, only the special instrument can
answer : but anything will do equally well, if a man
only wants to get rid of it.   Here it is not the
special function of the commodity, as such, that
makes the difference : that is left out of account :
the important thing is, that it should be readily

and universally transferable. The more general
and less particular it is, here, the better.

Now, the secret of money lies here. It is, as
it were, commodities *minus* their special qualities.
It is their general capacity. It is the expression
not of what is different, but what is identical in
them. They all differ endlessly, but agree in
one point, that of answering to demand. Money
is the embodiment of this fact. It can perform
the special function of no commodity: out of
society and commodities, therefore, it is useless:
but it can perform the general function of *any*
commodity; in society, therefore, it is omnipotent.
It is the quintessence of the power of commodities.
It is no metaphor, but the expression of the deepest
conceivable, analytical, economical truth, to say,
money is power. Money *is* power: that is exactly
what it is. Money is in the economical world,
precisely what motion is in the physical world: and
parodying Aristotle's famous definition of motion,
we may define money as *the potentiality of commodities*. This definition is the ultimate wisdom, the
truth κατ' ἐξοχὴν, the omega of Political Economy.

Now though it may seem ridiculous, nevertheless
it is true, that just because it could perform no
special function, it was, except to the man who at
the moment wanted any special function performed,
better and more welcome to everybody, than any
actual commodity. Everybody wanted it, because
everybody else wanted it too. Everybody knew
that he could not always reckon on finding a man
who wanted boots, but he could always find a man
who wanted money. Therefore, paradoxical though
it might seem, it nevertheless came about that

money, in itself less useful than any other thing, was in virtue of its relations more valuable than any.   This position it acquired early, and has never since lost.

Yet again.   Just because it had acquired this anomalous and supreme position, it had two very peculiar and ennobling rewards conferred upon it, in addition, which raised it still higher, in all the world's estimation, as well as in its own.   To it alone of all things was given the power of paying taxes and of making war.   This more than anything else made it indispensable.   When, for example, the King (Henry I.) had decreed that payment in money was to replace the old system of payments in kind, he made a change whose importance he was probably very far from foreseeing. From that moment, according as money was or was not plentiful, were the taxes easy or oppressive. For money had to be forthcoming when the taxgatherer called, and if it was difficult to obtain so much, the more of his produce had the producer to give to obtain it.   And yet again money, being of universal validity, now added a stimulus to accumulation.   To the heaping up of wealth, so long as it consisted of perishable commodities, there was a limit.   No one could find it to his interest to accumulate sheep or oxen, grain or stuffs, whose value was destroyed by moth and dust, time and casualties.   But money would always keep its value. Therefore no one could have too much of it: the more he had, the more he still desired to have. Money became now synonymous with power, alike for the private individual and the State.   He who had money could at all times command the services of all. Money was the supreme Lord of the World : and conferred upon its possessors whatever human nature could desire, or human services perform. It was the universal instrument. That quality which placed it lower than any actual commodity gave it its prodigious dominion over them all : its strength lay in its weakness. Its absence of utility gave it at once universality and imperishability. For to become actual, i.e. a commodity, is to lose your power of becoming anything else. Once definitely this or that, Commodities had nothing to do but to be used and pass away : but money, being never any actual commodity, but merely the potentiality of any, did not perish in the using, but endured. Money stood to commodities in precisely the same relation as Samson with his hair stood to Samson without it : or better, as a loaded pistol to one already discharged. It held in itself the command over future destinies and possibilities. It was master of all eventualities. It was a guarantee against mishap, and an earnest of benefits to come. Its star was always in the ascendant. It carried with it hope and security. Commodities were always the setting, money the rising sun. Power, said Swift, which was used to follow land, is now gone over to money[f]. And Bolingbroke is constantly harping on this string.

To the corollaries and applications of these facts I shall return : here our concern with it is different :

[f] Land is the opposite pole of money : between these extremes lies every form of wealth. Land is the indeterminate possibility of wealth not yet formed : money, the quintessential and sublimated extract of wealth, divested of all its special qualities.

we are at present analysing the notion of value. These considerations will enable the reader to appreciate the wisdom of Aristotle's assertion, already quoted, that money has arisen in answer to *necessity :* here too structure has been determined by function. But what necessity? Let him tell us. There can be no exchange and no community unless there can be found some means of equating the values of commodities : there must be something therefore which measures all of them, and this is in reality our need, which binds all together : and money has come in to function as *the instrument or conveyancer of need.* There is the truth about money and value. Is it not strange that men should so entirely have missed a truth which when we approach the subject along the proper path seems to lie under our nose? Is it not more than remarkable to see to what an extent false methods can throw us off the scent? to see the laborious and ineffectual attempts of economists to found an essential notion of value upon what is merely secondary and derivative, such as power in exchange? If men had adopted the analytic enquiry into concrete realities, instead of a vain theorising from certain received dogmas, they would naturally have said to themselves : the law of nature is universal, that all structure arises in answer to function. Here then we have a structure so remarkable as money. There must be here too a *reason why,* for ' there ' are reasons and causes why and wherefore in all ' things.' What then is the necessity, the necessary function, to perform which money has arisen? Why, what can it be, but to express and make visible, concrete, external, our need for, or value of a thing?

That is in fact the truth. Money is simply the instrument, actuality, or realisation of demand, the vehicle of demand, the embodiment of value. Money is to value what the body is to the soul. Value is the soul of money[g]. The amount of money a man will give for a commodity is the exact measure of his value of it. The value of a thing, as Hudibras said with scientific accuracy, is so much money as 'twill bring. The value of a thing is not its cost of production, or the amount of money you must pay to make it : but the amount of money you can get *for* it : depends, that is to say, on the esteem or demand placed upon it by the man who is buying it, in comparison with his other necessities at the moment. Hence,—here comes in the point that the Economists have never perceived, the core of the financial question—the values, and thus the creation, of commodities are determined by variations in supplies of money. For it is important to observe that value, economically not expressible, is economically of no account. A man may *potentially* place any value he likes, great or small, upon commodities ; this is of no economic bearing, till it has been *actually* expressed. It is deeds, not wishes or words, that are wanted. A man shows his love for commodities by buying them : they pay no attention to anything but this. If, therefore, money be deficient in quantity, although men might retain the same regard for commodities ;

[g] Money being embodied demand or value (as value is the spirit or soul of money), exhibits exactly the old Platonic idea that *matter vitiates form :* for just because it is value materialised it is itself subject to impurities and variations which detract from its perfection as a measure of value.

although, that is, commodities might retain, potentially, their value in the eyes of would-be buyers : yet this 'would-be' will not avail : actually, commodities will lose their values, and hence cease to be produced, because men cannot afford to give so much money for them as before. For in actual economical life and real processes, the value of commodities depends upon the money tendered for them : depends, that is to say, not on their cost of production, nor upon other commodities, but upon money, which is not a commodity, but the actuality of demand for commodities [h].

The solution of all the perplexing enigmas which have defied solution on the principles hitherto dominant in economics flows, as I shall presently show, from this fundamental conception of value and money : and I shall show further from a different standpoint the truth of the analysis now arrived at. But in this place it is necessary to return, in order to attain to the proper point of view, to the essential nature of Wealth.

IV. Every particle of Wealth, every commodity or unit of Wealth, necessarily consists of, and is defined by, four causes or forces, which are, its

[h] Notice the confusion introduced into Economics by what the Economists call *Exchange-Value*. There is *Value*—that is, the mental esteem, appreciation, and demand for a thing and its qualities in the mind of a man considering it : and there is *price:* that is, money value, the commercial or concrete expression or realisation of the same fact : (when inexpressible in money, we say a thing is invaluable or inappreciable). But a thing like *Exchange value* which is neither of these two, but a kind of mechanical relation between two commodities, abstracted from men, is an abstract metaphysical entity which exists only in the writings of Economists.

matter, its form, its labour, and the function it
serves. This last, the function of the commodity,
may from one point of view be regarded as the
most important of the four: it is the soul of the
thing: its creative principle. Yet it would be
a fundamental error to attend to it alone. Certainly, the matter, form, and labour in a commodity
are determined by the function. Nevertheless,
these three causes are as essential to every commodity as the fourth. For no commodity can
possibly exist if deprived of these four indispensable components. They are all impotent divorced
from the others. All wealth must result from the
combination of the four. There can be no wealth
which is not under one aspect Matter, under another,
Form, under another, Labour, under yet another,
Use or Function. This is the Quadruple Principle,
the Fourfold Root, out of which springs the whole
mass of human wealth. *Flos de radice ejus ascendet :*
a flower shall go up from his root. And from this
point of view we see the absurd fallacy of those
economical and socialistic doctrines, which assert
that labour is the sole origin or source of wealth :
which derive the value of wealth from labour alone.
A true analysis annihilates this crass and indis-
criminating theory, by disclosing the fragmentary
and inadequate nature of its reasoning. So far
from labour being the sole source of wealth, it
is on the contrary only one, and essentially the
least significant, cause of wealth.

It is impossible to understand society, without
this principle : for the growth of wealth is nothing
but the evolution of the Quadruple Principle. This
principle is in fact the central conception of econo-

mics, which stands to economics in precisely the
same relation as the Copernican conception stands
to astronomy.   It explains exactly why the world,
considered economically, is constituted just as it is :
and exposes constructively the errors of previous
systems, which are all but so many abstract fragments and sides of the truth, unintelligible because
severed from that alone which can give them significance, the root idea, source, and origin of the
whole of economical science : for it all ramifies
from and finds its explanation in this central conception, and to trace the evolution of this conception is at the same time to explain the genesis of
our social system.   Not only economics but history
is to a large extent unintelligible without it.   And
being entirely without any perception of this truth,
economists have given us the most ludicrous statements of production and its requisites : confounding
the primitive barbaric form of production with the
highly differentiated form now obtaining : utterly
misconceiving the nature and meaning of Rent,
Capital, Money, Credit, Interest, and other economic categories.   They tell us that land, labour,
and capital are the three sole requisites of production : they deny that currency is capital : they
assert that capital is the result of saving—yet how
can wealth be saved except in the form of money ?
they deny that money is wealth, and yet assert that
it is a commodity, yet what is a commodity, but
wealth ? they cannot make head or tail of Credit,
just because they completely fail to comprehend the
true nature and function of money : their theories
of banking are utterly self-contradictory and suicidal, because they do not understand the part

money plays in the creation of wealth : interest
is a phenomenon that utterly baffles their efforts to
explain it on their principles : their explanation of
International Trade is pure nonsense: and their
whole system is a vast knot of errors and absurdities,
contradictory at once to itself and the facts and
practice of the world[1]. And yet the world, acting
on their theories, laboriously sets itself in a strait-
waistcoat, and brings upon itself gratuitous misery
and disaster, by twisting its commercial and financial policy into harmony with their mistaken notions.
Dearly has it paid for this : still more dearly may
it have to pay, unless it awakes betimes. Never
was anything bought for a heavier price than what
passes for Political Economy. So much misery
can Error inflict upon her misguided victims.

The test of a true and universal principle, says
Aristotle, is that it holds in any and every particular
instance taken at random. Just as a circle is always
a circle, whether it have a radius of one inch or ten
thousand miles, so always and everywhere, whether
we look at Wealth in the primitive barbarian protoplasmic system of production, or in the highly-
developed system of to-day, it is the same product
of four indispensable causes,—matter, form, labour,

---

[1] People try to excuse the Ricardian economics, by the
apology that its conclusions are true, only under ideal conditions. If that were so, why did Ricardo presume to come
forward and offer advice, or lay down the LAW, as to real
conditions? You have only to assume everything to be just
what it is not, and any philosophy is true. The sphere of
philosophy is the real, and the man who thinks of things just
as they are *not*, may be a mediocre poet, but philosophically
can only count as a fool. Was Ricardo, forsooth, a poet ?

and demand.   But these causes are of very different sizes at different epochs.   It is the confusion on
this head that has led economists astray.   We find
them united at first, separated at last: separated
but not divorced : differentiated, in order to perform their enlarged functions, into immense classes,
but not essentially changed.

In the rudimentary form, agricultural or nomadic,
venatory or piscatorial, we see early man plucking
fruit, growing corn, tending sheep or cattle, catching
fish, snaring birds and so forth : producing rude
wealth to serve his needs.   Here nature does much
and man little; and some of these simple forms
still necessarily remain.   What is sport to many
to-day, was life and death to primitive man.   In
these early forms only does it approximately express the truth to say that the requisites of production are two, labour and appropriate natural
objects, or three, land, labour and capital (excluding
from this term money).   I say approximately, because the statement is false even here.   Under
Labour are faultily assumed Knowledge and Demand : i. e. three of the causes are erroneously
jumbled into one.   For in fact in those early forms,
these three causes are united in the same individual.   It is not Labour, it is Man that 'makyth
wealth.'   But by omitting to take this into consideration, economists fall into fatal errors in subsequent more complicated forms of production.
Similarly, only in these early forms is the economical
use of 'capital' approximately accurate : meaning
wealth reproductively employed.   In these forms,
of course, money has not as yet made its appearance.   But if we define capital, as we ought to do

every *instrument of production*, as wealth in the strict and primary sense may be regarded as every *instrument of life and action*, we shall find, later on, that money is capital just as much as anything else : nay, that in a very significant and legitimate sense it alone is regarded as capital at all. But to this we shall return.

These low forms of wealth-creation, then, are very simple, nevertheless they contain in germ the essential elements of higher forms which are by no means so simple : but which will escape the notice of any one who has not correctly analysed the simple forms. The man who raises garden produce for a bare subsistence does in truth raise it from combining land, labour, and capital : i.e. the ground, seed, and his spade, to gain a required end. But it is pure nonsense to say that such a thing as, for example, a gunboat, is produced by 'land, labour, and capital.' Such a product never has anything to do with land at all, and any one can see, that even if we grant, what is not the case, that science may be included under the term labour, yet State necessities are an essential cause of the production of the gunboat, and these are not even suggested in the trinity. The true causes or requisites of production here, as everywhere, are material, form, labour, and demand or need : and what we must do, if we wish to understand the *raison d'être* of such an instance, is to analyse closely the four constituent elements that go to make it up.

Take first the material cause. It is philosophically and analytically a grave error to speak of the material cause of wealth as 'land.' The expression, derived from agricultural notions of wealth-creation, is even from a purely vague regard ridiculous : do not the sea, the air, the sun, cold and heat, contribute their *quotum?* If we are to be vague, let us be vague consistently ; let us say, the universe. But if we are to be scientific and analytic, what is the use of the term land ? Very few people are apt to reflect how immensely the original nature of land, the earth, has been changed by the way in which man has worked it to his ends : these being determined by moral, religious, personal and political ideas. 'Land' is not a thing homogeneous and everlastingly identical with itself, such as would subsist under any form of production. Therefore even *a priori* land is a bad term. But *a posteriori,* it is still worse. We only know a thing, when we know its proximate causes. To leave gaps is not to have a scientific knowledge : e.g., the cause of water is not 'gas,' it is hydrogen and oxygen in definite proportions, two to one. The cause of light is not 'land :' it is now wax and wick, now mineral oil, now zinc and copper connected by wires and immersed in a particular fluid, now friction, and so on. The cause of the ruin of Troy is not Helen ; it is the objection of Menelaus to let Paris take her away. And thus, every particular bit of wealth has its own particular material cause : *sine quá non.* The material cause of a table is wood or stone or ivory : that of a knife, steel : of a pudding, flour, raisins, sugar and so forth. That commodity which regarded as an end is wealth, regarded as a means becomes the material cause of a new commodity. 'The end of one beginning is the

' beginning of another end : ' and it is the last end
which conditions the first beginning of all. Here
we see what an insufficient and inadequate enumeration of the requisites of production it is to say
' land, labour, and capital.' The cause of log
rolling in Canadian backwoods is ultimately, the
demand for the production of ships, houses and what
not all over the world. Production on one side
of the world is determined and conditioned by action
on the other. From animals, one man produces
fleeces : these fleeces are materials to the dyer
or carder : these, again, hand over their products
to be the material cause of new products in the
hands of tailors, dressmakers, upholsterers : and
so on indefinitely. And observe that what came
last in the order of time came first in the order
of necessity. Just because there are so many
customers of all sorts at the end, are there so many
producers of all sorts at the beginning. The *raison
d'être* even of the material cause of wealth is the
special form of production and consumption existing
at the time. What an egregious want of insight
then does it argue to suppose that if the whole
constitution of society were changed the material
cause of the wealth would still be there. 'Land'
certainly would be there, but 'land' is not the
material cause of wealth. Land is the material
cause of a bare and scanty subsistence, that
is all.

Thus we see that the material cause of Wealth is
not land : but that it depends on, and is essentially
made what it is by, the whole dynamical play and
process of labour, power, science, and need, in
any society at any given moment. A man in

England makes, we will say, brushes from fibre. But he could not get this fibre from America, unless there were steam-boats, elaborate machines, a complicated banking system, an immense demand for brushes : all these things again depend on a host of conditions for their existence, which all ultimately resolve themselves into the same four causes. For every commodity is at once a result, the terminus of a long set of processes, and again the step or link in the chain of processes leading to a new term. Hence not only each product, but each process of production is structurally determined by its function : or what is the same thing, the needs or demands of customers at the end of the chain. And thus in one aspect the whole economical condition of society is dynamic :—a set of functions : and in another, it is a vast staircase of material structures : dynamics petrified and embodied. Viewed from the top, it is a graduated series of forms, all performing functions : viewed from below it is simply material, constantly passing into new forms. This is what Aristotle means when he says that matter and form, structure and function, are at the moment of active operation the same, but their essence is different. The *raison d'être* of the whole, the soul of Society, is the performance of necessary functions.

I shall presently show, that the failure of economists to comprehend the function of money arises from the fact that they have misunderstood the dynamics of production, here explained. In order that each productive process may have ready to hand the material and instruments on and with which it goes to work, the whole system must be working properly. Now, it is just money which works the machine.

But let us first succinctly consider the two causes, science or knowledge, and labour power.

Obviously, the power of transforming material into shapes that serve turns, essentially depends upon science, and when we know what has to be done, we still have actually to do it : apply power to effect the transformation. Thus Science and Labour are the two handmaids of the will to compel material to obey its wants. But they are two and not one : and the evolutionary process shows this by differentiating them. Science again naturally falls into two divisions, theoretic and practical. Theoretic science investigates and discovers the properties and powers of matter and the forces of nature; finds out how to utilise and apply matter and force. Hence, for example, steam, machinery, navigation, artillery, and so on. Practical science is essentially supervisional, forethoughtful: it introduces labour to the demand for it, transports material from place to place ; from here, where it is useless, to there, where it is valuable : facilitates production and the employment of labour and the satisfaction of demand, by moving commodities about, and devising ways and means, making enterprises, and so on. Knowledge thus becomes power. Inventors, discoverers, chemists, philosophers, merchants, agents, carters, railway directors and projectors, shipowners and shopmen—all these supply the indispensable element of science. Thus practical science stands on the border-line between pure science and pure power or force : but although pure science has no element of power in it ($\delta\iota\acute{a}\nu o\iota a$ δ'

αὐτὴ οὐθὲν κινεῖ), on the other hand some degree of science, i.e. skill or practice, is always found with labour power : it cannot act if it is blind. Even porters and coal-heavers must know the way to go to work. In machinery, again, hydraulic presses or mechanical automatic saws, hammers, drills, &c., we have force without human labour at all. From all this we see the absurdity of the claim that labour is the sole source of value and wealth. On the contrary, labour is merely the agent or instrument in the hand of science : to which, or rather to the *mediation* of which, labour owes all its employment. Without the eye to guide it, how could the hand know what to do, or how to do it?

Obviously, then, the degree of science in the com‑ munity, and the practical, business-like aptitude for designing, managing, providing, constructing, fore‑ seeing, in the individual members of the same : as well as, again, the skill, native or acquired, and character of workmen, their efficient condition, their political and social welfare, or any such circum‑ stances as influence their action as motives to make them take an interest in doing their work well, and so on : have a large share in promoting or retarding the creation of wealth in any community.

But in the last resort all depends on the demand, the final cause, the need for the commodities pro‑ duced, to serve which is their function, and the need for the services of the producers. To this great cause we must now turn.

The greater and more various the demand for commodities, the more employment will there be for labour which lives by ministering to demand. In this lies the true refutation of the old ' wage-fund ' doctrine, which reposed upon the ridiculous principle that a demand for commodities is not a demand for labour: the most curiously devised contradiction of the truth that ever puzzled the brains of two generations. Here we see the economical aspect of Darwin's law that diversity of character is an essential principle of evolution: that the more diversity there is in the character of the inhabitants of any country or area, the more life will be able to find support within that area. This is merely a case of the great law of biological evolution first discovered by Aristotle. It at once exposes the absurdity of the dogma that a demand for commodities is not a demand for labour. The *dictum* rests upon a radical misunderstanding of the *rationale* of the productive process. All production is essentially dependent upon and conditioned by the necessities of action which call it out. It is just to minister to life and make it good that all production exists. But the nonsensical division of labour into productive and unproductive prevented the economists from seeing this. All life is essentially action and not primarily production at all: hence by baptizing action as unproductive, and thus stigmatising it, economists are really stultifying themselves and the nature of the world and man. The end of production is not production, it is action. This is. its *raison d'être.* But according to this economical dogma, people must. give up action, and confine themselves to production, which only exists for the sake of action: i.e. they must give up that for the sake of which it is that they produce, and simply produce for the sake of producing! Or we may put the same point thus. If those who divide

labour into *productive* and *unproductive* mean by
this last expression simply something negative :
i.e. *non*-productive : the division is unimpeachable,
but an insignificant truism which tells us nothing.
It is like dividing things into *roses* and *not-roses*.
But if by *unproductive* they mean, as they do
mean, something positive : if they mean, as they do
mean, to cast a slur upon it, and to argue that what
they call '*unproductive*' labour exercises *no* influence
on the production—then it is a gross and vital
error. *There is no such labour in the world.* Action,
which is non-productive, is nevertheless indirectly
the essential cause of all production : all production
rests upon its needs.   There is no such thing as
labour that is unproductive in this bad positive
eeonomical sense.   All labour is either the final or
efficient cause of wealth.   Fighting is the reason
why military instruments are made : ploughing and
reaping, &c., the reason why agricultural instruments are made : praying, &c., the final cause of
churches : painting, music, &c., the final cause of
their tools : and thus generally, all productive
labour rests upon action, as its basis.   To call any
labour unproductive, in a scientific sense, is either
a miserable truism, or a proof of total incompetence.

   This is the consequence of omitting to take into
consideration the final cause, the end and reason
why of all wealth.   Everybody desires to live,
i.e. to act, and that as well as he can : that is to
say, the aim of his life is to consume 'unpro-
'ductively :' (though this word contains of course
an element of moral censure which is not in the
facts : as if, forsooth! it were a crime to wish to

live and act!) and this is what stimulates him
to exertion, to gain by producing, the means of
action. But conceive his horror, if he found no
one to buy : if everybody confined themselves to
producing, and nobody ever bought at all. Why,
the aim of the producer is to sell, to make profit
by selling. Is it conceivable that men should have
acquired great reputations as 'thinkers' of a high
order, who so ludicrously misunderstood life and
its processes as to lay down laws which negated it :
which, if carried out, would instantly put an end
to existence. Unproductive labour! what a name
to give to life! A fine man, riding on a magnificent horse : a beautiful woman, dancing at a ball :
a pretty child, playing in a garden : a regiment of
soldiers, marching along : a great actor, holding
his audience spellbound : a party of friends,
bivouacking by a river on a summer evening :
these are the fine flowers of existence which, all
unconscious of the ineffable absurdity of the thing,
these unutterable economists dismiss as 'unproductive labour.' The whole economical structure and
business of society has arisen and exists in order to
perform its function : the economists cut off the
function, never see it, and fondly imagining they
are able to explain the structure abstractly, i.e. out
of relation to its cause, pose as great thinkers, with
the grave dignity of men who will not be severe
upon inferior persons! O Momus, where are you?
did ever ancient Greece afford you such rich food
for an everlasting roar?

The truth is that all employment rests upon
consumption : that all Wealth - creation depends
upon the diversity of character, and diversity of

Demand for commodities. A highly-differentiated form of production, where competition is severe, necessarily implies a highly-differentiated society : great diversity of character in the members composing it. And as I have pointed out elsewhere, there is strict correspondence between the men and the commodities. To every different sort of man there are commodities answering. For the soul of commodities is the function they serve : and all Wealth is Wealth, only in relation to the men who use or demand it or buy it. To talk of 'social Wealth' as if Wealth was one great homogeneous lump is absurd. Every particle of Wealth has, just like every man, a definite character of its own : there is no such thing as social, i.e. general wealth. We may of course speak of wealth in the abstract : but wealth is no abstraction. It is rather the most real reality in the world. It is an accumulation of infinitely various structures answering to infinitely various demands. The failure to realise the connection is at the bottom of arbitrary socialistic schemes of division and distribution. You cannot carve the mass of wealth into so many equal portions. Its divisionary limits are fixed by diversity of character. The portions are, if they exist at all, essentially and necessarily unequal. You may, for example, sum up the wealth of the community, and estimate it at, say, ten thousand millions. But you could not subdivide the wealth as you could subdivide the money. For money is fractionally divisible and discrete, but wealth is not. Its nature limits its division. A loaf is worth, say 4*d*. : a carriage, say £150 : if now we think to divide up this £150 into portions of 4*d*. each, you will find you cannot: you will only annihilate that form of wealth : *with all the labour that depends on its production.* That £150 worth of wealth exists only because required in that form : and will not exist at all, if you taboo that form. In other words, the mass of wealth is as large as it is, because it answers to the functions which are required : if you annihilate the functions, the wealth correspondent to them will disappear. This is the heart of that fallacy, dear to demagogues, which supposes that a rich man might cut up and provide for many poor ones. It is not so. Abolish the rich man, and you will not be able to divide his wealth, for it will disappear : and with it, the employment of labour to which it gave occasion. The amount of existing wealth is inseparably connected with its form. You cannot change its form, and keep it the same in amount. For diversity of character is its condition : and it is impossible, as Aristotle said long ago, for any state to exist, whose individuals are all of one kind. They are essentially different in kind : as different and numerous as the necessities, capacities, and possibilities of human nature. To attempt to unify them is the old error of Plato : it is a denial of the evolutionary law of nature, that to different functions different structures correspond. And the essence alike of Nature and Society is the dynamical evolution of this law.

V. But let us look closely into the *actual operation* of this final cause, this demand of the person, answering to the function of the commodity.

The force which calls out all commodities from the womb of the infinite possibilities of matter ;

which sets the Idea to Work upon the Material, in
order to obtain instruments to serve it, is the Will,
Need, Want, or Demand of Man.   But of course,
so long as it remains merely potential, it can effect
nothing.   Mere desire, wishing, will do nothing.
We may long for commodities as much as we
please ; this will achieve nothing, unless we put our
demand into active operation, unless we actually
and definitely express and convey it.   Here then is
the crucial point.   On the one hand, it is obvious
that commodities *are*, in fact, produced in multi-
tudes.   On the other hand, we find that in order to
produce them, the power of demand must be actually exerted.   How, then, does this take place ?
At what point is it that this occurs ?   The answer
is, Money.   Money is the actuality of Demand :
the medium, or conveyancer, or vehicle, or mea-
surer, or instrument of demand.   Now, demand is
merely a synonym for value.   A man's value for a
commodity is his demand for it : and money is the
expression or outward visible sign of the inward
spiritual esteem.   Conversely, the value of a thing
is just the money it will fetch.

Here, then, we see the true function and the
immense importance of money.   The most vital
and radical error in orthodox economics is its
failure to understand money.   And this again came
about owing to the fundamentally erroneous method
of economical investigation.   Instead of analysing
the causes of wealth, economists started from abstract entities, of merely partial validity, where they
were of any validity at all : such as, for example
'labour.'   They thus cut themselves off from all
possibility of ever arriving at the truth.   The true

way was, to discover first the actual causes of commodities, and then find out where money came in.
Instead of doing this, they laid down abstract
dogmas about Wealth ; and, as these never included
the most essential cause of all, how could they
possibly pick it up afterwards ? how could they
possibly solve the problem of money and value ?
For it is just this cause which is concerned, in the
case of money and value ; it is from this cause they
arise, and on it they play.

Instead of proceeding analytically and going
backwards, the economists started with dogmatic
abstractions and went downwards,—argued, that is,
deductively from these. Instead of looking straight
at the facts of wealth, disentangling its causes, and
tracing them up to their simple forms, the economists began by laying down axioms drawn from an
agricultural and one-sided view of Wealth-creation,
and argued from them. As they had omitted
from their premises the really decisive cause, that
of demand, they could never reach it again. It
was not in the premises, and could not therefore
come out in the conclusion ; for you cannot get
out of the sack more than you put in. They
asserted that land, labour, and capital,—meaning
by the last expression, not money, but wealth
reproductively employed,—were the sole requisites
of production. They conceived wealth as being
therefore, somehow or other, first made, and, when
made, ready to be exchanged. Here came in the
notion of barter. One commodity was exchanged
against another, and money was devised simply
as a means of making exchanges more readily,
by providing a medium and measure of value.

But this value was, they said, determined by cost
of production.   Money only measured values
already determined.   Money was thus a sort of
otiose *deus ex machina* introduced between two
commodities preparing to exchange.   Indeed it
is hard to see what on earth was the use of it :
for both its own value and that of both the commodities, were all already determined by their
cost of production.   It followed, that it was of
essentially subordinate importance.   It did not
matter how much or how little there was of it.
If there was more, more could represent the same
value : if less, less.   Being itself a commodity, its
value also, like that of commodities, settled by
cost of production, buying and selling were thus
essentially identical with barter : the substitution
of similars, equal costs of production.   A purchase
and a sale were identical.   *Toute vente est achat :
tout achat est vente*, said Quesnay, the *fons et
origo mali.*   Commodities were purchased with commodities : hence, gluts are impossible.   All holders
of commodities could exchange them against others;
therefore a glut was a contradiction.   Commodities
were the market for commodities.   Money obeyed
the same laws as all other commodities.

The only objection to all this is that it is
radically, hopelessly, wildly, and glaringly wrong :
in flat contradiction to notorious facts.   Money is
not a commodity : it is *not* subject to the same
laws as commodities : commodities are *not* purchased with commodities : gluts *are* possible : it
makes, not no difference, but *all* the difference how
much or how little money there is in an industrial
community : a purchase is *not* the same thing as

a sale : buying and selling are *not* barter : the
principle of exchange is *not* the substitution of
equal *costs of production :* value is *not* determined
by cost of production : and so far from it being
true that commodities are first made, and then
money comes to exchange them, or 'circulate' them :
on the contrary, money is a decisive agent in their
production : without it they cannot, in a commercial
society, be made at all.

It is perfectly true that money was originally
devised, or arose, in answer to the need of facilita-
ting exchanges, by measuring values. But their
false conception of value led Economists astray
here. Barter was no doubt the primitive form of
exchange. But barter was not based on the substitution of similar costs of production. How on
earth could this be determined ? And what reason
would it furnish for making an exchange ? Two
men might agree that their commodities were of
equal costs of production. But why should this
lead to an exchange ? And what would lead, then,
to an exchange ? Why, of course, the fact that
each man *wanted* what the other man had, *more*
than he wanted what he had himself. But how
were they to agree how much value each placed
upon the other's commodity ? Here it is that
money comes in : it measures values, not because
these depend on cost of production, *but precisely
because they do not :* because on the contrary they
depend on the respective *needs* felt for the commodities. Money, however we may theoretically
account for its origin, came to be the medium in
which men reckoned their *need* or *value* of commodities.

No doubt, it was originally chosen because it was a thing everybody liked to possess : but the more it won its way, as *the* medium, the more would people like to have it. No doubt, metals speedily seized upon the position, because they were in themselves beautiful as ornaments, and easily carried about : easily divisible, permanent, and easily concealed. But observe, that as soon as gold and silver were recognised universally as money—the medium of valuation—they sprang into a peculiar position. Henceforth, their value as metals became a thing essentially subordinate to their value as the universal valuer and de-mander. From this moment anybody who possessed them could get what he chose in exchange for them. And just because everybody would give commodities in exchange for them everybody strove to acquire them. They were simply external lumps of demand : bodies endowed with the mysterious property of commanding everyone's services. The world became the slave of money : money became synonymous with power.

All things being estimated in money, direct barter, being clumsy and indeterminate, went more and more out of fashion. Everything was worth so much money. To get anything, you had either to make it yourself, or give money in exchange for it. You could make other things, give them for money, and then give this for what you wanted. But this, the commercial method, is a roundabout and laborious way. The short and easy method was to lay hold of the golden mean direct : by begging, borrowing, or stealing, gambling or specu-lating. Hence the development of begging, bor-

rowing, stealing, gambling, speculating, stockbrok-
ing, pawnbroking, and so on : all are but various
ways of getting hold of the golden mean. Hence,
too, the growth of fortunes : i.e. wealth in money.
Hoarding was now the thing. There was now
a motive for accumulation. No one could have too
much of the universal demander. The measure
of value of any commodity was now just what
money you could get for it. This was determined
not merely by the need of it felt by the purchaser :
but also by the amount of money he could spare.
For here came in the influence of the important
fact that sometimes there was more money about,
sometimes less. When there was little money
about, a man could not afford to give so much for
any particular commodity as at other times : because it would leave him less for other things.
And when he had plenty, he would give more
easily of it, and also buy more things. This
accordingly was a good thing both for himself and
the producer whose goods he wanted. Thus we
see at once that scarcity of money lowers the
value of commodities : not mathematically, as the
Economists say, but dynamically : i.e. a man cannot
afford so much for his commodity. Conversely,
plenty of money tends to raise the value of commodities, but will not necessarily raise prices, because if more commodities are wanted, more will
come, if they can, and this will again tend to lower
prices : but in the meantime the process will increase
employment. Thus as the one great necessity for
a producing society is to sell its goods, plenty of
money is a great benefit ; and too little money, the
greatest possible evil. On the one hand, the con-

P

sumer cannot afford to buy, and on the other, the producer cannot sell.

We see, then, that the radical fallacy of the Economists lies in this, that they have not, owing to an erroneous method, understood the function of money. Money is not a commodity, but the vehicle of demand for commodities. It is thus the most potent agent in Wealth-creation and distribution. For no one can buy commodities, if he cannot offer or promise money in exchange for commodities. And commodities, as we saw, are the material cause of new commodities. Hence no one can make commodities, unless he can get at the money with which to buy his instruments and materials. For commodities are not purchased with commodities, but always with money, which is not a commodity, but the vehicle and expression of demand for commodities.

Here comes in the truth as to Credit, Banking, and Credit Instruments. Capital means, as has been shown above, any instrument in production. In autonomous societies not yet based upon exchange, where money has not arisen, these instruments are simply previous commodities employed in making another. Such as, for example, food and clothes, tools, weapons, &c. But when society has become commercial, and is based upon buying and selling, the only way of obtaining commodities is to offer money in exchange for them. Accordingly, whoever wants anything, or to make anything, must first want money. Hence, because money is the indispensable condition of acquiring these required instruments, and because they can only be got, with money, Capital comes to be used exclusively for money, as being the sole means of getting commodities : the indispensable instrument for purchasing instruments : and in practice every one means money when he mentions Capital : that on which Interest is paid. The Capitalist is the man who has money. The distinction between Capital, meaning money, and Capital, not meaning money, but instruments of production, is indicated by the terms Fixed and Circulating Capital. The Economists, owing to their want of comprehension of money, have never been able to understand this distinction [k]. Fixed Capital means Capital which is fixed *in a particular form of production :* as machinery, plant, and so on. Circulating Capital means Capital which is not so fixed, but which can circulate from form to form : that is to say, money. To convert circulating or floating Capital into fixed Capital is simply to lock up money : to fix it permanently in a special form of production where it must stay. And sometimes this leads to awkward positions : when, for example, there is a rage for investing in one particular form of production : as, for example, railways, and every one goes in for them : then it is found that there are too many in the business : but they cannot get out then, for no one will buy. This is the *rationale* of the difficulty. The explanations given by Economists are all explanations that ex-

[k] J. S. Mill surpasses himself in this connection. He bases the distinction between Fixed and Circulating Capital on three different notions, which contradict one another. See his *Pol. Econ., Pop. Ed.*, p. 57. He is obliged to observe that the term 'circulating' is not very appropriate. Not very : *for his meaning.* According to one of his notions, Capital could not mean money : according to another, it could mean nothing else : according to the third, heaven only knows what it means.

plain nothing : because they try somehow or other to avoid admitting that circulating capital is money. They therefore give arbitrary meanings to the words *fixed* and *circulating,* which nobody means when he uses the words, and which are unnatural to the words.

To make Wealth, you must either have money or borrow it. You cannot borrow Commodities [1] : (hence, if it were true that Capital is not money, it would follow that *you cannot borrow Capital:* what a consequence !) you have to buy them : it is money that is borrowed. But now, you cannot get people to lend you this money for nothing. You must make it worth their while. You must give them something for its use; this is Interest. To this we shall return.

But here comes in a further development. If I wish to buy anything, I must pay money. But perhaps I have not the money. Would the seller wait a while for it ? I *promise to pay* him subsequently. If this will do, then trade can go on. I can get my materials, make my Wealth, sell it, and repay my debt out of the proceeds. This is the essential operation of Credit and Banking. All Credit is simply *a promise to pay money,* and Banks are simply the means of working the system of Credit. The function of Banks is not, as most people suppose, to receive deposits of money. This is a means, and not the end, the *raison d'être* of Banks. The function of Banks is *to lend money by creating Credit.* They advance money on enter-

---

[1] Of course, you can, in another connection, borrow commodities ; *i.e. hire* them ; and pay Rent : but this is not the point here. You do not pay Rent, but Interest, on Capital.

prisers' and merchants' securities before these have completed their transactions. The whole thing rests upon *anticipation.* Mr. So and So wishes to make Wealth. He borrows from the Bank on the security of his future profit : and, of course, an essential element in the transaction is the character of the borrower. The Bank charges a percentage on its loan, called its Discount. Thus the Bank makes its profit by lending : the merchant makes his, by borrowing : all the tradesmen and wage-earners employed by him gain : and the whole thing is done by means of Credit. For the Bank does not, except in rare cases, actually hand over the actual money, when lending it. It empowers the merchant to *draw upon it* for the money, if he requires it: i.e. it *opens a Credit* for him in its Books. He draws a cheque. This cheque is handed in, but in ninety-nine cases out of a hundred is not paid in money : it goes off and is cancelled against another. Thus the whole thing is performed, *without actual money.*

This is the *rationale* of Credit and Banking. To analyse it more fully, we must go back a little.

The fundamental delusion in Economics as regards Money (arising from its theory of value) is this : that it gets its value from the metal of which it is composed. On the contrary, the metal gets its value from its function as Money. It is because it is the material of which money is made that people all wish to get hold of the metal. De-monetise it, and it is of no use except as a metal : its function as money is gone. Who then would care to possess it ? The value of silver, for instance, has sunk, not because its production has quantitatively

increased, but because the nations have discarded it
as Money.   And the value of gold has risen, because, silver having been ousted, double and treble
work has been thrown upon gold.

This requires explanation.   It was stated above
that money was not subject to the same Laws as
commodities.   Economists ' maintain the reverse.
Their theory of value lies at the bottom of this
error.   Value being in all cases determined by cost
of production, and money being merely a commodity
among commodities, its value was on the same foot-
ing as that of the others.   But we have seen, in the
first place, that money is not a commodity, but the
instrument or vehicle of value and demand for commodities : and in the second place, that value is not
determined by cost of production, but by the relation
between the qualities of the commodity and the man
who requires it.   The function of commodities is
totally different from the function of money : and
their function, we should not forget to observe, is
the *raison d'être* or cause of their existence.   The
functions of commodities are all different, all particular : they all answer to special needs, and are
required only by special persons.   *The function of
the Commodity is special: the function of Money
general, universal:* it answers directly to no needs,
but indirectly, i.e. *through Commodities,* to all : it is
not only wanted, but absolutely necessary to all
persons, in civilised society ; for whoever wants
anything wants Money.   In this lies the *difference*
between Money and Commodities.   Commodities
all differ in respect of their functions, but are all
identical, in respect of their capacity of changing
hands : money is just the universal expression of

this resemblance, this side of commodities which is common to them all. Money is Commodities, without their special functions : Commodities, in an undifferentiated form : Commodity-power. Hence it does singly what they all do together : i.e. satisfies every sort of demand. Hence the shapes of commodities are essential to them : for all their shapes are determined by their special function ; they are what they are, in virtue of their shape : and without its own peculiar shape each would cease to exist. But the essence of money does not lie in its shape. Its shape is to have no shape : but as this is impossible, it has as little shape as it can : i.e., its shape is not determined by any need for the *material* performance of work, but as we might say, *spiritually*. Its shape, as Kant might say, is not phenomenally but noumenally determined. The essence of Money lies not in its formal action, but its invisible potency. Hence it is not its shape, but its quality and amount, i.e. its material potentiality, that is the main thing. Being merely a little lump of demand or value, it is not formal, but qualitative and quantitative considerations that make the difference here. It would not matter in the least, as far as the performance of its essential function was concerned, whether it were round, spherical, oblong, square, triangular, polygonal : nobody would care, except that some of these shapes would wear holes in his pocket : i.e. it is merely convenience which gives money its shape : convenience, that is to say, a reason not essential to money as such. For money does not act through its shape as such, whereas with commodities it is just the reverse ; they are through and through shapes, above all things shapes, just

shapes, and could not lose their shapes without
ceasing to be that which they are. What is essential to money is that it should be what it pretends
to be : just so much gold or silver : genuine.
A false coin deceives, it may be, all the senses but
one : it *looks, tastes, smells, feels*, just like the real
Simon Pure : but *is* not : it does not *ring* true :
that is to say, it is not its visible but its invisible
qualities that are essential to it. It must be, not
just anything, but exactly what the human mind
expects that it ought to be, in its inner nature.
And *in the abstract*, no doubt the human mind can
confer upon any material it chooses, the function of
money. But here comes in custom and tradition :
the hereditary prepossessions and time-honoured
uses, and daily work-a-day practice of nations cannot be rationalistically played upon, juggled with,
and lightly set at nought, in this case, any more
than others. Gold and silver are in possession of
the field. Nevertheless it is a vital error to suppose
that money gets its value from the value of the
metal in it, *quâ* metal. The metal gets, on the
contrary, its value from its use as money. Money,
then, is valuable as containing so much gold, but
gold not *quâ* metal, but *quâ* money material. De-
monetise gold, and where is its value ?

Here lies the reason why money is not subject
to the laws of commodities. The demand for money
is not, like that for commodities, definite, but inexhaustible. The demand for any commodity is
simply the demand for that commodity ; the demand
for money is the demand for *all* commodities.
Increase the supply of any commodity, and you
will infallibly lower its value, for the limit of de-

mand for any special commodity is soon reached. But this is not the case with money. Vast additional supplies in highly civilised commercial communities do not touch its value : for no man can ever have enough of it. All that they do is to increase enormously the production of commodities and the employment of labour. For as all production depends upon consumption, and to be a consumer a man must first be a customer, his capacity of buying essentially depends upon the quantity of money he can give : and thus in the question of *prices* lies the cardinal question of Political Economy, and the welfare of a productive community.

All this has been completely misunderstood by Economists from Smith down to to-day. The Physiocratic dogma that commodities are purchased with commodities : and the semi-Physiocratic agricultural error of stating the requisites of production to be land, labour, and capital (from which term money is excluded) blinded them to the truth. This is why they have condemned the Mercantile System. They did not understand the function of money in the creation of Wealth, neither did they pay any attention to another function that money alone could perform in the days of that system, and which alone it can perform still. It was the instrument of war : the weapon *par excellence.* Who had money, could fight : hence, who parted with his money left himself defenceless. This was why the Mercantile Theorists held, truly, that the side which gained money in international exchanges, gained : and the other side lost. Hence their theory of the balance of trade. And most certainly they

Body and Soul.

were right.   The whole development of the English constitution has hinged upon the power of the purse.   The Stuarts were beaten because they had no money.   It was the want of money which made Edward I. lean upon his Parliaments for support. It was the payment of money which made the middle-class Englishman hate the Pope.   It was the fact that the Pope and King were rivals for the money of their subjects that set them by the ears. Want of money beat James II. and the Jacobites : the power of money and the Bank of England kept William III. on the throne and secured the Revolution.   England beat Napoleon with her money. The development of Banking made Scotland, and saved England in spite of the Napoleonic war.

Here again we come back to Banking.   It was inevitable that the orthodox Political Economy should find this a stumbling-block.   For how could any one comprehend Banking, who ignored the function of money in the creation of Wealth, and denied that the increase of money was a benefit to the country ?   The essence of Banking is, simply, the multiplication of money, without mines.

If I have money, I can buy : if not, not : unless the seller will take my promise : give me Credit. I can write upon paper, ‘I promise to pay so many ‘pounds, either on demand, or in a definite time.’ If I am believed to be able and willing to pay : if my credit is sound : this promise will be taken by people who know me as readily as money.   This is the essential structure of Credit.   The function of credit is to enable purchases and sales to go on, business to be transacted, without the actual use of money.   For want of this, production would come to a standstill. Credit enables us to do without money that which intrinsically we can only do with it. Credit is essentially identical in function with money. It is the performance of money's function by proxy. Money must be there, but only potentially or in spirit. Credit does without money, not absolutely, but relatively. Credit cannot replace money, but must rest upon it, as a basis. Money is to Credit what substance is to shadow : or, more accurately, what act is to power. Credit is potentially money, but not actually. It is the expansion, the velocity, the wings of money. But it only can exist, in so far as money stands, or is believed to stand, behind it. Upon this CONFIDENCE rests its efficacy, its power, its validity. In times of destruction of confidence, panic, political apprehension, the potential, Credit, is robbed of its atmosphere and dies : only the actual money then avails. It is in critical times that the truth appears : that the superstructure vanishes, and the pillars of gold and silver stand firm. Credit only possesses a reflected glory, or delegated authority : it has *potestas*, but the *dominium* is money's.

Banks, as we saw, are nothing but machinery for the working of Credit, for basing Credit upon Money. Many have thought that if Credit can be based upon Money, there is no reason why it should not be based also upon other things, commodities : as, for example, upon land. But now, this will furnish us with an admirable corroboration of the view of Money which I have been advocating. It has always been found, *in fact*, that any attempt to base Credit upon anything but Money ; on any Commodity, for instance, has been a disastrous failure. And

therefore, Mr. Macleod says, perfectly truly, that
a true theory of Money and Credit must explain
this. It must show what it is that constitutes the essential difference between Money and Commodities.
It must explain why it is, that Credit, which works
perfectly when based upon Money, refuses absolutely to be based upon Commodities. Now, this
is just what no Economist has ever been able to do.
Even Mr. Macleod, who sees the point, fails to
achieve the desired end : although he thinks his
own solution the true one. The truth is, that there
is an essential difference between Money and Commodities. The truth is, not as Mr. Macleod says
that Money is Debt, but that Money is *Demand*,
and Commodities, the *things demanded.* Credit can
be based upon Money, because Money is the *power
of demanding*—whatever its holder wants. But all
holders of Money want different things. Therefore
no particular thing will do instead of Money to
satisfy all, because Money alone will answer every
demand. Here lies the reason why Credit can be
based upon nothing but Money : why all attempts
to base it upon land, like those of Law and Cham-
berlayne, or any other Commodity whatever, are
foredoomed to failure. Let the reader judge whether this be not a complete verification of the truth
of that view of Money here established : for only
this view of Money can possibly explain the facts.
We find that Credit will not work when based upon
Commodities, while it works excellently when based
upon Money. There *must* accordingly be some
essential difference between Money and Commodities : and, as I have shown, there is. The
function of Money is demand in general. There-

fore any body will take *promises to pay Money*
freely : because these give them the power of getting anything they choose in exchange. But no
one will take *promises to pay any particular Commodity* instead of Money, because, whatever it is,
very few people want that particular Commodity :
consequently, it is not readily exchangeable or nego-
tiable : that is to say, Credit based upon Commodities will not work.

It is well worth our while to consider this carefully, not only because it contains the gist of the
whole theory of Money, but also because Mr. Macleod is a recognised authority on Banking, and
by far the ablest writer on Economics in modern
times, in spite of the fact that his system has gone,
in some directions, wildly astray, and is far more
correctly described as Mathematical than Political
Economy. When we find that in Mr. Macleod's
opinion, Money is Capital, Money is Credit, Credit
is Capital, and both Money and Credit are at once
Wealth and the representatives of Debt, we are
apt to lay him aside as maintaining views palpably
absurd. But the absurdity is not so great as it
appears : it is half true, half due to a want of
sufficiently close discrimination. If we define Capital as any Instrument in Production, it is unquestionably true that Money and Credit are Capital,
and may even, in a sense, be called Wealth, though
only indirectly. But that Money is Credit, ('money,'
says Mr. Macleod, 'is only the highest form of
'Credit,') or that 'currency is debt,' is not true, nor
is it difficult to point out the cause of this error.

'If,' says Mr. Macleod, 'a paper currency succeeds which is based solely upon bullion, and fails

' when based upon bullion and Commodities, which
' are both articles of value, it necessarily follows
' that we must search for some conception which
' shall *include* bullion and *exclude* commodities. And
' this is precisely what we have done. We have
' found that a paper currency is based upon bullion
' as the specific representative of *debt* and not as
' an indifferent article of value. *Bullion is the*
' *representative of debt*, and commodities are not.
' Paper currency is the representative of debt.
' Paper currency and bullion are homogeneous quan-
' tities, paper currency and commodities are *not*
' homogeneous. . . . There can then be no possible
' doubt that we have at last obtained the true
' conception of the nature of a currency. *Currency*
' *is the representative of debt and not of value.*   Now
' this result is not doubtful, or a matter of opinion,
' but it is a certainty.' (*Elements of Political*
' *Economy*, p. x.)

The mixture of truth and error in this passage
is most instructive : still more so is the very positive
conviction of · certainty in the conclusion ; for, as
I shall have no difficulty in showing, instead of
being a certainty, it is certainly an error : and
this should teach us how careful we ought to be
before making sure of any scientific train of reasoning.   It is unquestionably true that paper currency,
or Credit, is the representative of debt.   William
Cobbett, as far as I know, was the first to point
this out, in a most characteristically dogmatic little
pamphlet entitled '*Paper against Gold*,' in which
he maintains opinions that are undoubtedly erroneous with an amusingly cocksure conviction that
they are all right.   Paper currency is debt, but

this is exactly what bullion is not. Mr. Macleod's error is precisely analogous to that of a man who should maintain that a statue is the same thing as its pedestal. Paper currency and bullion are *not* homogeneous quantities. They are, on the contrary, unhomogeneous. Paper currency is a set of *promises to pay bullion.* The first *is* debt: the second is not : it is the thing itself : the thing owed. Credit *is* debt : but Money is not : Money is Demand, and Credit is the debt, or owing, of Money. As soon as we see this, we see also that Mr. Macleod has not performed the task he set himself. For if paper currency be debt, why should it not be debt of commodities, as well as of bullion ? Mr. Macleod's question still remains unsolved ; it is still just where he took it up.

The true solution is the one I have given : but it should be recollected that if Mr. Macleod did not answer the question, at least he saw that it ought to be asked, and so far he is a long way ahead of other Economists. Bullion is *not* debt, and it *is* the representative of value : it is the vehicle or embodiment of demand. Bullion differs from commodities in this, that everybody wants bullion, and only some want Commodities. People do not want a *promise to pay* any *particular* article of value but *value in general:* for the former would not be universally taken, not easily disposed of, and so would not be accepted in payment, just because it would suit very few people, comparatively speaking : but bullion suits everybody. Credit is Debt, but it must be debt of the required sort : it must be bullion, i.e. *any* commodity required, and not one hard and fast particular commodity, that is owing.

Here is the fallacy of Law's scheme or any similar
scheme of erecting a paper currency on a commodity.
And it is obvious that Mr. Macleod has confounded
money with the promise to pay it. Money is not
Credit : how could it be? far from it. Money and
Credit are identical in function, but essentially different in their material nature. They both *effect
demand.* But though they agree in this, they do
not agree in all respects ; absolutely, as Aristotle
would say—Money is no more Credit than sunlight
is moonlight. The one stands upon its own legs ;
the other upon the first, without which it cannot
exist. How can a *promise to pay* a thing be identical with the thing itself? How can a man lift
himself up in the air? The solution of Mr.
Macleod's difficulty is not to be found in the false
identification of bullion and paper currency. It lies
in the difference between Money and Commodities.
And this difference consists in the difference between
their functions, and values : between that which all
the world wants, and that which only some want.
Bullion being the concrete realised embodiment of
demand, and commodities being the things demanded, the moment a commodity is substituted for
bullion in the *promise to pay*, Credit loses its universal quality, and retains only the particular value
of the commodity in question. Hence it will no
longer perform that function which is its *raison
d'être :* to perform which it came into existence :
i.e. effect demand in all cases. And therefore it
must of necessity fail ; issue in panic, disaster,
financial ruin.

The truth is, that the attempt to base Credit upon
Commodities essentially involves the negation of

the very *raison d'être* both of Money and Credit:
and must therefore of necessity be suicidal. If
Money was, as Economists tell us, merely a Commodity, then no one could ever explain why Credit
should not be based upon Commodities other than
Money: though in practice this is always found to
be impossible. And perfectly truly, for in fact
Money is not a Commodity. It is the power of
demanding Commodities. Just because it is so,
everybody who wants Commodities either to consume, or to use as the instruments for producing
a further Commodity, must first obtain this *power
of demand.* This is the *raison d'être* of Credit.
There is not enough metallic Money to accommodate all producers. Were Money to be confined
to the volume of metallic Money, Wealth-creation,
in the degree in which it exists and acts at present,
could not go on, and consequently immense numbers
of people who live by producing would die. Now
Banks are simply the instruments for enlarging the
volume of Money, by operating Credit. Banks cannot make £5 out of £1; but by their means £1
does the work of £5. Banks do not and cannot,
except in rare special instances, lend actual Money
to borrowers. They 'open Credits' for them: that
is to say, they give them the power of claiming
sums of Money. But in ninety-nine cases out of
a hundred, this Money is never demanded, so long
as the borrower knows that he can have it. He
does not take the *Money* from the Bank. He
writes a cheque or draft, which is paid in to another
Bank, and by a system of cancelling cheques
and bills, the great bulk of payments, Banking
liabilities, is effected without the actual agency of

Money. Bankers live on averages. They know that not one in a hundred will actually want hard Money : so that they can, relying upon this, accommodate, say, a hundred people with a loan of £100, though they may actually possess no more than £1,000. The business being all carried on in Credit,—cheques and drafts,—every hundred pounds is enabled to do the work of a thousand. The borrowing producers buy their required commodities not with the body but the spirit of Money : with cheques, not coin : bills, not bullion. And this is why so small an amount of bullion can support so vast an amount of producing and trading in Commodities of all kinds.

Now any one can see that when this system is established everything depends upon the efficiency and security of Banks. People take cheques, drafts, bills, instead of the actual money, because they believe they could have the gold if they chose. They take the chance of the future, rather than the actuality of the present, because they are confident. But when, from any reason, people doubt the security of Credit, they will not take *promises to pay:* they will only take pay,—the actual cash. It is manifest that the very nature of Banking makes it absolutely impossible for every claimant to get his money, if all claimants ask for it at the same moment. No Bank, however sound, however solvent, could exist for a single day, if all who had claims upon it came in a body and demanded payment at the same moment. For the essence and function of a Bank is to promise money in excess of what it has : to erect upon a basis of Money a superstructure of Credit. The failure of a Bank does not by any means necessarily argue that it has been fraudulently managed. Every Bank must fail if all its Creditors come on it at once. If a Bank's reputation is discredited, it can be broken at any moment. No amount of metallic reserves can possibly enable any Bank to pay its liabilities in money. It was never the intention, never within the power, of any Bank to do any such thing. It engages to pay Money, on receipt of securities and deposits that are not Money, and cannot be turned into Money except under favourable circumstances. It may hold millions of securities, worth ever so much money, and yet be unable to pay a shilling. It calculates that in ordinary times so much Money on an average will be sufficient to meet ordinary demands, and so much it keeps by it : but it cannot possibly keep Money equal to its liabilities. It would not be a Bank if it did : further, it could not, if it would. There is not coin or bullion in the world equal to the liabilities of even English Banks.

When its trade has once been thoroughly based upon the lending and borrowing of Money, and thus upon the system of Banking and Credit, there could not possibly be a more frightful disaster for a nation than the sudden annihilation of her Credit. It would be national death. All Wealth-creation, for want of the *means of demand*, would instantly cease. Therefore the most fundamental business of the statesman in such a country should be to see that in the event of panic, temporary loss of confidence in Banks, means should be provided to enable them to tide over the crisis. Now the fundamental error in English financial legislation has been that its

authors did not understand this.   Sir Robert Peel
and his advisers understood nothing about the
question.   They had not the dimmest conception
of the process of Wealth-creation, or the part that
Money played in the creation of Wealth.   They
thought that commodities were bought with commodities.   They did not comprehend the mechanism
and function of Banks.   They were possessed
by a vague and unintelligent fear of paper credit,
'over-issues,' and so on : they looked upon paper
money as essentially dangerous, doubtful, and mysterious.   When gold left the country, they never
imagined it might be going away to pay for commodities : they looked upon the drain as an infallible
sign that our money was depreciated, because they
argued that no one would send away gold to pay
a debt as long as some other commodity was
cheaper : as if a man could pay a debt of pounds by
sending soap or candles !   They made it the aim
of all their efforts artificially and forcibly to restrict
the supply of money available for commerce, never
dreaming that they were thus throttling and en-
dangering the producing power of the nation.   The
fact is, that here, as always, Peel was halting between two opinions.   Either he ought to have recognised that, all trade being carried on by the borrowing of Money, the first essential was to secure and
ensure that there was enough : or else he ought
to have abolished Credit altogether and limited
trade to cash payments.   This is, in fact, the inner
tendency of his legislation.   By making Bank-notes
increase and decrease with the inflow and outflow
of gold Peel showed perfectly clearly that he was
totally ignorant of the true function of Money and

the necessities of trade. It is not only unsound and insecure trade, over-speculating trade, that lives on borrowed money; it is essential to all trade to do so. No one now-a-days keeps money by him. Everybody rests upon the Banks. The most wealthy trader in the world may be quite unable to pay ten pounds without the assistance of the Bank. And by robbing Credit of its elasticity, reducing its volume to that of gold, raising the interest on borrowed money, and making it legislatively impossible to get money from the Bank, Peel was in reality cutting at the root of all Wealth-creation. The Bank Charter Act is a monument of ignorance. The man who made that Act wrote himself down as emphatically as ever Dogberry did : he proved in black and white that he was totally ignorant of the whole economical structure of society. Wealth-creation exists by means of Credit facilities : destroy them and you annihilate Wealth, Trade, and Industry. The whole system of Credit is a system of Debts, reposing on a small basis of metallic Money. The Bill whose avowed design and inevitable tendency is to minimise Credit just when it is most required, to confine vast trade operations within the limits of a constantly lessening gold supply :—why, the Black Hole of Calcutta was nothing to it. You might as well enact that as the gold left the country, so many tons of machinery should be smashed up by the myrmidons of the law. For the currency of the country is as important as any part of a machine. The whole economical machine, and every machine, works by its means. Viewed economically, society is a vast organ of production ; an immense piece of

mechanism pyramidal in form. Every finished
commodity becomes in turn the material of some
further productive operation. Hence unless at
each step the producer is provided with the accepted
medium, the vehicle of demand, to enable him
to purchase his materials, the whole thing must
come to a stand. Money and its reflex, its deputy,
Credit, are essential and indispensable agents in the
creation of wealth.

VI. Not understanding this, economical authorities fell into hopeless confusion over ‘ Capital and
Currency,’ which at this point it is as well to
pause over. By Capital all the world means and
understands money. This is just what orthodox,
Political Economy refused to allow. Capital according to it was Wealth reproductively employed :
but as money was not wealth, so neither could it
be Capital. That Currency was not Capital : that
Money was a Commodity : that Commodities were
Wealth ; and yet that Money was not Wealth :
what a confusion ! what miserable contradictory
thinking. Here appears a fundamental contradiction between the theories of economists and the
practice of the world. As usual, it is the theories
which are to blame. Nay, they cannot even preserve themselves from falling into the practical way
of looking at the matter : for when they are not
thinking about it, even those economists who most
sternly refuse to allow Money to be Capital, nevertheless use the term Capital to mean Money. Use
and the logic of facts are too strong for their
theories : which all arise from a radical confusion
and failure to trace with sufficiently strict accuracy
the essential notion of Capital.

Capital in its original meaning and *raison d'être* is every instrument of production, as distinguished from instruments of action. In early stages of society, when as yet exchange is only embryonic, and Money has not arisen, such instruments are of course procured directly by their employers : axes, food, clothes, and what not. In later stages, when society has been definitely based upon buying and selling, and Money has taken its place as the universal mediator, it becomes impossible to get any instrument of production, except through Money. Hence Money, in itself not a direct instrument of production at all, becomes indirectly the instrument *par excellence.* It monopolises the signification of the term Capital. By its means all other agents are procured. Thus it alone is looked upon as Capital, as the *sine quâ non :* and the Capitalist is the man who has Money. Further, Interest, the correlative term of Capital, is paid upon Money, and upon Money alone. Payments upon other instruments are not called Interest but Rent. To this we shall return.

That Capital properly means Money is proved not only by the fact of universal use, but also by the fact that the term only makes its appearance concomitantly with the power of Money. Capital is misapplied, when it is applied, as by the Economists, to early stages of Society. The term which subsequently turns into Capital is Stock. Stock, a word Adam Smith is fond of, is what the Economists mean by Fixed Capital : *i.e.* Capital which is not purely general and universally applicable Circulating Capital or Money : but Capital fixed in one form. Capital, used absolutely, with-

out any qualifying epithet, now means Money.
There‾is of course a border-land where the meanings of 'Stock' and 'Money' shade off into one
another. But the popular meaning of Capital is
Money, and there never would have been such
terrible confusion in Economics, had economists
attended carefully to terminology, and not used
words of ordinary acceptation in peculiar arbitrary
meanings. There is always a reason why, in
popular language; always a true *apperçu* in ordinary terminology. The true meaning of Capital
is Money, regarded as the indispensable instrument,
without which no produce can be produced. And
when a man has converted his Money into any
particular form of Wealth, any particular instruments of production, he is said to have *sunk* his
Capital in them. He has risked it, by changing
its form, from the pure generalised expression of
value and demand, from the pure general instrument of production, into an actual definite form :
and so it must stay. Now he must make Money
with it, not by lending it, but using it. Now he
will not get Interest, but Profit. For the Capitalist
makes his Interest by parting with his Capital :
but the Entrepreneur makes his Profit by keeping
and using his—*Fixed* Capital, not Capital absolutely.
    Now, all this will help us to clear up another
difficulty in Economics, due to a want of comprehension of the term Capital. Capital, we have
always been told, is the result of saving. How,
then, in the first place, if this is so, do not Economists see that Capital must mean money? For
how is it possible to save Wealth, Commodities,
to any appreciable degree ? how can anything

be saved except Money? who can save perishable
and bulky, troublesome commodities? And where
is the motive to save Commodities all of one kind?
Any one can see at a glance that the motive for
saving and accumulation begins with Money : with
the possibility of accumulating a thing which is
not corruptible, not anything definite, which does
not *lose value by time*, but will in the future retain
all its power, being merely a concentrated essence
of desire. To save Money, and Money alone, is
to lay up power, the power of doing and getting
what you please. Thus we find the accumulation
of Wealth, and Money, making their appearance
together, for the two are in reality inseparably
connected. The economists, then, who tell us that
Capital is the result of saving, ought consistently
to have maintained that Money is Capital, for it
is a corollary of their proposition. But they did
exactly the opposite.

There is, however, more behind. The thesis,
that Capital is the result of saving, is only a very
small part of the whole truth. It is true enough
that saving will accumulate, and that ' savings ' are
in a way already Capital. But this is a trifling
matter : that Capital which was only the result of
saving would be a small and insignificant affair.
In fact, the doctrine only shows how totally those
who maintained it failed to understand their giant
subject. I do not refer here to what has been
pointed out as an ironical criticism of the doctrine :
viz. that great fortunes have been made by means
very different from that of saving : that the spoliation of the Abbey Lands, at the Reformation, the
swindling sale of Church Lands, in the Revolution,

bribery and corruption, gambling on 'Change and
so forth, have been the methods by which Capital
has been accumulated. These things are true
enough : but they are abuses and, scientifically
speaking, accidents ; and we must not press accidents into the service of economical science. But
I refer here to the essential mechanism of economical
production itself: which is so radically misunderstood by these economists. It is not a merely
negative saving, that will account for the facts : it
is a positive cause which generates Capital. The
secret lies in the play of Banking.

Through the agency of Banking, a certain sum
of money, say £1,000, is made to perform the
function of £10,000. Now, suppose that ten men
borrow £1,000 from the Bank, engage in trade,
succeed, repay the Bank. Here are ten men using
the *same* £1,000, by means of Credit, to produce
wealth. Ten men are enabled to purchase their
instruments and employ the required service, by
the agency of Banks, where only one could have
done so before. It is, therefore, not saving but
Banking, which provides the means, generates
Capital, and promotes the production of Commodities. It is Banking which enables men to
get the means of producing, and thus creates the
demand for commodities and services of all kinds.
It sets the Idea to work upon Material. Wealth
can only make its appearance when it is called for,
or demanded. Without money, men cannot ask for
it. This is what Law meant, when he said that all
Scotland wanted to get on was more money. He
was perfectly right, and his prediction was verified,
as all the world knows, by the Banks started in

Scotland, and the system of Cash Credits. Yet just because they could not understand the mechanism of production and the function of Banking, economists and historians have always loaded Law with their ignorant abuse. Even Mr. Macleod, who knows all about Cash Credits, and enlarges on their merits, and the benefit they have conferred on Scotland, most strangely fails to understand how right Law was in this respect. His errors we have already dealt with. But what are we to say to the fact that Ricardo, the prime cause of all the ridiculous financial legislation of this century, when he was asked by the Lords' Committee in 1819: 'Do ' you not know that when there is a great demand ' for manufactures, the very Credit which that circum-' stance creates enables the manufacturer to make ' a more extended use of his Capital in the pro-' duction of manufactures?' actually replied: '*I* ' *have no notion* of Credit being at all effectual in ' the production of commodities : commodities can ' only be produced by labour, machinery, and raw ' materials, and if these are to be employed in one ' place, they must necessarily be withdrawn from ' another.' And can there, then, be no more made ? Then being still further asked whether Credit might not be efficacious in creating an additional quantity of machinery or raw materials, Ricardo answered: '*Impossible:* an individual can purchase machinery, ' &c., with Credit : he never can create them[m].' Observe the blank, hopeless, incurable idiocy of the man : his absolute incapacity of seeing the obvious points : yet this inconceivable blockhead

[m] McCulloch's Edition of Adam Smith, p. 530.

has been held to be a great authority on questions,
of which he could not so much as master the
simplest preliminaries. Labour, machinery, and
raw materials, forsooth! why, what sets these to
work? what, but the demand for commodities.
And how can the demand act, without Money or
Credit? To such preposterous incapables can men
attribute great economical genius.

The Wage Fund theory, now abandoned, yet
both held and abandoned for equally fallacious
reasons, is merely another case of the failure of
orthodox Economists to understand Capital. When
men can get money to employ labour, they will do
so, provided they see their way to profitable enterprise: and being thus provided with employment
and money the labourer will purchase commodities
for himself. The whole thing rests on the possibility, through the agency of Banking and Credit,
of anticipating the future. The failure to comprehend the operation of money, and the way it
acts under a system of Banking, is the cause of the
ridiculous Wage Fund Theory: a theory which
rests, too, on a statical conception of Society and
Wealth-creation, and a complete misappreciation
of the continuity of processes in the dynamical
alembic of a complicated industrial system. Wealth
is not made by fits and starts and jerks: its creation is not discrete, but continuous: and this continuity rests upon the foresight of what is coming.
If merchants foresee a large demand, they will
produce to meet it: and the possibility of this, the
point of connection between past and future, the
nodus of the whole question, is Credit and Banking.
If it were not for these, the Wage Fund Theory

would be true. It is just precisely the possibility of anticipating, through the agency of Banks, which gets over the limitation of Capital paying wages to a past accumulated Fund, and enables it to increase and expand up to any limit guaranteed by future prospects and the calculation of coming Demand. The money which production works with is not the accumulation of the past, but the creation of Banks, resting on the confident expectation of the future. Hence, through Banking, the Wage Fund is really conditioned by the Demand for Commodities ;—the exact antithesis of the old dogma, that a demand for commodities is not a demand for labour. That dogma conclusively proves that its disciples did not understand Credit and Banking. It was either a transparent and most miserable truism, or a radical and vicious error[a].

Similarly, it is nothing but the fundamentally erroneous conception of Money, Credit, Capital, and Currency prevailing in Economic Dogma which lies at the heart of the financial difficulty now puzzling the world, and the 'still vexed Bermoothes,' Bimetallism. Acting on the theory that commodities are purchased with commodities ;

---

[a] A concise epitome of the true origin and sources of Capital will enable the reader to understand clearly what is said in the text. The economic dogma, that *all Capital is the result of saving*, is only a mere fragment of the truth. Not *all*, but only *some*, Capital is the result of saving. All Capital is the result of either 1. Saving; or 2. Banking, as shown in the text; or 3. Profitable enterprise; that is to say, that where demand for any commodity is very great, the producer may realise thousands over and above his expenses: and this becomes Capital, but is the result, not of *saving*, but of *making*.

that money is a commodity; that it makes no difference how much or little of it there is : acting, that is to say, on a total and criminal ignorance of the true functions of Money and Credit in Wealth-creation, the financial legislation of 1819, 1844, 1872, and onwards, has all tended to minimise and restrict the supply of money, and thus strangle and stifle the creation of wealth°. It will not be long before the world awakes from this fatal delusion and rectifies its conception of the authors of those tragic farces, the single gold standard, and the Bank Charter Act : which have proved fatal to thousands of excellent families and sound commercial houses in this nineteenth century, which has in so many directions plumed itself upon superior lights when it was only presumptuously silly.

Socialism again is based, *quâ* economical, on just this radical economic error. It entirely fails to understand the mechanism of Wealth-creation. It takes from Political Economy its capital : its stock-in-trade : the argument, Labour makes Wealth. Therefore, argues the Socialist, labour should take what it makes. Unfortunately, the thesis is fallacious. Labour does not make Wealth. On this point I may refer the reader to my book on *The Principle of Wealth Creation.* Yet orthodox Political Economy has nothing to answer to Socialism : for it is based upon her own premises. But we, who have thoroughly analysed the process of Wealth-creation, can not only answer, but weigh

---

° I have fully exposed the fallacy of the single gold standard in a little book entitled *The Corner in Gold* (*Parker*), to which accordingly I refer the reader.

Socialism in the balance and find it wanting.
Wealth is made not by labour, but by material,
science, labour, and demand. This demand depends upon Money, Credit, and Banking, and so
again, material, labour, and science essentially depend upon demand, both potential and actual, and
upon each other. The evolution of all these factors
essentially produces, and involves, society just as
we see it : a society highly differentiated in all
its parts. The structure is made by its functions.
The Wealth created essentially follows and shadows
the nature of its Creator : and *operari sequitur esse.*
The great and varied production of Wealth is
determined by and involves a great diversity and
inequality of human characters. A vast system
of Wealth-creation is impossible in a state whose
members are all alike : and the more alike they
are, the less can Wealth be in amount. Accordingly, in vainly attempting to keep the Wealth,
and yet get rid of that which is its *raison d'être,*
in attempting to unify Society more than is possible
or expedient, the Socialists are really betraying
their own hopeless incompetence to deal with the
problem. They are like men who should attempt
to get rid of the sun and still think to preserve
its heat and light : like men who should endeavour to abolish the realities, never conceiving
that their reflections in the water would vanish
at the same moment. For the production of the
World dogs its action more unerringly than ever
sleuth-hound did : men make what they make
because they are what they are and do what they
do. The work of the world is determined by its
play : its industry by its leisure : and the old

mysterious Etruscans knew more than the Socialists, when they allegorised the greatest truth in human knowledge, that Function makes Structure, by representing a butterfly drawn in a car by two industrious ants. Man makes his instruments to serve his ends. Wealth is a vast accumulation of instruments, for production and action : how can you have the instruments and the production without the action? the Structure without the Function? the umbrella or the parasol without the rain or the sun? It is function which is the creative soul of the world.

VII. And now, having gained an insight into the essential mechanism of the Principle of Creation, the law that function makes structure, as exhibited in the sphere of common or general needs, Economics : before turning to the consideration of the same Principle in the sphere of special needs, or Æsthetics, a few words are necessary upon the distribution of Wealth. As I have treated this with sufficient detail in the companion volume to this book, and as further, distribution is not the question with which we are here essentially concerned, I shall only pause here to examine one point in that problem, that of Interest; partly because it is essentially connected with Capital : partly because it illustrates admirably the thesis of this book : partly because I omitted to notice in *The Principle of Wealth Creation* the particular point to which I wish to draw attention here. On Distribution in general I shall only say here, that being essentially conditioned by and wrapped up in Creation, it is quite impossible to treat it adequately, until the creation of Wealth and its mechanism are fully understood. Wealth is distributed in and by the process of Creation. Every one who shares in production naturally tries to get as large a share as he can, and in general it is the amount of the need felt for his contribution to the product which determines his share : as Aristotle puts it, the division of Wealth will be based on the relative proportions contributed by the common producers to the result : the violation of this proportion being injustice. And yet more ; any attempt to violate this proportion, this analogical distributive justice, will only prove detrimental to production altogether. An arbitrary system which attempts to make the rewards 'equitable,' not according to the necessities inherent in things, but according to a harmonic theoretical ideal : e.g. which attempts to disregard special qualifications and endowments and reduce all contributors to the level of their 'common humanity,' is bound to destroy its own end, by stopping creation. You cannot buy genius for the price of common minds. If the honours and rewards are the same for all, there will be no energy. Napoleon will not serve for the pay of a common soldier : a Christopher Wren will not be attracted to architecture by the prospect of ranking with a mason or bricklayer : and so on. Equality kills genius and originality, initiative and enterprise : and the justice which is the bond of society is not a Procrustean Platonic absolute dead-level arithmetical equality, but a free and spontaneous organic Aristotelian proportional equality. What annihilates States, as Aristotle admirably says, is just the sophistical misuse of this term equality. Persons equal in some respects

demand equality in all : and persons unequal in
some respects demand inequality in all.   Both claim
more than their due.

Those who share in production and get a share
in the product, to enumerate them, are the Landlord
with his Rent, the Capitalist with his Interest, the
Labourer with his Wages, the Entrepreneur with
his Profits, the Tradesman, Merchant or Transport Agent, with his Price, the Inventor or Patentee
with his Royalty, the State with its Taxes, and
other indefinable variations on these great typical
contributors.   All these various shares are cases
of value : and the man who has correctly analysed
value has no difficulty in determining whatever
scientific element there may be in these various
shares.   In all cases alike it holds that the Value,
whether it be Rent or Interest, Wages or Profits,
Price or Reward, is a resultant of the relation
between the Qualities of the Thing valued and the
Needs of the Valuer, *in comparison with his need
for what he has to give for it ;* that is, his command
over *money.*   I shall here confine myself to an
analysis of what we may call the *Antinomy of
Interest.*

VIII. Interest is of course the sum of money,—
a percentage—given for the use of money : hence
its name *usura,* usury, interest.   As all the world
knows, it is only in comparatively recent times that
public opinion and law have ceased to condemn the
practice of usury : and in fact, although the law has
removed its prohibition, public opinion still retains
its old impression.   A certain doubtful aroma still
hangs over the conception of Interest, still more of
Usury   there is, as it were, a cloud over its exist-

ence. All this only finds its explanation historically. From the earliest times usury has been
condemned, and the animus against it played a
large part both in Greek and Roman History.
The earliest and greatest of all economists, Aristotle,
disliked and condemned it on philosophical grounds.
The production and provision of Wealth to minister
directly to needs, he called natural : but the production of commodities for the sake of gaining
money by their exchange he considered to be a
distortion of the true end ; something unnatural.
Accordingly he condemned the making of money
by trade. ' To provide oneself with wealth, from
' fruits and herds, is natural to all men. But this
' act being, as I said, divisible into two provinces,
' trading for money and economy proper, and the
' latter being necessary and laudable, the former,
' commercial exchange, being rightly condemned,—
' since it is not natural, but based upon mutual
' over-reaching—petty usury is most justly abhorred,
' because the gain arises from the money itself, and
' this is not the function money ought to perform :
' for the cause of its origin was the need for facilitat-
' ing exchange : whereas lending at interest makes
' it more : whence it gets its name : for interest is
' the offspring of money ' (there is here an un-
translateable play upon the word), 'so that this
' sort of wealth-creation is of all the most contrary to
' nature.' And a little before this passage he explains the ground of his dislike still more clearly :
viz. that commerce seizes all the arts, and turns
them into tools for making money : thus degrading
them and subordinating their true function to
money getting : substituting their ' venality ' for

intrinsic worth, as the basis of their estimation and their *raison d'être*.

There was a true insight lying at the bottom of Aristotle's criticism here, as I shall show in the next Book: and those who puff aside Aristotle with an air of cheap wisdom only show that genius sees further than its critics: indeed the prophetic genius of Aristotle was all the more remarkable in that the truth in his criticism foresaw and anticipated a solution which was less obvious then than it is now. But to continue. The Fathers of the Church carried on this view, not merely following Aristotle, but also the moral code of Christianity: indeed, both Old and New Testaments agree in condemning—on different grounds however—the practice of usury and money lending. 'The prohibition of ' usury is indeed, as Roscher says, the centre of ' the whole canonistic system of economy[p].' The Angelic Doctor, S. Thomas Aquinas, 'the Aristotle ' of the Middle Ages,' as Michelet calls him, argued elaborately against it, and his authority was followed, not merely for its own sake, but because it was in harmony with public opinion. Calvin was the first theologian to take the opposite side: a significant fact, indeed. To oppose Catholicism and Aristotle in all matters was a general maxim of Reformers: moreover Protestantism, in one aspect, is essentially a time-serving religion: it had to make its formulæ suit the material ends of those who took it up. Further, the economical development of society was undermining the ideas on which the whole condemnation rested. Gradually

[p] Ingram, *Hist. of Pol. Econ.*, p. 28.

necessity carried the day : though the legal condemnation of interest died hard ; and indeed, in
a sense, is not dead yet.

When a particular and possibly paradoxical view
maintains itself with indomitable tenacity through
long ages, and carries the votes of genius of the
first order, no less than that of common men, there
must be a reason for it. Here, as always, the shallow,
impertinent rationalism of orthodox Political Economy only displays its own original and native
incapacity, in its absolute condemnation and de-
nunciation of Interest in earlier ages, and the airs
of superior lights which it puts on when discussing
the 'errors' of its poor benighted fathers. Here, as
always, structure finds its explanation in function.
And in order to make the point clear I shall take
the liberty of borrowing an illustration from the
admirable book of Dr. Cunningham on the *Growth
of English Industry and Commerce,* a work which
stands in marked contrast with the theoretical rub-
bish-heap of Political Economy, being based throughout on the solid and fruitful ground of interpreting
ideas by their conditions.

In January 1377, Ralph Cornwaille, of Broad
Street, complained to the Mayor and Aldermen of
the City of London. He had borrowed £10 from
Walter Southous, giving security for the repayment
of the debt, and giving still further security by getting his friend John Tettesbury to stand behind
him. At the time of repayment, he tendered the
£10, but the unconscionable Walter Southous
refused to receive it, 'persisted in his demand for
' £2 more, and sued Ralph before the Sheriff to his
'great wrong and damage.' Accordingly, Ralph

complained. 'The wrong that rankled in his mind
'.was not that the interest was extortionate, but that
' he was called upon to pay interest at all, to return
' anything more than he had received ; and his view
'.of the case was fully endorsed by the City author-
'ities before whom the matter was reopened.'
Ralph Cornwaille was declared free from all obligations in connexion with the debt, and Walter
Southous was condemned to ' be imprisoned till he
'.had made over double the £2 which he had tried
' to get by usury as a forfeit to the City of London.'
This will enable us to understand the force of the
odium against the Jews, who existed by usury ; as
indeed they were prevented from existing by any
other means.

What a different view is here from that of modern
men ! Dr. Cunningham says on the point : ' Walter
' Southous demanded full security that the money
' should be repaid at a definite date, and there his
' conduct met with full approval from city men at the
' time. He was perfectly justified in seeing that the
' money was fully secured. But when he went
' further than this, and charged for the use of the
' money, public opinion did not support him.
' Why should he, his money being safe, be repaid
' for an action that involved no risk and no priva-
' tion ? ' [These fourteenth-century men had never
heard of the great economical truth, Capital is
Abstinence, and Interest its Reward.] ' Of course,
' if there was risk, or if the borrower "broke day "
' and caused inconvenience, there was a reason for
' making a charge ; but where, as here, there was
' no risk and no real privation, there was as men
' thought no justification for taking usury, or interest

' as it is more commonly called in the present day.
' " *No risk, no gain,*" was their maxim of lawful
' traffic.'

So far Dr. Cunningham[q] ; and let us now see
whether we cannot carry the analysis still further,
and lay bare the essential antagonism in the two
views still more completely.

On the one side it is obvious that the system of
money-lending leads to a general state of things, in
which the lender or usurer reaps profit without any
risk, trouble, or exertion of any kind of his own.
This is the moral point of view from which those
who condemned and who condemn Interest look at
it.   And who can blame them ? Does it not seem
hard that some men should sit still, and yet share
in the gains accruing from the risks undergone, the
labour, energy, prudence and invention exhibited
and expended, by others ? It goes without saying
that we have here a fact contradicting the moral
sense and conscience of every man who has got
one.

And yet on the other hand it is most unquestionably true that the endeavour to remedy this state
of things from the moral point of view alone would
be most disastrous to the welfare of the world : and
this is just what gives the question its absorbing
interest and political importance. For however
hard the thing may seem, nevertheless, if those
who actually do the work and take the risk could
get no money, they could produce nothing ; they
could take no risk and do no work, and could
neither make Wealth nor any gain for themselves.

q Cunningham, *l.c.*, vol. i., p. 325, sqq.

It is therefore obvious that it is a good thing for them to pay interest. The tax paid to the holder of money is the essential condition of their production. Now suppose that it were forbidden by law to lend money at interest. It is perfectly clear that not one man in a thousand will lend money for nothing. Accordingly, if the law is kept, Wealth-creation will stop : if it is broken, that is itself a great evil ; and further defeats the end aimed at : nay more, it will tend to make Interest higher than it would otherwise have been : for men who break the law run a great risk, and must insure heavily against the chance of detection.

Let the reader reflect upon this, for, by heaven and earth, it is worth his while. Let him meditate over this economical ANTINOMY—which is not, like the Kantian antinomies, a palpable fallacy, but a fact—till he sees how both sides of the question have truth on their side. It will teach him what value to place upon the superficial condemnations uttered by theoretic writers upon points of view opposed to their own. It will enable him to bring home to himself the futility of demagogues, whose whole stock in trade consists of moral platitudes. It will teach him to appreciate statesmen whom perhaps he formerly misinterpreted and depreciated, statesmen whose insight into social evils is not more apparent than their apparently inexplicable refusal to adopt moral or political remedies. For statesmanship, like other things, is determined by its function, and no statesman can be correctly judged by any one who has not mastered the preliminary condition, which determines all a statesman's views : who has not fully grasped the portentous fact, that evil is the negative condition of good ; and who has not seen and savoured the wisdom of the old dark saying that the tares must grow up with the wheat. He who has not merely noted but *felt* this, and he .alone, is on the road to political wisdom : wisdom, justified of her children, and accordingly reviled by the time-serving incapables and moral pedants who have borrowed the feathers, aped the functions, and degraded the epithet of statesmen in this age of sophisms and sentimentalisms and shams. For all things are defined by their work, and their capacity of doing that work. We must not allow ourselves to be deluded by words. Time was when a statesman meant one who understood the state and its necessities : but we have changed all that. The modern Statesman does not require either diplomatic finesse, or social insight, or financial sagacity, or patriotic sympathy : these things are by no means the essential. If then we enquire what is the true function and capacity of the statesman now-a-days, we find that a statesman is one *who has the capacity of catching the votes of the vulgar:* and for this nothing is required but the combination of vulgar prejudices with glib loquacity. Anything further than this is likely to interfere with the true end of statesmanship. And the reader should observe, that this is not an epigram : it is merely an analytical definition, which he can verify for himself by turning to the newspaper.

BOOK III.

ÆSTHETICS, OR THE WORK OF ART. THE PRINCIPLE WORKING IN THE PECULIAR OR PERSONAL SPHERE.

ἡ γὰρ χεὶρ ὄργανόν ἐστιν ὀργάνων· καὶ ὁ νοῦς δὲ, εἶδος εἰδῶν· καὶ ἡ αἴσθησις, εἶδος αἰσθητῶν.

De Anima, iii. 8.

BOOK III.

ÆSTHETICS, OR THE WORK OF ART. THE PRINCIPLE WORKING IN THE PECULIAR OR PERSONAL SPHERE.

I. HITHERTO we have considered the working of the Principle of Creation in Society only in the sphere of common or general needs : we have now to examine it, and discover the peculiar nature of its operation in another sphere. We have investigated the Commodity : we turn now to the Work of Art. It is true that works of art may be and often are commodities. Yet none the less is there, as we shall see, a most essential distinction between them. A work of art is or should be only accidentally a commodity, and wherever circumstances compel Nature, and forcibly turn this accidental relation into an essential one, the degradation of art is the inevitable result. Works of art have laws of their own, and refuse to obey the laws of ordinary commodities, except at the price of degeneracy. But for all that, works of art are Wealth as much as, and many will say far more than, any commodity. And indeed, it is not only astonishing in itself, but a proof of the very fragmentary and incomplete way in which the subject of Wealth-creation has been conceived and handled, that the subject of art has been so

totally omitted. Not without reason have Adam
Smith and his followers been accused of Philistinism : one might know their works by heart,
yet never dream that works of art formed any
part of the wealth of man. But that man shall
not live by bread alone, contains more truth than
is dreamt of in the philosophy of orthodox Political
Economy. And this weak point in their enquiries
appears in a still more glaring light in Socialistic
theory and propaganda. When Bazaroff, in ' Fathers and Sons,' lays it down that a good chemist
is twenty times more useful than any poet, and
declares that Raphael is not, in his opinion, worth
two kopeks : when the old Liberal Idealist in
' Demons ' finds himself hooted as behind the
times by an audience of 'advanced opinions' for
asserting that Pushkin is worth more than a pair
of boots :—these are but truthful pictures of the
Socialist tendency, already latent in orthodox economy, to disparage all but mere manual labour
and creature comforts : a *reductio ad absurdum* and
an exposure of the radical deficiencies of a Political
Economy which has omitted from consideration
a whole side of wealth : the only side which en-
titles humanity to hold up its head and plume
itself on its attainments. Strike out the productions of genius from the sum total of Wealth,
and what have you left worthy of attentive consideration ? Are the statues and the temples of
the Greeks, the castles and the cathedrals of the
Goths, the painting of the Italians, the music of
the Germans, the literature and philosophies of
all countries and ages, of no value ; no part of
wealth ? Yet where is the orthodox economist who

has given to them a moment's consideration? And if a 'science' of wealth leaves them out, leaves out, that is to say, all its best part, what are we to think of its critical acumen, or its conception of its field? Why, it is just the apathetic and material deadness to this side of the subject which has impressed upon economical literature that essentially low and soulless shop-keeperish view of life, which cannot fail to strike and revolt any one capable of appreciating the genuine worth of things, who looks however superficially into the subject. It is this lack of any reckoning with the moral and æsthetic side of humanity in Political Economy which lies at the bottom of the diatribes of Carlyle, Ruskin, Kingsley, and similar thinkers, against the dismal science : and though there was in what they said much of impatient and irritating want of logic, there was also much of truth, and that of the deepest ; a treasure entirely overlooked by people like Ricardo, J. S. Mill and their commentators. So did the cock in the fable sapiently reject the pearl of great price which he came upon while scratching his dunghill for his commodities.

With works of art, no less than commodities, the same principle holds that structure is determined by its creative function. But the difference between them lies in this, that their functions are different in kind. Both are called into existence by demand. But the demand which summons the commodity into life and being is merely the general or average demand of the ordinary man, the demand of the Many : the demand which creates the work of art is on the contrary that of the special man, the demand of the One.

Every commodity is essentially a time-server.
The condition of its existence is that it shall, like
Pilate, please the multitude.   Thus its production
must of necessity be determined by and follow
closely the pleasure of the million.   Here, numbers
carry the day.   That commodity best survives in
the struggle for existence which appeals to the
larger number.   It obliterates its competitors.
The great evolutionary principle of the extinction
of minorities comes into play.   (*Origin of Species*,
p. 126.)   Rare species, says the Oracle, will
be beaten by the commoner species.   Here then
appears the deep gulf between the commodity
and the work of art.   The commodity aims at
the fittest: the work of art at the best.   From
this peculiarity flow all the disadvantages which
reason, history, and experience prove to hold in the
case of the artist.

The Commodity is unscrupulous, ready, versatile:
does not set itself up, is not proud; has not a stiff
neck.   It fawns and cringes to its circumstances.
It aims at serving everybody, and being all things
to all men.   It is hail fellow, well met, with the
world.   It makes no pretence of being better than
its neighbours.   It is ready and willing to be a tool
in anybody's hands.   It adopts all colours, all
shades of religious or political opinion, with callous
egoistic indifference.   Aristippus-wise, it yields to
all contingencies.   It subordinates all things to the
preservation of its own existence.   It has no principles.   To all who enquire of it respecting these,
it replies in the words of Artemus Ward : *'I hain't
got enny, not a prinscrpul.   I'me in the show
bizness.'*   Hence, as it is so universally democratic,

obliging, obsequious and convenient, everybody likes it. It never attempts to blame or criticise the world, but pays it that greatest of all compliments, imitation : it dresses itself *à la mode*, adopts any fashion which the world enjoins. It shadows and reflects as in a mirror, and even hastens to anticipate, every desire that men can express. The world feels for it that agreeable sympathy existing between partners in crime. In the presence of the Commodity, it feels quite at its ease.

But the Work of Art,—how different from this ! Proud, cold, exclusive, critical, fastidious, impatient, imperious, autocratic : essentially aristocratic : turning away with ineffable disdain from the many, expressing even by its silence its inexhaustible contempt for the vulgar : currying no favour : seeking to please no one, to serve no one, but its own ideal : self-centred : capable of breaking but not bending : absolutely useless for all common purposes : nay, worse than useless, according to the old Italian proverb : *tanto buon che val niente :* in whose presence the world feels ashamed as of one who is a silent and eternal condemnation of itself : refusing to bow the knee to ordinary laws, customs, prejudices, manners : refusing to admit the division of labour, and to be produced, like the Commodity, by the combination of many workmen : going its own way and perishing in its obstinacy rather than abate one jot of its pretensions : like the old Roman senator, sitting silent in his irony, and regardless of consequences, preferring death to dishonour, smiting the irreverent Gaul who took him by the beard : constant as Julius Cæsar, or the Polar Star, to its own law : awakening in all lower natures the

s

superlatively exasperating sense of inferiority, and
the still more exasperating sense of an unfathomable,
indefinable, impassable gulf dividing them: patient
and suffering, calm, nay, ironical, flippant, sarcastic,
crushing down with superhuman energy the fiery
tumult of passionate rage and despair into the
bottom of its heart: master of itself: fearing one
thing only, lest it should contaminate the purity
of its ideal by being betrayed into any expression
of weakness before its eternal lynx-eyed enemy, the
malignity of the common herd:—how can the Work
of Art complain, if its punishment is as terrible
as its consciousness of immeasurable superiority
is sublime. It will not fall down and worship
Satan; nay, it is superior to virtue, reckless of
happiness: and therefore bitter is the pang.
Uneasy lies the head that wears a crown. Golgotha
and Gethsemane, and the terrible loneliness—and
what is the reward? Will the poor and tardy
applause of the undiscerning vulgar, whose praise
is perhaps still more unutterably loathsome than
its blame, make up to the genius for his horrible
torture, when he finds himself alive in a world
of dead? Could the everlasting fame which now
glorifies the name of Shakspeare, even if he could
hear it, rolled round as he is with rocks and trees
and stones, make up to him for the insufferable
patronage of this or that noble lord in his own day!
Could the roar of the excited crowd that welcomed
Lord Beaconsfield home from Berlin console him
for the years of agony during which, to use his own
terrible simile: 'IT SEEMED TO ME THAT I WAS
'POURING WATER UPON SAND, BUT IT SEEMS NOW THAT
'THE WATER CAME FROM A GOLDEN GOBLET?' Could

the noise of the populace who read his novels fill
the hole in the heart of Sir Walter Scott, which his
inexhaustible strength led him so entirely to keep
out of his writings that fools cannot even appreciate
it? What could fame do for the immense sadness
of Michael Angelo? Why was Napoleon old at six
and twenty? In vain did he offer hecatombs to
appease his demon : he was driven on : yet could
Marengo or Austerlitz wipe away the effects of those
years of horrible desperation, restore the liver that
the vulture had devoured? Such a curse lies upon
those who have drunk at their birth from the pool
of imagination, and are seized with inexhaustible
thirst ; who carry to their graves the inexhaustible
craving for things other than the common. What
business have these madmen here? Is not this
world enough for them? then, in God's name let
them e'en get away to a better. We'll have no
cavillers here. Aye : and is it even so? Seest thou
yonder knot of conspirators, pressing round Cæsar
in the Curia? or that dark band of inquisitors,
glowering at Galileo in the dungeon of the Holy
Office? there you may see the everlasting contest
between bigotry and genius : the commodity and
the work of art. For the work, as Aristotle said
long ago, is the embodied spirit of the worker : the
worker puts himself into his work. And again he
says : the free man is the man who is his own
master, and not dependent upon another : but the
nature of man is in general slavish. If then there
is anything in what the poets say as to the divinity
being jealous, it would come in here : and this would
be the meaning of the fact that men of genius are
shortlived : *the gods will permit no mortal to be free.*

There lies the deep significance of the unpopularity of the work of art. It refuses to be bound by the universal law of Natural Economy, that 'one 'thing is for the sake of another.' The cause of all things, as Darwin and Aristotle tell us, is the necessity for their existence, the work they have to perform. Now all the senses and organs of the human being, nay the intellect itself, came into existence originally to serve the needs of the body to which they belong : to do that work it must do to keep itself alive. This is their original *raison d'être* and the law of their being. The cause of existence of reason itself is utilitarian. For the *raison d'être* of community is safety, as Aristotle says : and the *raison d'être* of speech or language, which is to reason merely what the outside is to the inside, convex to concave, is just the necessity of *communication* between members of the community as to their common damage and advantage. The essence of speech is communication. Hence it follows necessarily that first, no animal not social can have speech : for there is no need of it : second, that the essence and gist of speech is the proposition : speech begins with the sentence : thirdly, that any animals possessing it must eventually gain supremacy over all others, provided they be of a sufficient size. For upon reason depend all the achievements of man. Now the point for us is this : that the artistic use of all the senses and organs of man turns its back upon their true and original use, and is, as it were, ashamed of its origin, despises its parents. It will not lend itself to utilitarian ends. And consequently Nature takes her revenge. For man's existence would instantly cease, were the artistic use of his organs to pre-dominate over the utilitarian. This is the deep mystical reason for the cloud that always hangs over the artist, and the artist's life. It is similar in kind to the reason for the fact that, socially speaking, the woman who falls is a Pariah, while the man is not. Shallow people who inveigh against the injustice of this do not see that the reason for it is deeper than reason: it rests on the mystical feeling of the members of the community that its life depends upon the purity of its women.

Upon this radical distinction between the Work of Art and the Commodity rests the fact that as civilisation develops, art in general tends to decay. For it is only the commodity that admits of the division of labour: the work of art, in essentials, must come from one man. Here, brain, desire, eye, and hand must all work together: only on this condition will the result be a unity, stamped with the *cachet* of genius. To dissociate these, is to turn the work of art into a commodity. But now, it is impossible that the business of the world, and hence its evolution, should rest upon special demands. It must of necessity be based upon common or general demands. In early stages of society, when as yet production has not been differentiated, this distinction does not appear, except in embryo. All early production is, so far, more artistic than its later development, in that being a small affair the product is the work of one and not many producers. All early commodities, though owing to deficient science they may be less directly adapted to a utili-tarian end, less strictly accommodated, are yet just for that reason more artistic. They bear a freer and more *personal* character. This is why old glass, old china, candlesticks, weapons, clothes, ships, implements of all kinds, always preserve an æsthetic value, apart from their special use, long after they have been superseded and gone out of fashion : in similar modern instruments, on the other hand, there is hardly any æsthetic element: they are too business-like : too strictly utilitarian : too much branded with the stamp of the commodity, to retain anything artistic. And thus it is that as time goes on, the production of commodities growing larger and larger, and hence necessarily requiring further and further division of labour, there arises a wide gulf between the work of art and the commodity. The latter carries the day, for numbers are on its side : *suffragiorum jus habet.* Now it is that any one who with his eyes open chooses to devote his life to artistic production does so under the risk of starvation. No one is to blame for this : it is a consequence of the nature of things. The artist being essentially one who aims at pleasing *himself,* realising *his own* idea, cannot expect to work with the security of the man who makes it his whole and sole object to cater for *others.* Lucky for him, indeed, if his genius conquer its fate : if he obtains recognition before he is dead.

And here appears the temptation, the choice of Hercules, for the artist. Will he stick to his ideal, choose her and work for her, and her alone, regardless of consequences, in spite of poverty and misunderstanding, struggle and possibly death ? Or will he succumb, and turn aside, Atalanta-wise, to snatch at the golden apple? This is the eternal pitfall, spread by Nature (who does not love artists) for them all. Gogol has given us a typical illustration of the point, in his little story of the obscure painter. On the one side loneliness, hunger, cold, perhaps universal condemnation, domestic and eternal squabbling, false accusation, genius, the purity of the darling idea, the hope of everlasting fame, and the consciousness of intrinsic worth :— on the other, security, well-being, ease, happiness, notoriety which passes with the vulgar for fame, the degradation of the idea to the level of common demand, and everlasting gnawing self-condemnation and remorse. ' All these things will I give thee, if ' thou wilt fall down and worship me.' A hard matter, in very truth : he had need to be strong who dares this quest. Not to all men have the gods granted the power to resist the Devil. And this it is which is celebrated by poets, and evinced in the mythology of all nations. This was what the Lord spake unto Joshua : Only be strong and of a good courage. This was what Disraeli, in whom the old Jewish spirit lived, and who found in the sacred writings of his race the consoling power that sustained him throughout his struggle with folly and prejudice, meant, when he took for his motto, *forti nihil difficile.* This was what Spinoza meant, when, thinking doubtless of his own stern choice between philosophy and ease, he wrote, *omnia præclara tam difficilia quam rara sunt.* This is the meaning of the old Eastern legends, copied and elaborated in Western stories of chivalry and Holy Grails, which show us knight after knight, princes and calendars, ' sons of kings,' going upon terrible quests, and failing for want of inner self-restraint. All fall, when they enter the palace of Temptation.

This is the esoteric meaning of the Faerie Queene, and the Pilgrim's Progress. This is that which was shouted by the demonic voices in the legend of Thomas the Rhymer :

> Wo to the coward that ever he was born,
> Who did not draw the sword before he blew the horn !

This is the core of the unutterably beautiful old Middle Age legend of Tannhaüser, who yielded to the earthly Venus and was lost : a parable the type of endless poetical fictions, from Orpheus and Eurydice and the Sirens to Carmen and Ladislas Bolski. For woman is the everlasting tempter, who drags man . down to her own level, and after making him the tool of her egoism, and robbing him of his best, throws him callously aside, like a squeezed orange, for some new caprice. And then in vain he bellows in his rage : it is too late ; he hears ringing in his ears the chorus of demoniacal laughter : 'the bite of the apple has made ' thee ours.' Why didst thou taste? *Illico post coitum auditur cachinnus diaboli.* And this is the moral that lives for ever in the Greek myths of Perseus and Ship Argo, so beautifully painted anew by Kingsley : ' Rashly and angrily I promised, but ' cunningly and patiently will I perform. . . . Then ' he thought of Medusa and the renown before him, ' and he leaped into the empty air. And behold, ' instead of falling, he floated, and stood, and ran ' along the sky.'

But woe to the faint-hearted : 'who die in the ' Unshapen Land, where no man ever finds their ' bones.' This is the case with those who turn their art into a commodity : and prostitute their mistress,

turning aside to worship Venus Venalis. Of this
we have only too good an example in modern literature, which has in very truth reached the Nadir.
The function of modern literature is to please the
sovereign people : and it is to be devoutly hoped
that it performs that function. How can anything
rise into notice, now-a-days, if it does not pay ? And
how can anything pay, but such as pleases the
greater number? The best and the fittest are here
in direct contradiction. The best cannot possibly
be the fittest, just because it is the best : that is to
say, one out of thousands : but it is just these
thousands, or rather millions, *quem penes arbitrium
est.* And who can blame the publishers ? they
must live, even though art has to become a trade,
a tool, to save them. *Kto venovat ?* Who is to
blame? ' Neither Bacon, nor Newton, nor Locke,
' nor Descartes, nor Gibbon, nor Hume, nor Adam
' Smith, nor Montesquieu, nor Berkeley, nor Butler,
' nor Coleridge, nor Bentham, nor Milton, nor Words-
' worth, could have made a living by their works,'
says the historian [a] ; and his list might be extended
indefinitely ; nay, even Aristotle, if he were expressly raised from the dead to instruct the world,
would speedily have to rejoin the majority, if he
had nothing but the sale of his works to trust to for
a living. It is puerile, and marks a want of comprehension of the world and life, to abuse this state
of things. It is impossible to establish any system
by which genius shall be made secure, and the work
of art identified with the commodity. Nevertheless,
in an age where the market is flooded with books of

[a] Lecky, *History of England,* i. 457.

every description, literature must of necessity decay:
for, just because it is in the minority, a work requiring alike for its production and its enjoyment intellect, culture, insight, discrimination, imagination,
breeding, lies buried beneath the mass.   Yet as the
world refuses to admit that there can be anything
wrong with the majority, and every one must therefore praise what pleases the majority, we find the
most ironical contradiction between phrases and
facts.   Books destitute of every qualification, books
betraying in every line ignorance, illiteracy, vulgarity, false sentiment, cheap wisdom, innate and
original mediocrity—masquerading in the garb of
genius, books destitute of every faintest vestige of
style, insight, taste or criticism, are every day be-
lauded in the papers, God knows by whom, in language that sends one hurrying to buy them, expect-
ing to discover a new Scott or a second Pascal.
Under the magniloquent language lurks the very
pitifullest reality that ever deserved indescribable
contempt.   And the reason for this is obvious.
Function makes Structure.   The original and true
function of criticism was and is to analyse and
appreciate works of art on their merits.   But the
function of modern journalism is not single but
triple.   It must above all first please, amuse, and
chime in with its public : it must, next, provide
a living for the talented writer : and last, stuffed
in at the end, and an entirely secondary, nay ter-
tiary consideration, comes the actual not appreciation, but *de*preciation of the work, written perhaps
by some tenth-rate nobody, absolutely ignorant of
what he is talking about, who, skulking behind the
grateful wall of the anonymous column, damns *ex*

cathedrâ anything he cannot comprehend. The Liberty of the Press! The Press is no longer a free agent : it is the tool of material religious and political interests : from a work of art it has become a commodity : this is the fundamental condition of its being, its *raison d'être*. It is hardly possible to pick up a paper without being immediately struck by the disingenuous tone of one writer who is seeking to evade by quibbles some obvious conclusion, or another vainly attempting to conceal under a cloud of verbiage the fact that he has derived his whole knowledge of the question he is discussing from the book of the author he is depreciating. What man who knows anything now-a-days is deceived by newspaper criticism? he takes it for what it is worth, something intrinsically quite *insignificant*, using that word in its true sense : its praise or blame equally worthless in itself, equally significant by the way, as indicating merely the tendency of the paper in question, and always capable of being predicted beforehand. The one essential for the newspaper is to preserve at all costs an air of absolute freedom and independence, as well as an appearance of universal knowledge ; and the spectacle is almost too much for the augur behind the scenes. Behind the sublime attitudinising, as though of a Cato or a Chatham, he sees only too plainly the miserable form of a Rigby crouching and cringing to his callous and contemptuous owner and patron, the public. The only way in which it might be possible to remedy this state of things would be to forbid by law any one to publish a comment or criticism of anything without signing his name at the bottom of the page : and limit all anonymous matter to pure statement of matter of fact and news. Half the authority of the ' Press ' would then vanish at once, for if the world only knew who were the persons who speak under its cover, no one would pay any further attention to anything they said.

II. The aim of the artist, the true artist, is to realise his ideal : to embody, as it were, his soul, in stone or colour, words or sounds, action or achievement. It is contrary to his nature to make concessions : he refuses to be bound. The conventional is the antithesis and the death of the artistic. Genius is led only by its own instinct and laughs at all rules. This is a commonplace, and yet one which is almost never understood. The rules by which genius refuses to be bound are those of other men : on the other hand, it is a slave to the rules regulating its own species of art : but by instinct, not pedantically or consciously. Genius is at once absolutely bond, and absolutely free : free, in relation to those hard and fast maxims and rules which are erected by inferior criticism on the observation of works of art, which rules . are always based more on the letter than the spirit : yet a bondslave to the true and inner necessities dictated by the nature of things in his special province, just because he cannot help himself, or disobey his demon. Genius is a law to itself, and yet it obeys its own laws with the most uncompromising fidelity, recognising them by intuition. Napoleon sets military ' rules ' at nought, but obeys the true laws of war better than any rule-keeping mediocrity : this is but a type of the procedure of genius in all art. Now, this capacity

of recognising the true necessities, this insight into
function, cannot be acquired : it may come out, as
we say, by education, but if it is not there to start
with, nothing can put it there. *Poeta nascitur non
fit.* Genius is not experience but instinct, and
arises out of the depths of the organic nature, who
produces her results not in the short compass of
the single life, but the subtle processes of ages.

For Nature does not imitate : she creates : so
does the artist. The doctrine which flourishes
now-a-days, that art is imitation, closely connected
with which is the doctrine that genius learns how to
do its work by experience, is radically absurd, and
though presenting a specious appearance, really
superficial to an incredible degree. If we want
to find out about genius, we must not ask mediocrity to tell us what it is : and this is the doctrine
of mediocrity. The faculty of the artist is not
imitation but *divination.* He does not copy, he
creates. It is true, that his result is like the works
of Nature ; (though observe, that in the arts of
music and architecture there is nothing to copy
from, and therefore ' imitation ' in this case fails entirely ;) but the very reason why the genius can
achieve this result where small men cannot is that
he does not follow Nature from the outside, but
the inside : he does not slavishly *imitate her result*,
but *works in her method:* he knows beforehand
how she does things : the *vis creatrix* is in his
soul. If it were not so, he could not see it in
Nature : for each sees in Nature only so much as
he brings to her. Why does the artist present
us with pictures, far more ' true to Nature ' than
we could ourselves produce, if not just because he

knows what is hidden from the eye ? Hidden, that
is to say, not in the totality of its effect, but
requiring for its depiction the pre-established
harmony which enables the genius to put it there,
because he instinctively knows Nature's ways of
going to work. Thus, for example, Dostoyeffsky
gives us a set of Nihilists, and these are not
copies, but creations built on an intuitive perception of the methods of human nature in general,
and Nihilists, that is, men swayed by certain social
and political ideas, in particular. The real artist
is not limited by his experience : he anticipates
it, having the fountain whence it flows within
him. Genius may be compared to the magic
mirror which reflected things that were not to
be seen in the scenes it was turned upon, and
which an ordinary mirror could not show.

Now, the divining power, which works its wonders not by copying Nature's results, but her
processes, by working in and on her own lines, is
nothing but *a native and original gift of discerning
and understanding the true and proper correspondence of Structure with Function*—Nature's *dynamical* method. And just as Nature's actual products are limited, whereas if occasion should arise,
there are unlimited illustrations of her principle still
up her sleeve, which she could produce if put to
it : so neither is the artist limited to reproducing
Nature's actual results, but may draw upon his
imagination for ' the light that never was on sea
' or land.' It cannot be too often repeated : imitation is the principle of bad art : divination, that of
the true. But just for this reason, and it might
have been anticipated, we find imitation loudly

proclaimed as the essential principle and function of art in these times. For certainly, it *is* the principle of most modern art. And just because it is so, we find that the arts which really most obviously refute the theory (though all art does so equally, if properly understood) and make it ridiculous, the arts of architecture, sculpture, music, epic and dramatic poetry are those which flourish least in our day, whereas painting and the novel, which can flourish to a considerable extent on imitation, are in great vogue. The novel is merely the imitation of common life, painting, merely the careful reproduction of nature and persons : both in a low sense of the word art. Accordingly, we find that whereas builders, musicians, and sculptors are so rare, the world is literally deluged with great painters and novelists. For as the test of worth is now held to be popularity, and as the only pleasure in art which the multitude can find lies in comparing it with something they have seen before, it naturally follows that photography becomes the principle of art : everybody pronouncing an artistic work *good*, just in so far as it reminds him of something within his own experience. But this is the degradation of art. Not Imagination, but Imitation is the goal. Not great passions, great actions, but the small passions and insignificant actions of mean and inconsiderable souls, are the thing depicted. For art that sets itself to imitate, and to please the multitude, must necessarily follow the majority : whereas the great is essentially something above the average. This is why, in ultimate analysis, the only form of true and real art left in literature is the satirical. For a genius reduced to

portraying mediocrity, 'our common human nature,'
must at least despise it ; this makes its portraiture
tolerable. Who can endure mediocrity painted by
itself in admiring worship of its own utter insignificance? Nay, the 'abstract individual' theory of
philosophy has stripped man of all his 'lendings
and trappings,' the heroic buskin : and what can
we think of naked and ugly little unashamed humanity, with no dignity lent to it by fictions and
opinions, creeds and beliefs ? The Man gone, who
can worship the Individual? whose God is no
longer heroic Zeus, but King Vortex. The
satirical criticism of Goethe, Disraeli, Dostoyeffsky
is the same thing at bottom as the whining of Shelley
and Byron. Scott is great, because he refuses the
philosophy and keeps his eyes chiefly on the heroic
past. But the unendurable style is the modern style,
' the literature of the Victorian age,' where humanity
sees its own face reflected in the glass, and yet falls
down and worships it, without the excuse of Nar-
cissus ; never suspecting its own ugliness, and un-
enlightened by the humour, the infinite jest in the
thing. *Der Mensch erkennt seine Fehler eben so
wenig wie eine Affe oder eine Eule, die in den
Spiegel sehen, ihre eigene Hässlichkeit erkennen.*
Truly function makes structure : and art based
upon imitation issues in such down-hill trudging as
the literature and painting of to-day. Where is the
artistic production requiring imagination, where the
building, the drama, the sculpture, the speech with
the faintest indication of greatness of soul in its
whole composition ?

And in another respect here as everywhere men
mistake the means for the end. The artist, as we

saw, is essentially the man bound by no law, but
that of his genius, the essentially unconventional
man.   But he is so quite unconsciously, and without
malice prepense, because of his genius : his genius
is the cloak that covers the multitude of his sins.
But the sins without the cloak ? Mediocrities who
have no genius are only too eager to ape the artist.
This disregard of all conventions is easy to acquire.
Moral predigen ist leicht, says Schopenhauer : *moral
begrunden,* and he might have added, *darstellen,
schwer.*   To adopt all the peculiarities of the artist,
without the inner spark, is just the characteristic
of the modern genius, whose portrait appears at
the beginning of his deathless works.   Maudle and
Postlethwaite meet us at every turn.   All the
outward visible signs without the inward spiritual
grace : the *raison d'être* not there.   Hence arises
the most ineffably sickening of all forms of human
society, the *coterie,* the *clique,* the mutual admiration
society : 'Societies of Authors,' 'Literary Men,'
and so on.   Everything æsthetic becomes covered
with the horrid slime of these living whited sepulchres,
and consequently every one with any real instinct
for the things acquires a loathing for the words
connected with them.   The Beautiful and the True
have become *Bulwer-Lyttonised.* Nothing is easier
than to read up a few books and have the technicalities of music, painting, and what not at your
fingers' ends.   But no amount of technicality will
constitute genius.   Nay, more ; technical knowledge,
except in the case of genius itself, is actually a bar
to achievement, and an obstacle to true criticism.
It is not the man who builds the house but the man
who lives in it, that is the best judge of the house,

says Aristotle : and his remark is universally true.
The technique is only the scaffolding, but the work
of art should show none, and is best judged by one
who has no knowledge of it.   It may seem paradoxical to say that artistic study unfits a man for
judging a work of art, but it is true for all that.
'Out of the mouths of babes and sucklings hast
thou ordained praise.'   The mediocrity who has
acquired some technical knowledge, and does
perhaps a little dabbling himself, is inevitably
impelled to attach importance to technique as such :
further, it gives him an imaginary superiority, and
instead of judging the work as a whole, he judges
bits at a time.   This, for example, is the reason
why not one woman in a thousand is a good judge
of dress in her own sex : she knows too much
about the technique, and looks too curiously into
details : she studies the effect, with the eye not
of an artist, but of a milliner or anatomist.   But
the true way to judge a work of art is to forget
that it ever existed in pieces, or grew in time :
it must be considered abstracted from its causes,
ideally, as something absolute and eternal.   Plato's
point of view, which is just the popular point of
view erected into a dogma, and which is scientifically
so jejune and worthless, is the right one here.
People all think of forms as something absolute :
only Aristotle saw the truth.   But art is not science.
Taste and not technique is the necessary condition
of true æsthetic criticism : and those who, destitute
of taste, 'go in for art' in whatever branch, must
necessarily fall back on the only thing left them,
technique.   But this, just because it is conventional,
is almost always opposed to the true spirit of art.

A work may be technically perfect, and yet artistically detestable. And though, speaking ideally, the true artist should have perfect command over technique; for as Aristotle said, the three requisites of production are natural abilities, education, and practise; as a matter of fact we rarely find this to be the case. Genius is often technically careless and impatient. The conception of a work is white hot and glows : cold and laborious is the execution. And so, rarely do we find the two consummate. Homer nods: Shakspeare and Scott are slipshod now and then : many great cathedrals betray the same thing : indeed a very furious and impetuous imagination chafes and frets under technical restraint like a wild horse : on the other hand, an overscrupulously exact and pedantical finish is only too often the stamp of second-rate genius, not too exuberant to rebel at delay. The work smells too much of the lamp.

There is, in fact, not exactly a contradiction, but a fearful chasm, between conception and execution. To pass this gulf, the artist must be endowed with invincible tenacity : and this is the meaning of the often-quoted saying that genius is the power of taking pains. Of course, genius is essentially nothing of the sort, but if it is without this, it will not perform its task. Industry is not the essence, not a cause, but a corollary of genius. Just as Aristotle tells us that money is not happiness, but that you cannot be happy without it : so too neither is genius hard labour, but no work of genius can be produced without it. Many a divinely gifted artist has carried his secret to his grave for want of patience and industry and self-control : on the other

hand, no amount of these will put genius into a con-
scientious dullard. The head and the heart, which
conceive, require the hand to execute, and the will
to drive all on. And the differences of artists lie
in a great degree in this, that in their work now
one, now another of these qualities predominates.
But nearer to my heart is the irregular genius that
mars its work by impatience than the ultra con-
scientious elaboration due too often to a coldness
of the inward fire. Compare Shakspeare with
Milton, Scott with Merimée, Dostoyeffsky with
Turgenieff. A very great excess of imaginative
power is almost incompatible with laborious execution, regularity, formal excellence. Shakspeare,
said Wordsworth, *could* not have written an epic,
for his wealth of imagery would have killed him.
Matter, or Power, and Form are in contradiction,
when the former is superabundant. Theoretically,
the two should be both on an equality, in harmony :
but practically, we have nearly always to choose
between them. Exuberance, hurry, recklessness,
extravagance, a want of pruning and revision,
a lack of proportion : these are faults, indeed, but
they grow only in rich soil : Alexander and Cæsar,
Shakspeare and Scott, Wolsey and Michael Angelo,
Mirabeau and Napoleon are, we feel instinctively, on
a higher plane than Wellington, Milton, Sophocles,
Marlborough, Richelieu : Gothic with all its errors
is nobler than Grecian architecture, and so on. Let
those speak who know : is not the best part of
genius that which is suggested rather than carried
out [b] : that which cannot find adequate expression :

[b] Therefore it is, that sketches are in a way better than any
finished picture. Compare Comyns Carr's *Essays on Art*,

that which remains ever potential, never succeeds in becoming actual? For material is stubborn : imagination a goading demon : life is short : accidents many: pleasure a Siren : and death, sure. Happy the man who does not cease to be, before, as Keats hath it, his pen, his chisel, or his brush has gleaned his teeming brain.

The aim, then, of the artist is to realise as fully as the obstinacy of matter and the impetuosity of his own soul will allow him, his ideal. And as there are infinite spheres of expression, in which he may move, this ideal takes various forms, and these determine the various arts : which roughly speaking we may enumerate as architecture, sculpture, painting, literature, music : all of which issue in the creation of a definite product, and which we may call the productive arts : but there are other arts of action, equally deserving of the name of art in the highest sense, whose spheres are the stage, politics, and war. For the great actor, the great general, the great statesman must have the creative instinct in a degree as great as any productive artist. They too have to realise their ideals : and in truth, when we come to think of it, we may well doubt whether the result achieved by a Siddons or a Cæsar, a Hannibal or a Sulla, does

---

p. 79 *sqq.*, and Ruskin's *Modern Painters*, iii. 144, and v. 37.
' Imperfect sketches, engravings, outlines, rude sculptures, and
' other forms of abstraction possess a charm which the more
' finished picture frequently wants.' 'In a small Greek coin
' the muscles of the human body are as grandly treated as
' in a colossal statue ; and a fine vignette of Turner's will show
' separate touches often more extended *in intention* and stronger
' in result than those of his largest oil paintings.'

not for the difficulty and the glory of its final
accomplishment surpass that of any other artist,
and is not creative in a higher sense than any of
them all: though from its very nature, the result
here cannot endure: for it is not fixed in stone
or marble, but in men, who change and die.
But durability, as it has been well said, is not to be
regarded as the test of merit in human affairs.

Let us then cast a glance at these various arts,
and see whether we cannot throw light upon
them from the point of view of our essential principle. But the reader should remember that it is
only in connection with this principle that they are
here considered : only in outline, in vindication of
that principle: and he must not quarrel with the following discussion for not being what it is not meant
to be, nor demand more of it than the limits of the
enquiry and the nature of the subject admit. The
creations of art, regarded as part of the wealth of
man, and considered in the light of their creative
principle, which is the same for all forms, differently
as it may clothe itself,—this is the aim now before
us. And further, we should avoid much empty
dispute and confusion in these matters, if we remembered that it is impossible entirely to dissociate
the purely artistic effect of any work from that
which it receives in· addition from historical and
personal associations. This is the case even with
the arts which must trust mainly to form for their
effect, as architecture and sculpture : or form and
colour, as painting : how much more, then, with
literature and music, which appeal to all the moral
emotions ? There is something special and peculiar
in every spectator, every listener, every critic, which

mingles in the effect that every work of art has upon him : often, too, this 'something' entirely escapes analysis. Nevertheless, it is possible, and valuable, to state with a certain exactness the province and function of each several art.

III. Architecture, the great man's art *par excellence*, is, broadly speaking, the art of building : more narrowly, the art of realising or embodying in stone, aided by light, shadow, and the colour of the materials, the ideas of grace, harmony, proportion, and power. The sphere of this art is very limited ; but just because it is so, it can attain better than any other art to that exquisite simplicity which has so inexhaustible and indescribable a charm for us : an effect more potent, more purely artistic, than all that can be produced by the more elaborate and various appeals of arts that have a wider scope. A beautiful building may be aptly described as a poem in stone, and Goethe's comparison of Cologne Cathedral to frozen music is well known. We must not allow the happy turn of expression to conceal from us the wide difference of the two arts : and yet music and architecture have two most remarkable and essential points of affinity. In the first place, they have this in common, that, unlike all the other arts, they have no prototypes in nature. There is no copying here : for the fact that mountainous stones and crags resemble buildings is an accident. But the second point of resemblance is still deeper : both music and architecture are *impersonal*. They both appeal to us *powerfully*, i.e. dynamically, rather than actually : the basis of their appeal is the potential, in Nature and ourselves : the potency of their effect rests upon what is conveyed through them ; and just as architecture speaks to us of the *power* of Nature's materials, so does music speak to us of the deep potential capacities of our own nature, the *material* of emotion, as it were : there is nothing in either of them special, personal, or limited, and so insignificant. They both rest upon an essentially mystical sentiment : and in the presence of both we have a secret consciousness of our temporary and fleeting nature, (which has nothing to do with the *size* of buildings ;) as though we felt an inward uneasiness about our existence : which really, as regards its structure, *is* fleeting ; and is permanent only in virtue of that which is potential : that which may quite as well be other than it is. For at bottom, matter is deeper and more fundamental than form : more enduring, more terrible, more sublime : and this is just what Music and Architecture hint to us, though they speak in a language which reason, just because it has only to do with form, and only came into existence to serve it, does not understand. But this is why architecture is the great man's art : for all great men are mystics, and neither sculpture, painting, nor literature can ever satisfy them : for these are too exclusively human and superficial : whereas Mysticism rests upon what is *sub*human : organic and dynamic nature.

The sphere of architecture, we saw, is limited : now, to do great things in a very limited sphere of operations is essentially the badge of a master mind. And architecture is not only essentially limited, in respect of the ideas and emotions to which it can appeal, but there are also special and accidental limitations which trammel it still further.

It is, to begin with, a very costly art, the erection
of a great building being a work of great expense :
and further, it is always more or less hampered by
its *raison d'être*, for owing to considerations of cost,
as well as other reasons, a building is almost always
designed to serve some utilitarian end : which has
somehow or other to be combined with its artistic
aim. Yet again, climate has much to do with the
effectiveness of any building : a clear sky and little
rain being favourable conditions, whereas, on the
contrary, fogs, smoke, rain and so on, rapidly transmogrify any building, however beautiful. Lastly,
situation is, one might almost say, half architecture :
for, architecturally speaking, a building ought to be
placed where a good view of it can be commanded.
The Greeks understood this far better than the
moderns, in general : although the builders of
minsters and cathedrals never imagined, when they
erected their glorious structures, that in course of
time their works would be almost entirely robbed,
in many cases, of their external effect by the growth
of horrible little huts and houses all round them,
making it completely impossible to view them ap-
propriately. The monks who built the old abbeys
understood the value of a fine situation well : what
would their feelings have been, could they have
raised the veil of the future, and seen the ignorant
and brutal iconoclasts instigated by John Knox and
similar horrid rascals at work sacking their brother-
hoods and battering into ruin some of the noblest
works that were ever raised by man to be the glory
of God and the proof of his own divinity. Certainly, buildings more beautiful than what those old
ruins of Dryburgh, Melrose, Coldingham and else-

where must have been, it were hard to imagine :
well worthy of that immortality of another kind
which has been conferred upon them by Sir Walter,
in whom their spirits found an everlasting shrine.

But to turn from these limitations and conditions, which all add to the difficulties of architecture, to its intrinsic function.   The fact, that
it is not its *utilitarian* end, which the building,
considered architecturally, must be constructed to
meet, has misled some into very strange delusions :
Mr. Ruskin, for example, in his *Seven Lamps of
Architecture* shows us to what an extent a man
of artistic taste may go astray, for want of critical
discrimination.   In his haste to get rid of the
directly utilitarian aim of the building, Mr. Ruskin
actually asserts that building is only architectural
when it is useless : he tells us, that ornament,
because it is useless, and only when it is so, adds
to the architectural beauty.   A greater absurdity
was never printed : it is the very reverse of the
truth.   Anything whatever is bad, architecturally,
if it is *useless :* to pile on *useless* ornament is just
exactly where the degradation of an architectural
style begins.   Every detail of architectural form
and ornament should be determined by its end :
an end not utilitarian, but architectural : utilitarian,
that is to say, in another sense : having reference,
not to the base uses of man, but the form of the
building itself as such.   To express the meaning
accurately by a comparison, we might say, that
a building should resemble, not a tame or domesticated or pet animal, but a wild one.   Its form
must be determined by considerations utilitarian
indeed, but not from an extraneous or human point

of view: from its own. It is the opposite of
Mr. Ruskin's view which is true, and evolution
might, had his eye been open, have taught it him.
Not by useless ornament, but without it, does
architecture achieve its end, the reason of its being:
and few indeed are the Gothic buildings from
which we might not wish, speaking architecturally,
much, maybe intrinsically curious or beautiful, removed. The truth is, that Mr. Ruskin has confounded architecture with sculpture, and a great
part of what he says becomes perfect nonsense
unless we remember this[c]. And it is the same
with much of his doctrine respecting colour and
ornamentation. In such a matter every one must
be left to his taste. But whatever may be the
intrinsic beauty or excellence of the additional gold
or silver, sculptured or coloured ornamentation,
I would appeal to the critic: let him turn suddenly from any highly decorated and carved architectural specimen — if you will, Venetian: and
contemplate, either really or in imagination, a

[c] Mr. Ruskin, it may be noticed here, confuses throughout
æsthetic and moral ideas in a most puerile way. He writes
on art as if he were teaching children to be good. Sacrifice,
for example, has nothing peculiarly to do with architecture.
Mr. Ruskin makes it a 'Lamp.' A man must give ungrudg-
ingly of his best, says he, and give himself wholly to his work.
Of course, but this is not architecture: it goes without saying
with all work of any kind. He becomes ridiculous when he
goes so far as to say that a man should give architectural
material *because* it is expensive. This is as bad as it would
be to give bad material because it was cheap. Cheapness
and dearness have nothing to do with it: what should be
given is the material best suited to achieve the artistic aim
of the building.

plain grey column, the shaft of some pillared arch throwing up its graceful curve, in severe and Doric simplicity, against green foliage, sleeping in moonlight and shadow, or burnished like gold by the sun, and judge which best achieves the architectural end. On some minds, at least, there will never be a momentary doubt: anything which tends to remove the attention from the whole to a part is architecturally a mistake, whatever from the point of view of sculpture or painting its merit may be. Nothing can be a more decisive test of true creative genius in any art than the power of refraining, of rejecting superfluous beauties. A really great artist never subordinates the whole to its parts : never hesitates for a moment to throw away his riches into the sea, so that he may save the life and soul of his work : while on the other hand, minds less dominated by the pure æsthetic idea can with difficulty, or not at all, refrain from *improving, i.e. spoiling* the whole by hanging as it were chains and gewgaws to its neck. The ornate style is always bad. No ornament is ever architecturally justifiable except when directly calculated to assist us in achieving the sole and true end in view. In themselves, no doubt, sculpture, paintings, and what not may be full of the highest beauty, or the most fascinating historical or moral associations. But everything must be bought at its price. The more there may be in a building to occupy the virtuoso, the longer it may take to 'do' it, the richer it may be in artistic and antiquarian curiosity, so much the less is a building a work of art. Modern buildings are almost always not one but many : many, not so much from their size, for size is nothing, but from the multiplicity of their artistic attempt: which was therefore foredoomed to failure. Such a thing could never spring from an artistic conception, but only indicates a restless desire, perhaps ambition, to build.

Closely connected with this is a point which touches the very heart of the matter. The architect, says Mr. Ruskin, should copy the forms of nature [d]. He is thinking here half of painting, half of sculpture: in connection with these there is a grain of truth in his rule: but as regards architecture, none. With admirable insight, on the contrary, Mr. Fergusson tells us, that the architect should never copy Nature's *results*, but only her *processes* [e]. This is the genuine *aperçu:* this is the philosophy of architecture. Mr. Fergusson was not thinking, when writing this, of the peculiar principle, universal in Nature, which it is the aim of this book to illustrate: he was thinking of nothing but architecture: and yet the reader will see that it is in exact harmony with all that has been said: a verification all the more valuable because independent and unconscious, especially coming from an architectural authority like Mr. Fergusson. This is the true law of architecture, as it is the law of all art. And what exactly is its meaning? This, that the creations of the architect should resemble

[d] *Seven Lamps*, p. 64 (ed. 1855). 'Whatever is in architecture 'fair or beautiful is imitated from natural forms.' *Ib.*, p. 94, 'the value of architecture depends on two distinct characters: 'the one . . . . the other, the image it bears of the natural 'creation,' and so on.

[e] Fergusson, *History of Architecture*, vol. i. p. 33.

those of Nature, not as being modelled upon them,
but as being instances and specimens of her universal method of creation, according to which her
structures are all made by their functions. The
building should be no miserable copy, but itself :
it should obey its own function only, and be thus as
natural as any animal or any tree.   What, then, is
it to be natural? When we look into Nature, we
see everywhere unfettered spontaneity, an autonomous and self-willed impulse, absolute freedom
from within outwards ; and yet none the less is all
this freedom in strict self-control, strictly obedient
to the ἀναγκὴ τοῦ διὰ τί: the law of each particular
organic nature. What more free, more graceful, more
self-willed, more independent than the movement
of a cat's paw? And yet, free as puss may think
herself, she is really bound in iron necessity : for
every other cat moves in precisely the same characteristic and cat-like way.   Is not the hawk as it
hangs on the breeze, or the porpoise as it rollicks
along, leaping and playing, in the sea, the very
embodied spirit of liberty? and yet in every
motion it obeys stern necessity, for each acts after
its kind, and you cannot tell when you stand on
deck, and watch, whether this porpoise which you
see now is the same as that which you saw but
now, or another one.   But nothing perhaps can give
a more striking impression, can bring home to the
mind with more force the sentiment of this union
of freedom and slavery, of complete anarchy and
complete obedience to law, than to contemplate a
number of flowers of the same species gradually
growing and budding and blowing, making themselves under your very eye, and all in the same way.

Now this union of opposites, this attainment of free and airy spontaneity with absolute truth and fidelity to the laws determining his art, is the true τὸ καλὸν for the artist. His work should be no imitation, but an original, illustrating Nature's creative principle as well as her own productions : but never copying her result. A building copied from Nature would only be a caricature and a hideous unlovely abomination. To copy her letter is to miss her spirit : and spirit must work with hand, said Lionardo da Vinci, or there is no art. Nature must be mimicked not from the outside, mosaically, pedantically : but understood and reconstructed from the centre outwards. Nature's products, like a King of England, can do no wrong, because they obey unwritten laws. The two aspects are admirably illustrated for us in Pre-Raphaelitism and Turner. Both are, in a way, realists. Yet the former, by attempting to imitate Nature from the outside, produces nothing but ridiculous caricatures. Nevertheless beneath this method lies a perception of the truth, which Turner understood. There is more of the inner spirit of Nature in Turner, even though he attempted often too much, than in all the painters in the world : not because he imitated more, but because he knew beforehand what Nature was aiming at, and how she went about it. His divining power is behind his eye. If Spenser be the poet's poet, Turner certainly is the philosopher's painter.

Now this is the heart of all that is good and true in Mr. Ruskin's praise of Turner, although the essential principle is not in Mr. Ruskin. All Mr. Ruskin's rules of art follow from the law of nature,

which is also the law of science, and the law of art,
that function makes structure. When Mr. Ruskin
contrasts the stones, trees, leaves, clouds, or
branches of Turner with those of Claude and
others, he is right in fact, but wrong in explanation. What he says is not what he means. He
says, art should imitate forms, results : he ought
to say, art should imitate processes, comprehend
functions : only thus is it creative. It is true that
the creation will be in *result* imitative ; in the best
sense. Turner's boulder, for example, is more like
a boulder than Claude's because it looks *heavy :* its
weight has got into the picture. Turner *felt* that
it was heavy, and must look so : he did not attain
this result by mere copying. Just so, his branches
hang like Nature's, because they express weight.
Nature's appearances can only be represented by
the man who feels her realities. The reality is
hidden : the appearance, visible : but the appearance is dictated by, gets its look, tone, and character from, the necessities of reality that do not
appear. All this is absolutely a sealed book to
Pre-Raphaelites, and to the great majority of bad
artists in every sphere. That which is not seen
must be expressed : it is infinitely more decisive
than that which is, in the making of the artist.
This is the eternal paradox of art : *the artist is the
man in whom this perception of the invisible scaffolding of Nature, this hidden play and balance of
forces, is innate.* Upon this all depends. Alike in
art and in philosophy, in politics and in war, the
great worker is the man who understands the
dynamics of Nature : who knows that the key to
structure and form lies in function and potentiali-

ties. Who can draw a cliff, but the man who *feels*
its weight? Who can create a dramatic scene or
situation, but the man who *feels* the tendencies of
human nature? Who can analyse economy, or
govern a nation, but the man who *feels* the tendencies of events, the necessities of politics, the dynamical energies and strivings of realities?

And in architecture, as in other directions, this
law holds. Not imitation, but the intuitive sentiment of correspondence between every structure
and its causal function, is the principle of creative
architecture. It is not ornament and decoration,
nothing externally added, but the outward stamp
and inward character of balance, poise, sweep,
power, weight, grace, proportion, harmony, sym-
metry, clean and delicious, or magnificent and mas-
sive adjustment and coadaptation :—these things
are the goal and glory of a great building ; and they
are seen in natural bodies, but will never be attained
by a servile imitation of her results. All but this is
secondary. Colour and ornament are entirely subordinate to these, and only truly admissible in so
far as subservient to the end. This is why (though
here each must speak for himself, according to the
measure of his capacity to savour the truth of
things), colour is, strictly speaking, to be limited in
architecture to the natural colour of the material.
A building all of one colour, and that its own, is
the best. It loses in unity whatever it gains in
added colour. To colour a body variously may be
otherwise successful ; but it *must* always disturb
the architectural effect : the relations of balance
and weight which give the building its unifying
character. Different colours inevitably and irresist-

ibly suggest diversity of weight and material : still more so if they are laid on from the arbitrary conception of the artist. Colour is antagonistic to form : painting out of place destructive of architectural beauty. Of colour in painting anon. But of colour in architecture and sculpture this at least may be said, that we can no more colour a building or sculpture than we can 'paint the lily.' Why? Because it then immediately becomes a thing glaringly artificial and unnatural. Nature's secret escapes us here. We can only colour arbitrarily : we cannot connect in this particular the inward with the outward : hence to colour a building or sculpture is to make it false, false as it would be to colour a lily. For all structure that is not perceptibly spontaneous and original, jars against our sense of beauty, and colour in this case must and cannot but be arbitrary. Here of course tastes will differ: for my part, I can but say that I can never see colour on a building without experiencing the same feeling of disgust which is aroused by paint on the face of a woman. The true building is all of one colour, or almost all : grey, or white, black, or ruddy : even different materials should be employed with caution, for differences of colour inevitably suggest, as we said, different weights, and densities : thus destroying, or tending to counteract and annul that sense of balance which is the soul of architectural beauty. And the reader should remember that just as many a fool gets the reputation of a wise man, and many a woman passes for a Lucretia who is no better than she should be, so many a building is praised which has nothing architecturally beautiful about it.

And as with colour, so is it with sculptural ornament and decoration. However intrinsically beautiful it may be, it is always an architectural blot,
unless and in so far as it directly contributes to the
architectural end. As a general rule, it may be
laid down that the good in sculptural decoration
lies in such carving, moulding, tracery, and so forth
as is *in* and *of*, but not *added to* the architectural
form or basis. All work which tends to aid the
chief design by rendering it lighter, more graceful,
more airy, soaring : which helps to throw it out
into relief by the aid of light and shadow : adds very
greatly to the effect of the whole, provided it be
always subordinate to that effect, and does not go
so far as to weaken and emasculate the whole, give
it a gymnastic appearance, or tend to draw away
attention from the work to the personal merit, as it
were, of the piece. But on the contrary rich and
detailed ornament of all kinds which is positively
added on to the whole, and superfluous to the main
design, only succeeds in destroying all. No doubt
what is lost on one side is gained on another : and
those in whom the historical or antiquarian sympathy predominates over the artistic will not readily
agree to a principle which would rob many a building of much of its interest. None the less is it true
that Gothic architecture sins very much by over-
doing its ornament and decoration : and the clusters
of foliage, grotesque figures, emblematic and sym-
bolic sculptures of all kinds that are dotted all over
it mar as well as make its effect. They may add
largely to its religious significance ; but this is
metaphysics and not art : so would ethical maxims
printed on the wall, though not quite so directly.

For a moment we may abandon ourselves to the
charms of beauty, arrayed in all the costly magnifi-
cence that wealth can command or fashion dictate ;
but the spell disappears when familiarity has
destroyed the novelty, and we turn everlastingly
back, repentant and ashamed of our desertion, to
offer on our knees the apple to divine simplicity,
as she stands resting on the rock of Nature, cold,
white, pure and stony, magnificently patient,
biding her time.. All her rivals do but dazzle and
disappear, but she, what she is to-day,. that she was
yesterday, and will be to-morrow : something that
defies our analysis and commands our homage :
altogether indifferent whether we leave her alone
or stand before her lost in admiration and despair.
For nothing really excellent need ever hurry :
sooner or later its turn will come.

Such is the power of those creations of Art which
derive the source of their beauty from the same
fountain as the creations of Nature, and of those
alone. The indescribable charm which haunts
Nature's products lies essentially in this, that they
never aim at effect. Nature never anywhere aims
at beauty : it results, comes of itself without intention. Beauty is a corollary : it comes to those who
do not seek it, but who do their duty. Not a single
detail of structure is ever ornamental : to ornament
for the sake of ornament would spoil all. Nature
does her duty, suits her structures to their functions,
and beauty follows like the reward of virtue, like
the Legion of Honour to the sentinel who thought
only of defending his post. The very essence of
her consummate beauty lies in the fact that she
makes no effort after, no boast about it, sets no

store by it : there is no *arrière-pensée* here : she is
naïve, open, and absolutely without *pose*. Each
natural creature attends strictly to its own business,
and is not ashamed. Hence its beauty. And so is
it with genuine art : let it think of no other thing
than simply performing its function, and the rest
will follow.

But at this point it is necessary to notice the all
important principle, a principle valid equally for
nature and art, especially architecture, and which is
forced upon both by the nature of things : I mean
the Aristotelian and Darwinian principle of *correlated variation*, which we discussed in the First
Book. Structure is not, they tell us, determined
throughout and altogether by function : it is so in
essentials ; but then, these being what they are,
necessarily involve corollaries : that is, parts correlative and subordinate to those that are essential.
The architectural importance of this principle is
very great. For it is found that in the arrangement of any building, the form of the chief points
necessarily involves and implies and defines those
that stand behind. For example, the early Gothic
builders found that their attempts to work out the
principle of the pointed arch necessarily obliged
them to have certain correlative openings not
originally contemplated. The formula they found
to rule over their labour was this : If certain principles are to be pursued and attained, then certain
corollaries and concessions become necessary. And
this is the case with all creation, all formative
energy : let the statesman or party leader answer
for it : but above all, with architecture. A building
entirely one in its *ensemble* is as impossible as an

animal : one, that is to say, through and through
determined by function, in which everything is
essential. Something must always be superfluous :
it is as it were a percentage form has to pay to
matter : the price of the latter's consent to take
form. The skill of the artist lies in so working out
his idea as to subordinate this element as much as
possible. *On a les défauts de ses qualités.* The
knowledge of the disadvantages thus necessarily
accompanying and hampering advantages, is the
supreme knowledge of the artist in any art. The
palm of victory is rightly awarded to genius which
can as it were turn even this refractory element to
good account, which can attain the greatest possible
amount of the true end of architecture at the least
possible sacrifice. This is the soul of composition,
or, as we might accurately call it, organisation : it
is not merely in his true conception of the end, but
in his *grasp*, or power of seizing his work in its
totality, that we discern the master of his art. It
is just the absence of this which leads directly to
the decay of art, by allowing the artist to look only
at the result in bits, all of which may be separately
above and beyond praise, and yet the whole a failure.

And this leads us directly to the solution of a
question, which has often been debated, yet as far
as I am aware has hitherto remained without an
answer—the question, namely, wherein lies the true
distinction between *fancy* and *imagination*. Every
one feels, without being able to account for the
feeling, that such a distinction there is. And in
truth, the distinction can only be perceived and
made clear, from the point of view afforded by the
thesis of this book. Fancy and the fanciful are

notions exactly analogous to those of chance, haphazard, luck, accident. All these terms essentially imply a negative relation to the term *design.* When, for example, we say that anything happened by chance, by accident, luckily—we do not mean that it did not happen of necessity, for this is not the opposition involved : we always mean to contrast the event with a given design. A man aims at a rabbit, and unluckily chances to kill his friend : he takes a bridge by storm, and luckily it happens to give his general the means of victory : he tries to catch a train, and arrives late—thereby avoiding death in a railway accident—and so on. The element of chance always lies outside the design, but implies a negative reference to it. Now, what chance and luck are to design, that is fancy to imagination. The fanciful in result or execution always implies a negative relation to the law that function makes structure : always implies, that is to say, *the absence of correspondence to function.* The fanciful element in art always signifies isolation, arbitrariness, structure undetermined by function : intrinsically very beautiful, it may be, but capricious and erratic : unfettered by rules and laws : not required by the subject in hand. And this is corroborated by the popular feeling that fancy is, as it were, free, irresponsible, abnormal, wayward, autonomous. A fanciful mind is one that runs off the subject, wanders and strays from the main point : catches at explanations, ideas, analogies that want solidity and connection,—i.e. that do not answer to the need or function in hand. Fancy is thus just the opposite of Imagination, and indeed, a far lower and more common faculty. Fancy shoots at random : Imagination always aims at a mark : for example, Dickens is fanciful as compared with Dostoyeffsky, an author whom he otherwise resembles in many points : his characters are whimsical, odd, amusing, but unreal ; not imaginative : they are the children of originality and fancy, but not based on that deep constructive, imaginative, sympathetic intuitive insight into the essential realities of things and natures of men which the Russian possesses in so marvellous a measure. Gothic ornamentation is very largely of this fanciful description : imaginative ornament, a far higher reach of genius, is rare. But the ordinary mind finds more pleasure in the fanciful than the imaginative. For any one can appreciate the first ; whereas to appreciate imaginative power it is necessary to possess insight into the nature of the sphere in which it is exercised. Aristotle, for example, is imaginative : Plato, only fanciful [f] : Shakspeare or Scott, imaginative : Shelley, fanciful : De la Motte Fouqué, imaginative : Hoffmann, fanciful ; and so on. Hence it is, that the grotesque, the ridiculous, the quaint or curious, all but varieties of the fanciful, caricatures and comicalities are readily recognized and enjoyed : while on the contrary the imaginative, because it requires sympathetic interpretation, and demands a certain basis of knowledge of its field in the spectator, is not so readily received, but must wait perhaps for years to

---

[f] The reader to whom this may seem paradoxical should remember, that imaginative thinking does not lie in thin visionary arbitrary Utopian dreaming, but in large analytically constructive insight, which leaves out no circumstances possibly influencing results.

meet with recognition. And all the more, because
imagination is always terribly in earnest : hence all
men of real imagination are lonely : whereas fancy
is *bon garçon*, a good fellow, constantly grinning
and playing antics : never scrupling to break
a scurril jest in the most sacred and solemn moments : nay, maliciously choosing just these for its
outbreak. This is the spirit so frequently seen in
Gothic architecture, where the solemn effect of
many a silent religious nook or arch is rudely, and
as it were boisterously, broken into by grinning
goblins and uncouth devils, shooting out the tongue
and startling the quiet meditations of the spectator
by malignant and disturbing scoffs and jeers.

The point is well illustrated by a comparison of
Greek with Gothic architecture : for comparisons
are not odious when the object is not depreciation,
but explanation. Of all nations, the Greeks best
understood the true province of pure art. The art
of the Greeks is at once the purest and the most
imaginative, the least fanciful and most natural of
all. Their temples, for example, are exquisite
models of proportion and harmony : though they
lose in power by not making use of the arch. The
rectangular form of their building could never, in
point of grace and power, compete with Gothic
curves. But in this as in other points the barbarians show both their strength and their weakness. They spoil the purity of their fundamental
conception, in itself far more beautiful than that
of the Greeks, by overloading it with matter foreign
to its own nature. They attempt to turn art into
symbolism, and hide the beautiful simplicity of
contour under a multitude of fantastic and alle-

gorical garments. It is the old story: here as
always the Barbarian, as against the Greek, shows
a higher moral spirit, but less mental freedom and
perception of form. Black night, Oriental mysticism,
and iron feudal oppression have entered into the
soul of the Goth : suffering and superstition poison
his taste and transmogrify his artistic productions.
' What the artist is potentially, that his work actually
expresses.' Gothic architecture, as Michelet says
in his wonderful History of France, is the record
of the Passion. It attempts, in fact, to express
more than is artistically legitimate or even possible
in stone : ideas not only æsthetic, but metaphysical
and religious. This gives to it as it were a wider
public, a more democratic and popular appeal ; but
it only conquers by stooping. A genuine son of
Hellas would have felt uneasy in contemplating it :
he would have felt, yet not perhaps been able clearly
to explain, that form was here disfigured by feeling :
that the province of art had been invaded by sen-
timental vulgarity : that the idea was marred by an
unseemly want of self-command and knowledge of
limit ; as though he were listening to some orator,
spoiling the effect of a great idea by uncouth gestures and bizarre expressions, which idea nevertheless shone through, inarticulately, in spite of its
medium. And in truth Gothic architecture stands
half way between the purity of Greek, and the
sombre and gloomy abominations of the Hindoo
or Russian style, which express nothing artistic,
but only a dark and oppressive superstitious awe :
curious from a philosophical or antiquarian point of
view, and presenting extraordinary evidence of
industry and patient sculptorial skill, but utterly

repulsive, artistically speaking, and destitute of taste. On the other hand, Mohammedan architec-ture with its peculiar horse-shoe arches and pointed minarets displays in some ways a finer sense of grace and beauty than all the others, especially in its simple forms : though here too excess of orna-ment mars the effect. And in general, we may see how the Greek qualities are those of harmony and proportion : while grace is the essential feature of Moorish, and power of Gothic architecture. The impression of sublimity in Egyptian building arises chiefly from its colossal size.

So much, then, as to architecture, which is of all the arts perhaps the most instructive from the point of view of the central idea we are analysing. For the work of this artist, just like that of Nature, results in an original and completely independent body, not imitated from anything, not tested by reference to any model ; but whose excellence de-pends upon the degree in which its structure an-swers to its true and peculiar function, that of expressing those ideas of grace and proportion, harmony, balance, and reciprocal relation of part to part, which are appropriate to and conditioned by its material. The pleasure we experience at seeing a panther noiselessly leap with ease from point to point over immense spaces, is precisely the same in kind as that which we experience in con-templating a lofty roof springing out of and resting on a single pillar : in both cases it depends essen-tially upon the underlying sentiment of *weight* in the bodies, and would vanish instantly were we told that the panther's body was as light as a balloon, or that the roof which seems to be so heavy were

made of cork or paper. Herein lies the reason why
brick, wood, and similar materials are architecturally
a mistake. It might seem that iron, being heavy
like stone, would equally serve its purpose : and
yet an iron building would certainly not produce
the same æsthetic effect as one of stone. Why is
this ? It is because we know and feel that stone
inevitably tends and strives to fall, and will do so,
unless the balance is preserved : whereas iron, being
continuous and not discrete in its particles, may
stick up in any direction without falling, being supported by its cohesive force in its lower extremities,
and thus weight here does not determine the result.
But all balance and all grace in architecture essentially depend upon weight ; apart from the weight
of their materials, the forms of arches, domes, and
so forth have no reason for their existence. Iron,
which imitates these forms without possessing their
inner necessity, displeases us, and with reason.
And on this account, too, it is, that on the one hand
those buildings would please us best which we
knew to have been built entirely without mortar or
any binding, but which held together entirely by
the weight and composition of their materials :
while on the other, leaning towers, such as those
of Saragossa and Pisa, are entirely abominable,
simply *tours de force*, violating the very inner nature
of all architecture, and jarring on us like a false
note in music.

IV. Widely different as they are, there is nevertheless a close relation between architecture and
sculpture, the art of carving wood, marble, stone,
and other material into shapes imaginatively and
fancifully beautiful. A certain amount of sculpture

is thus indispensable to architecture, for in the wide
sense of the word all cutting, carving, or chiselling
falls under the notion of sculpture. In a narrower
sense, sculpture is regarded as being peculiarly
concerned with the forms of men, animals, and
plants : organic life, real or imaginary. The erroneous view of art which places its aim in imitation
finds apparent support in the arts of sculpture and
painting. Of the latter anon : here we confine
ourselves to sculpture. Now, there is just this
amount of truth in the theory, that certainly, in
representing organic forms, the realities are always
at hand to serve as a test of the sculptured result.
But—not to mention the fact that sculptural ornament may entirely neglect reality and set itself
to realising the fantastic—here too imitation alone
will never produce any artistic result. Closely as
the artist may study models, both externally and
anatomically, his work will never be worth anything,
unless imagination teach him how to use his material. The types of nature must be to him not so
much models, as hints. It is not so much what
nature actually shows us, that he will endeavour
to produce ; but that which he shows us will always
be such as nature might have shown us, under
suitable conditions. His creation will be natural
even when unreal. For nature is often hampered
by unfavourable conditions, which she must obey ;
especially in the case of man : this is what Aristotle
means when he says that it is Nature's object to
produce the best, but not unfrequently she fails.
The artist is he who sympathises with her, enters
into her soul to interpret her and learn her methods :
only the power of sympathetic imagination will

enable him to divine and as it were anticipate how she would act in any given case. Here too the law holds that it is not the finished *results*, the forms, but the *processes*, of nature that the artist should imitate. He who can divine what, under given ideal conditions, would be her action, he who can imaginatively seize the structure which her forms would take in answer to ideally noble or sublime or peculiar conditions, is the sculptor *par excellence :* provided always that his hand can execute what his head can conceive. For in no art is matter so obstinately difficult as in sculpture : viewed as the conquest of mind over matter most unquestionably sculpture is the highest art : and this is why it is the rarest. Just because it appeals so directly to the eye, trained by the experience of ages to estimate [g], even in imperceptibly small degree, nature's balance and proportion and finish, a fine sculpture is the artistic ideal. The combination of boldness and delicacy, ease and sweep, with scrupulous and minute accuracy ; the infinitely laborious and patient toil which must nevertheless entirely conceal itself, so that the result shall appear as though instantaneously created ; the keeping of the temper ; the real, living, spirited animation of

[g] People are apt to attach far too much importance to technical learning, as the qualification of a critic : and pay no attention to the fact that the education of the eye has been going on for millions of years. It is not the little rationalistic technical furniture acquired in a few years of the individual life, but the great deep popular capacities of the organic nature, in a good specimen, that make the critic. Not merely *vox populi*, *vox Dei*, but *oculus populi*, *oculus Dei*. Just as true metaphysics lies in language, so does true judgment and criticism lie in the organic faculties.

a result obtained through a process contradictory
of it : the grace, fire, passion, or soul of the end
contrasted with the plodding, pedantic, exasperating
dulness of the means ;—all this makes executive
excellence in sculpture next door to impossible.
The labours of Hercules are nothing to the labours
of the sculptor. No other artist has a tithe of the
struggle of the sculptor : no other finds such an
infinite distance between his ideal and his grasp.
Nor can he ever expect repayment in proportion
to his expenditure : for sculpture must always be
the least popular of the arts.

Apart from the unique excellence required in
the execution, the sculptor's peculiar endowment
and faculty is taste. This appears in the result :
the laborious execution, on the other, appears
by its absence, negatively : the less it appears,
the more we know it to have been there : the
more living and unfettered the result, the more
we guess the difficulty to have been overcome :
the easier it appears, the harder it was. *Ars
suprema celare artem.* But with taste it is the
reverse. Taste is the sculptor's quality, and
taste is just the point in which the Greeks are
most decisively and superlatively great. No
sculptures of any age or country can stand beside
the Greek without suffering : their supremacy in
taste is as undeniable as it is inexplicable. They
alone, we might almost say, had any taste at all.
Of sculpture, more than any art, may it be said,
that there is but a step between the sublime and
the ridiculous. It is further impossible to define
taste, or say how it is to be attained : it can
only be felt. It lies in no part of the whole, but

pervades it all : and yet the charm vanishes, if
it be not there.   The slightest suggestion of
its opposite, which just because it is negative,
has many names, the gross, the boorish, the
vulgar, the commonplace, the wooden, the *lourde*,
ruins all.   We can only describe it by metaphors :
it is that which we see in all flowers, in most
birds, in some animals.   How infinitely hard to
render it in stone !   It is not merely difficult, but
impossible, except by some divine chance the
artist hit the mark.   The sculptor must be one
beloved by the Gods.

And yet sculpture has still an obstacle to en-
counter, and one which goes far to render it
almost impossible ; one which it can never conquer, but must compound with.   Just because it
creates models and specimens of living forms ;
just because it approaches so infinitely close to
reality, it almost inevitably suggests a contrast
and comparison of its creatures with the realities
in a point to which it never can attain : *motion.*
Comparisons, here above all, are odious.   It is
an inevitable defect essential to all sculptures that
the more lifelike and breathing they are, the more
do they challenge comparison with what they can
never rival.   Half the charm of natural objects lies
in their motion, but this is for ever denied to
sculpture.   Well did the author of the legend of
Pygmalion pitch upon the everlasting torture of the
sculptor : *if only his creation could move !*   It was
not all nonsense when Byron exclaimed,

' I've seen much finer women, warm and real,
Than all the nonsense of their stone ideal.'

For he here touches to the quick the weak point

in all sculpture, its want of motion. There will always be a sense of *gêne*, which nothing can ever banish or do away with, which sticks in the mind like some faint unpleasant flavour left in the mouth, in the contemplation of figures ever on the point of moving, but never reaching it. We feel instinctively as we look at them that something is lacking. It is as though we were tied, or struggling in a dream to run or escape. They are meant to move: they are built for motion; nay, they want, they strive to move: why, then, do they not? Alas, they cannot.

And here, as it seems to me, though here, again, we can but repeat the old *de gustibus*, lies the reason why statues ought not to be coloured. To colour statues is to remove the last partition that divides the stone from the life: and by bringing them still nearer to reality than ever, to make them less real than before. The feeling of uneasiness which lay like a disturbing element in our pure contemplation of their immobility before, now rises into positive discomfort. Exasperation, almost anger, now succeeds to that which before was melancholy and regret. Before, the artist confined himself to form, and form is not yet life. But when we go further, and attempt to mimic the very hues and warmth of life, inseparable from motion, we arouse a positive and glaring contradiction between the ideal and the real: and the ideal turns out to be after all only a caricature. Fools, exclaims old Hesiod, who know not how much more is the half than the whole: there is indeed a limit beyond which art may not proceed: *non datur ultra*. Orpheus looks back, oversteps the forbidden line, in his yearning for complete fruition, and loses his Eurydice, who

x

returns with a shriek to the hated halls of Dis.
For all genuine and complete achievement, and all
sublime reward, rests upon self-control : nor can
any one call out his realised ideal from the dark
realms of the formless who has not strength to
refrain.   And yet genius is just excess of passion !
Who can wonder, if that which involves the blend-
ing of two contradictions is so rare ? But as to
statues and their colour—let who will colour his
statues, but let me not be there to see !

And this inability of sculpture to attain to motion
explains why we find most permanent and undying
pleasure in those figures and groups which have
caught the instantaneous moment of repose.   Not,
indeed, that sculpture should confine itself to the
representation of bodies absolutely still, or even
sleeping, though perhaps here it would most completely attain its end : but that the moment which
is naturally motionless in any action, one that suits
it for a dramatic *tableau*, is best fitted also for sculp-
turesque presentment.   This has always seemed to
me to be the essential defect in the Laocoon : for
here the figures, writhing and striving with the
serpents in their agony, would certainly never be still
for a moment : and we feel this when we look at
it : it is an error of taste.   But horses prancing on
the freize of the Parthenon, and similar momentary
poses, do not create the same unpleasant impression,
because sight is so rapid that even in real life these
positions photograph themselves on the eye.   Still
even here, the æsthetic effect is a little hampered
by the feeling that they ought to change their position, and we never can rid ourselves of this.   We
are never in more entire harmony with any sculp-

ture than when it represents death. For here, there is no more motion, but the object lies still and quiet for ever. This is the æsthetic reason,— though a mixture of religious sentiment enters into the matter,—for the inward peace and satisfaction aroused in the mind by old tombs of knights and their ladies : there is no lie here, no self-deception : the marble speaks truth at last.

V. Architecture and sculpture, being compelled to trust to form alone for their result, must work within very narrow limits : for this, among other reasons, they are the least democratic of the arts. With painting, we enter upon a wider sphere. Painting, the art of representing on a flat surface by means of form and colour any such ideas, objects, characters, or emotions, as find their legitimate expression through form and colour, is the most popular of the arts. Partly because it appeals directly and immediately to the eyesight, of all the senses that which gives us most information and pleasure with the least trouble, partly because it is the least expensive, and partly again because it requires less ability and less labour to produce a tolerably satisfactory result in this than in any other art, if it may be called the democratic art : and in fact the terms *art* and *artist* are applied in popular parlance primarily to painting and painters. Of all the arts this is the one which gives most colour to the theory that art is imitation. And this much at least may be conceded, that skilful imitation alone in this art will give very pleasing results. Yet here, no less than elsewhere, the highest achievement is possible only to imaginative construction.

The width of its province is not the least of the

qualifications that recommend painting to the suf-
frages of the many.   Thousands of people who are
quite incapable of appreciating architecture, music,
sculpture, or literature can take pleasure in pictures.
Their scope is as universal as the field of vision.
Scenery and landscape, portrait and character painting, historical, allegorical, ethical or religious, tragic
or comic, sublime or grotesque, subjects all fall
within its sphere.   Painting is like a pedlar, who
has a ware in his pack for every customer.   Nor,
regarding art from a strictly critical point of view,
have we any right to exclude anything whatever
from its ken.   Raphael or Turner, Albrecht Durer
or Reynolds, Blake or Kaulbach or Cruikshank—
the painter may paint what he chooses : from the
painter, *as such*, we have no right to demand that
he shall paint this rather than that : provided
always that the subject, whatever it may be, be
treated with that degree of artistic and executive
excellence, and in that spirit which is proper to it.
But from another point of view, the case is altered.
From the point of view, not of the execution, but
of the subject ; not of the painting, but the painted ;
not, that is to say, of the painter *quâ* painter, but
the painter *quâ* artist, there arise differences of
rank.   No one would ever think of the noble, the
sublime, or the beautiful, nor even of the terrible or
awful, in connection with Hogarth or Wilkie, Teniers
or Landseer.   Regarded as imaginative creators,
everyone would give to different artists higher or
lower niches in the temple of fame : and rightly :
for though it might seem a sort of paradox to say
so, it is not painting that makes the painter : it is
creative genius.   The ideal painter will combine

both excellences, but where this is not so, the true
critic will choose the former, and choose well. For
the true function of all art is to realize the ideal,
and it is better to hint at a high ideal, than to give
thorough and complete expression to a low one.
All art is more or less incomplete : it hints rather
than speaks out. No one knows better than a
consummate artist how infinitely far below conception even the most perfect achievement stands : so
much so, that even what it is given to him to attain
is attained, as it were, θείᾳ τύχῃ, by some undesigned happiness. Since then this is so ; since even
the most finished result is, relatively to the ideal it
sought to express, but a suggestion and a sketch,
it should seem that the highest ideals are least
susceptible of completest definition, and the further
we go in the direction of definition, the more likely
we are to obliterate our original conception. This
is the really deep reason for the fact, which must
have struck every student of art, that the unfinished
studies and sketches, the stray fragments of imagination caught and jotted down under happy inspira-
tions, but never worked out, of great masters, often
possess an indescribable fascination that we miss in
their larger works, even in their masterpieces. For
on the one hand the rapid sketch comes, as it were,
warm from the forge and no frigid and perhaps
erroneous detail spoils it, while on the other much
is left to the imagination to fill in, and imagination
is free, while execution is bound. For the further
we go in filling in the sketch, the more do we
recede from the divine conception ; and is it not
the case,—let those answer who have striven to fix
an ideal,—that the best part of all is just that which

beggars all description and defies translation into the language of material? No finished picture ever touches one so near, as many a rough and inspired sketch, where with a few broad essential strokes and features the artist has caught a spirit that would have evaporated long ere he succeeded in imprison - ing it in an elaborate *magnum opus*. For time is the great enemy of the genuine artist. Especially is this true of Turner, a poet painter if ever there was one. The very reason of his failure, in many of his larger paintings, is that he was attempting to fix upon the canvas something utterly beyond the power of brush and colour to express: while on the other hand, in his studies and vignettes, the letter had less dominion over the spirit, and thus he was enabled to throw his soul upon the paper : to do more by attempting less. Moreover, the further we go into detail, the less can we cope with the difficulties that beset us. But on the other hand, it should never be forgotten, that everything actual is superior to what is merely potential : to realise is harder than to suggest : and from this point of view, execution becomes more important than conception. The truth is, that, ideally, both should be supreme : where one predominates over the other, it is impossible to lay down any law that should guide us in our choice. Sometimes, ex- quisite execution may pardon a want of imaginative power : sometimes, we may forgive great executive defects in one who has ' imagined much.'

And on this principle rests the paradoxical truth that in landscape especially light and shadow alone, black and white, will often produce a more artistic effect than colour. For natural beauty depends to a large extent upon colour, whose infinitesimally continuous and infinitely various tints it is quite impossible to seize ; and upon lights, which no conceivable skill of hand or tractability of pigment can do anything but caricature. For example, the low evening sunlight striking through a pine forest, or sunrise on hill and moor. In such cases, Nature's very choicest and commonest feats, which she performs with the most reckless and spend-thrift extravagance, as if to mock and baffle all attempts to follow her, who reaches after the impossible is foredoomed to failure : it is better, and marks a truer sense of art, to aim only at what is practicable. To confine oneself to light and shade, without attempting colour, is no sign of a want of colour sense : on the contrary, the more exquisite the sense of colour in the artist, the stronger will be his conviction of the total impossibility of reproducing it : the less time will he waste in verifying his misgivings, and proving by experiment the desperation of his forlorn hope. But what he cannot achieve in full, he may in large measure effect by suggestion : contenting himself with grasping the basis of the miracle in its lights and shades, and leaving it to the spectator to fill in sympathetically the lacking tints, from the combined power of memory and imagination. This again is the reason for the apparent and familiar anomaly, that an engraving often gives us a keener æsthetic pleasure than the original painting from which it was taken.

The beauty of Nature gives to landscape painting in some ways a higher position than any other branch of this art : on the other hand, its difficulty, rising into impossibility, lays it open from another

point of view to the opposite charge of being less
artistic than any other form of painting, just because
it can, to begin with, never effect its aim so adequately as these, and may further degenerate into
commonplace by basing itself on unimaginative
mimicry.   Nature we have always with us, and
who would barter the reality for the copy, however
skilful?   Moreover, a flat surface is after all always
a flat surface, and in spite of all the cunning of per-
spective and foreshortening, it necessarily comes
about, that the more space we take in, the less
adequate can be the treatment.   The stereoscope
proves how little any painted picture can really
represent an extensive view.   But now, the sense
of space is half the charm of scenery.   If, therefore,
realism in the vulgar sense of the word, exact imitation of nature, were the true aim of art, it would
follow that a stereoscopic photograph was higher
art than any painting.   But this is a *reductio ad
absurdum* of the theory.   On the contrary, it is the
true function of art to give us imaginatively what
is not to be found in Nature.   Therefore the pre-
valence of imitative landscape painting in our day
marks a want of artistic imagination : the old
masters turned to ethical subjects as the sphere of
the noblest form of the art : and indeed, landscape
painting, such as is not mere conventionality and
caricature, is a comparatively modern invention.
Turner is great, not because, as Mr. Ruskin says,
he is imitative, but just because he is not : he is
imaginative.   His paintings are poems.   Realistic,
indeed, he is : true to Nature, even where he is
least imitative : but never realistic in the commonplace sense, never photographic.   He does not

imitate Nature's results, but her processes. He
creates ; he does not copy : he gives us the light
that never was on sea or land, but *as it would have
been*, could it be found. For all true art is realistic :
not, that it copies, but on the contrary, because it
creates imaginatively in the spirit of realism. No
true idealism is arbitrary : it is idealistic of the real.
And Turner is the prince of landscape painters,
because he understood this. Realism idealised :—
this is the true vocation of art ; and few indeed are
the painters who can cope with landscape. Vulgar
imitation is as common as it is abominable : but
creative realism is as admirable as it is rare.

The noblest forms of figure painting are historical
and ethical : portrait painting is a kind of cross
between the two. The art of the portrait painter
lies in so depicting his particular character as to
universalise him : in Aristotelian language, catching
not merely what is actual, but what is potential in
him : slavish reproduction of the individual, on the
other hand, is not art but a mere knack : cleverness
and nothing more. This will always be caviare to
the general, who think, not without reason, that the
first business of a portrait is to be like the original.
And so, indeed, it is : but then the question is,
what do you mean by *like ?* As any particular man
is not only a unit, an individual, but also a character, the true portrait painter is he who can so catch
the character of the individual as to express this.
For it is only in so far as it expresses character :
only so far as the individual trait is characteristic,
that it is artistic. The individual, merely as such,
is always mean and insignificant : it is as a specimen
of the race, as a man definitely of this or that kind,

that he becomes full of moral meaning. Now, character diverges away from the common type; beauty, on the other hand, intensifies it. Character is the quality of a man, beauty that of a woman. This is why female figures are more appropriate for sculpture than painting : with male, this cannot be said : the portraits of men are however a higher and more difficult form of art than those of women, because character is a higher and more noble thing than beauty. Character in woman is to character in men what moonlight is to sunlight : a thing pale, uncertain, faint and shadowy : not that women have no character ; every woman has, rather, something, some *point*, special to herself : but hardly what we mean by character : because action is not the function of woman, and character is the correlative of action. Sex is the thing of primary importance in a woman : therefore it predominates in them all, and is only slightly coloured by special qualities in each : but nobody ever thinks of sex in the case of men. They stand or fall by character and action. This is why women are peculiarly styled ' the sex :' they have monopolised the word, as they would monopolise everything else if they could. A proof of all this is the fact, that a woman whose face or manner expresses character more than is customary seems almost masculine : we feel that something is wrong : she is not the same as the rest. The more character, as a rule, the less beauty : but all women, give them their choice, would choose beauty first. Their instinct tells them what their function is : it is simply sexual ; to attract men. As soon as a woman is married, her goal is achieved : but a man's marriage is only

an incident in his career : he may achieve *his* end
either with or without it. Hence with men the
resemblances are superficial, and the differences
deep : women on the contrary only differ superficially ; at bottom they are identical. Therefore
it is that we always speak of women in the lump,
and base our inferences respecting any one woman
on the known characteristics of the sex; for in spite
of commonplaces about the caprice and uncertainty
of woman, and the difficulty of 'knowing' women,
the truth is that nothing acts with such apodeictic
certainty after its kind as a woman, and the difficulty of knowing women does not arise from their
depth, but their superficiality : their motives escape
us by their extreme triviality. Just as Napoleon's
army puzzled themselves about the secret mysteries
lying hidden inside the Pyramids, and when they
went in, says Bourrienne, they found—that there
was nothing to be found : so do men, arguing from
their own depth, delude themselves about the difficulty of fathoming the heart of woman, while all
the time the deception is analogous to that of
a mirror, which seems so deep because it reflects
the profundities that stand above it, being itself
a mere surface. On the other hand, we never
assume that we can tell what any particular man
will do, till we have made his acquaintance, and
seen what sort of a man he is. And the reader
who with particular cases in his eye disagrees with
all this, should recollect that exceptions prove the
rule : and ἢ θήριον ἢ θέος : a woman is always
either a woman or a saint.

The cardinal defect in portrait painting is that it
is an abstraction, and thus compares unfavourably

with historical or ethical painting. Characters in life are always in 'action, and thus expressive : whereas in their portraits they are still, isolated, in attitudes, and doing nothing, or, what is the same thing, doing something fictitiously for the sake of appearances and the portrait : this always lends an air of stiffness and unreality to the very best portraits, which is much increased when the portrait is only half length. We never see people in bits, but all together. Our conception of any particular person's character always rests upon the whole man in action, and can never be adequately expressed by the face alone in repose. Accordingly very few portraits can ever enable us to feel sure we have any certain knowledge of the character they represent, and a stolid, stupid, wooden, phlegmatic person is the best subject for portrait painting, regarded as the means of conveying exact information as to what the subject is like. This is proved by the extraordinary differences that are presented by portraits of many a well known character, so that they hardly resemble each other at all : for instance, those of Napoleon. And in fact, we never really know what people are like till we know them personally, because the mere dead expression of the face in repose is hardly ever adequate to the character. And thus the good portrait painter must always compose, rather than copy the face at any one moment, by living for some time with his character, and throwing into the face more than is actually there at any particular instant : which will always make stupid people say that he has flattered his subject. But he must flatter his subject, in this sense, otherwise his portrait will be no portrait, but a mere photograph ; and nothing could be a better proof of all this than the well-known fact that photographs are always liars and stupid deceptive caricatures : there is nothing harder than to find out what people are like from their photograph. Photographs are good only for people who have seen the originals, because then they supply what is wanting. As a very fine example of what is said here, I shall instance Millais' portrait of the Earl of Beaconsfield, which is totally different from all his photographs and other portraits, but which expresses admirably and completely the *real character* of the man, as evinced in the totality of his life and writings. This is what a true portrait should be ; the quintessence of the life of the subject. We should feel, as we look at it, with an intimate knowledge of the whole history of the man, that it is *there*, expressed in the portrait. And the bust of Julius Cæsar, in the British Museum, always impresses me in the same way.

Far higher than portrait painting proper stands imaginative ethical painting, though indeed the former at its highest power is simply a special case of the latter : for example, Vandyck's Charles I., or the portraits of themselves by Lionardo da Vinci or Albrecht Durer. And indeed, ethical painting is but portrait painting : the two are related as potential to actual : thus the former, as Aristotle says, has a wider province and a deeper meaning. The special function of the ethical painter is to depict character and expression of all kinds, legitimately finding their due expression through form and colour : that is to say, it is an artistic error to attempt in one art what can only be truly and adequately performed by another : for example, to depict characters in scenes or situations whose point lies less in form than in sound or motion, or where we feel that the characters are unnaturally still, or inarticulate. The choice of such subjects always argues a lack of instinctive or imaginative taste in the artist, who is thus thrown back upon accident, conventionality, or the *interesting*. For example, there is nothing artistic in the feeling which leads a man either to paint, or to buy a picture representing sportsmen in the act of shooting at partridges. The essence of this lies not in contemplation, but in action : honest Tony Lumpkin however loves to have a ' picture ' recalling his favourite pastimes to his mind. It all depends upon the spirit in which the artist has approached his task, whether scenes representing common life are æsthetically good or bad. For example, the spirit of Hogarth is always truly ethical and philosophical : on the other hand, the great majority of analogous paintings is equally commonplace and detestable : people without the slightest artistic taste simply trying to put action or anything familiar upon the canvas, because it is interesting to those concerned. This is not art, but ' shop.' The productions of Dutch artists are largely of this kind : looking at their ' domestic ' interiors ' one wonders why the honest painter did not rather make a list of all the things in his room and suspend it in a frame upon the wall. On the other hand, even furniture, tables, chairs, and what not may be artistic subjects in the highest sense, provided that they are introduced and contemplated from an ethical standpoint : for example, if the artist intends to bring out, through the sentiments of familiar and common objects, a feeling of absolute repose, loneliness, or the absence of some personality. Thus, a picture representing for example, Wallenstein just assassinated, the murder-ers gone, everything quite still, would gain by the most accurate representation of all the furniture, which in moments of passion and emotion stand as it were looking cynically on : what fearful stories could not old arm-chairs and tables reveal to us, had they but voice ? This occurred to me very forcibly when I was listening, in the Château at Blois, to the old man recounting the murder of the Duc de Guise : close by stood an old oak settee, beautifully carved, with the *porc-épic*, or porcupine, of Louis XII. on the back. A per-ception of character in furniture, for it has much, will heighten the general effect. Or again, a pic-ture representing the Empress Joséphine, stand-ing motionless and alone, steadily and fixedly gazing at the door by which Napoleon has just left, after telling her of his divorce project, would require the eloquent silence of inanimate objects to express the mood. For here the aim of the artist is to express ethical mood, and everybody who has at one time or another received some fearful shock, such as seemed to paralyse while it stirred to emotion, knows how curiously, as if in pure irony, the mind seems at such a moment frivolously to turn aside and examine and atten-tively consider external objects of no significance around it. Thus a man just on the point of being beheaded or hung will count the faces of the spectators, or examine, it may be, the pattern of the executioner's coat, or perhaps smile at some grotesque expression on the face of the nearest boor who has come to gloat over his last agonies. And the intuitive knowledge of this indirect expressiveness of outward objects is the essential quality alike of the dramatic author and the dramatic artist. Consider, for example, the well-known

' Rolled round in earth's diurnal course
With rocks, and stones, and trees.'

What are rocks and trees to her? Little dramatic as was Wordsworth's genius, here he has reached the core of dramatic expression, which rests always on the imaginative and intuitive sentiment of the close relation between the actor and his surroundings. So, too, Lear's *Pray you, undo this button.* In literature, none have so profound a sentiment of this sympathetic relation between character and inanimate objects as the Russian novelists. Dostoyeffsky is the very devil, and this is just what is meant by realism, of which more anon.

Ethical painting finds its highest expression in the Italians, above all in Raphael. The spirit of Christianity, of ascetism, of renunciation : that peace which the world cannot give : the serenity of the saint who has finally subdued his passions, and the resignation of the religious soul, which having weighed the world in the balance and found it wanting, has attained to inward calm and patience : the untroubled quiet of faith that has long ago emerged victorious from all doubt and anxiety, lives in his Madonnas and Saints. And yet it is impossible to deny that a certain conventionality,

a certain unreality and anti-natural mysticism lurks
in these artists and their Holy Families. Incom-
parably strong and intense on one side, their
imagination was yet confined within narrow limits.
They never really penetrated into the inner shrine
of that religion in whose cause they incessantly
laboured : their treatment of sacred subjects drawn
from Catholic tradition and Christian legend is
always philosophic, traditional, never intuitive. A
false unreal glamour, as of courts and riches, antagonistic to the essential spirit of Christianity,
surrounds it all. Instead of poor obscure Jews,
despised and rejected of men, the Founder of
Christianity and his circle invariably appear as
well-to-do Italians. The constancy and everlasting
sameness of the conventional idea is a little wearisome and irritating to anybody but Vasari. The
whole treatment is in fact inherited from the illu-
minations of the Middle Ages, a stereotyped
formalism. Christianity from the point of view
of Raphael's pictures and cartoons is a delusion,
a dream, and an impossibility. And in fact there
is really a contradiction between form and matter
here. Christianity cannot be idealised, cannot lose
reality, without losing all : the very core and essence
of it is that it was *real.* If it is not real, it is
nothing. Regarded as an ideal, it becomes absolute
foolishness : there is no ideal but the Greek ideal :
sorrow and care, disappointment, agony and bitter
repentance—all these things only appear in the real
and actual world. Why do we turn from the real
to the ideal? only because this is so. Therefore
it was necessary that if the southern intellect, sensuous and impressionable to colour and form,

adopted a subject so essentially opposed to its genius, the result should be a contradiction. We see how Michael Angelo strives as it were to get away from the Christian to the Greek and Pagan ideal: he has no inward sympathy with the one, everything with the other. Had their atmosphere been Pagan and their thoughts free, what would they not have accomplished? As it is, they are attempting the impossible, the reconciliation between Christianity and art, sensuous art, that lives on colour and form, joy and indulgence, light and the garish world. It is not painting, but music, through which religious emotion finds its true expression.

Historical painting is the highest form of the art, and the rarest. The universal love of the stage reposes on the same foundation: for the scene is merely a historical painting that has quickened into life; and conversely, the painting is merely a gorgonised scene. Every one remembers the criticism of the Greek priest upon Titian: Your scandalous figures stand quite out from the canvas: they are as bad as a group of statues[h]. Now, just as dramatic poetry, which is history actualised, is the highest form of poetry, so is historical painting, which is always dramatic, the highest form of painting: for here imagination is supreme. No small man can ever imagine or represent a big one, either in real life, art, or as an actor on the stage. Historical painting includes all other forms of the art. Its subject is the whole field of human life and character, in its highest and most significant illustrations: its passions, emotions, situations, are not those of

[h] See Gibbon, *Decline and Fall*, cap. XLIX.

commonplace mediocrity, but special life, greatness
and genius. Pity and fear, terror and admiration
are the strings on which it plays. What element
of the sublime can possibly enter into middle-class
existence? Who can care two straws whether 'the
individual' lives or dies, except his relations? But
Columbus, looking out westward from his cockle-
shell over the unknown sea, with his mutinous
mariners crowding behind him : John Hus, pleading
for his life before the Council of Constance : Coriolanus, cursing the mob : Cæsar, carelessly smiling
and talking to the conspirators : Sulla, descending
from the rostra, in the Roman market-place :
Napoleon, standing motionless on guard, while the
tired sentinel sleeps beside him : Mary, Queen of
Scots, on the scaffold : Harold, with the arrow in
his eye : Ahitophel, putting his household in order :
Loyola, preaching in Venice : Becket, facing his
murderers : Wolsey, parting with the King : Abelard,
giving Heloise lessons in old Canon Fulbert's house:
Peter the Hermit, at the head of his 'believers : '
Henry III., crouching at Canossa : Louis XI.,
praying to his little leaden images : Hannibal, hear-
ing the news of Metaurus : Joseph, declaring himself
to his brethren : John of Gischala, emerging from
the caverns of Jerusalem : James of Scotland, meet-
ing the Highland woman at the ferry : Jephthah,
catching sight of his daughter : the Douglasses,
leaping from the table at the sight of the black
bull's head : Haroun Alraschid, strolling in disguise
through the streets of Bagdad : Beaumarchais, examining Mme. Goezman in Court : Harpagus,
gazing without emotion at the fragments of his son :
Philippe Égalité, passing his own house on a tum-

bril : Pharaoh's daughter, discovering Moses in the
bulrushes : John, among the Barons at Runnymede :
the Roman *fetialis*, receiving the insult at Tarentum :
Colonna, striking Pope Boniface with his iron
gauntlet :—history furnishes an inexhaustible store
of the richest materials for art : but they are still
only material, to be spoiled by incompetence or interpreted by genius.   Moreover, although Aristotle
tells us, and rightly, that poetry is more philosophical
than history, yet on the other hand we should remember that imagination is here powerless, except
on the basis of history.   For these things cannot
be invented.   The individual, as such, is intrinsically insignificant : he can acquire dignity and
sublimity only in so far as he represents a cause :
only in so far as he embodies an idea, or stands
forward as the champion of a principle.   This is
what makes him a great man, and great art deals with
great men.   But these conditions cannot be wholly
imaginary : for they would in that case appeal to
no one, and instead of being sublime or terrible,
would only be ridiculous, or even meaningless and
unintelligible, and so of no effect.   This is why the
characters of fiction that are wholly fictitious can
never impress us in the same powerful way as those
of history.   And the practice of great poets shows
us this plainly, for they instinctively turn to history
for their tragic material.   So too the greatest critic
that ever lived, Aristotle, requires the characters
of Tragedy to be of high rank.   With Comedy, on
the other hand, the contrary is the case : nothing
is required here but the qualities peculiar to common
men as such.

Lastly, we must take note of allegorical painting,

which endeavours to express imaginatively moral or religious ideas, and which from its very nature must always be to a certain extent conventional, that is, based upon ideas of local and temporal rather than essential significance. Art of this kind must always be either very bad or very good, and requires for its realisation a very peculiar sort of originality. As, for example, the curious *Riders of the Apocalypse*, by Cornelius, or the strange Knight of Albrecht Durer, on which Fouqué based his inimitable Sintram : or, still better, the works of that weird indescribable genius, William Blake, which show us this kind in perfection. As instances of the grotesque side of this form of art, Kaulbach's illustrations to Goethe's *Reineke Fuchs* are worth notice : they catch in a wonderfully subtle and inimitable way the humour of the old beast fable, such as we see it in Æsop and Bidfai. The difficulty of allegorical painting lies in the impossibility of clearly understanding the relation between form and the abstract idea : and yet when we turn over Blake's illustrations we often feel as if he had just this inexplicable faculty of discerning the appropriate form in which any particular moral or religious conception should be clothed : so much so, indeed, that it seems as if the idea in question could often be suitably represented only just in that form in which he has chosen to express it, and in no other. A kind of second sight seems to be needed here : this much at least is certain, that nothing can possibly be more vile than the commonplace in this field. The power of detecting, or representing hidden analogies, which escape us even while we experience their effect, a faculty in art akin to that of the mystic in philosophy, is at the bottom of it: without which, allegorical painting degenerates into mere sterile symbolism, of no more inner significance than algebraical formulæ or anagram.

With regard, now, to all these various forms of painting as an art, the reader must observe that only the subject, not the manner, falls within consideration, from the point of view of this book. Any one who fails to note this will very much misinterpret everything that is here advanced: indeed, a few words in this connection will not be out of place. In all forms of art, from our point of view, technical excellence, workmanship adequate to the subject, is necessarily assumed; for our business here is to discuss the function of art regarded as aiming at an end, and the technical qualifications of the artist lie entirely outside our ken. But the tendency of the critic in all art is to exalt the manner at the expense of the matter: while, on the contrary, the vulgar think more of the subject than the treatment. The former tendency is illustrated by such aphorisms as 'art for art's sake' and similar epigrams: as if the thing of primary importance were the form rather than what it conveys—the spirit! There is a deep truth in the popular view. An intimate familiarity with processes and methods leads the critic to forget the cardinal truth, that painting is not an end but a means. But wherever this happens, degeneration in art necessarily follows. Just as the first business of a hat is to protect the head, while by dropping this native and original function out of sight, and attending to artistic and subordinate ends, the form of the hat may be actually modified till at length it becomes less and less fitted to perform the function which gave it its existence, less and less of a hat: so too, if we neglect the true function of art, which is to realise the imaginative, and centre our gaze more and more upon the conveyances rather than the conveyed, upon, that is to say, the form and manner rather than the spirit, we shall end by worshipping the insignificant, the trifling, the ugly, the absurd, or even pure nothing at all: a process which has been exemplified by some modern schools of art. But the great achievements in art were accomplished by men who were thinking primarily of what they wanted to express, and only secondarily of how to express it: the opposite process leads to vapid inanity, empty verbiage: 'culture,' without genius: style, mannerism; much ado about nothing: vain effort and parade, with no result: laborious and artificial composition, without any inner instigating idea. The essential merit of all style, execution, and workmanship is that it shall be, if not unconscious, at least directly dictated and suggested by the necessities of the thing to be so conveyed, the spirit: felt, not excogitated: spontaneous, not elaborately devised. But where this natural sequence is reversed, and the subject is chosen as the mere parade-ground for technical talent, nothing but mediocrity can ever be attained. The worst of all styles is to have a conscious style. Instead of Shakspere and Bolingbroke, we have now Tennyson, Browning, Macaulay: instead of eloquence, rhetoric: simplicity is replaced by critical purism: earnestness disappears, and the κτῆμα ἐς ἀεί degenerates into the ἀγώνισμα ἐς τὸ παράχρημα. This is the predominant manner in all modern life. Ceremony, where it endures, is no longer dictated by the felt necessities of the case, but arbitrarily forced in from above, and smacks of the unreal. Because here structure is not honestly and naively determined by function, but kept up, like a game, after the function, the life, the *reason why* of all, has disappeared. Just so art, whenever it is regarded not as a means but an end, though apparently taking a very high standpoint, is really cutting its own throat. The first condition of all true art is that the means shall be determined by the ends, the manner of expression by the imperious and uncompromising desire of the artist to realise some ideal that makes a slave of him. Reverse this : drop out of sight the ends, and concentrate all attention upon the means, and you have no longer any art, or any genius, but only critics and criticism. The critic, in a high sense of the word, is catholic, tolerant, comparative, admits all ideals, so that only they be truly executed : but this is not the nature of the artistic genius. It is intolerant, exclusive, knows no ideal but its own, and thinks of that only : the artist and the genius are always men of one idea. No man ever has two ideas worth anything. This he labours to express, and expression comes to him because he is striving to fit it to his idea, to clothe his idea, and cares nothing for expression in itself. Expression, like a woman, gives herself to those who make light of her. But how can any one produce lasting works, who is considering, not how to clothe his ideal statue in fitting garb, but who uses any stray wood—*e quovis ligno*—as a peg whereon to hang and exhibit the clothes—Academy Pictures ?

VI. We may turn aside here for a moment to cast a glance into the bric-a-brac, or old curiosity shop, of the minor arts. Holding a sort of distant relation to plastic and pictorial art, yet not properly falling within their sphere, these exercise nevertheless an important influence upon life, and achieve sometimes really beautiful results. Such things as curios, antiques, china, ware, glass, cups, rings, snuff-boxes, the carvings and stuffs of China and Japan, Indian ivory and boxes, old weapons, bowls, jars, statuettes, lace and candlesticks, vases, furniture, mats, arras, hangings, tapestry, and the whole of that multifarious class of *objects* which are properly regarded as within the province of the virtuoso, deserve notice, for they often embody extraordinary skill and artistic fancy, and give us keen pleasure. These stand on the border-line between the work of art and the commodity, and show us, in fact, what the commodity was in old days, when all production savoured of the artistic, and the division of labour was as yet not paramount. Their artistic value varies indefinitely. But just as it has been observed that it is the multitude of small things rather than the isolated big ones, that really colour and make up life, so we might very well say that these minor and less ambitious works of art have a primary claim upon our attention. The things that immediately surround us have a constant and unnoticed influence on our lives: taste, like virtue, is the daughter of habit, of repeated acts. Now, all these objects are far more the product of fancy than imagination. Here, there is no imperative necessity of correspondence, no underlying ground of being,

or reason why : nothing archetypal : but all is wayward, capricious, anomalous, even to the grotesque
and absurd, nay the positively ugly, downright
caricature : form is dictated not by any deep sense
of function, but the good will and pleasure of the
workman, arbitrary and unconfined license. We
see here, in fact, structure escaping from the law
that binds it to function : these rudimentary forms,
as Darwin might say, are highly variable : structure
becomes plastic, irregular, fanciful, and even amorphous, just because there is nothing to determine
it but the potentialities of matter and the caprice of
the artist. And this is the deep reason why these
minor arts can never rise to the dignity of the great
arts[1] ; they aim at no realisation of high and
determinate ideal, but sport and trifle, as it were,
with sacred subjects beyond their ken, like kittens
playing with chessmen, or puppies worrying a cardinal's hat. Yet on the other hand this very absence
of seriousness and light airy thoughtlessness has
itself a charm. For though a great critic has told
us that *ernst ist das Leben: heiter ist die Kunst:*
nevertheless the solemnity and bitter earnest of life
lies always just below, and lurks within art, which is
serious and severe, or else it is no true art : and in
its presence close attention always involves a strain,
of which we are not conscious till we turn by
contrast to a sphere into which it does not enter.
And hence there is nothing so invigorating, so
unconsciously refreshing, no such tonic for the mind,

[1] Herein lies the deep ground of distinction between men
and women : women can never recognise any sphere but the
arbitrary : men are always more or less aiming at bringing their
lives into correspondence with external necessities. Fancy is
female : imagination, male.

as to live surrounded by pretty things, even though they may have no high claims to artistic merit : for the soul retains this much of its old vegetative life, that it grows and clamps itself to what is nearest to it : and as this is, so is the soul.

VII. When now we turn from the plastic and pictorial arts to that of music, it is as though we were entering a different world. The field of the former was the whole universe of form and colour, and all that pierces through them. With music, the whole visible world vanishes : it is as though we closed our eyes : and in truth, we never appreciate music so well as in the dark. For music is the art of appealing to the emotions through sound ; of embodying the feelings of the heart in sound. Further, though we cannot explain how it comes about, music achieves its aim more certainly and directly than any other art. All the other arts must appeal to the heart, if at all, through the head : but music speaks directly to the heart. It requires no interpreter. In all the other arts, we must first understand, and then only feel : but music we feel without understanding. Neither words nor pictures are capable of reaching the core of feeling : they can only hint and suggest, through the imagination : but music is the embodiment of feeling : feeling is the very soul of music. Music is Feeling : the two are identical : opposite sides of the same fact : and all music which is not directly inspired by feeling in the first instance, all music that is scientifically composed without this, is neither music nor not music : it is nothing at all : it is simply gymnastics, suitable for the intellectual pabulum of the young gentleman who holds the function of music to be the expression of thought [k]. For music is essentially not rational, but ethical. And the powers of music are coextensive with the powers of the human soul. There is no conceivable moral disposition which music cannot express. Music stands there to convict every rationalist of foolishness. Here are we, with our characters and passions, doing and suffering, and the accidents of life sweep over us, educing in us states and emotions, infinitely various and different in each different individual, as an Æolian harp swept by the wind, or the billowy waste of waters by the changeful gusts of every casual breeze; taking colour ethically as the sea does physically :—and there is music, which mocks us like echo or a glassy mirror sending back to us with exact correlative repetition every shadow passing over us. 'Dark- 'ling we listen,' and the tears stand in our eyes: tears it may be, of rage or pity, enthusiasm, desperation, remorse, or sublime devotion. But the greatest philosophers of all ages have striven to solve this inexplicable community and pre-

[k] It is the modern musical cant to hold just the opposite of this: to talk about music expressing 'thought,' and to call emotional music 'sensual,' to emphasise the technical side. Those who hold good music to be that which has 'thought' in it need not read anything said here about music, for they will disagree with it all. For my part, I am convinced that people who estimate music by what they call the thought in it, understand neither what music is, nor what thought is. It is passion that is required to appreciate music: reason has nothing whatever to do with it. But now-a-days, people are over-educated for their intellect, and sling technical terminology about the more, the less they have penetrated to the interior understanding of the point.

established harmony in vain. Aristotle, as usual,
is on the track: why, he asks pertinently, why is it
that music, being mere sound, resembles moral
character? And Schopenhauer's mystical explanation is well known: it has moreover, the great
recommendation of being endorsed by Wagner,
who held Schopenhauer to have understood music
better than any other philosopher. Yet Schopenhauer's explanation is, in fact, no explanation, but
an exposition of the fact, that music seems to have
a direct and immediate relation, or rather connection,
with the Will, the Self. Yet no one can ever tell,
why. The fact is there: it is ultimate: one of those
primordial facts in the universe, through which it is
impossible to penetrate. The more we think of it,
the more impossible does it seem to arrive at the
how of this mystery. Why is a minor key
melancholy? there is a problem which baffles all
attempt at explanation. The Sphinx was a poor
creature: had she been a musician she might have
been alive still: her puerile enigma was nothing
to this.

Music does not appeal to the head, but the
heart: not to the ideas, but the feelings: that
is to say, it is not an intellectual but a moral
art. This differentiates it from all the other arts,
and makes it infinitely deeper and more universal
than them all. For intellect is merely superficial
compared with character, which is organic. Further,
intellect is the principle of difference and discord:
but morality is the principle of unison and community. Sympathetic appreciation of the other
arts essentially varies with various intellects: but
it is not intellect which enables us to appreciate

music. To the intellect it does not appeal : people of very different intellectual power can equally appreciate music : people may be, and often are, intellectually on a very low plane, yet musical in the highest degree. Music is not a rational art. Its function is not to realise ideals that satisfy the intellect, but the heart : music will express simply, directly, and exhaustively what, if we try for a hundred years, we shall never express in any other way, either pictorially or reasonably ; it is potent where language is not merely impotent but ridiculous. It is observed to exercise a strange influence even upon animals : and a well-known physical experiment proves that to every musical note a special vibratory movement corresponds in matter, such as can be tested.

And here it may be permitted to hazard a conjecture, though many a reader will perhaps regard it as fanciful rather than imaginative. The Pythagoreans believed in a 'music of the spheres.' Now let us consider, how the essential principle in this book would apply to the stars. If all structure and all form be such as it is, by reason of the necessity of corresponding to its function, what would be the function which determined the form of the heavens? which dictated the regular motions and orbits of the stars? what is the function of the heavenly bodies? what is that duty which they must perform, *on pain of death?* Chaos, it is obvious, might return again, and yet the *matter* of the heavenly bodies would remain : but not their form. Chaos, then, would be to them what death is to organic bodies : and their life, therefore, is to prevent this Chaos from coming

about. What, then, is the function of the heavenly
bodies, but harmony? They move and roll as they
do, for the sake of harmony. Harmony is the
function of the universe : that which is the *raison
d'être* of its form. Does it, then, seem so un-
reasonable as at the first blush might appear, to
hold that, could we but hear it, this harmony is
musical? or is it the mystical perception of the
truth, that music is so deep, just because it is
the upper, the illuminated side, of the great organic
fact of nature, that harmony is the supreme law?

From a strictly musical point of view, we have
no right to say, that music should appeal to one
emotion rather than another. But from the ethical
point of view, we class music, and rightly, as higher
or lower, according as the emotion to which it
appeals is ethically sublime or the reverse. From
its very nature it follows, that apart from this
ethical standpoint, there is not and cannot possibly
be any objective standard of music. It does not
appeal to the external, but the internal sense.
Hence futile as most argument is, especially in
regard to taste, nothing is so essentially futile as
argument about music. There are no canons of
music, but men. Each man is his own law in
the matter. Music that misses its effect is simply
noise and nothing more. To the ear that cannot
'see' anything in it, Beethoven's Moonlight So-
nata is neither more nor less than a row. For
observe, that music, considered with regard to
its end, is sound, in the strictest sensational sense :
sound as heard and felt, not sound as consisting
of vibrations. Music is vibrations : but vibrations
are not necessarily music. The mathematical

relations and expressions are nothing to the purpose: these are the material of music, but its *raison d'être* is its moral effect on the listener. There is therefore no test or criterion of music except its effect: its result as heard. It is therefore pure nonsense, and a mark of insufficient insight, to lay down rules beforehand with which music is to comply, or by its adherence to or rejection of which it is to be ticketed good or bad music. The ear is the ultimate appeal. There is no such thing as music in theory apart from music in practice: there is musical taste, and no other law. Teach harmony for years: you will never enable the disciple to create music: on the other hand, genius will laugh at all rules, in music as in war. It is true that genius will be a slave to those rules which really are laws of music: it is true that every genius has the technicalities of his art at his fingers' ends. But how does he learn how to employ these technicalities? Instinct, and the co-ordinating power of genius, which enables him to separate a musical whole into its parts, to assign to each part its function, to combine all into a unity, all this is not in the rules. For what else is musical theory and rule, but a deduction arrived at by the analysis of the works of great composers? But who taught them the rules? And does not all art furnish in its history instances or cases where certain rules were held to be such erroneously, till genius came to throw them away? Genius acts always in the same way: it masters its subjects: then it goes to work in its own way, using instinctively what is good, neglecting what is bad: but neither in music, nor in any other art, can mere technical excellence make a work good. For just as the Sabbath was made for man, and not man for the Sabbath : so does music determine its technique, and not technique the music. Good music will be technically excellent, but not for that reason will it be good music. It is good music, because it achieves its end : has its due effect upon the ear of the listener : and as what will rouse one to madness, or melt him into tears, will leave another cold, it follows that there is no such thing as music, in an absolute sense. And the reason for this is, that the essence of music is not actual, but potential. Its power is essentially conditioned by the nature of its correlative, the listener : lies, that is to say, not in itself, but another. Only in relation to this other can it actually become music : take him away, and it is music no longer. And this is peculiar to music ; for all other arts can achieve their actual result independently of any appreciation : but music alone, till it meets its appropriate respondent, remains merely potential : φωνᾶντα συνέτοισι.

Had this essential potentiality of the musical art been remembered, had the essential correlation between music and men been steadily recollected, a great deal of misunderstanding and dispute would have been avoided. Πάντων ῥυθμῶν μέτρον ἄνθρωπος,—men select by instinct the music that is congenial to them. National music follows the national character. And what is true of nations is equally true of individual men. According as they lean by nature to gaiety or melancholy, to sordid pleasure or sublime contemplation, to cheap and sensual gratification or soaring ambi-

tion, to simplicity or grandeur, to love or war,
so will they turn to Mozart or Chopin, music-hall
ditties or Handel, Strauss or Wagner, old ballads
or Beethoven, Anthea or the Marseillaise. There
is more cant in music and musical professions than
in any art in the world. Nineteen out of twenty
persons who flock to musical performances go there
for reasons other than musical. Some go because
it is the thing: some to admire feats of musical
gymnastics; some, because they have nothing else
to do: some simply to say they have been:
some because they are taken: some, to flirt or
make love : how few, from really musical attraction.
And of all arts, music is the one which may say
from its heart, God preserve me from my friends.
To acquire a tolerable mechanical and soulless
proficiency, learn up the technique, and talk musical
shop, is the easiest thing in the world, and the most
insufferable : in general you may measure a real
musical taste by its absolute silence on all these
points. Of all arts, music can least bear profana-
tion, and yet of all it is the most profaned. From
the glib technicalities and fatal prestidigitation of
the 'musical' young man or maiden, Good Lord,
deliver us : such is the heartfelt prayer of every one
who has a real love of music in his soul.

Music, appealing directly to the feelings, does not
require words, which can only reach the feelings
through the imagination, and do not really add
anything to the effect. Every piece of music is a
song without words : while every tale told in words is
only a special illustration of what music gives us in
general. For music, unlike words, speaks in
a language which is understood by all. Words

are the variations : music, the theme : and to every theme there are innumerable possible variations. In the song, appropriate words furnish a running commentary upon the text of the music. The opera is merely a higher and more elaborate power of the song. The aim of opera is to combine music with a special dramatic illustration of that passion which it expresses in general, and so make music and dramatic action reciprocally interpret each other. The essential merit of opera lies in the fidelity with which the music strikes as it were the keynote of the passion which is specially exemplified in the drama : the music being to the action just what the law is to a special case. Of all musicians, Wagner most fully realised this true function of operatic music. For the highest function of music is to interpret the highest and most sublime characters, emotions, or passions : and these are to be found ready to hand in the old heroic legend. How admirably was the joyous gaiety of Mozart suited to catch the spirit of *Figaro*, the adroit, ready, universal versatile barber of Beaumarchais! How marvellously has Bizet expressed in his *Carmen* the desperate sacrifice of military glory to love that takes all and then betrays : the note of inexpressible sadness and remorse, as of one who has staked his all upon a card which has failed, and wittingly fallen into error which his fate makes it impossible to repair! Or look, again, at Tanhäuser, the most beautiful of all legends, interpreted as none but Wagner could have interpreted it. Poorly do those critics understand their trade, who have objected to this opera that it is sensual. Sensual! why, the very keynote of the legend is the conflict between the sensual and the spiritual element in man! Throughout the whole runs the infinite solemnity of the Middle Ages. The remorse of the sinner, the chorus of Pilgrims, the martial ardour of nobility, the sublime purity of Wolframo and Elizabeth, especially as rendered in that most exquisite of all unearthly human songs, the greeting of Wolframo to the Evening Star; the bitter repentance of Tanhäuser. How infinitely sublime the legend! how deep, how serious, how unutterably solemn, and yet alluring, the music! what bewildering sorcery, what ineffable disappointment, disillusionment and remorse, does not the music of Tanhäuser reveal to us! This is the peculiar prerogative of genius, that it rises everywhere equal to its subject.

Music, as it is the most divine of the arts, so does it stand in certain respects at a disadvantage: it has always to be executed, and must therefore always be received through a secondary medium, and not direct from the hands of its creator. In this respect it resembles the work of the dramatic poet. How great, then, the disadvantages of opera: for here all, actors, voices, instruments, drama, scenery or setting and music, must all work together to produce the effect; and small wonder that excellence should be rare, where it depends on such a multitude of well-nigh incompatible components. Fine singers are rarely good actors: setting is costly: again, there are few operas in which there is not much padding, in which there is not much that is wearisome and non-essential: hence opera must always remain more of an ideal than a real. Remembering this, we should always be thankful to genius for giving us so much, rather than apt to cavil for that we have not more : and this, which holds in all art, is above all true of music, and especially of opera. For to attain perfection in this kind requires the combination of so many different sorts of genius and talent, that we should count it a special favour of the gods, when all its components are so happily suited as even to approximate to success. No other work of genius requires anything but genius to achieve it : but here genius can do nothing, unless luck assists it. And therein lies the innate and original defect in all opera. For just because it is so infinitely hard, it can but seldom attain its end : whereas music of other kinds, songs, fantasies, sonatas, oratorios, and so on, being less dependent upon accessories and combination, can within their sphere best hit the mark they aim at. And therefore in general we enjoy these far more than indifferent opera : for in them the purely musical effect is not ruined and rendered impotent by jarring accompaniments. *Corruptio optimi pessima.* Perhaps no artist ever felt a more desperate sense of the distance between what he would have done and what he could actually effect, than Wagner. Imagination can conceive nothing surpassing the ideal opera, the perfect and pre-established harmony between dramatic action and musical commentary : yet what more grotesque caricature of this ideal could there be than some attempts to realise it?

VIII. Lastly, we have still to consider literature, an art which from its infinite variety is more easily described than defined. Its field is the whole world of the real, as well as the infinite world of the imaginary. In general, its aim is to reveal to us by means of language the nature of the world and man, macrocosm and microcosm, either actual or potential : and according to the manner in which it seeks to do this, it assumes, broadly speaking, the forms of history, poetry, and philosophy. History describes the real ; philosophy endeavours to explain or interpret it ; while poetry pictures the imaginary or ideal. Such are their several appropriate functions. But, inasmuch as human nature is the medium and basis of them all, and men can rarely, perhaps never, entirely separate the real and the imaginary, each of them is coloured by and partakes of the other two. There is no history which has not an admixture of the poetical and philosophical : no philosophy untinctured by history and poetry : no poetry that is not also historical and philosophical. For the three are in reality but different faces of one and the same idol, which is man himself, or his surroundings. Thus shall we often find that the poet is most historical then, when most poetical : the historian most real, when most poetical : the philosopher then most truly philosophical, when both historical and poetical. For all attempts to analyse and discriminate, to separate and isolate in order to know, do in reality divorce things from their concrete relations, which are all in life inextricably blended together. Such attempts can never be more than hints, which the wise will understand, but out of which the fool will compose arbitrary mosaics, in which strong dividing lines must always appear, that are unknown in nature.

The proper function of history is simply to narrate : to describe things as they are or were, adding nothing of its own. In the sphere of Nature, as Natural History, it collects the facts on which philosophy and science are based : heaps up a thesaurus of material for science to reduce to order and explain. But as the proper study of mankind is man, so history proper has come to signify the annals of mankind : and according as the account deals with the state or nation or one man, it appears either as history or biography. The latter, if related by the man himself, is autobiography : the former may take many forms according as it confines itself to bare narration, or partakes more or less largely of philosophy, by adopting special points of view. From the ethical point of view biography, above all autobiography, is infinitely more valuable than any history : nay, even from the political standpoint, a really good biography is deeper than any history can ever be. For we must have the history, to understand the biography ; that is, we get the former in the latter : whereas history, under the influence of false political and philosophical theories, is wont to smother, disregard, and eliminate the biographical element, the influence and bearing of particular men, the special characters of significant actors, in history.

History is, or should be, the mirror of politics : it is the record of the actions and fortunes of men combined in political groups or societies. Now, every political event is the outcome of *all* the forces tending to produce it. To leave out even one will falsify to a certain extent the historical account. These forces, now, may roughly be divided into two kinds : first, the large general influences or

conditions affecting the great mass of the men concerned : and secondly, the particular characters,
motives and genius of the principle leaders in the
political life of the time considered. To omit
either element is equally unscientific. But two
one-sided schools of history have done just this
in modern times. One school ridicules the influence of individual character, and ascribes every
result to the action of great general forces alone :
another, known as the ' great man theory ' neglects
the general causes, and seeks to concentrate the
historical gaze exclusively upon great individual
characters. Both these extreme views are easily
seen to be superficial. It is just as certain, *e.g.*
that Napoleon could never have played his Imperial
part, except coming when he did in a period of
revolutionary agitation, *i.e.* that the great man
requires to suit his times; as on the other hand
it is, that the absence of a special and peculiar
character would often have changed history, as *e.g.*
Themistocles at Salamis, Henry VIII. in England,
or Peter the Great in Russia. We see, too, the
same thing still better negatively : for example,
had Charles II. had a son, the Duke of York
would not have come to the throne, and then
where would the Revolution have been ? Without
Mahomet, what were Islam ? What, if Clive had
never gone to India, or been ill at the moment
when he marched on Arcot ? If Hasdrubal had
not been defeated on the Metaurus, or if Fabius
Cunctator had died, before the time came for his
policy to save Rome ? In fact, any one who really
views history with a philosophic eye can see, in
general, that history is a resultant not merely, as

the Bishop of Chester says, of the national character, the national institutions, and foreign influences, but of all these in combination with another factor, the special character of prominent or
influential individual men. For example, Fred-
erick the Great, or Bismarck, in Prussia : Peel,
in England. And it is to be observed, that the
special character on which all turns is by no means
necessarily a great man : he may be a very particularly small one. For small men are like small
states, which, according to Christina of Sweden,
are impotent to do good, but potent for mischief.

But there is a still deeper point of view, which
shows us from the strictly scientific and biological
standpoint how much history has been falsified by
necessitarian philosophers, who have endeavoured
to apply to history the mathematico-mechanical
method : *not distinguishing the various senses of
the term necessity.* These philosophers, in fact,
do not understand that distinction between *absolute*
material necessity, and *conditional* organic necessity,
which we endeavoured to analyse and unravel in
the first Book of this work, which to misunderstand is to misunderstand all, and therefore it is
necessary to recall it here. Where our historical
salvation is concerned, no apology is required for
a little vain repetition. Aristotle alone explicitly
understood and stated this : it is the cardinal fact
in him : though the same thing is latent in the
Origin of Species. The essential distinction, then,
as stated in his own incomparable way by Aristotle, is this : things are determined, or follow,
with absolute necessity, from that which *is :* they
are determined, with conditional necessity, from

that which *is to be*. The former is the law of the material world, *quá* material : the latter, of the organic world, *quá* organic. Matter cannot help itself, it cannot be other than it is : but organic bodies can very easily be other than they are. Viewed as a mere lump or congeries of matter, it is all one whether the human body, for example, is fed, starved, ragged or clothed, warm or cold : whether it remains whole, or is cut in two, and tastefully disposed on opposite sides of a bridge. Dead or alive, whatever happens, it must obey the laws of its material constituent particles, as such. But *if* it is to remain whole, *i.e.* with a view to a certain condition of its organic nature, certain extra necessities, conditional on this required form, arise. If it is to work and function, it must eat, drink, and so forth. This is the great organic law, known only to Aristotle, that STRUCTURE depends on and is determined by the necessities of FUNC-TION. Now, states are organic bodies, and what the senses and intellect are to the organic body, that are special characters and special political heads to the state. This may continue to exist as a state, or it may perish. But *if* it is to con-tinue as such, political necessities arise which must be fulfilled and obeyed. *Adaptation is necessary.* But now, these political necessities may or may not be understood by the men at the head of affairs. When there are able men to comprehend them, and adapt their measures to them, the state flourishes : when there are not, not. And accord-ingly it follows from the deepest organic point of view, that history depends essentially upon individual character. Look, for example, at Poland, in 1772.

Its existence, as a state, was threatened : *if* it was to preserve its life, certain political changes were imperatively necessary. The Czartoriski family saw this, and laboured to save it : but they met with opposition from other nobles which neutralised their efforts, and so Poland fell. Look at Russia. If, at a certain period, she was to regain her freedom, from the Tartar yoke, certain action became necessary. Ivan the Great was the man who comprehended the situation and did the deed. So did Louis XI. in France. Or take an opposite case. In 1792, if Prussia were to rise, Poland had to be kept down. ' Möllendorf said, what every Prus-
' sian without any exception of party will say, that
' this country (Prussia) can never acquiesce in the
' establishment of a good government in Poland,
' since in a short time it would rise to a very
' decided superiority[1].' Nor indeed is it necessary to multiply instances. This 'political necessity' is the soul of history, and every practical statesman knows only too well what it means. When it is correctly comprehended and obeyed, the nation flourishes : if not, it suffers or decays : and this all depends on the wisdom or unwisdom of its rulers [m]. How then could history be truly interpreted by modern historical philosophers who are entirely ignorant of this conditional organic ne-

---

[1] See Fyffe's *Modern Europe*, i. 35. Despatch of Eden from Berlin, July 17, 1792.

[m] ' Financial difficulties may lead, and have often led, to
' great historical results. But by a single blunder in the conduct
' of our foreign affairs, the most provident arrangements of the
' finances ever planned may in a moment be cancelled or
' destroyed.' *Speech of Disraeli in* 1868.

cessity, as the ultimate political law; and therefore endeavour to apply to history the principle of absolute material necessity; thus necessarily obscuring and neglecting the paramount influence exerted by individuals over the march of events and the national welfare?

Now, this explains why it is that political genius can do without experience. The knowledge that tells us how to use experience, as Bacon says, is more valuable than experience itself. Knowledge of history, in itself, is just as likely to lead the statesman wrong as right, because he may argue falsely from cases that are not entirely parallel to his own. It is not experience, but reason, and intuition, that make the true statesman. The necessity follows from the nature of the case, i.e. if a knife is to cut, it must be sharp: if the state is to flourish, it must *be* or *act* thus or thus. The argument in the head of the statesman is not mere *probability*, derived from observation of similar cases in the past (which may be deceptive analogies), but *necessity*, derived from intuitive comprehension of the needs and possibilities of the state in the present : and this can only be discerned by native genius, eye, and insight. It was not experience that taught Themistocles his policy : it was not experience that taught Kozma Minin or Joan of Arc : Cæsar and Hannibal, Stein and Bismarck drew not their inspiration from experience. A real statesman does not study history to accumulate *cases* more or less alike, but to discover the *method*, the way in which statesmen of a previous generation have seen and met their political problems.

History does not furnish models, but hints : the statesman, like all other artists, does not imitate results, but processes. Just so, the true historian is the man who understands and exposes these political necessities, and the way in which they were or were not seen and provided for : such are Thucydides, Commines, Polybius, Macchiavelli, Mommsen, Rulhiére, the Cardinal de Retz, Ranke, Brewer, Sismondi, and others who have appreciated this primary function of the historian. On the other hand, such historians as Tacitus, Buckle, Carlyle, Froude, Macaulay, Hallam, whatever be their merits in other departments, have not the dimmest idea of it. They are thinking about style, 'laws,' Providence, literary effect, party, and similar nonsense : they teach us no political knowledge at all. And this is why the letters, despatches, and biographies of statesmen, either written by themselves, or by other statesmen (meaning by that term those only who are capable of discerning these necessities), are more valuable than any histories : such as the letters of Napoleon, Disraeli's *Life of Bentinck*, Bolingbroke's Works, the letters of Christina of Sweden (one of the greatest of statesmen, although a woman), and many others. In general it is worthy of notice, how the average intellect, which is quite incapable of appreciating any political necessities at all, derives no political instruction at all from history ; it does not ask this from historians, but turns by preference to the writings of 'historians' who aim at literary or sensational effect, or the establishment of some religious or political theory : all of which are loathsome to the true historical critic. Literary, philosophical, ethical, dramatic, religious, sensational—all this kind of history and biography is, compared with real political history, comparatively easy, and much more to the taste of the vulgar than the genuine article, which is only savoury to those who are looking for it, who ask from it that which it can, and its imitators cannot give. Thus a really great historian is infinitely rare, because he must combine the tact and insight of the statesman with the diligence of an antiquary and yet be without ambition. Style is altogether a secondary object : but now we put it first. For everybody can tell approximately what a style is ; but not one in a thousand critics has any political insight at all. Aristotle says admirably of style, in words which are true to-day ; ' the ancients wrote πολιτικῶς, but the moderns ' ῥητορικῶς : ' that is, they were thinking of realities, and the style came of itself, suited itself to these : but we are thinking of theories, or even the style itself, and with the result that is before us : form without spirit : flabby verbiage, thin, frigid commonplace, stereotyped, phraseological and unreal.

Poetry may be roughly divided into lyric or meditative, epic or narrative, and dramatic, and has probably been developed in this order, originating perhaps in songs and hymns to the gods. The function of lyric poetry is to depict words and emotions as such ; of epic, to tell stories ; of dramatic, to make the stories tell themselves, by action. Poetry is commonly felt to be somehow or other essentially connected with rhythm, metre, and rhyme, and distinguished, in this respect, from

prose. Nevertheless, this condition is not really
essential to poetry, as such. Regarded as creative,
poetry may just as well be prose or rhyme: the
original meaning of *poetry* being just our old word
'*making:*' for example, Spenser praises Chaucer
for his 'excellent skill in making.' We shall be
less inclined to make a difficulty of this if we
recollect that poetry was originally intended to
be spoken or chanted, not written and read: it
appealed to the ear, not the eye: hence Homer's
ἔπεα πτερόεντα. Under these conditions, it would
obviously gain immensely by being metrical: this
necessity, on the other hand, becomes less of a
necessity, as in course of time poetry directed
its appeal rather to the eye than the ear. Accordingly, early poetry and those forms which
represent early and original poetry, and still con-
serve early tendencies, seem still to require the
aid of metre and rhyme in a more peculiarly essential manner than others: whereas narrative and
dramatic poetry are no longer thought to be essentially bound up with rhyme and metre: and these
do, in fact, gain in freedom, even if they lose
otherwise, by neglecting it. For rhyme and metre,
though they add powerfully to effect, yet hamper
simplicity and directness, by imposing restrictions.
Indeed it is partly just the feeling of the consummate art with which these restrictions have
been surmounted that leads us to value good
metrical poetry so highly. Further, metre facilitates quotation and memory, besides having something pleasing in itself. So too has an old style
which has completely disappeared, yet in its day
was regarded as the great beauty of poetry, I

mean alliteration. Still, as life grows prosaic, and
art realistic, narrative or dramatic poetry in rhyme
or metre strikes us with a certain feeling of unreality and contradiction, and so these tend ever
more and more to be written in prose. In fact,
no rule is possible in this matter. Poetical genius
will instinctively discern the form suited to its
matter.

Lyric poetry, understood widely, includes both
passionate and contemplative or meditative feeling : the emotional outpourings of Burns and
Shelley, and the calm perception of Goethe or
Wordsworth. The excellence of this sort of
poetry lies in its unity and intensity, combined
with beauty of expression. It goes of course
without saying that the negative condition of all
effect is that the feeling shall be sincere. Sincerity
is no positive poetical qualification ; but insincerity
makes all poetry impossible, and will ruin it,
though the poet had every other gift in perfection.
The perfect sincerity of many an old anonymous
lyric makes up for all that it may otherwise lack :
much modern poetry, on the other hand, is destroyed by this want alone. Exquisite examples
of the lyric are, for instance, Goethe's *Kennst du
das Land :* Wordsworth's *The world is too much
with us :* Shelley's *Lines to an Indian Air :* the
songs of Burns and Shakspeare : the odes of
Catullus, and so on., And this kind of poetry
will always preserve in a sense a sort of claim
to be poetry proper : for here the poet gives vent
to his uncontrolled yearning and passionate long-
ing, or enshrines as it were in a golden phial some
divine glimpse that he has caught of the inner

light, some quintessential drop of imaginative insight embodied in words of perennial charm. The briefer, the better for unity: to be short is here above all a virtue : and no poetry has ever understood this better than some of the incomparable epitaphs in the Greek anthology. The Arabians too, to judge from translations, seem to have been masters in this kind : many of the little scraps of poetry scattered through the Arabian Nights possess a quiet, melancholy charm all their own : as an example, I may instance the lines in the exquisitely beautiful story of Azeez and Azeezeh, about the tomb in the garden of red anemones.

Epic, or narrative poetry, though in qualitative intensity it does not compare with lyric, yet requires a more fertile and various imaginative power. The story teller in all ages has been everybody's favourite, from Homer and the Arabian Nights down to Mr. Rudyard Kipling. Now the way a story is told is half the story. Who does not know how often a story is spoiled in the telling ? Or who does not think, at the very mention of story telling, of Homer and Herodotus —for Herodotus is an epic poet—of the Arabian Nights, of the Middle Age Romances and the Norse Sagas, of Sir Walter Scott, of Alexandre Dumas, of Charles Kingsley,—for in these was the spirit of the old epic ? But some one will say : epic poetry ? and where then are Vergil, Milton, Dante ? Although it may seem somewhat paradoxical, none the less is it true, that these are not epic poets at all. To suppose so, is to mistake the letter of epic for its spirit. The epic spirit

does not lie in its metrical form, but in its heroic
action.   Indeed, Shakspeare is more truly epic
than either Vergil, Milton, or Dante.   The essence
of epic is life and action.   Homer's first aim was
to tell his tale, and the form in which he conveyed
it was determined by the necessities of the time,
and the nature of his audience.   But these authors
pedantically cling to a form that has no longer any
inward justification : it is no longer living, but
arbitrary and imitative.   Hence, whatever else
they may be, the *Divina Commedia, Paradise
Lost*, or the *Æneid*, are not epic poetry.   The
spirit of action is not in them : they smack of
antiquity, artificiality, imitation, learning, pedantry ;
they do not rest upon broad and deep popular
sympathies, but appeal only to special culture.
Licentious and degraded as he was, Petronius had
more of the true epic in him than Vergil :
Hudibras, though inverse and ironical and grotesque, is far more the epic of its age than *Paradise Lost*.   In such an age as the nineteenth
century, even to attempt 'epic poetry' is proof
positive that you are no epic poet.   The true
epic of our age is to be found in the writers who
throw aside the letter to attain the spirit : in
Westward Ho ! or *Hereward the Wake*, or *The
Heroes*, we discern the old Homeric and Scan-
dinavian ring.   And indeed, Kingsley came within
an ace of being a very great man indeed.   The
hot old fiery life of the heroes stirred within
him, and ran down into his pen : he is half a
pagan : he chants : his prose runs into rhythmic
harmonies, while our hearts beat, and our eyes
redden : his pages ring with battle-shouts and

mighty deeds of derring-do. But his Protestant prejudices are ruin to his art. On the other hand, *Paradise Lost* is a kind of lyrical exposition of the Bible, with reminiscences of the British House of Commons, and the debates therein : the *Æneid* a vile soulless piece of pedantic imitation, the work of a scholar who never had a spark of battle or strife in his composition : the *Divina Commedia*, intense and passionate as it is, is nevertheless an epic *à rebours :* related to the true epic spirit of heroic action just as asceticism and religious meditation are related to the full energetic assertion of life. Yet the man who has not within him a genuine instinct for action, a sympathy with adventurous daring as the true end of life, will always be apt to place these artificially cultured blossoms higher than the genuine wildflower : for on the one hand simple stories of great and noble action will not touch him, while on the other he will like the contemplative attitude, the critical meditation, the associations of learning, and so on, that he finds in the 'literary epic :' this in reality means that he prefers lyric to epic poetry : or may be due to old associations, which are more powerful than anything in determining literary taste. In his case the word 'epic' is but a word and nothing more.

Dramatic poetry is epic raised one step higher : in the former, the narrator tells the story : in the latter, the narrator disappears, and the actors speak for themselves. But in true drama, where all is before our eye, there is this disadvantage, that much that can be imagined cannot be represented. All kinds of impossibilities may pass muster, if

cleverly managed, in a narrative which would immediately appear ridiculous on the actual stage.
Horrors, which excite pity or terror in imagination, would if enacted disgust us : *nec coram populo.*
Similarly, the imagination can feign more cunningly
than any scene painter, and has, in fact, in every
direction, a freer scope. Therefore there are
limitations in drama which do not confine narrative, and accordingly to succeed in this field is
hard : above all in tragedy. For in this, whatever
is not sublime is ridiculous : whereas in comedy,
the ridiculous, even if unintentional, does not spoil
but assists the effect. Anything is good which
raises laughter. Therefore it is that there are hun-
dreds of good comedies for one good tragedy.
Further, all characters, high or low, are fit subjects for ridicule : so possible is it in this world to
raise a laugh at all things in heaven and earth ; so
essentially has Vanity marked us for her own. But
how few are the characters that command our admiration or deserve our pity ! This is why Aristotle said that great characters are alone suited for
tragedy. He was thinking of a tragic effect in
which there should be nothing mean or sordid, no
admixture of the grotesque, no element of humour,
still less of comic, but pure, sublime, dignified :
Prometheus Bound or Agamemnon. This was
the character of ancient tragedy, at the critical
moment of which no one must feel inclined to laugh,
but sit overawed and terrified at the mysteries of
fate. And therefore the subjects had to be choice :
the characters had to be something passing the
limit, overstepping common measures. But modern tragedy, though indeed it turns by pre-

ities of Kings and Queens and persons of high
degree, yet—shall we say spoils or heightens?—
the effect of the catastrophe by placing the sublime
and the ridiculous side by side. Horror becomes
grotesque : here is Death the Antic, scoffing at
State and mocking at Courts : suffering not his
victims even of the highest rank to fall with dignity. There indeed is the sting : *ridiculos facit.*
Could even the most heroic hero die superior to
the shocks of fate, did he but know the pitiable
figure he cannot choose but cut?

The function of the tragic differs from that of
the comic poet only in that they appeal to different
emotions[n]. The aim of tragedy is to rouse our
awe, pity, or sorrow : that of comedy, to make us
laugh. But they do this both in the same way :
the function of both is to hold the mirror up to
nature, the nature of man : to reveal to us life and
the world, by combining significant characters in
a common action, or a common catastrophe. The
characters are not an end but a means : the end is
the working out of the action or plot. Just as the
end of the Iliad is to work out the Wrath of
Achilles, that of the Odyssey, the return of Odys-
seus ; so the end of Othello is to reveal the suicide
of jealousy : of Macbeth, the wages of crime : of
Julius Cæsar, the murder of Cæsar : of Coriolanus, the fall of pride : of Romeo and Juliet, the

[n] In Plato's Symposium, Socrates endeavours to convince
his drunken companions that the same man will be best both
in tragedy and comedy : a result which was not verified till
Shakspeare, but is thoroughly correct.

course of true love : of King Lear, the misfortunes
of virtue : of Richard III., ambition ; and so
on. Tragedy, just because it is serious, must be
much more of a unity than Comedy. Comedy,
therefore, can neglect the end for the means, and
turn off to side issues : it can thus accentuate its
characters and develop them out of connection with
the main plot, and so is more varied, democratic,
and inconsequent : finishing up perhaps with nothing at all : ending in smoke : as you like it, what
you will, a comedy of errors, much ado about
nothing. All this is quite proper to Comedy, but
fatal to Tragedy. Tragedy must have a definite
and necessary issue, essentially arising out of the
main action, or else it is nugatory, and there is no
tragic effect. Therefore a comedy may be, in itself, a very bad one, yet act very well on the stage,
if all the actors are very good, for their own characters will carry it off : but this will not serve in
tragedy : the play must be tragic in its quality, or
no acting, however admirable, can make it so.
Similarly, to act tolerably in comic scenes is very
easy, for any exaggeration, idiosyncrasy, or originality will chime in and perhaps happily suit-the
effect : but to play tragedy well is hard, for here the
actor must play up to his part, and hit the right
mark, strike the true chord, or he will spoil all.
In comedy, he may remain himself : in tragedy, he
must impersonate his proper character, or the whole
play will be ridiculous. The tragedy and its author
are more than its actors : these are but interpreters :
but in comedy, the author may be nothing, or very
little, and the actors all. For there are a thousand
ways of making people laugh, but there is only one

way of making them weep or shudder : you must stab them to the heart with iron truth.

Therefore consummate excellence in tragedy is rightly regarded as the supreme gift of genius, for it requires not merely the deepest knowledge of men, which many have possessed, but the power of making characters express their nature in action, which is a very different matter, and few indeed have been able to achieve it : so much so, indeed, that Shakspeare is in this field what Aristotle is in another, not merely first, but all: he stands alone. The Greek tragedians, indeed, worked on magnificent material. But what they really give us is ethical legends expressed quasi-dramatically and lyrically : they convey a moral lesson, in metrical form, but the dramatic element is an altogether secondary and subordinate matter : regarded as dramatic, the Greek tragedies sink altogether into insignificance, however sublimely the ethical tone may be pitched. The effect, e.g., of the Agamemnon or the Prometheus Bound lies in the idea, not in any dramatic element, nor in the dramatic form : this is often altogether ridiculous, both as regards the Chorus and the puerile στιχομυθία. In fact, we must approach the Greek tragedies from quite another point of view than the dramatic, if we are not to find them absurd. They are elaborate cameos from Greek mythology. Aristophanes had more of Shakspearian exuberant fancy and action than any of the Greeks : but then he is not a tragedian. Calderon's tragedies, again, are religious and philosophical allegories : so too is Goethe's Faust, which dramatically regarded is altogether ludicrous : all that is best in it is taken from Marlowe and spoiled in the taking, for the true spirit of Faust, rebellion, anarchy, presumptuous daring, Satanic pride, was in Marlowe, and was not in Goethe, cold, pedantical, egoistic prig that he was ; as a critic, superb : as a man, unendurable. As to French tragedians, the mathematician who asked with a shrug of Racine's Iphigenie *Qu'est-ce que cela prouve ?* appears to have been much misunderstood : he was no doubt an admirable literary critic with a turn for caustic humour, and meant in this malicious question to paint the general spirit of French tragedies. For certainly they resemble nothing so much as theses written to prove a point. Their characters do not act, they harangue to each other, and deliver ethical orations : they express ethical sentiment in general but show no sign of it in particular. And it is curiously instructive to see how Moliere does precisely the same, whenever he attempts anything higher than Plautian burlesque and buffoonery. His *Avare,* his *Tartuffe,* and his *Misanthrope* act at all moments with a logical and pre-established avarice, hypocrisy, and misanthropy : on each character we seem to see a paper ticket, *I am a wicked miser,* a *vile hypocrite* or whatever it may be, hanging round the neck : the plays are rigid, syllogistic, mathematical deductions from the ideas: we feel quite safe : we know that every time the characters appear they will open their mouths and utter some general and undeniable proposition respecting their own character, while never once *acting* like the true character they represent. Moliere's *intention* is that they shall be hypocritical, avaricious, and so forth : we can see that : and so the characters have to do their best to appear so : but it is all humbug : they are not really anything of the kind : the author had not the very slightest dramatic power of presenting character through its manifestation in action ; his only method, therefore, is necessarily to make them talk the talk. In fact, the French dramatists have never understood the one essential precondition of all dramatic exhibition of character : viz. that in life men do not as a rule *know themselves*, and hence a man's discourse is almost always in exact antagonism to his action : he does not know his own motives. His character appears not in, but through, his words. French tragedy, in fact, is a feeble and misplaced imitation of Greek, without the deep religious ethical sentiment or poetical expression. It is thus neither one thing nor the other, and vile, like all imitation. The essence of dramatic power lies in expressing the required effect through the action, and not by means of moral sublimities or declamations : the spectator must not feel that the dramatist *wishes* to produce this or that effect, that it is *designed,* but the effect must evolve itself spontaneously and naturally out of the situations, to which the words ought to be in entire subordination, as though suggested by the events, and the whole should spring naturally from the play of character and its motives under given circumstances. And all this depends on the *dramatic grasp* in the poet, that organising imagination which is the cardinal power and requisite alike in the musical composer and the statesman, the architect and the general. A tragedy should be not a line, but a solid concrete whole : no thin abstract, but a many-sided reality. The test of a real dramatic mastery over character is this : that the characters should appear to possess, just as they do in life, innumerable *potentialities* in other directions and of other significance than those which are actually called into play : they ought not to leave upon us the impression of having been created with capacities for *this particular occasion only :* with only just one set of qualities each, all different : they should have infinite possibilities in them : then we feel the reality and the effect is true. Just because Shakspeare knew this, are his effects so powerful : he is *the* tragedian. Where shall we find anything to compare with the effect of Macbeth's terrible ejaculations to the ghost of Banquo at the banquet ? any parallel, however distant, to Lear's funeral orations over Cordelia ? any conclusion so heartrending as Othello's ? any outburst like that of Coriolanus to the mob ? any eloquence like Antony's ? any overwrought frenzied fury like that of Hamlet unable to control himself in the player-scene ? Where is the LIFE in other dramatists ? Why, Shakspeare is different from the others not only in degree but in kind : he is altogether of a different species : he is not in the same intellectual plane. He and Aristotle are the Great Twin Brethren : the one gives the intuitive and poetical expression, the other the scientific and philosophical explanation, of that truth which is the heart of reality. For just as Aristotle saw that power is deeper and more fundamental than act ; that the capacities and possibilities of doing are more than any particular result done : so did Shakspeare achieve his triumphs through his instinctive

perception of this. Only because he understood
character in its powers, capacities, and infinite
possibilities was he able to create such true, natural and unspeakably touching *particular* effects.
Whereas other dramatists, not having this instinctive knowledge of the potentialities of character, but
imitating as well as possible definite special results,
only succeed in producing thin, frigid, abstract and
arbitrary compositions, which we may applaud, but
with cold hearts. For if you prick them, they do
not bleed : only sawdust or stuffing runs from their
staring seams.

It follows necessarily from the very nature of
tragedy that it can only flourish in an age whose
sympathies are with great action, the correlative
of which is great passion : and must fade away,
degenerate and disappear in an age of sensational
pleasure-seeking, nihilism, middle-class envy and
social equality. '*La democratie, c'est l'envie.*'
There are no great men now : what would be
the use of them ? they are *de trop*, kept out
of the ring by the sharp-sighted cunning of oligarchical officialism and the votaries of Red Tape.
*Si quelqu'un excelle parmi nous, qu'il aille exceller
ailleurs*, says the prophet. There is no more
adventure, no high endeavour, nothing to do worth
doing : the hum-drum existence of bourgeois business and pleasure swallows up all, sucks all into
its vortex : every nature not congenial to this
condition, not after this type, is considered to be
mad : and thus as a rule subsides into irony,
sarcasm, *insouciance*, cynical *dolce far niente*. In
such an atmosphere tragedy is impossible. Great
men were, in the old days, everything : now, they

are only fools. Their chief use was, little as they
could have guessed it, to bring grist to the mill
of the future publisher, who should employ legions
of small men to reveal to the world big ones, in
half-crown volumes with fancy covers, all in a
series. Great warriors and statesmen, prophets
and philosophers, are here reduced to scale : one
inch to a mile. Men of iron will and superhuman genius are expounded to us by 'rational'
milksops and 'judicious' pedants, for whom every
man of action feels a contempt that is not loud but
deep : your Strafford and your Wolsey, your Wallenstein or your Graham of Claverhouse are here
gravely called up, hectored, lectured and dismissed,
patted on the back or it may be reproved, by mild-
mannered, civil-spoken, drawing-room, tea-party,
ethical, economical, æsthetical, metaphysical, gastro-
nomical gentlemen, nay, even ladies—ladies! without any the faintest suspicion that there is anything
ironical, anything discrepant, in the business. All is
as it should be in this best of all possible worlds.
O boue humaine ! And is tragedy to be written
in an age like this? is tragedy a flower that will
spring in the soil of mock humility, hypocrisy and
moral cowardice? The buskin will never flourish
on the stage, where the mask has left the stage for
real life. '*Souvenez vous seulement, et n'oubliez
'jamais, que la pitié, le bonheur, et la vertu, de même
'que la patrie, la religion et l'amour, sont des
'masques . . . De quelle religion êtes vous ?—
'Oubliez votre foi, et par sagesse devenez athée.'*
    Certainly, in such an age, tragedy is not *à
propos*. But if, then, we ask ourselves what form
of literature is best adapted for its expression, in

what direction we must look for its characteristic literary outcome :—if it be true, as it certainly is true, that structure follows function :—the answer is, the *novel.* The novel is to our own age what the plays of Shakspeare were to one, the poems of Homer to another : the literary expression and reflex of its endeavour. It is a kind of combination of the epic and dramatic forms, adapted to the needs of a sedentary age that has been educated, i.e. taught to read. It is a mistake to confound the novel proper with the romance or the tale. The primary aim of the latter is to tell a story, and its field is the unknown : story teller and story listener alike turn by preference to distant ages and far-off climes, to marvels and adventures : they love the picturesque and the bizarre, they delight in local colour and peculiar character. The excellence of this kind lies, in short, in constructive imagination and simplicity of style. With the novel, it is quite otherwise. The true function of the novel is not imaginative but critical : it aims at interpreting common life. What we demand of the novel is precisely Touchstone's query : Hast any philosophy in thee, shepherd? The good novel, whatever be its subject, is that which embodies deep and genuine criticism : conveyed by means of pictures of common life. But observe, that the function of the novel is not to reflect, to photograph, but to interpret. Even when it reflects, it does more : it reflects reflectively : and in this, though it were unaccompanied by a single word, lies the criticism. The bad novel, which, if we go by majority, the modern law of truth and justice, may essentially claim the name of novel for its own, is just the novel without its *raison d'être :* the form without the spirit; shell without kernel. It gives us a perfectly commonplace story, varied by far-fetched absurdities, with nothing whatever below : no significance, no criticism, appealing to its reader on no grounds whatever exept the resemblance of its author and its characters to themselves : it deals with cheap sentiment,—the sentiment of the drawing-room song, —births, marriages, and deaths : perhaps horses : if it is very daring, a little tame illicit love-making gives it a fatal fascination for school girls, maiden aunts, and the clientéle of the circulating library. The name of this novel is legion : its safety is in numbers : it is simply a means of killing time, a preservative against ennui : an instrument by which publishers and circulating libraries make their living. Any human being can produce this sort of thing who has a pen and paper, and an interest in his own existence, its eating and drinking, flirting and sporting. Neither in the production nor the consumption of this species of ' Wealth ' is there any element of the æsthetic or critical : the emotions it appeals to and the interests it springs from are purely personal : like those of the sportsman or epicure looking at a dead partridge. These novels are wealth in one sense, and the very reverse in another. They are commodities, and if it be their function to sell well perhaps they are more valuable to the publisher than the good would be : for these are rare, whereas novels are many, and numbers carry the day. The lower you go down, the more general you make your appeal, the larger will the golden harvest be. The biggest fortunes made in trade are those that minister to the commonest and most vulgar desires : hence monster shows, cheap illustrated papers, and so forth. This tendency of commercial societies to twist the true function of all the arts into the single one of making money was long ago noticed by Aristotle : it must of course lead to degradation, for money can only be made by following the dictates of the multitude. That is to say, the artist abandons his Psyche, and worships *Venus Venalis et Vaga.*

The true novel, the novel which is determined not by the desire of notoriety, nor the need of dollars, nor the personal likings and dislikings of writers and readers, but the critical appreciation of life is very different from its bastard imposture. A good novel is one of the highest forms of art. Jane Austen and Turgenieff, Scott and Dostoyeffsky, Lord Beaconsfield and Tolstoi exhibit to us in various ways the novelist's faculty at its highest power. This faculty is simply that of seizing, and having the power to present imaginatively, human life in all its forms from an æsthetic or critical point of view. The attitude of the author to his work is the first characteristic of real genius in the field : the second is, that the work should be essentially realistic : the third, that it should display, as its essential underlying note, that quality which appears now as humour, now as irony, now as sarcasm or bitter satire, according to the native spirit of the writer. All these three points are in reality different sides of the same fact, but nevertheless distinct sides. A few words on each point will make the meaning clearer.

The first point, the attitude of the author to his work, is of all the most difficult to describe in words, and yet most undeniable in fact. Authors of marked originality in every respect never attain to it. It lies not in but behind the words : and it cannot be acquired : you have it, or not. This critical attitude, which is essential to all art, is above all manifested in the novel and the drama. We have only to think of Dostoyeffsky, or Scott, in connection with Balzac or Thackeray, to feel it at once. The latter authors are not superior to their characters : they sympathise with them : but this is fatal. A really great artist preserves a wholly independent relation to his characters. There is no sentimentality whatever in a great artist : there always is, in the writings of lesser men. The true artist looks at men not as one of them, nor with the eye of curiosity, but critically. He loses himself in their creation, yet always retains in his work that undefinable superiority, as of a Demiurgus to his creatures. Of all novelists, Scott and Turgenièff are the most perfect artists : Dostoyeffsky and Lord Beaconsfield the deepest critics.

And this brings us to realism. Nothing is more curiously misunderstood than the meaning of realism. What is Realism ? Mr. Howells is right in judging the Russians to be the greatest masters of realism in the world, but his criticism and his imitation show us that he does not understand in what realism consists : its method. Realism is not photography. Exact and photographic servile imitation of gestures and mannerisms will not produce any but pre-Raphaelitic, e.g. pseudo real-

ism. Realism rests, not upon the imitation of
results but the comprehension of methods : upon
the intuitive perception of concrete realities ; and
imagination, not imitation, alone can give it. The
realistic artist can select with unerring instinct
those features, material or psychological, which are
essential to any required effect ; on which it
depends. He can see, not because he has an
eye, but because he knows what to look for, knows
beforehand how things are done. Copying will not
reach it. Balzac and Thackeray seem realistic
enough to a crude observer, but they are not : their
scenes and treatment are all abstractions. Zola
is not a realist, but merely a sensational dauber.
Realism does not lie in piling up the horrors of
real life : neither does it consist in keeping very
close to common life : the most ideal picture in
the world may be more realistic than anything in
Zola. Realism consists in grasping the correspondence between structure and function : it knows
that everything is, by its relations to other things :
and it understands how to present all that it presents in just those relations which are essential.
It understands how surroundings act upon the
mind and its moods. It understands accident,
and the part it plays in life. It understands the
association of ideas. It never gives us abstractions. It looks not at one side only of any event :
but understands it all round : alike what is there,
and what is conspicuous by its absence. Thus
it can produce positive results by negative
methods : it can describe, for example, by touches
in no way apparently connected with the subject
in hand, *which would not occur to an unimaginative*

copyist [0], because it comprehends the organic relation between all the component elements of an
effect, and can foresee, from its knowledge of
human nature, what any special character would
do under given conditions. Sympathetic intuition
is the faculty which does the miracle: and this
is merely a synonym for realism. The most
exhaustive description which was ever elaborated
and written down by Balzac, or one of his school,
cannot touch us so near as a suggestive line or
epithet used by Dostoyeffsky or Disraeli: for the
first is only observation and photography, the last
is psychological divination, imagination, black art.
A story told by a true artist never seems consciously designed: it happens, just as in life: it
presents itself as a series of undesigned coinci-
dences: we experience no feeling of constructive
design in perusing Scott or Tolstoi: all is natural,
real, and so, impressive: for where the story is
obviously constructed, it disgusts us: we feel
intention and are put out of tune: there is deception. The artist is not a *composer:* he is a seer,
and he relates visions. Every one capable of
appreciating good work will understand what is
meant: those who are not need not puzzle over
it: they can read their Balzac or whatever it be
in peace: there is room in the world for all.
But as instances, take, for example, the chapter
entitled '*Among us*' in '*Demons:*' the questioning
of Madge Wildfire, in the '*Heart of Midlothian:*'
the death of Bazaroff, in '*Fathers and Sons:*' the
opening chapters of '*War and Peace:*' any scene
in which Mrs. Norris appears in *Mansfield Park:*

[0] For example Lear's, *Pray you, undo this button,* is realism.

or any scene in *Tancred*, especially the latter half.

Lastly, that humour, which is the finest flower of literature, infinitely deeper and broader than the mere sparkle and conceit, superficial and verbal play of wit, springs out of the combination of the critical attitude and the realistic treatment, and lies not in the words, but in the sentiment underlying the actions represented : it is felt and not seen. Always subtle, it takes many different forms. In Jane Austen and Sir Walter Scott it is genial and playful : in Turgenieff, sad : in Disraeli, it becomes bitter, withering irony : in Dostoyeffsky, the deepest of all, malicious indescribable satire : his characters are nearly always tragic, yet usually forced into grotesqueness by the comedy of errors : the ineffable ridiculousness of humanity even in its misfortunes rises before us : and yet he says no word to that effect. His humour stabs. In Tolstoi, humour is replaced by mystical seriousness. There is nothing 'funny' about authors like these ; we do not smile, much less laugh, in reading them. A laugh has always something vulgar in it : laughter is foreign to art. Just for that reason art can never be popular : and this is why we turn from all these authors, now and again, with a sense of relief, to the buffoon. *Ernst ist das Leben:* the artist who works at it must approach it seriously, and so must its spectators. We find in the absurd and the farcical, in caricature and grotesque fancy, in Dickens or Mark Twain, or clowns of all kinds, the very opposite of art : the Saturnalia of æsthetics : and we love them just for that reason. They represent the unbending of the bow. But they can lay no claim to be art. The very lowest conceivable conception of art is that which demands from it amusement. *Amusement!* People who ask only for amusement should let art alone. Life may be better than art, but the two things are not the same, and those who prefer life to art will always be the majority. The artist, however, does the reverse : he is a fool : he subordinates life to his art : he is always in dire and bitter earnest, and probably is not given to laughing. He never makes a joke of his art—*to himself.* To subordinate his art to the claims of life : to turn it from the expression of ideals into the means of amusement,—as if he cared about amusing the people !—this would indeed be the wisdom of the 'sensible man,' but for the artist, it would be the sin against the Holy Ghost. What are other people or their business or pleasure to him, save exasperating interruptions that waste his time and break the thread of his imagination ?

Remains only, that we should consider the subject of philosophy. But inasmuch as this whole book is an essay on the subject, little need be said about it in this place. It goes without saying to any one who has followed me thus far, that I regard Aristotle as the only philosopher who ever really understood the economy of nature. And this he did because of his method : because he was no mere phraseologist : because his whole philosophy was based upon a deep enquiry into biology, or the science of life. Only in comparatively recent times have we regained the evidence that places us upon the platform to appreciate him. Before his time, nothing was known about the economy of nature. After his time, the world sank back into barbarism : and the philosophers of the Middle Ages and of modern times, who endeavoured to refound philosophy, did so without the necessary scientific basis. It is only since 1801, the year in which Lamarck proposed the word *Biology* to denote the whole science of life, that the Aristotelian point of view has been gradually regained : and, mainly through the agency of Darwin's *Origin of Species* has his logic of science been re-established. For in biology lies the key to all natural and political economy : and this is just the thesis of this essay.

And now, having passed in review the productions of art, let us pause to take stock. Here is a whole mass of Wealth, whose value is certainly not to be measured by its cost of production, or the demand for it. Here there can be no talk of 'homogeneous human labour,' of Capital and Interest, of Wages and Profits, Diminishing Returns, Machinery, Combination or Division of Labour. Yet are not the productions of art wealth, and that in the highest sense of the word? Do they not make life better, nay, are they not its choicest flowers, without which life would be but a bare and disgusting workshop? Who is there into whose life these do not enter in large proportion? Shall we reckon up our wealth, and omit this? Why, what is life, but a series of actions, enjoyments, memories and reminiscences? for as action sinks into memory at last, so does it issue from and depend upon memory at the outset. Memory is the condition of all : and while it composes at least half of man's life, it makes up

certainly two-thirds of woman's. What then are
the stores of memory? To whom are we indebted
for the marvellous panorama which history and
legend roll out before us? Whom have we to
thank for the countless visions that brighten the
dull background of existence, but the artist? The
paintings and the sculptures, the buildings and the
music, the poetry and the history and the philosophy of Egypt and Assyria, Greece and Rome,
England and France, Scandinavia and Germany,
Spain, Italy, Russia, Arabia, and others—are these
nothing in the tale of wealth? Will machinery
or human labour evolve you these? Are the
accumulated wisdom and the accumulated beauty
of ages to be left out of account, when we calculate
our Wealth, because they are not subject to the
ordinary laws of demand and supply, prices, profits,
wages and all other economic categories? These
things not Wealth: why, they are Wealth in the
supreme sense : and yet we are told with unutterable gravity, by economists, that the essence of
Wealth is Labour, or Exchange Value. No mention of the Idea that gives form to the matter : no
account of the fiery consuming heart's Desire, that
gives birth to the Idea.

But, as we have seen, this, and this only, is the
difference between the Work of Art and the Commodity : that the former requires, for its production, both labour, genius, and demand, nay even
material, of a special and superior kind. The
Work of Art is merely the Commodity, raised to
a high power ; nor can any definition of wealth be
framed which shall include the Commodity and
exclude the Work of Art.

BOOK IV.

ETHICS AND POLITICS, OR THE COMMONWEALTH.
THE PRINCIPLE WORKING IN THE MORAL AND
POLTICAL SPHERE.

ἕνεκα ἄρα θατέρου θάτερον.

Phys. Ausc., ii. 8.

BOOK IV.

I. In any attempt to arrive at scientific conclusions in matters ethical and political, we should be equally on our guard against two opposite errors, both equally fatal to a right appreciation of the truth, which here, as always, lies in the middle between extremes. The one has been the vice of the predominant political theories of modern times, and it lies in ignoring the fact that the economy of nature is the basis of the economy of man : that 'man,' though the highest, is nevertheless an animal, an organic being, and subject therefore to the general laws of organic nature, whatever else of special may be peculiar to him. Artificial schemes of political economy, arising in an age completely ignorant of the true relation of man to his 'poor cousins in the country,' could not fail to go entirely astray. But conversely, modern speculation has tended to throw us into an error on the opposite extreme. In their anxiety to prove man an animal, modern philosophers have often forgotten that he is indeed an animal, but something more. Some part of him is his own. Evolutionists nearly always make this mistake : Aristotle never did.

Though we must never overlook the resemblances between things that are different, still less must we forget the differences. The differences, just because they are differences, are the most important. Man is no God, but neither is he a beast : and mysticism shows us that it is just when he is most inclined to fancy himself a God that he becomes most of a beast. And in fact, Aristotle, in whom nearly all modern difficulties are anticipated, and many solved, actually found it necessary to make this very objection to one of Plato's wild delusions : ' It is preposterous,' he says, ' to have recourse to ' beasts, in this case, as if they were to be a model ' for man[a].' But this is a favourite proceeding of the divine Plato, and it is precisely the assumption that lies under much speculation, ethical or economical, of the present day. But it is a false and degrading argument : better never trace the higher back to the lower, better to discard the investigation of origins altogether, if it is only to lead to the confusion of the higher with the lower, of result with origin : a method equally false in science and fatal in practice.

Consider, for example, Nature's scheme. Nature knows nothing of morality. She is individual, physical, essentially *immoral*, if we may, by anti-cipation, apply to her a conception which as yet has not been evolved. ' I will have mercy and not ' sacrifice,' is a law unknown to plants and animals. Nature says, on the contrary, I will have sacrifice, and no mercy. No quarter. *Opfer fallen hier.* What qualities does she favour in this world of

---

[a] Politics, ii. 5.

battle, of strife, of force, where the weakest must go to the wall, and all must live by their wits ?

> All kinds of creatures stand or fall,
> By strength of prowess, or of wit.
>
> .   .   .   .   .
>
> For why ? because the good old rule
> Sufficeth them, the simple plan
> That they should take who have the power,
> And they should keep who can.

Nature loves injury, wrong, fraud, hypocrisy, trickery and deception, outrage and spoliation : every means that will ensure success, and preserve the individual at the expense of other lives. Thus her politics are essentially Liberal and Anarchical. Robbers, thieves, murderers, misers, gluttons, torturers, hypocrites,—hawks, tigers, sharks, ants, crayfish, snakes, ichneumon flies, dragon flies, praying mantides, spiders, and lions—these are specimens of Dame Nature's dear darlings. The God of Nature is the Devil of Man. In that region of unrestricted competition, might makes right ; ἡ φύσις δαιμονία ἀλλ' οὐ θεία, says the Oracle. In that demonic whirlpool of struggles for life, there is no honour. There it is, that, according to the old Greek satirist, Zeus having ceased to exist, or rather never having come into being, in his place King Vortex reigns supreme. His subjects, the creatures of Nature, what are they but living weapons, constructed for strife, attack or defence. Heraclitus is right. Strife made them, and strife is the breath of their nostrils. Strife is the father of things.

Here, then, we can clearly discern the nature of

that radical error which is the heart of the Liberal theory of politics : a theory which has dominated the political speculations and the historical practice of the last three hundred years.

The essence of this theory is identical with that of the theory of knowledge and the theory of being refuted in the First Book. It is essentially individualistic, and founded on a misunderstanding of the nature of man. In fact, it substitutes rationalistic individuals for real men : eviscerating these, alike of their physical and moral *character*. The Cartesian *Cogito ergo sum* is the starting-point of moral and political as well as logical nihilism. In every department of the philosophy of human life and action, the true starting-point must be not logical but biological : but of biology Descartes knew nothing. He did not only know nothing, but he did not even know that he knew nothing : he never suspected his deficiency : he gravely proceeded, none the less, to erect Dogmatic theories of human nature without possessing any essential information on the subject. But if we excuse Descartes for condemning what was totally above his comprehension, and attempting to base explanation upon and solve the problems of the organic world by a superficial rationalistic quibble, denying, such was his fundamental principle, everything he could not distinctly conceive (the cloven foot of the *mathematician :* as if, forsooth ! we were to deny digestion, or any fact of the kind, because we do not understand how it is done !) that excuse cannot be extended to the miserable pettifoggers of our own day, who still continue in an age of comparative physiological enlightenment

to ring the changes on his old dictum (θεσεις
ληκυθίζειν) and exhaust the patience of the world,
while they degrade its philosophical reputation, by
the *crambe repetita* of their thin ideological pseudo-
philosophies.

When Descartes asserted, at the very outset of
his Meditations, that the whole scheme of existing
knowledge had to be torn up by the roots, it did
not occur to him that he was violating the whole
of his own principles at a sweep when he went on,
after this sceptical preliminary, to lay down
a positive dogma of the highest grade as to the
nature of man. He began by doubting, and ended
by believing, all: this well-known epigram is as
true as it is pointed. If he was so ignorant as all
that, he ought to have seen the propriety, on his
own principles, of *restraining the will* and *refraining* from dogmatising on subjects of which the very
elements were unknown to him. How could he
fail to see the absurdity of a man self-confessedly
ignorant of all the facts of nature immediately proceeding to lay down positive dogmas as to the
essential nature, of all things in the world, of his
soul! Is there anything in all philosophical literature to equal the monstrous absurdity and arrogance
of his *Cogito ergo sum:* always of course assuming
that it is not mere truism? That marvellous
miraculous problem which stands at the summit of
organic nature, and pervades it all, of which only
a long biological preparation can enable us to see
the difficulty, much less to explain, is settled by
our ready reckoner in a trice. Thinking, the last
and highest function, the apex of organic nature,
the rarest and most valuable capacity of man, is

turned by a *presto !* into his essence. Every fragment of his nature, except that, is cut away,
ignored [b]. I think, by all means, but I who think
am a man, and what is a man? *Nescio,* says
Descartes : an animal, says Aristotle, but the
highest. Just so, says Darwin : and with Darwin
we regain what we loved long since, but have lost
awhile, our moral and organic nature, and the true
method of investigating it, which Aristotle carried
at one bound to the pinnacle of possibility. We
get back man as an organic being, man as a *political animal.* We get back, instead of the rational,
the real. We get back the whole world, the world
of action and passion and creation. Where is it,
where can it be, in the Cartesian system? Most
significant is it, that the Cartesians should have
accused Newton of introducing unknown causes
into nature : he did, in truth, introduce the first x,
the first element of the real, into mathematics.
Why is it that the last of the Cartesians, the
nihilist Schopenhauer, commends himself to us
as of all his school the best thinker? the man ' who
' had seen the world?' Because he has at least
established the paramount, the omnipotent power

[b] Aristotle would have disposed of Descartes, and exposed
the superficial quibble very shortly by adding to his *Cogito ergo
sum—quâ cogitans.* But how about me, not *quâ* thinking, but
quâ acting, loving, being, and suffering, *quâ* living and dying,
quâ growing and begetting? Cogitating, my dear Descartes,
may persuade you of your own existence, but it will not do
us much good. It is a description, no explanation at all.
A fine explanation, indeed, which places the explanation of
the fact in the fact to be explained ! This the death of metaphysics !—why, it is the perpetuation of it. So little does
Comte understand the logic of science.

of the *other* side of man, the self-will as well as the conscious ego : because he has rooted his philosophy in the heart rather than the head : in the organic depths rather than the superior shallows. And who shall say nay to him ? Is not the self-will of the cogitator far more essential to him than his thought ? Schopenhauer's great work is, indeed, on the strictly physical side, open to criticism. But if we put this aside, and confine ourselves to the human and ethical meaning of the word ' World,' then we may fairly say that the ' *World as Will* '*and Mind-Picture* ' is the quintessence of all ethics and religions : the still mirror of this transitory life, with all its trouble, sorrow, pain and sickness. What, forsooth, is the reason, the conscious, and self-conscious self, but a mere weapon 'in the hands 'of the Will ? ' That is Schopenhauer, and that is Darwin. *Cogito ergo sum :* what, being, thinking ? no indeed, being is doing : everything *is* as it does, and because it does: *esse* is not *percipi : percipi* is only a particular sort of *esse ;* ESSE is AGERE. This is Aristotle, and all Creation is on his side. *Opinionum commenta delet dies: naturæ judicia confirmat.* Time which obliterates the fictions of Descartes, ratifies and approves the judgment of Aristotle.

Descartes had indeed a dim perception of his own fallacy. ' *Ainsi je m'imaginai que les peuples* ' *qui ayant été autrefois demi-sauvages et ne s'étant* ' *civilisés que peu à peu n'ont fait leurs lois qu' à* ' *mésure que l'incommodité des crimes et des querelles* ' *les y a contraints ne sauraient être si bien policés que* ' *ceux qui dès le commencement qu'ils se sont assemblés* ' *ont observé les constitutions de quelque prudent* '*legislateur.*' In this passage of his *Discourse on Method* he indicates the political tendency of his own principle, namely that the thing to do is to revolutionise from the bottom, and reconstitute on arbitrary principles. Not organic growth (of which he knew nothing) but arbitrary creation :— there is the Cartesian, the Rousseauesque revolutionary scheme. But it strikes him dimly that there is danger ahead here. '*La seule resolution de se* '*défaire de toutes les opinions qu'on a reçues aupara-* '*vant en sa créance n'est pas un exemple que chacun* '*doit suivre.*' And, he continues, as the world is composed of two sorts of persons, the one sober and modest, the other apt to believe themselves more clever than they are, and without patience, (*Cogito ergo sum* did not give Descartes, after all, self-knowledge, for here he paints himself exactly ;) these '*s'ils avaient une fois pris la liberté de douter* '*les principes qu'ils ont reçues et de s'écarter du chemin* '*commun, jamais ils ne pourraient tenir le sentier* '*qu'il faut prendre pour aller plus droit, et demeurer-* '*aient égarés toute leur vie*^c.'

Most true, indeed : not every one is a safe subject for the Cartesian catharsis : to emancipate oneself totally from all one's received and inborn customs, beliefs, and what not, is not an example that every one should follow. Unfortunately, each of us considers himself exempt from the prohibition, the one man in a million who can adopt this process without danger. Hence, the Cartesian method logically issues in absolute isolation, negation, abstraction. The individual stands alone amidst the chaos of the world : a vanishing unit : a speck

<hr>

^c This is precisely the theme of Dostoyeffsky's '*Demons.*'

of self-consciousness, without a tie to link him to the fleeting shadows that crowd around him. Instead of constituting a link in the moral and physical chain of relations, the percipient subject stands in *no* relation : it is absolute, and all its surroundings, its neighbours, depend upon it. And here it is, that as if to give the lie to these abstractions, up from under the rationalistic rises the real egoism. The individual consciousness having determined thus satisfactorily that it is itself the only reality, puffs away its prejudices, like a child dismissing its fear of ghosts, and proceeds to assert its Self and its own existence to the denial and exclusion of others. Behind the Self of consciousness arises the Self of will. In this lies the true foundation of the principle of unrestricted competition : a principle which is not the salvation, but the utter destruction of any state in the world.

Thus we find that the Cartesian rationalistic position coincides in logical result with that which identifies man with the brutes : though they start from opposite ends of the abstract method. Descartes, by drawing a magic circle around the rationalistic speck at the summit of the organism, cuts the individual off from any moral or political relations, and reduces the world to the play of isolated egoisms : just as, on the other hand, by entirely neglecting the special nature of man, and attending solely to his animal nature which is indeed the basis, but only the basis, of his being, the evolutionary struggle for existence levels him to that out of which he has arisen. Both systems err in mistaking the nature of man, and both come to the

c c

logical conclusion: war of all against all, and the
Devil take the hindmost.

And this leads us naturally to the consideration
of the political system of Hobbes, who is the original founder of the Social Contract theory, and
out of whom modern rationalist politicasters, Rousseau and the rest of the troop, have but quarried.
Upon the foundation of this war of all against all,
which Hobbes maintained to be the ' natural ' state
of man, depends his theory : viz. that in order to
escape the evils of this miserable condition, in
which the life of man is and must be ' nasty, mean,
' poor, brutish, and short,' men have long ago entered
into a compact and sold their birthright of liberty
for a mess of pottage : i.e. resigned the absolute
authority into the hands of one who shall be responsible for keeping the peace.   ' For men natur-
' ally love liberty *and dominion over others :*' it is this
last half of the sentence that the Revolutionary
theorist never remembers.   Therefore having given
up their power, they have no longer any power to
escape from the terms of the compact, and may
therefore never rebel.   All that their collective
representative may do, is RIGHT, and they must
obey.

But who is to determine when the sovereign has
broken the contract ?   This was the dangerous
question that lurked in the speculations of Hobbes.
And his opponents drew from his-own theory consequences the very opposite of his own.   They
decided that ' the people' (under which meaningless abstraction, fit only to beguile ' the people,'
crouch all kinds of villainous usurpations) might
expel a sovereign who had broken the contract.

The sovereign people should decide the matter. And accordingly it is this theory which has really been a primary cause of the history of the last two hundred years. Within Descartes' abstraction and the Hobbesian rationalistic compact was hidden the egg, out of which in due time should develop Russell's right of resistance and Carrier's panegyric upon 'insurrection, holy insurrection :' and all that infernal and arrogant, equally foolish and insane Whig politics, which ends by converting men from peaceable citizens into rebels when out of office and despots when in it. The philosophy of revolution, as displayed in the history of Europe, has yet to be written. It is uniform. In 1640, in 1688, in 1789, in 1825, in 1832, in 1871, the process is precisely similar. Under the screen of principles the most entirely virtuous, high-sounding, patriotic, philanthropic, philosophic, a gang of knaves, using folly as a stalking - horse, cunningly cloaks nefarious dynastical designs. The sin of the Stuarts was not that they were bad kings, for they were not : their crime was that they were kings at all. The opposition to them was not created by their evil deeds : but anticipated them : it was *a priori*, and its strength lay in the fact that it rested on a theory. It was composed partly of men who really believed in their theory, and aimed at 'freedom,' i.e. the substitution of a republican for a monarchical form of government, not knowing, owing to a want of political insight, that a republic is not a more free, but a less free, form of government than a monarchy, and only another name for the jobberies of an interested clique : and partly of men who knew this only too well ; who had their own aims in view, who wished to encroach upon the supreme authority and substitute for *one* king, whose interest was in the main identical with that of the nation, *many* kings, not called kings, whose interest was very different from that of the whole : who aimed under cover of the ambiguous cloak of the word 'people' to hide their design of usurping the royal authority, and freeing themselves from irksome restraint. The Revolution was actually based by its authors on the theory of an original contract. *Civil and religious liberty!* These were but the banners flaunted in the air to deceive the general eye. Religion never stood in greater need of reformation than when it had been reformed by the reformers : liberty was never less enjoyed by the 'people' than after that 'kings 'having been driven out, consuls,' i.e. the Whig oligarchy, had been created, and the reign of liberty inaugurated. It was not their factious opponents, it was the Stuarts who were the real supporters of civil and religious liberty : their destruction inaugurated the advent of civil and religious despotism. They fell because they strove to prevent a minority, an enthusiastic party of bigots and self-seekers from forcing their despotic views and interests upon the nation : but these last succeeded in throwing the colour of good over the evil : of making the worse appear the better cause. Shaftesbury is the true type of the Whig, forcing on theoretical politics by playing on the passions of the multitude. The theory is specious, but the practice iniquitous. Jacob the supplanter is obliged to clothe himself in the skins of Esau. Kings might err, but their representatives might betray. But theory alone, though it may afford a specious pretext, will never ensure the success of a revolutionary attempt. There was more behind. Both in the French and the English revolution the cry of liberty was but the watchword of a rising interest. Theory, to get itself adopted, requires to chime in with the interest of a minority, but a coming party. The law of history, unnoticed by every writer except Aristotle, who knew it well, is just this : *that the potential strives to become actual.* Under cover of a popular theory the Whig oligarchy and the banking interest in 1688, the commercial and manufacturing interest in 1832 and 1846, crept into power.

The theory of a social contract is now exploded : everybody has been taught to look upon it with an appropriate contempt. But it seems to have escaped observation that there really was a relative justification for Hobbes, if not Rousseau. Curiously enough, the theory was not all theory. A state of war, and a social contract : well, that was, almost exactly, the feudal system. Dr. Cunningham tells us : ' The feudal system of England was therefore ' one of contract between the King as centre of ' the whole, and each of his tenants [d].' He speaks of it, again, as 'a national system of defence on ' a basis of contract.' Sir William Anson tells us that 'the Feudal System was a contract in which ' the fidelity of the subject was the consideration ' for a promise of good government by the King,' and again, ' Feudalism invested the relation of ' King and subject with a contractual character [e].' So, too, Ranke says, ' Whether men's union in

[d] *Growth of English Industry and Commerce,* vol. i. p. 115.

[e] *The Crown,* pp. 7, 8.

' a State in general depends on an original contract
' is a question for political theorists, and to them
' we leave its solution. On the other hand, how-
' ever, it might well be maintained that the English
' constitution as it gradually shaped itself assumed
' the character of a contract.' And again, ' ever
' since the times of Magna Charta there had
' always been in the English constitution an ele-
' ment which had the character of a compact : and
' never had this appeared in a stronger form than
' that which it assumed in the Settlement (of 1688).
' Definite rights were reserved : definite expecta-
' tions expressed : on these conditions the crown
' was offered and accepted [f].' And much similar
evidence might be accumulated, were it necessary.
Hence as it seems, the Hobbesian theory of a contract was not so historically ridiculous as some
have pronounced it.

His theory, in fact, as to a natural state of war,
and a social compact, is not so much historically
as philosophically wrong. Its radical failure was
the misunderstanding of human nature. Man is
not an individualistic but a social animal [g]. A political animal is the definition of man. And this was
the fundamental doctrine of Aristotle respecting
man. The state, he says, is a natural institution,
if, that is to say,—and the limitative addition shows

---

[f] Ranke, *History of England, Eng. Trans.*, i. 56, and iv. 518.

[g] Here lies the gist of Hobbes' error. He starts from the
abstract individual and binds the individuals together only
by a rationalistic contract. But as Aristotle would say, the
sentiment of community is not λογικὸν but φυσικὸν—*i.e.* the
community is the prior, and the individual only appears by
differentiation from the community.

us what a cautious thinker Aristotle was,—*if* the original communities out of which it arose were so too. Now, in some cases, this is not the fact. The Norman Conquest had swept over England, and introduced the element, not of φύσις but of βία and ἀντίφυσις. And here lay just the amount of justification for Hobbes' theory of a contract. Nevertheless, though there was this slender justification for Hobbes, still his theory fails just because it is theory : it is arbitrary : it is not according to the scheme of nature. Hobbes confounds men with animals. He misunderstands human nature : a thorough and accurate comprehension of which must be at the base of all sound political theory. It is true that we may maintain, not without reason, that man is naturally an enemy to man. So, too, may we maintain, with equal reason, the exact contrary, that man is naturally a friend to man. The fact is that these theories are too vague : we must be more particular.

II. Man is the measure of all things : of the things that are, how they are : of those that are not, how they are not. This is politically the sum total of human wisdom ; if it be properly understood. 'Man,' 'humanity,' is a mere abstraction : it is non-existent : but there are men. Now, who ever found a man living in isolation ? Men always exist in States or Communities. Isolated, man is the weakest of animals : just because it is union that constitutes his force. Language proves it. For what is language ? simply the power of *communication*, that is to say the precondition of forming *concerted plans*. Hence the mere fact that he talks proves undisputably that man always was a

social animal.   For an isolated individual needs not
to communicate ; his strength lies in himself.   Just,
therefore, because language is essentially the *exter-
nality*, the *imparting to another*, the *sharing* or *community* of thought, Descartes' position becomes
utterly ridiculous.   For the fact proves that the
essential nature of man lies not in himself but in his
relation with others : that he IS, *by means of and for
the sake of others*.   Language is thus not only the
strongest weapon of man, but the irrefragable refutation of abstract individualistic, egoistic, nihilistic
theories.   Language is the bond of society, and is
essential to every human being.   It is fact which
completely upsets all the Descartes-Berkeley-Hume-
Kant-Schopenhauer-J. S. Mill philosophy.   For
the first problem of all philosophy is to harmonise
with and explain facts.

From the evidence of language alone, then, it
follows that the theory of Hobbes is as false as it is
true.   Man is a friend to his own kith and kin,
an enemy to strangers : that is the real universal
proposition.   The man of whom Aristotle speaks,
the ἀφρήτωρ, ἀθέμιστος, ἀνέστιος, is just what the
modern Scots used to call the ʻkinless loon :ʼ one
who had no relations, and hence no disposition
to show favour : Ishmael.   It is natural to man to
befriend his kind.   *Homo homini Deus* as well as
homo homini lupus.   Men are what they are,
because their neighbours are just what they are.
It is pure abstract nonsense to talk about individuals.   There are no such things in human
society.   When they seem to be individuals, men
are really lunatics, madmen : ἰδιῶται, *private
persons*, the Greeks called them, with that depth

of nomenclature which is only found in languages like the Greek, which enshrine the native aboriginal perceptions of things.

A man is an unintelligible abstraction, unless we qualify the general with specific limitations, either mentally or verbally: English men, French men, and so on. A man is what he is, only by reason of being one of a number. His native language alone goes far to making him the sort of man he is. Blood, race, or the principle of heredity, combined with circumstances, or the influences to which he is from his birth upwards subjected, whether of time, place, or companions, mould him to a special form. It is mere want of insight to suppose that argumentation based upon our common human nature, abstraction being made of its special qualifications, can lead to anything solid or in conformity with reality. It is the qualifying circumstances that determine the result. What then can possibly be more futile than theories of 'the State,' or 'Man' in general? Every State is essentially conditioned by its men, and again, no reasonings about men can ever begin till we know of what special sort of men we are to speak. Till then, it is all *ignoratio elenchi*. Are they English or Chinese, Greeks or Russians, Jews or Turks? Until we know this we know nothing, for it is only when we know what is the nature of the man's peculiar State and atmosphere that we can discern what is his function, and until we know what that is, we do not know anything essential about him.

Those who like logical accuracy and clearness may look at the matter in this way. The end of man is to DO, and in order to DO, he must MAKE,

and therefore also KNOW.   Hence according to the
conditions of his existence at any special time or
place, so must his doing, or activity, take its peculiar colour, and this will alike determine, and be
determined by, the nature of his making and knowing : his production and knowledge.   But the conditions are the masters of the whole.   They
constitute that ἀνάγκη τοῦ διὰ τί, that overruling,
tyrannical divinity, conditional necessity, that shapes
our ends, rough hew them how we will.   Under
such a system of things as obtained, for example, in
the eleventh century A.D., a man's doing was primarily determined in a military direction : his first
function was warlike ; for above all things he had
to preserve his life amidst a clattering *mêlée ;* it was
never safe for a moment.   Under modern conditions, all this is entirely changed : the difficulty is
rather to lose your life than to preserve it.   What
puerility, then, are all *abstract* theories of the State
or the Man : still more, the Individual !   Is it not
as clear as day that these theories can never so
much as win their way into public attention, except
in so far as they chime in with the needs of the
age ?   A theory succeeds when it fits the times, or
serves a turn.   Any one who supposes that the
abstract theories of Adam Smith, Karl Marx, John
Locke, Hobbes, Rousseau, and others succeeded
because the world was attracted by the *absolute*
truth in them still lacks the fundamental *aperçu*
in politics and philosophy : for there is only one
absolute truth : it is, that all structure is made such
by its function, a law which is higher or deeper
than all other truth, for even truth must conform
to it, or be neglected.   For Truth, even when it is

truth, is as a rule accepted not for that reason, but because of its services.

If then we consider that a State or Nation may be defined :—and here let me beg the reader to remember that it is only of *real* States or Nations that we are talking, and that in this matter only just such a degree of accuracy and determinateness is to be expected as the subject admits of, for very rigidly accurate definition is here impossible :—if, I say, we define a State or Nation as a number of men with their wives and children, who are actuated by the sentiment, grown up gradually [h] under the influence of time and place, of a half-real, half-imaginary *community* of language, religion, descent, sympathy, interest, action and passion, past and present : we shall, I think, see at once that everything for the individual man depends upon the nature and relations of his community in itself and to the world at large. Only from a thorough comprehension of this, from a full and clear comprehension of what sort of thing is the State or Nation of which he is a member, and *minus* which, apart from which, he is a non-entity, can we discover what is a man's special function, what is his DUTY. For this is the main point : a man's first duty is to his country. I say, to his country, for it is to his participation in the benefits derived from common union that he owes all that he is. Is it no birthright to be an Englishman [i] ? And on the

---

[h] στασιωτικὸν δὲ καὶ τὸ μὴ ὁμόφυλον, ἕως ἂν συμπνεύσῃ· ὥσπερ γὰρ οὐδ' ἐκ τοῦ τύχοντος πλήθους πόλις γίνεται, οὕτως οὐδ' ἐν τῷ τύχοντι χρόνῳ. *Pol.* v. 2. O prophetic soul of Aristotle, here is the epitome of the history of Ireland.

[i] Mr. Lecky (*Hist. Eng.* i. 178) says excellently well : 'All

contrary, the vain and shallow rhetoric about 'rights
' of man,' and ' our common human nature ' is seen
at once to begin at the wrong end : it is, scientifically, abstract nonsense, and morally, in ninety-
nine cases out of a hundred, either mere meaningless cant, or the cloak under which is disguised pure
egoism.   A man who has to feel such pan-humani-
tarian emotion will almost certainly end by caring
for nobody but number one.   The rights of man
and universal philanthropy are seen when closely
inspected to involve in practice the interests of
a handful of knaves, and that war of all against all,
against which and out of which it is that the culti-
vated policy of nations has come into existence.

For Function makes Structure : every institution
religious, legal, political, organical, has arisen in
answer to definite needs and grown : it is the product of the final necessity acting upon the original
arbitrary element furnished by chance or chaos.
For here, too, necessity can only form what is
supplied to her.   Natural Creation can only produce, like the bear, by licking her cubs into shape.

The *raison d'être* of the economical structure
of society was examined in the second Book,
and also in my *Principle of Wealth Creation :* and

' civic virtues, all the heroism and self-sacrifice of patriotism
' spring ultimately from the habit men acquire of regarding
' their nation as a great organic whole, identifying themselves
' with its fortunes in the past as well as in the present, and
' looking forward anxiously to its future destinies.'   And when
on a subsequent page, he tells us that ' stupidity is essentially
' Tory,' which is certainly true, he might have added with
equal truth that virtue, as well as wisdom and good government
are essentially Tory.   That which is the common basis of them
all is *habit.*   See below.

now I shall endeavour to illustrate the *political structure* by reference to the development of English constitutional history. Equally good, perhaps in some ways better, and more deeply interesting illustrations are furnished us elsewhere : but in a case of this kind it is perhaps well to remember the advice of Bacon : Read the ancients for what is best, the moderns for what is fittest. Nothing certainly could be more fit than for English people to know their own history : yet what has hitherto been presented to them as such is simply a monstrous caricature ; an elaborate and to a large extent deliberate lie. And that it should have been so, is merely a further proof and illustration of our cardinal truth. For the vicious political theory based upon rationalistic Liberalism has always naturally refused to read any history that contradicted it, and hence the preposterous and 'systematic' lying of historical writers, who all do but 'flatter the big beast,' and seek to curry favour with the public. But let us, on the contrary, ' conceal nothing out of a desire to ' curry favour, but make use of the actual facts.' For the rationalistic theoretic politics has this among other things of absurd in it : that nothing about it can endure. Only that can endure which is based upon realities : only that structure really built to answer necessary demands : only that can exist which is capable of doing its work : and on the contrary, no structure can ever be permanent which is rationalistic. For example, hard work and practice will make the arm of the blacksmith brawny, because his arm is here doing its proper work. But on the other hand the mutilation of the foot by the Chinese never tends to produce any lasting alteration; for this mutilating process is merely rationalistic : the structure it produces is arbitrary, which answers not to any end of the foot, but contradicts it : hence nature never takes any notice of the fact, but goes on reproducing feet after her own fashion, for the Chinese to whittle away at in their delusive possession. Just so is it with political institutions framed, not by the natural necessity of things, but in accordance with the arbitrary rational fancies of unpolitical mischief-makers and bigoted busybodies. For the very essence of *theory*, in the bad sense of that word, as opposed to fact, lies in the want of inner and spontaneous adaptation to necessity : e.g. a theoretic structure, such as Sir William Temple's Privy Council Scheme, or Siéyès Consulate, or many of the revolutionary governments of modern France, is framed apart on rational grounds, and then superimposed from outside and above upon the facts; and thus it can never endure : durability can only belong to a system dictated by the inner necessity of events. And this is just the difference between a good and bad statesman, Julius Cæsar and Plato. For the visionary and puerile laws and institutions of the latter, as well as those of all his school, though they present an appearance of great moral sublimity and deceive weak thinkers into insignificant applause, stand in direct contradiction to the essential tendencies of things in general, and the nature of men in particular, and hence no man of any political judgment ever took them seriously; whereas it was just his profound insight into the needs of the time that justified the usurpation of Julius Cæsar and gave permanence to the system inaugurated by him. For in human affairs there is, as it were, a logic, the logic of circumstance, the iron dictation of necessity, against which all attempts must split and shipwreck, which run counter to it : except in the case of those that are strong enough to master the circumstances contradicting them by the aid of military force. Yet even this, just because it is arbitrary, is always precarious. Thus Sulla's constitution fell to pieces, the moment after he was dead ; thus the Whig Revolution of 1688 tottered and staggered for fifty years after that a combination of fortunate accidents had established it : thus, too, Napoleon was in reality beaten by the fact that he went too far : up to a certain point he was the thing demanded by the circumstances ; but in going too far in his personal caprices he awoke against him the inner tendencies of events : the spirit of the age broke his dominion, strong though it was ; it slowly and ironically loosened, as it were, the desperate grasp he strove to tighten on the world, with irresistible force. He struggled in vain against a mighty impersonal agency to the existence of which he would fain have closed his eyes : but like Thor, lifting the whole earth, unknown to himself, or the Slavonic Svyatogor, struggling with the terrible Villager's Son, the fact that he could prevail even so far as he did, proved him to be of more than mortal strength.

If then we turn for illustration of the nature and origin of political institutions to English History, it is necessary to warn the reader at the outset, that he will not find the history of England in that school of historians who have hitherto made the

popular conception of English history: historians
whom it would be invidious to name. That school
of history to which the popular exponents of
English History belong is dominated by various
essential errors [k], which are all in essence resolvable
into a denial of the fundamental law of organic
economy, which it is the object of this book to
explain and illustrate, the law that function makes
structure. They have, to begin with, a fundamentally erroneous conception of the nature of society,
which at once vitiates all their political understanding. They divide Society into the King and the
People; as if all men but the Monarch were on the
same side, and homogeneous! as if all who opposed
and rebelled against the King were thereby necessarily on the side of the People! Whereas the truth
is that Monarchy has always been triple in its nature,
the King, the Nobles or Upper Classes, and the great
body of the common people. But owing to their
total failure to apprehend this obvious truth, these
historians fall into a fundamental political and historical error. They look upon the King as the
enemy of Liberty and the People; whereas the

[k] The political *niaiserie* of Hallam, Macaulay, and their
'constitutional' school is as naïve as their criminal lack of
social insight and sagacity. The artless ingenuity with which,
while totally ignoring the dynamical law of history, they
credit every party opposed to the King with large unselfish
public morality and zeal in the cause of 'the people' is too
amusing. The King is always a 'tyrant' and everything he
does 'tyranny:' a dark, mysterious libel-label which turns
all the good he does into evil. As if, forsooth, only Kings
could be tyrants! as if petty tyranny were not ten times worse
than anything the King could do! as if legitimate authority
is to be branded tyranny, and every insubordinate rebel a
sublime patriot!

truth is the exact contrary, the King is the natural ally and protector of the people, and it is the intermediate oligarchical party, which is hostile to both. Just because the King aims at enforcing equal justice on rich and poor, high and low alike, he incurs the enmity of the oligarchical party. They therefore proclaim him a tyrant, and spreading specious phrases over their real designs[1], they present their nefarious machinations against the supreme authority as being ' popular' in their tendency. Many a good King has lost his throne and gone down to history as a tyrant because he was not the enemy, but the friend, of justice, liberty and the people. Such were Pedro the Cruel, Charles the First, Mary Queen of Scots, and many another, and this is the key to the history of England, and especially that of the Stuarts. But the historians, totally blind to this, or deceived by lying authorities, actually mistake oligarchy for its

[1] ' The gloss of zeal for the public service is always spread ' over acts of oppression, and the people are sometimes made ' to consider that as a brilliant exertion of energy in their ' favour which when viewed in its true light would be found ' to inflict a fatal blow to their rights.' Edward Livingstone (quoted in Bryce's *American Commonwealth*). As for example, in 1215, 1832, 1846, 1792, 1688. ' The people' are always deceived.

Buckle, for example, would have us believe that the Stuart Kings of Scotland were destroyed by ' the people' to gain liberty. That the nobles who destroyed the King were not the people's allies, but their oppressors; that the King was the real friend of ' the people,' and their natural ally and protector against the wild turbulence of the great feudatories, never occurred to Buckle, and yet he thought himself a great historian! He is rather the *beau ideal* of knowing nineteenth-century self-ignorant omniscience.

opposite, popular government, and in writing the
history of England under this delusion give to
every political event of importance a false colour.
Everything becomes in their pages exactly what it
was not.   ' If there be one legislative quality more
' valuable than another it is the power of dis-
' criminating between the cause and the pretext.'
They utterly confound the cause and the pretext,
being utterly destitute of political insight : for
an antiquarian is one thing, and a historian another.
Hence the enemies of the true liberties of the
nation are panegyrised as its friends, and its friends
as its enemies : hence Wolsey and Charles I.,
Charles II. and Bolingbroke are denounced, while
Pym and Cromwell, Shaftesbury and William of
Orange are extolled as the champions of liberty.
Liberty! Yes, ' men do naturally love liberty, *and*
' *dominion over others :* ' pity, that the second half
of the aphorism, which throws so glaring a light on
the first, should be invariably forgotten by the partisans of licentious liberty.

And in close connection with this want of
political insight, this lack of comprehension and
understanding of abstract ' liberty,' is a heartrending ignorance of human nature.   Everything is
presented to us in what are called ' constitutional'
histories, or ' philosophies of history,' as happening
impersonally.   The pages of *e.g.* Hallam would lead
us to suppose that the King was a wicked and
' unconstitutional' plotter against the peace and
well-being of all his subjects, while the House
of Commons was a large, absolutely moral, absolutely united person, doing all with supernatural
wisdom, generosity, foresight, and self-abnegating

care for the interests of the people. That it was composed of many different individuals, each with his own end in view : that it might be at variance with itself : that it might be actuated by mean, bigoted, or sordid motives ; that it might be a tool in the hands of two or three artful Macchiavellian politicians: that these might be ambitious self-seekers and ambitious mischief-makers : that thus it might after all 'represent the nation' still less than the King, and be merely the '*instrumentum 'regni*' of a party or a class; that if Kings might abuse the prerogative, 'representatives' might betray their constituents ; that irresponsibility might be a failing of the House, no less than of the King ; that Parliamentary Government might be simply many Kings instead of one : that its interests might be in direct antagonism to those of 'the people :' that it might be ten times as despotic and tyrannical as the King : that 'arbitrary ' power' may be exercised by a knot of placemen in the pay of the ministers, no less than by the King :—all this and much more is conspicuous only by its absence in the pages of Hallam or Macaulay.

Certainly the rarest and most valuable of all qualities is the power of rightly interpreting facts : for upon this depends all science and all art, all prudence, all action, and all history worthy of the name. The fundamental necessity for any one who wishes to understand the history of England is to *unlearn the bad:* get rid of the delusion that people are any more free under a republic than a monarchy: throw to the winds the wretched sophism that the King is a wicked tyrant, and a usurper of the rights and liberties of 'the people.' The very contrary is the truth. We owe everything to our Kings. The King is the original source and fountain of our justice and our liberty : the maker of our commerce, the founder of our nationality and security. To the Crown we are indebted for all. To the Williams and the Henries, the Edwards and the Charles, who conquered us and held us together, gave us laws, thrashed us and took our money, loved us and chastened us, gave their laborious days to patient thinking over our army and our navy and our trade, we owe it that we stand in our present unexampled imperial position. And yet a parcel of superficial rationalists in the nineteenth century, without either any spark of historical or political insight, or any discerning gratitude to the great men who made it possible for them to be proud of the name of Englishmen, disparage monarchy and serve up a vile demagogic caricature as the History of England [m], attributing the whole evolutionary process by which we gained

[m] In his anxiety to prove 'the people' the source of all that is good in our constitution, Green, the most *popular* of English historians (in every sense of the word), completely misses the heart of the whole thing. To baptize the Norman Conquest as 'England under Foreign Kings,' and assert emphatically over and over again that *all* that England subsequently became lay already formed in the primitive Anglo-Saxon character and institutions, marks a total want of historical science and perception. The truth is that the early 'English' society was but the chaotic material. The Norman Kings supplied the formative idea (compare Stubbs, vol. i. p. 247) and the conditions of the organisation, its *raison d'être*, was war. England owes her peculiar nature *more* to the Norman Kings than any one else. *Foreign Kings !* As if England was England in 1066 !

our wealth, our laws, our learning, our nationality and our glory to the comparatively recent and entirely self-interested nostrums of bigoted quacks and short-sighted traders.

The true theory of English history and its evolution is admirably expressed in the old and much vilipended Tory aphorism : *a Deo Rex, a Rege Lex:* provided that we properly understand it. *A Deo Rex:* here is the original arbitrary element, the beginning of the evolutionary process. God gives the King : he comes, as Carlyle would say, by Divine right : the right of might. *A Rege Lex:* when we have got the King, our Lord and Master, then out of him by successive unfolding come all our liberties and privileges : *and without him we should not have had any.* It has been said, and said well, that the defeats upon the Thames and the Avon were probably necessary preliminaries to the victories upon the Sutlej.

A Deo Rex. William of Normandy came over and seized England for his own. It was then his property, and well he and his descendants looked after it. Stark men were they, and well is it for us that they were so. Not without reason was Delolme of opinion that we subsequently acquired so much freedom because we were ruled by the Normans with a rod of iron. *Blood and Iron,* says Bismarck, are the things to build with. We verify the epigram. We were saved from anarchy by the Normans [n]. Our liberty came not to us suddenly, suddenly to die down and wither away, as it did abroad : it grew slowly, and was therefore rooted

[n] 'The Norman Conquest restored National Unity at a 'tremendous temporary sacrifice.' Stubbs, *Hist. Eng.* i. 203.

deep. The fear of the Lord is the beginning of wisdom. Just in so far as the King was strong were we well off; when the King was weak our ' freedom,' i.e. our miseries, began. Freedom meant the lawless and arbitrary violence of an anarchical and licentious Baronage. When Commynes praised our government in the time of Edward IV. was he thinking of it in the same way as those who have so triumphantly quoted his testimony in our own day ? Not in the least. It was the strength of the monarchy which had rendered possible the praises of Commynes. Good government, because strong government : that was a state of things Commynes noted : it struck his eye, because it was unfamiliar : it did not exist abroad, as Louis XI. found to his cost. And to whom did we owe it ? To William I., Henry I. and II., and Edward I. The English constitution was a work of art : and the Norman supplied the idea. And are we to call the Normans *Foreign Kings* ? Why, the fallacy is exactly akin to that prevalent economical sophism which makes Labour the sole source of Wealth. The Saxons would never have made England. *A Deo Rex.* The Norman furnished the Genius of England's future : the soul that created the body. *A Rege Lex.* The King's Court, the *Curia Regis*, originally directly simple and personal, looked after the Justice, with a keen eye to Finance. He had a gift for Finance, had the Norman King, and he knew that the best Finance is based upon Justice. The Justiciar was the King's offshoot. As time went on, the Court grew and differentiated to answer to its growing functions. Function makes structure. Lords and Commons, Courts of Justice, Army and Navy : they are all National : all these, and all their corollaries, we owe to the Crown. To the Stuarts, again, we owe it, that while their subjects were running mad and enforcing their bigotry, political and religious, upon the monarch, the naval and colonial power of England bounded ahead. Their policy was the policy of the future : they fell before the madness of the time. Our Abbeys and Cathedrals, such as the Commons have left of them, were built by Normans. Our art, what might it not have been, had Wolsey and Charles I. had their way ? and what is it now ? But our civil and religious liberty ? that surely was the gift of the Revolution ? On the contrary, it was the gift of the King. Charles II. vainly strove, after the Restoration, to control the factious bigotry and intolerance of the religious and political sects that refused to tolerate any one but themselves. The Stuarts lost their crown because they championed an oppressed minority : the civil and religious bigots and traitors who called in William of Orange were tyrants to a far greater degree than the well-meaning but dogmatic and unwisely sincere James. The Venetian oligarchy cared not a straw for civil and religious liberty, nor did William III. *He* wanted a *locus standi* for his Continental policy : *they* wanted a tool to effect their oligarchical designs. The basis of the opposition to the Stuarts was a bigoted refusal to tolerate Roman Catholics. The Tories were indeed honest bigots, but the Whigs were disloyal knaves. They played upon the prejudices of the vulgar—especially the London mob—to bring the

King into discredit : the one thing they were determined upon was to show no mercy to the religion which they had robbed of its patrimony, the
Abbey lands : which it held in trust for the people.
They hated the Roman Catholics with the hatred
of the injurer for the injured, according to the
well-known law : *proprium humani generis est
odisse quem læseris.* But what was the value of
their cry of liberty ? Why, these gentlemen who
had made a standing army their pet grievance (as
if the Stuart Kings could have resisted anarchical traitors with no force!) established their
liberty with William's Dutch troops °. They who
had played the injured patriot and the careful
economical watch-dog, and cut the King of the
money necessary to government (in a time of
rising prices) saddled the nation with vast taxa-
tion and a national funded debt. They who
had virtuously abused Charles II. for taking
money from Louis XIV. (which he did because
he could not get it anywhere else ; they drove him
to do it), having at the time some of the filthy lucre
in their own pockets (the cause for which Russell
and Sidney died on the scaffold!), turned England
into the mere tool of William's Dutch and Continental policy. They kissed the ground before the

---

° Κινοῦσι δὲ τὰς πολιτείας ὅτε μὲν διὰ βίας ὅτε δὲ δί ἀπάτης, διά βίας
μὲν ἢ εὐθὺς ἐξ ἀρχῆς ἢ ὕστερον ἀναγκάζοντες. Καὶ γὰρ ἡ ἀπάτη διττη·
ὅτε μὲν γὰρ ἐξαπατήσαντες τὸ πρῶτον ἑκόντων μετα βάλλουσι τὴν πολίτειαν,
ειθ' ὕστερον βίᾳ κατέχουσίν ἀκόιτων. Pol. v. 4. This is exactly
the Revolution. The Whigs achieved it by the aid of the
Tories : these afterwards found they had been deceived and
wished to undo it, but then the Whigs and William maintained
their position by force and fraud. They had the money and
the advantage of occupation : still they only *just* won.

man who distributed English soil and money to his foreigners, who pensioned Titus Oates, the dirty scoundrel who had by his infamous perjuries brought innocent men to the scaffold, the tool of their trumped up plot, and scare of being massacred by the Roman Catholics, who were not more than four to a thousand of the population. They had expelled James especially on account of his exercising the dispensing power :—an exercise impolitic no doubt but unquestionably legal and constitutional :—their new master, for they found he *was* their master, made use of that power to a far greater extent than James. They denounced and exaggerated James' cruelty : was it then so black, compared with Glencoe ? They had never repaid an atom of gratitude to the Stuarts, who had made our navy with which we beat the Dutch. William III. utterly neglected it[p]. They had ousted a King on the plea that he was a tyrant, and denounced, with a pharisaical puritanism, the iniquities of Kings and Courts; they inaugurated a period in which a grinding oligarchical tyranny threw the benevolent dispensation of the Stuarts into the shade, and veiled its incredible corruption—when it did not openly, shamelessly, and cynically preach it—under a screen of popular humbug and mystification[q]. They had expelled a line of Kings who were above all careful to preserve

[p] See especially J. S. Brewer's *English Studies*, p. 168, and passim. Brewer was a historian in the highest sense of the word.

[q] The Whig policy from the days of Pym downwards is simply stealthy encroachment on the royal prerogative, under theoretic pretexts. See, for example, Hearn's *Government of England* (p. 160), on their mysterious policy as to the right of *electing* the Premier, ' abandoned as noiselessly as it was

the nation from continental complications, and
looked seawards for its future: they introduced
a dynasty, whose connection with Holland or
Hanover cost the nation untold sums of money,
absolutely barren of return. What in fine did we
gain by the Whig Revolution for civil and religious
liberty? We gained a Venetian oligarchy, a Dutch
finance, slavery and degradation, darkness and
social misery for the body of the people, a despised
and parasitic Clergy, a privileged Brahminical order,
corrupt and dead to all higher things, and in ultimate
result, that social question which now defies our
solution and threatens our national existence.

But if the nature of the English government can
only be explained on the principle that structure has
arisen in answer to function: if theory is unable
to cope with the difficulties, and only in history,
i.e. in the organic evolution of the whole, is the true
raison d'être and explanation of its existence to be
found; how much less can merely rational or
theoretic considerations explain to us the nature
and formation of the English Church? Let us look
into the matter, for nothing could be more worthy
of our closest attention. Nothing could be more
futile than the attempt to account for the Church
of England on rational grounds. The Church of

'maintained.' But the truth is simply, that if there is no
justification for the royal authority, there is no justification for
any. Anarchy is the only alternative.

It is most curious to see how identical all down history is
the spirit of the Whig party: a factious and anti-national,
unconstitutional party, necessarily requiring to lean for support
on theory and extra-national props. In the days of Pym, it
leaned on Scotland: in 1688 and onwards, on the Dutch; in
the days of O'Connell, on the Irish, as it does now.

England has, in fact, no rational basis at all. She is not a *rational* entity, but a *national* and *real* institution. No man could ever, on rational grounds, become a member of the Church of England: nor again could any member of the Church of England, guided by purely rationalistic considerations, justify his position. Such considerations could only and inevitably turn him into a Sectarian: as indeed history shows by copious instances. The Church of England has no rational foundation: this, which her enemies cast in her teeth, does in reality constitute her glory and her strength.

Consider her origin. She owes her independent existence to Henry VIII., beyond all question the most execrable ruffian, the most whimsically grotesque, the most superlatively wicked and capricious tyrant that ever existed outside a dream[r]. Words cannot paint the unique. Because the Pope would not be either bullied or cajoled into humouring his lust (rendered additionally abominable by its cruelty and hypocrisy) by setting aside his marriage; because he found in the Pope a moral barrier, Henry VIII. dethroned the Pope and set himself up as the Supreme Head of the Church, in order to give the sanction of the Church, i.e. his own, to his own villainy. A more outrageous and insolent piece of absurdity was never perpetrated in the face of

[r] The writings especially of Brewer, Canon Dixon, Hubert Burke, and Gasquet have settled this question for ever. I find it impossible to examine the true record of Henry VIII.'s villainies without a feeling of positive sickness. It is only when reading of him that we can truly appreciate Rabelais. Dr. Brewer knew how deeply Rabelais had penetrated into the mixture of farce and solemnity which was the spirit of the Reformation.

humanity. This indeed was something altogether
'new and strange.' It is idle to assert that Henry
VIII. was but doing what his predecessors had
done before him. They had never dreamed of
such a thing. It is true that English kings—as
William I., Henry II., Edward III., and Richard
II., had expressed in strong terms their claim to
supreme jurisdiction in matters ecclesiastical[*]. But
this was a totally different thing : the supremacy
of the civil over the ecclesiastical jurisdiction.
None of these Kings ever dreamed of usurping
the *spiritual* functions of the Pope. But this is
precisely what Henry VIII. did do. He who had
been the willing son of His Holiness, who had been
as vain as a peacock of his title of Champion of the
Faith, now, when his evil passions met with an
obstacle in the head of the Church, turned and
rent the Church asunder. In order that religion
should sanction his crimes, he had himself to become the mouthpiece of religion. Then he could

[*] There is nothing in history more ironical than the career
of John. He set at nought the authority of the Pope, and
his rebellious subjects exclaimed against his wickedness: he
submitted to it, and his rebellious subjects made that, too,
a crime : and they disobeyed the Pope themselves. What the
barons, lay or ecclesiastical, wanted was not liberty for the
nation but *license* for themselves. Hagiological history has
transfigured Magna Charta, in whose case we ought to recollect
the words of Renan, '*dans les hommes élevés à la dignité de
' symbole, il faut toujours distinguer la vie personnelle et la vie
' d'outretombe, ce qu'ils furent en réalité et ce que l'opinion en
' a fait.*' Averroes, p. 432. The real nature of Magna Charta
is shown by the conduct of the Barons in the next reign. The
truth is that, under the influence of modern Protestant
anarchical theories, historians have entirely misrepresented the
events of John's reign.

do what he liked. But the idea of reforming the Church, morally or doctrinally, never entered his head. All he wanted to do was to turn it into an instrument, a tool, an engine in his own service. But here he would have met, and did meet, with a new check. The nation would never have submitted to his new-fangled immoral papacy, had he not found means to make it also subservient to his will. He found these means. He threw to the upper classes the Abbey lands, as a sop to appease them : he shut their mouths with the Abbeys and Priories and Chantries of the Church [1]; and as for the lower classes, when they rose in defence of their old religion and their kind old friends, the monks, he put them down with barbaric severity by the aid of foreign mercenary troops. Instead of the old Pope, who with all his faults lived at a distance and let them alone, the English people got a new Pope, King Stork for King Log, a fierce, sanguinary, and atrocious tyrant, who despoiled them of all they had, and hung, burned and quartered them for objecting.

Of reformation no faintest suspicion ever entered his head. He slew with a boisterous and hideous alacrity (*'hang him up, hang him up !'*) both those who denied his supremacy and those who attempted

---

[1] 'Our Abbeys and our Priories shall pay this expedition's 'charge.' (*King John*, Act. i. Sc. 1.) The epoch is far more correctly described as that of the 'New Proprietors' than the 'New Learning.' When a modern writer tells us that 'the 'shrines and altar plate of York Cathedral were sent to the 'mints to be issued in base coin,' he epitomises the age. It was probably not only of money, but of men, that Sir Thomas Gresham was thinking when he enunciated his famous law, 'bad money drives out good.'

any the slightest innovation in doctrine. Wolsey, the great Cardinal who had raised him to a pinnacle of glory, and Katherine of Arragon, fell at the divorce, and with them Henry's good genius died : or rather, we should say, with them disappeared all the genius and all the morality of his reign ; for left to himself, he soon showed how little of either he possessed. Fisher and More, two of the noblest men that ever lived, were sacrificed to his supremacy. From that moment Henry never had any but dirty and unscrupulous, greedy and insatiable tools and cormorants to serve him. His ministers, civil or ecclesiastical, were there, ready and eager to baptize all his outrageous crimes with the professed formulæ of religion and law.

And here now we come upon the difficulty. On the shoulders of Henry VIII. lies the blame for all the subsequent fearful disasters in Church and State. He was now in an untenable position. People began to say *Quo Warranto?* By what authority doest thou these things? The old Pope we understand, though we might condemn him ; a moral reformation, a recasting, in the spirit of purity and earnestness, of error and backslidings, a reconstitution and reorganisation of religious truth and doctrine, we understand : but who are you? Who made Henry VIII. Pope of the English Nation! Is the authority of the Pope to be cast aside, only to install a new Papacy, differing from the old one only in its sanguinary robbing and murdering to enforce immoral complaisance and winking at its own hideous crimes? No, a thousand times, No. And in fact, little as he intended it, Henry VIII., by making the ecclesiastical authority of the King a farce, and yet tying it of necessity to the civil, really ensured the fall of the supreme civil authority of the realm. The Puritan crusade under the Stuarts laid both together in the dust. For this was just where the knot lay. Henry's ecclesiastical polity was simply Catholicism *minus* the Pope. But this was seen and felt by all to be impossible. ˙ There was no religion or sincerity in it : it was political only. Accordingly it could not survive its author. No sooner was the arch-buccaneer dead than his policy and his last instructions were cast to the winds by the gang of sharks and pirates who succeeded to his power behind the authority of Edward VI. Their policy was dictated primarily by the impossibility of any reconciliation with a Church on whose spoils they were battening ꭢ. A Protector who tried to pull down S. Margaret's in order to build himself a house was likely to be hostile to the old religion. And

ꭢ 'The spoil of the Church was now become the only
' resource of all their operations in finance : the vital principle
' of all their politics : the sole security for the existence of their
' power. It was necessary by all even the most violent means
' to put every individual on the same bottom, and to bind the
' nation in one guilty interest to uphold this act and the authority
' of those by whom it was done. In order to force the most
' reluctant into a participation of their pillage, they rendered
' their *paper circulation* compulsory in all *payments*. Those who
' consider the general tendency of their schemes to this one
' object as a centre, and a centre from which afterwards all their
' measures radiate, will not think I dwell too long on this part
' of the proceedings of the National Assembly.'

For '*paper circulation*' and '*payments*' substitute '*Anglican*
' *Church*' and '*religious services*,' and this description by Burke
applies exactly to the English 'Reformation' of the Church
of England. How does history repeat herself !

this lies at the root of the position. When Mary succeeded, she was allowed to re-instate the old faith on the distinct understanding that she let the new proprietors keep their ill-gotten gains. (*The Reformation!*) But this involved a contradiction, and as soon as Elizabeth replaced her, some means of founding a quasi-logical basis for the 'new 'order' had to be devised. As far às her own personal inclinations went, and that was not very far, Elizabeth was a Catholic. *But she was the daughter of Anne Boleyn: she was the fruit of the crime.* Moreover, her personal wishes counted for least in the general situation. The circumstances in which she found herself were imperative. Her line was no free choice: it was above all a political necessity. She existed upon sufferance: the sufferance of the new proprietors. Both from the religious and the political point of view her policy was throughout one of balance and expediency. There was no choice: necessity held out the bowl. She had no great idea to realise: she compounded with events as they came[x]. To return to Catholicism, apart from the fact that it would have branded her as illegitimate, and thus *de jure* dethroned her in favour of Mary—*hinc illæ lacrimæ—et spretæ injuria formæ!*—would have ultimately involved restitution of its goods: to go forward was equally dangerous, for where were you to stop? *Hence the English Church.* It is essentially an apology excogitated to give some show of reason to a set of *faits accomplis.* It is mere hypocrisy to try and eliminate the four hundred

[x] Cf. Cunningham's *Growth of English Industry and Commerce*, vol. ii. p. 10.

years of Latin Christianity, and go back to Saxon and British England for the English Church. To its Roman connection our Church owes all its buildings, its achievements, its venerable age. Had, indeed, a good and pious King destroyed the monasteries and got rid of Rome, in order to achieve noble national aims : had the destruction of the Catholic organisation been, as Wolsey wished it to have been, essentially a moral reform, an endeavour to renew the spirit of religion and apply the resources of the Church to religious, educational, or other high and noble purposes, to bring its structure into harmony with new functions —the case would have been altered. But such was *not* the case. The appeal to early times, and antiquated, long-forgotten origins, was merely excogitated *after* the facts, to provide some sort of justification for a series of atrocious crimes. These were the essence, the apology was the accident, of the matter. Elizabeth had in some way or another forcibly to establish an Anglican Church, whose structure had necessarily to be determined by its function : and its function was, to suit the political necessities of the new proprietors. What a function for a Church! What an abysmal fall from the great civilising function of the Roman Catholic Church! But Elizabeth was obliged to cut her coat according to her cloth, and base her ecclesiastical system not upon a moral and rational inquiry into truth, not upon high social functions, but negatively, upon an avoidance of extremes, dexterously egg-dancing amidst a thousand causes of offence. Catholic as against the reformers ; Protestant, as being essentially hostile to Catholics ; the product

E e

of compromise; the convenient engine of State
necessity; the tool of interested views; the child
of diplomatic steering and material calculation;
such was the unavoidable conclusion, the Anglican
Church. The logic of circumstances gave it its
form. It could, and it can, exist only in connection with the State to whose action it owed its
origin. This was its *raison d'être*. And if, in the
next century, the Puritan, reforming, rationalising
rebels confounded the Stuart zeal for Anglicanism
with an attempt to reintroduce Roman Catholicism,
they were not without excuse. For in truth its
differences from the old faith lay in practical
exigencies, and not in rational or irrational dis-
agreement, like their own. And on the other
hand, it was more abhorred by Rome than all the
sects [z]. For Rome knew perfectly well the true
reason for its falling away : she knew the difference
between the cause and the pretext : the true
motives, lust and covetousness, and the laboriously
woven cloak of hypocrisy thrown over the horrible
ulcer already formed and spreading. Was there
nothing to palliate the attempts of Roman Catholics
to restore the past? Why, I say it was a sacred
duty, and regarded as such by every Catholic just
in proportion to the sincerity and depth of his
religious conviction.

Odisse quem læseris : there was the soul of the
persecution of the Roman Catholics in the seven-
teenth century. The material interests of the
upper classes combined with and employed the
sectarian bigotry of the lower, mainly town, popu-

---

[z] See Dryden's *Preface to Religio Laici.*

lation to oppress the old Catholic party. But
in human affairs who gains time gains all. 'The
' mighty years in long procession ran :' and the
English Catholic Church, the child of crime and
violence, personal ends and sordid tyranny, gradually became associated, as the Church which it
had displaced had been associated, with an English
gentleman's early childish notions of respect and
veneration. But there was this difference : the
English Church was inseparably bound up with
the State. Church and King became an indis-
solubly rivetted single idea. The two became
inconceivable to his mind apart. And this is
logically the case. The Church of England has
no *raison .d'être* apart from the State. She represents the State on the side of its social duties,
and this is just her true function ; a function which
in this century she has begun to realise and to
perform in a manner worthy of herself. On her
due performance of this function depends her
existence. She has awoken from the lethargy in
which she sank after the glorious Revolution of
1688 : and is thus making reparation for the terrible
injury caused to the cause of the poor, morally and
educationally, by the events to which she owes her
birth. For two hundred years after Henry VIII.,
being deprived of her property (which passed from
the hands of those who held it in trust for the
people, on the maxim that *property has its duties*,
into the hands of those who held it merely for
themselves, on the maxim *property is liberty*), the
Church was in a degraded condition : witness the
condition of the clergy in England in the seven-
teenth and eighteenth centuries. But now there

is no body in the State which performs its social
and religious functions more fully and unweariedly
than the Church. And we need not regret that
a cloud hangs over her origin, or echo the wish
of Dryden, that her inborn stains were washed
away. This is the guarantee of earnest and enduring services. She stands in the position of
a wife, whom the consciousness of early faults
and doubtful antecedents urges to repair and
make up for the past by a faithful and sincere
performance of her duties to her children passing
the common.

My object in these observations on the constitutional history of England is to succeed in imparting to the reader the conviction that neither
the State in general nor any of its institutions
are susceptible of a rational explanation, but
are only explicable through the method of *real
definition*, that is, the accounting for structure by
function, for what is, by the analytical investigation of how it came to be so : or in other
words, that 'The State' is a non-entity : but
that there exist States, which are nothing but
structures that have been formed in course of
time, and grown gradually to their necessities,
internal and external. Only the thorough insight into this truth will enable us to comprehend the futility of all general and rationalistic
theories of the State, from Plato and Hobbes
downwards. Nothing is at once more useless
and more simple than the construction of any
such theories of the State. But just because
they appear complete and magnificent, each *in
se totus teres atque rotundus*, just because they

are purely abstract and require no deep imaginative insight into special circumstances and the puzzling complicated nature of things and men, the vulgar mind turns to them more readily than to the really valuable political writings of statesmen who were thinking not of abstract but applied politics. The vain and visionary verbiage of Plato, Rousseau, Comte, and others of that ilk, will always fill a large space in ' Histories of Politics ' as being complete theories of the State : though there is really more political wisdom to be gained in any half-dozen pages of the Cardinal de Retz, or one of Lord Beaconsfield's novels, or a pamphlet of Lord Bolingbroke's, though these are marked by a total absence of any theory of the State such as might qualify them for fifty pages in a History of Political Theory. For what inspires all really valuable political writing, and breathes in its pages, is just the profound and intuitive perception of the truth, that, *abstracted* from its function, or its evocating necessity, no structure has or can have any meaning, much less existence. Of what value, then, are pedantic and frigid general lucubrations and systems of politics? What use are these, if a State be, as it is, essentially a product of time? if no State can possibly leap full grown into existence, just because there can be no State without a past, which past has made it what it is : in virtue of which past it is just what it is, that is, a State of a peculiar kind ? A special creative theory of the State, in fact, is an absurdity : one, such as implies that structure is absolute, and of absolute value : unrelated to function. This absolutism, in fact, this

form *minus* function, is exactly the Platonic, as
opposed to the Aristotelian, view : precisely the
same, under all its varieties, whether it be found
in Plato's own pages, or in real life : as, for instance, in modern times, during which some
mystical and absolute value has been attached
to 'constitutional' government and its forms, in
themselves, and absolutely, as such : and everywhere people have striven to force it upon all
sorts and conditions of men, regardless of the
essential distinctions, which make that which is
adapted to one race absurdly unsuitable for another.   But there seems to be in the human mind
a radical propensity to *absolutise* structure : to
consider it as something independent and valid
in se : men seem to be radically unable to understand that structure is nothing but that which
does work : and that you cannot have the structure,
where the work is not wanted to be done.   It is
the need for the doing of the work that creates
the structure : but what preposterous folly to
attach abstract value to the structure, and endeavour to produce it arbitrarily, where the function or work it should do is not wanted ! Yet this
is just the thing that people are constantly attempting to do in politics.   The attempt is just as
ridiculous as it seems to us to be, when we read of
some low barbarian savage potentate, who inhabits
a sweltering tropical clime, and whose national garb
is his dark skin, adopting a pair of military trousers
with a gold band, and a tall hat, together possibly
with boots.   The poor untutored Indian attaches
some absolute value to these structures : and we
laugh : yet in morals and politics we do precisely

the same. There has only been ONE philosopher
in all history who understood the truth of the
matter. And perhaps the most astonishing thing
about Aristotle, in whom all is astonishing, is
just this : that though a philosopher, and one who,
when it is necessary, can wield abstractions with
a masterly ease that leaves all other philosophers
far behind, he yet ranks, as a political writer, with
statesmen. Not Thucydides, not Macchiavelli are
more penetrated with the sentiment of reality, of
the limiting and qualifying effect of circumstances,
of relativity, in political affairs. Aristotle is the
only philosopher because he alone is always and
everywhere absolutely without pedantry : being in
this respect the exact antithesis to that prince of
superlative pedants, that King of uncompromising
politicasters, the divine Plato.

It would be easy and deeply interesting to illustrate this point by a careful and wide historical
review. But notwithstanding the temptation to
make an excursion into the pleasant fields of
history,—above all, in this connection, into those of
Russia and Poland, which present us with exactly
opposite object lessons on this very head,— brevity
is the soul of wit : and enough has been said to
convince any one willing to be convinced—and
nothing will convince those who are not so—of the
truth, that a State and its institutions are real and
not rational things ; or conversely, that the greatest
error which can possibly be committed, is to attempt to rationalise the State : to turn it into a
body of individuals : to forget its organic nature
and the overwhelming importance of bearing in
mind that the institutions of a country are the truest

and most valuable portion of its wealth. This which I state here as a historical and scientific fact, is nevertheless also the true Tory principle. The art of the Whig has, on the contrary, always been based upon the negation of this; it turns the institutions of the country into engines of oligarchical government, under cover of popular cries. The demagogue, on the other hand, is one whose delusion lies in supposing that by getting rid of all the old institutions of the country 'the people' will be 'free.' He never suspects that it is just these institutions which are the guarantee of liberty, and that liberty without institutions is at once a snare, an impossibility, and a tyranny. The individual, *as such*, can enjoy no liberty. This was the discovery made after the Revolution was over in 1795[a]. The only man who can enjoy liberty is the man who is a special sort of man : i.e. privileged by his birthright to share the *liberties* of his country, and the benefits of its institutions. All

---

[a] *e.g.* in Fyffe's *History of Modern Europe*, vol. i. p. 46, we read 'Men left their homes (to fight for France) in 1792 in ' order that the fruit of the poor man's labour should be his ' own, in order that the children of France should inherit some ' better birthright than exaction and want, in order that the ' late won sense of *human right* should not be swept from the ' earth by the arms of privilege and caste.' Magnificent! But on p. 103 we read, that on the establishment of the Directory in 1795, ' the rich and the gay consoled themselves with costlier ' luxury for all the austerities of the Reign of Terror. The ' labouring classes, now harmless and disarmed, were *sharply* ' *taught* that they must be content with such improvements ' in their lot as the progress of society might bring.' Eh ! was the Revolution then a failure? Poor deluded lambs of labour! then after all it was not you, not man *quâ* man, that derived benefit from the Revolution? Who was it?

history proves it, and the man who understands it is a statesman : the man who does not, not. For the individual, *as such*, there is and can be neither political liberty, nor moral duty.

III. For now it is time to examine the ethical significance of our principle, and determine not only the corollaries that follow from it, but also the doctrine of conduct which it involves : which we shall find to be nothing but the doctrine that structure is made such by its function, in other clothes. Nor can anything be a more decisive proof of the truth of this principle, than to find that it is equally valid and fruitful alike in the economy of nature and that of man, that it furnishes the key alike to economics and politics, æsthetics, and ethics. And when we comprehend it, in the ethical field, we shall understand why moral philosophy is such a chaos of conflicting opinions. For how could any one arrive at a satisfactory conception of conduct, unless he started from a correct analysis of human nature ? The conduct of men can only be deduced from the nature of men. And here, as usual, our master is Aristotle.

And first then as to the deep inward significance of the principle itself in the ethical sphere. What it says is this : that all created things are merely the material forms, the corporeal embodiments of functions : they arise to perform peculiar and special duties, in answer to the necessities that call them forth : these are their souls. ' Let it be understood,' exclaims Dante, 'that God and Nature make no-' thing to be idle. Whatever comes into being ' exists for the sake of some operation or working.' And conversely, the cessation of this is death.

Things sink back and disappear, lose their individuality, become nothing, and merge again into
the universal sea of the formless, when those necessities that held their material particles together
cease : or when they themselves lose their capacity
of performing their function. The great law of
Nature, moral and physical, the *raison d'être* of all
things is expressed by Aristotle thus : EACH THING
IS FOR THE SAKE OF ANOTHER. Now when we fully
realise all this, we suddenly become aware that this
fundamental doctrine of Aristotle's is nothing but
the definite and clear philosophical expression of
the thought which lies at the bottom of all oriental
mythologies, and forms the kernel of the ethical
teaching of the old nature worship. The presenta-
tion of the central idea in these religious myths is
related to Aristotle's thought as the glimpses we
catch of objects reflected in rough and stormy water
to the exact and beautiful mirror of the same in
a quiet unfathomable mountain tarn. But the objects *are* the same. This principle of creation is
that which is signified by the Hindoo Trimurti,
Brahma, the Creative Principle : Vishnu, the Preserving Principle, and Shiva, the Principle of
Decay : all being summed up in the neuter form
of the whole three, Brahman. All these are but
mythological forms of the same principle of generative evolution and decay, which Aristotle expresses
by naming the creative principle ἡ τοῦ διὰ τί ἀνάγκη;
the Necessity of the *Raison d'être*[b]. We see the

[b] Cp. Fustel de Coulanges, *La Cité Antique, ad fin.* ' *Nous*
' *avons fait l'histoire d'une croyance. Elle s'etablit : la société*
' *humaine se constitue. Elle se modifie : la société traverse une*

same thing shadowed in the Semitic myths of
Astarte and Adonis, the Egyptian Isis and Osiris,
Horus and Apis : the cosmogonical accounts of the
Babylonians and Assyrians, embodied in Genesis ;
in the dark obscurities of the old Chinese religion,
with its doctrines of Ying and Yang, and its worship of Tao [c]: and the various more or less degraded nature and fetish worships of the world. It
is this deep perception which gives to ancient
religious systems an attraction so much more
powerful than those of later times, which have lost
the old insight into natural relations, and are often
but superficial rationalistic arbitrary fancies reposing upon no deep intellectual penetration into
Nature's *arcana.* This thought again is that which
is embodied in the proverb : *vox populi vox Dei:*
and which again Shakspeare, the Aristotelian poet
(just as Aristotle is the Shakspearian philosopher)
expresses when he makes Hamlet say :

> ' There's a divinity which shapes our ends
> Rough hew them how we will.'

For by this divinity he means exactly that which
Aristotle calls τὸ θεῖον : the necessity which calls
out and fashions all attempts at construction, and
which is the supreme Lord Paramount of all action
and creation. We do but row, says Butler, we are

' *serie de revolutions. Elle disparait : la société change de face.*
' *Telle a été la loi des temps antiques,*' and of all time.

   [c] Cp. ' The natural political, social, and moral orders of the
' world are not only closely connected with one another, but
' they are perfectly identical. . . . . There are three fundamental
' beings, the heaven, earth, and man, who must be in harmony
' one with another.' *De la Saussaye, Science of Religion,*
E. T., p. 346.

steered by fate. And this is the true meaning of Fate : which is not absolute mechanical material Necessity, but formal, creative, conditional necessity ʽΗ τοῦ διὰ τί ἀνάγκη, χρωμένη οἷον ὀργάνοις, ποιεῖ.

Upon the full understanding of this depends our moral, political, and philosophical salvation. In this lies that social mysticism, which puzzles superficial rationalistic critics so much in the writings of real political philosophers : which appears in authors widely different in all other respects : in Dostoyeffsky and Burke, in Lord Beaconsfield and Proudhon, in Pascal and Schopenhauer. (In Aristotle it is not mystic but clearly understood.) On this depends the true and radical opposition between Tory and Whig views of politics ; and the solution of the dark and disputed questions of the relation of the Individual Man to the State : the duties of the individual man : and in general the whole difference, wide as the poles asunder, between the rational and the real. For no shuffling and juggling with abstractions will ever enable us to reach realities : those who start from the individual will never be able to understand man. Out of individuals we never can get the State, except a ‘State’ which is an abstract entity : as unreal as the individuals of which it is forcibly made to consist.

For there are no such things as individuals. There are men : and these men live in communities, states, or nations, which are all different. They differ in language, race, historical tradition, sentiment, religion, custom, fashion, climate and civilisation, and idiosyncrasy. Time and events and the law that harmonises every structure to the necessities of its situation, make every state a peculiar thing. It grows into existence gradually. Nothing more false was ever said than that the State is nothing but the individuals composing it. It is the individuals composing it, *plus* the composition. This which seems nothing, is everything. The 'individual' grows up in the atmosphere of the State: he is moulded into his form by its myriad influences. As a unit, he is well nigh powerless against the irresistible, because unconscious, strength of custom, tradition, use, wont, inheritance. He sucks in the national point of view, the national sympathies and antipathies, the national prejudices and cultivation with his mother's milk. He is made what he is by his environment. The collective idea [d]—if the expression may be permitted, to denote the sum total of the national idiosyncrasy—shapes him into conformity with it. It is only in later years, when his character has been all but formed, that he begins to rationalise, to estimate things and ideas from an abstract, absolute, rational point of view.

Now, only in this way can we attain to truth in the sphere of ethics. The strength of the national, political, or social idea is too great for the individual man. It is beyond his power. Every separate member of the community might for example hold, from the abstract standpoint, that some special custom or point of manners was absurd. Nevertheless, collectively they would all continue to obey

[d] The reader will not confound this with Socialistic absurdities. Socialism is just as rationalistic as Individualism: they are opposite ends of the same false, foolish, theoretical stick.

it : because in such cases the individual opinion and
action is pitted against the whole of the rest of the
community: each only knows a handful of his
compatriots, and therefore no one can take a first
step : no one is strong enough to inaugurate a
universal change. The thing cannot be done *on
a plan.* This is that mystic influence of large bodies
of men which makes them act as it were providen-
tially, entirely independently of each man's individual opinion : *which therefore makes each man act
not rationally, but really;* this we express when we
speak of fate. The State is *not* merely the sum of
the individuals composing it : on the contrary, just
because the State has a character ($\check{\eta}\theta os$) of its own,
each man is obliged, even were it against his will,
to obey and conform to the social idea. Thus
custom and conscience do make cowards of us all.

Now here we have the point of essential distinction between the true statesman, or the true
novelist, and the false one. The true statesman
knows his people: this is what Shaftesbury was
praised for : 'his strength lay in his knowledge of
' England.' He knows not merely human nature,
but that species of it which is his material in
particular : and cuts his coat accordingly. The
pseudo-statesman, on the contrary, frames his
measures from a rationalistic,—it may be highly
moral,—conception of 'humanity.' Similarly, your
true novelist never draws abstract individuals : he
knows that characters are abstractions, except in
their proper setting. The bad novelist, on the other
hand, gives us abstract individuals. The distinction
may be accurately expressed by the Latin words
vir and *homo. Homo sum, nihil humani a me*

alienum puto has a fine ring : but it is the principle
of bad art and bad politics : and a sure sign of
decay. *Homo* is an abstract entity : unqualified
by conditions. *Vir*, on the contrary, is real ; a man.
Paradoxical as it may seem, it is none the less a
deep truth, that the artist who wishes to draw
character must beyond áll know and depict everything else as well : *i.e.* the character *alone* is false.
No one ever understood this like Sir Walter
Scott. A knowledge of human nature does not
merely imply an abstract knowledge of individual
character : it involves a knowledge of the relations
of things, social and political, apart from which
there is no such thing as character at all. This
is why lady novelists are so terrible. True character
painting in novels is as rare as true legislation in
politics. They both rest upon the same basis :
an intuitive perception of the special correlations
of men and things : and this is Imagination. The
creation of abstract characters is mere child's play :
what is hard, is the concrete. Therefore popularity
is the worst test of excellence, in art or politics ; for
not one man in a hundred is capable of judging.

Every State then is a peculiar unity, and has
a peculiar spirit of its own, a tone, a character,
a way of looking at and doing things, a hereditary
idea, or rather, an inherited multitude of various
ideas and customs, which makes its individual
members what they are. Therefore we can seé
at once that it is utterly impossible to understand
the ' individual ' apart from, abstracted from, his
State. Abstract him, and we have cut ourselves
off from all possibility of explaining him : his
structure is now an insoluble puzzle : we have in

him no longer a real man, but an entity: the
springs of his conduct, his motives, the *raison
d'être* of his constitution, are gone.   Therefore
Aristotle says that one who lives alone, a member
of no State, is either a god or a beast; either
above or below the level of a man.   And the depth
of this remark can best be appreciated when we
consider special instances: such as *e.g.* Spinoza
or Bakunin.   Was Spinoza above or below humanity? Did not Bakunin and his followers, by
aiming at something above the level of possibility,
end by falling below the level of beasts? Does
not the man who attempts to rise above patriotism
and profess universal philanthropy end by caring
primarily for his own interest? The truth is that
out of a State a man is a non-entity and an absurdity.   Let no one quote the Jews, the standing
miracle, as men without a nationality: scattered
though they are, they have as strong a sentiment
of nationality as any other sort of men.

The life of a nation is built up, or we should
rather say, building up, long before it arrives at
the consciousness of its nationality.   Its definitely
conscious national life dates always from some
striking and peculiar man, event, or situation out
of which it rose victorious.   Henceforth it proceeds
on a fixed and settled basis of ideas and actions.
Thus the Greeks, especially the Athenians, awoke
in the battle of Marathon, a Greek Spanish
Armada.   France dates from Joan of Arc: Russia
from Ivan III.: and so forth.   But the ancient
history of the Jews presents us with the best instance
of all[e].   Jehovah, their national god, was the symbol

[e] Cp. Dostoyeffsky's *Demons*, p. 232 (Russian Edition).

and index of their nationality, as Moses was their founder. And in Christ, the old national spirit saw the cosmopolitan, rationalistic spirit rising up in opposition to it, denying its ritual and the efficiency of its customs and moral code. Christianity was the death of national life and character. It substituted the individual for the man, *homo* for *vir*, an ideal for a real morality. The Christian theory was profoundly atheistic and immoral, from the point of view of the good old national man. Its *intention* was pacific : its *tendency* essentially warlike : not peace, but a sword, lies in every philosophy which attempts to dissolve the faith in the State and reduce the world to rationalistic individuals. The individual turns away from all ties of kindred or nation, and centres in himself. From this time morality disappears, and sanctity, *i.e.* mysticism, leading to the wildest immorality prevails. For there is no morality, apart from the State. Morality is the true relation of the man to his kindred and his State, and to aim at extending it to the whole human race is only to annihilate it altogether, by throwing him back, in the wild and immeasurable sea of being, upon his own nature. Christian morality began again, only when its rationalistic basis had decayed and dissolved into nothing, and the CHURCH had arisen on its ruins. The Church, becoming organised, again became politic, again human [f]: and now entered upon that magnificent

---

[f] Religion had necessarily to stoop to conquer. For the soul of Christianity being the denial of the world, the organisation of the Church was the death of religion : since it had to adopt and adapt itself to all the worldly politico - economic categories.

course of education and civilisation which is essentially connected with Rome. The truth as to the
distinction between Protestantism and Roman
Catholicism lies here. As Protestant holiness drew
nearer to primitive Christianity, it lost its social
value. Protestantism is essentially an anti-social
religion. The English Church is justified in her
contradictions by the fact that she has retained the
social idea of Catholicism ᵍ. The social tendency
of Protestantism in religion is precisely the same
as that of Cartesianism in philosophy : isolation,
individualisation of the man. Centred in himself,
he degenerates into vain and sterile egoism, out
of which he cannot get : for beginning with the
abstract individual, we can never get away from
him. True morality and true religion are essentially
social and political : they start from the man, not
from the individual : from the man as a social being,

ᵍ For example, Fyffe is constantly declaiming against *priest-*
ridden nations and the state of things due to centuries of priestcraft, in pre-revolutionary Europe. But on closely inspecting
his own book we find (p. 411) that ‘ the people adored their
‘ Bishops and Clergy in the Tyrol. Nowhere could the Church
‘ exhibit a more winning example of unbroken accord between
‘ a simple people and a Catholic Crown.’ And again (p. 26),
‘ Hungary was the only part of the Austrian dominions in which
‘ the peasant was not in a *better* condition than his fellows in
‘ North Germany.’ Again, ‘ the French peasant knew no such
‘ bondage as the Prussian serf,’ and (p. 27) ‘ the comparative
‘ freedom and comfort of the peasant in the *Southern* States.’
Again (p. 362), ‘ nowhere on the continent is there a labouring
‘ class so stripped and despoiled of all interest in the soil, so
‘ sedulously excluded from all possibilities of proprietorship as
‘ in England.’ What ! then, apparently, it is not priestcraft,
but Protestantism, that is most to blame ! *Et voilà justement*
comme on écrit l'histoire.

conditioned by and related to all others near him, reciprocally dependent on each other : a biological growth, and not a metaphysical entity.

For here appears the point which links morality on to the fundamental thought in this essay. Structure is what it is because of its functions : it is what it is, only because of these : it is, in fact, non-existent apart from them, being only embodied function. Now what, in a biological sense, is function, is, in an ethical regard, duty. Just as engineers call its function or work the Duty of a Machine : so is the Duty of man nothing but his true function, ethically expressed. Apart from his conditions he can have neither functions nor duties : he becomes, metaphysically, an abstraction ; ethically, a non-moral entity : for a self-sufficient isolated entity can have no duties. How, then, can any one ever get any basis for moral action, on the Cartesian or Kantian principles ? The thing is absurd. Thus it has often been shown, and quite correctly, that Kant's Ethics are palpably sophistical, and only indicate the complete contradiction between his intellect, which was weak, and his feelings, which were strong. The latter told him that there must be a ground of moral action ; whereas the former was imposed upon by specious but entirely fallacious sceptical arguments. But there is no morality for the theoretical egoist. Goethe is the true type of the Kantian critique,— a cold-blooded, pedantical, callous and inhuman critic,—from a moral point of view. There is no morality except for *men: i.e.*, ethics are, either an absurdity, or they must be based on the biological nature of man : upon the law, *all things are for the sake of others.* For if not, where is the moral relation? If each is, not for others, but for itself, then where is the moral bond? Man being a member of a community, reciprocally limits and is limited, has rights and duties which follow from that fundamental fact. But if he be a mere rationalistic intelligence, a Cartesian self, all is lost. And the history of moral philosophy during the last three hundred years is simply a proof of the total incapacity of philosophy to fix the foundations of morality, if not based upon the organic nature of man. It is vain endeavouring to extract, by juggling of any kind, a moral doctrine out of either Cartesian or mechanical philosophy; for they do not contain it. The world threw away at the Reformation the only philosopher who held the key of the fatal problem.

Was it, indeed, wonderful that an age of dense physiological ignorance should, — even had there been no other reasons, — fail to comprehend the Aristotelian doctrine of virtue? How could a generation that sought to explain man on rationalistic or mechanical principles appreciate his extraordinary insight into the truth that virtue rests not on the logical and metaphysical, but the biological, real, and organic nature of man? Character, says Aristotle, is simply a higher power of habit; moral character, i. e. virtue, is simply a habit, and men become virtuous by constant performance of virtuous acts, till they grow to them : till they acquire the permanent habit of doing them in the appropriate spirit. *The man is made thus or thus by his reiterated actions :* this is the fundamental organic law of man's moral nature. It is simply a case of the evolutionary process, considered in the First Book. Not without reason did the Jesuits, the greatest educators that the world has ever seen, base their moral philosophy upon Aristotle, the one philosopher who knew the vital import of true education — not knowledge, but action — in the formation of character. It is not knowledge, not learning, rationalistic and discursive, that makes men virtuous : it is doing virtuous acts. Train up a child in the way he should go. Born with capacities and potentialities for good or evil [h], the child will become this or that, according as he is led or made to do constant actions of this or that kind. Thus repeated action, i.e. custom, is not a little thing : it is everything. ' It is by playing the flute that we become both ' good and bad fluteplayers. Practice makes perfect. ' And to perfection there are three things requisite : ' natural abilities, education, and practice.' And how should we know what to do ? Aristotle answers in the *exact* words of the Gospel : ' Do unto others ' as you would they should do unto you [i].'

The Protestants fell into inextricable difficulties over the great question of *faith* and *works*, just because they rejected the assistance of the one great moral analyst who knew the truth [k]. On the

[h] Compare Balzac, Preface to the *Comédie Humaine*. On a point like this, Balzac is an authority.

[i] ἐρωτηθεὶς, πῶς ἂν τοῖς φίλοις προσφεροίμεθα, ἔφη, ὡς ἂν εὐξαίμεθα αὐτοὺς ἡμῶν προσφέρεσθαι. *Diog. Laert. in vita Arist.*

[k] 'Luther's most earnest remonstrances were directed not ' against bad, but "good workes," and the stress laid upon them ' by the advocates of the old religion. If that religion had been ' in its practice so generally corrupt as it is represented to have ' been by modern writers, such denunciations were idle.' Brewer,

one side they accentuated faith, without works, and fell into mysticism and immoralities of all kinds. On the other, they accentuated works, without faith, and lost the soul of virtue. The truth lies in the harmony of the two. There are two factors, the actor and the act. Viewed externally, the act is the main thing : from the point of view of others, its *raison d'être*, the nature of the *act* determines what is virtue. But this leaves still undetermined the nature of the actor. For it is not enough to do virtuous acts : they must be done virtuously. One swallow does not make a summer, nor one virtuous action necessarily argue virtue in a man. A vicious man may do a virtuous act, but not therefore is he virtuous. Internally, the nature of the act must be determined from the *spirit* or *intention* of the actor. The intention of the actor must correspond with the nature of the act : then there is virtue. *Fides et opera.* The two cannot be separated. This is the great Aristotelian doctrine of the intention, or ethical spirit of the actor, which has been made familiar to all the world, in a way, by Pascal's *Provincial Letters.* But Pascal treated the Jesuits with gross unfairness. Doubtless, they abused the precept, but not to the extent he made out. He represented these theoretical casuistical puzzles as practice. But at bottom their doctrine was perfectly good and sound. The two sides of the correlation, the act and the spirit of the actor[1], must be

Henry VIII., vol. i. p. 254. See Michelet's admirable *Life of Luther, passim.*

[1] Mr. Herbert Spencer, for example, considers in his *Data of Ethics* only the nature of the act, or conduct ; and neglects entirely the spirit of the actor, which is equally essential.

taken together. If we neglect the former, we fall into the dangerous doctrine of Abelard, that *crime lies in the intention.* If we neglect the latter, we have no virtue, no ethical character: a bad man may be identical with a good one.

And as with virtue, so is it with greatness. Who or what is a great man? He who does great things? But he may do them accidentally. To leave out the spirit is to mistake notoriety for fame. The truly great man is he who does great things greatly. Chance may elevate a small man, who has blurted out some idea, or stumbled upon some course without knowing what he was about, into a great position: but he is not a great man, though he may *per accidens* do great things. The great man is he who does the thing with a full consciousness of what he is about. On the other hand, chance may deny to the really great man his sphere of operations. Walpole, *in esse*, plays a great part, but he was the very reverse of a great man. Bolingbroke, *in posse*, was a great man, but his schemes were shattered by a malignant evil star. Cæsar was great, both *in esse* and *posse*. It is true that the world, which never goes to the bottom of questions, but always judges by success, esteems the *esse* all, and pays no heed to the *posse*. There is just this much of truth in its view, that after all, actuality is more and higher than potentiality. Nevertheless, from the ethical point of view, this is not the case. Here, *posse* is superior to *esse*. And this is the deep ethical significance of the old *victrix causa Deis placuit, sed victa Catoni.* For chance has in many ways the ultimate *arbitrium* in the real world, and can with a dexterous twirl throw

all into confusion : but the capacity of virtue, or
the capacity of genius, is not within the domain
or power of chance. The great and good man
may die on the scaffold, or come to an untimely
end : the mean soul, the scoundrel, may die in the
odour of sanctity, or succeed, and be pointed at by
the finger of those that pass by : none the less,
virtue is virtue still, and genius, genius.

> 'For Loyalty is still the same,
> Whether it win or lose the game :
> True as the dial to the sun
> Although it be not shined upon.'

A Charles I. may perish on the block, and
a Henry VIII. live out his cruel lecherous life
and die a bloated mass of carrion in his bed : Bruno
may burn, and Socrates may drink the hemlock,
while the mediocrities and sneaking toadies of all
ages lie under tombstones recording all their
virtues : but at bottom, there arises in every breast
the deep inexpugnable sentiment that this is
a lie : that success is not the test of merit, and
reward is not the proof of excellence.

And if men had listened to the teaching of
Aristotle they would have seen the solution of the
apparent contradiction existing between the intuitive and the utilitarian school of morality. The
truth is that there is no real contradiction : the two
are complementary sides of the same fact. The
good of a thing, says Aristotle, is that which preserves it. This is its physical organic good. This
therefore must be the *tendency* of all moral action :
its *result :* but this is not the spirit of the moral
actor. That is always altruistic and self-sacrificing.

The essence of morality is both *preserving* and *sacrificing*: preservation of another ; sacrifice of self. Nor is there any contradiction : the two are indeed absurd apart. To leap into a raging flood, or a burning house, to save the life of a man, is a noble act. Why ? Because, first, life is *preserved*, and this is the *utilitarian end* of the act : secondly, life is risked or sacrificed, the leaper thinks not of his own interest, but that of another. This is the *spirit* of the action. But if we remove the utilitarian element, the morality, the nobility, disappears. The actor becomes, not sublime, but ridiculous and foolhardy. To leap into the flood, or the fire, where no life is to be saved, *i.e.* where the utilitarian end is not, is not morality or heroism, but mere folly. And this illustration is a type of all virtuous action. All such action is and must be in result, utilitarian ; in spirit, self-sacrificing. Aristotle is the conciliation of the opposing views which have raged with such indiscriminate violence between opponents incapable of understanding the moral relation in its entirety ; incapable of perceiving the ethical significance of the truth that *each is for the sake of others*, in which aphorism the whole of ethics is enwrapped, and apart from which there is no ground for virtue. If each be, not for others, but for and in himself, virtue disappears, and egoism becomes the only law. But it is not so ; how could it be ? far from it : man is neither God nor beast, but a member of a community. His function makes his structure : and from the very contemplation of that structure we can see that his duties are, and also *what* they are. Will he deny it ? Why, the very denial itself, his capacity of speaking,

communicating, disproves his denial : language
alone proclaims the truth that his essence is not
absolute, not Cartesian ; but correlative, Aristotelian, biological, and moral.

And now for the conclusion of the whole matter.
The State, like its individual members, has a character : and its character too, like that of the individual man, is formed by repeated acts. While it
is young and growing, it may be educated and
guided in the right way. But when it is old, when
it has become 'set,' and acquired once for all its
habit, its formed and ingrained moral character,
then can it no longer escape from itself, its constitution (not political, but ethical), which is its
doom. It must go on as it chose to begin. There
comes a time when all subsequent struggle is un-
availing ; when the spirit of its institutions being
definitely fixed, it must of necessity 'dree its
weird' and move on in its self-elected path. Θέος
ἀναίτιος, αἰτία δ' ἑλομένου. Then, when it was
unformed, chaotic, plastic, it might have been other,
retraced its steps : but now, the chance has gone.
Just as the sick man might, long ago, have been
healed ; but after long perseverance in debauchery
and loose living, uncontrolled indulgence, and dis-
obeying the voice of his physicians, he is past
curing ; so must he lay the blame not upon
external causes, chance, circumstances, but upon
himself, who had not the force to resist temptation,
or the patience to wait, but sank into slavery by
following his passions, and snatching at the fleeting
and imprudent present, rather than fixing his eye
upon the permanent power of action, and the
enduring future.

Thus must it be : the more self-consciousness it acquires, the more does it find itself bound by iron automatic law ;

> ' Y teniendo yo mas alma
> Tengo menos libertad ? '

In vain will the State which has once let itself go, which has lost control over its fortunes by neglecting to preserve its internal authority and its external self-sufficiency and independence, seek to recover its balance. Just because life cannot wait, on it must go, obeying no longer the dictates of prudence, but driven by the inner necessities of its fatal organisation, by the irresistible forces spontaneously generated out of its own complicated operations, goaded along as it were by fiends, down the steep place into the inevitable lake.

APPENDICES.

APPENDIX.

APPENDIX, NO. I.

On the possibility of knowing the actual reality behind the delusive apparent sensible phenomenon.

AN ounce of fact is worth a pound of theory, which is only too often based upon a misinterpretation of the facts. When, therefore, we find a fact or series of facts through which a true theory shines out unmistakably, we should cling to it closer than ivy. So, then, with regard to what is said, on pp. 14—20, as to the fallacies of idealistic or sensational philosophy :—the philosophy which maintains that '*we know only appearances, never things in themselves,*' or that '*we know only our sensations,*' and denies the possibility of knowledge of what realities are, or even that they are, when not being perceived :—I fell on a passage in Mark Twain's *Life on the Mississippi* which exposes the quibble so admirably that I feel sure the reader will be much obliged to me for recalling it to his attention. And by the way, it is worthy of remark, how many philosophical fallacies arise and are perpetuated by means of fallacious and question-begging illustrations, and instances that are not typical, but specially suited to disguise the pitfalls.

Here is the passage :—

' By and by Mr. Bixby said—

' My boy, you've got to know the *shape* of the river per-
' fectly. It is all there is left to steer by on a very dark night.
' Everything else is blotted out and gone. But mind you, it
' hasn't the same shape in the night that it has in the day-
' time.'

' How on earth am I ever going to learn it, then ? '

' How do you follow a hall at home in the dark ? Because
' you know the shape of it. You can't see it.'

' Do you mean to say that I've got to know all the million
' trifling variations of shape in the banks of this interminable
' river as well as I know the shape of the front hall at home ? '

' On my honour, you've got to know them *better* than any man
' ever did know the shape of the front hall of his house.'

' I wish I was dead.'

' Now, I don't want to discourage you, but — '

' Well, pile it on me; I might as well have it now as another time.'

' You see, this has got to be learned ; there isn't any getting ' around it. A clear starlight night throws such heavy shadows ' that if you didn't know the shape of a shore perfectly you ' would claw away from every bunch of timber, because you ' would take the black shadow of it for a solid cape; and you ' see you would be getting scared to death every fifteen minutes ' by the watch. You would be fifty yards from shore all the ' time when you ought to be within fifty feet of it. You can't ' *see* a snag in one of those shadows, but you *know* exactly ' where it is, and the shape of the river tells you when you are ' coming to it. Then there's your pitch-dark night ; the river is ' a very different shape on a pitch-dark night from what it is on ' a starlight night. All shores *seem* to be straight lines, then, ' and mighty dim ones, too; and you'd *run* them for straight ' lines, only you *know* better. You boldly drive your boat right ' into what *seems* to be a solid, straight wall (you *knowing* very ' well that in reality there is a curve there) and that wall falls ' back and makes way for you. Then there's your gray mists. ' You take a night when there's any one of these grisly, drizzly, ' gray mists, and then there isn't *any* particular shape to a ' shore. A gray mist would tangle the head of the oldest man ' that ever lived. Well, then, different kinds of *moonlight* change ' the shape of the river in different ways. You see —— '

' Oh, don't say any more, please. Have I got to learn the ' shape of the river according to all these five hundred thousand ' different ways? If I tried to carry all that cargo in my head ' it would make me stoop-shouldered.'

' *No!* you only learn *the* shape of the river ; and you learn it ' with such absolute certainty that you can always steer, by the ' shape that's *in your head*, and never mind the one that's before ' your eyes.'—*Life on the Mississippi*, p. 36.

This passage, now, is so accurately in point, that it might have been written expressly for the purpose ; and yet, on the other hand, the value of its evidence lies just in the fact that it was written by a man who was not dreaming of anything that it might or might not possibly prove. It is an exact and complete refutation of the idealist, be he Berkeley, Hume, Kant,

Mill, or any other of the tribe. ' *We know only our sensations ;* ' *only appearances, never things in themselves ; we cannot know* ' *what lies behind the phenomenon.*' Why, my dear Sir, we can imagine one of these Mississippi pilots saying to our idealist, it is obvious that you never went up the Mississippi : on all nights, and three days out of six, that *is* exactly as it does not *seem* to be : it *seems* to be exactly as it *is not ;*—and we *know* what it really is, the constant reality amid the changing phantasmagoria of sense. In fact, the reader who will reflect upon this illustration will readily perceive the quibble, the play upon the meaning of ' *things in themselves.*' ' *We know only appearances, never things in themselves :*' this thesis is, in one sense, undeniable ; an obvious and silly truism : in another, the only valuable, sense, it is not only not true, but a palpable sophism. There is a sense in which a thing *is* just what it seems to be, and another, in which it *is not* what it seems to be ;—by confounding the two, Kant's *dictum* appears to be very deep, while in reality it is either absurd or a mere truism. Mirage, *quâ* mirage, is just what it seems to be ; regarded, on the other hand, as indicative of other things that look just the same, it is a delusion ; but this, instead of proving that we *can not* know the reality behind the phenomenon, proves just the opposite, that we *can :* for we distinguish between the appearances. Just so, certain insects are so exactly like leaves or sticks that it is impossible, by contemplation at a little distance, to know which is which : nevertheless, the deception lies, not in our perception, but its interpretation. The insect *is* exactly what it seems to be ; it only becomes a deception when we infer it to be another thing which looks the same ; something other than it is. Two things can perfectly well be identical, *quâ* their perceptibility, and entirely different, *quâ* everything else. All this is quite simple and straightforward. But who in the world, even if Kant had never been born, would ever have supposed that we could know, otherwise than as we know : that we could have a knowledge which should not be knowledge? If Kant means merely that things, in order to be known, must *appear* before us ; that we cannot know them, when and if they do not *present* themselves ; that knowledge is essentially, *quâ* knowledge, based upon a relation between perceived object and percipient subject ;—where, forsooth, is the discovery? Who in the wide world did not know that? But if, on the other hand, he means,

that we cannot have a knowledge beyond and behind appearances ; that we can never know what things are 'in themselves,'
i.e. irrespective of perception, or place ourselves in a position
which renders us scientifically superior to appearances, and
enables us to disregard them, because we know their nature,
in spite of the lying phantom which would otherwise deceive
us :—if this is what he means, then I say that he is talking sad
stuff, and the passage I have quoted above decisively proves it.
What, indeed, differentiates the master in any art or science
from the tyro, but the fact that one *knows*, the other only *supposes* or *conjectures*,—the one has penetrated to the reality, the
other judges by appearances ? As Mark Twain says himself,
à propos of the same subject : ' Nothing short of perfection will
' do for a pilot. He cannot stop with merely *thinking* a thing is
' so and so, he must *know* it : for this is eminently one of the
' exact sciences. With what scorn a-pilot was looked upon in
' the old times, if he ever ventured to deal in that feeble phrase,
' " I think," instead of the vigorous one " I know," ' (p. 59).

Just so have the 'feeble thinkers' of modern philosophy,
relying on vicious hypotheses, ambiguous terms, and a radically
false and clumsy psychology that confounds essential distinctions,
sold their Aristotelian birthright for a chaotic mess of Cartesian
pottage.

The truth is that here, as always, the want of method is the
cause of error. The critical analysis of normal and healthy perception is the only starting-point of sound philosophy: the
analysis of concrete reality, which resolves the complex into its
elements ; but does *not* start with the elements, and dogmatically
pronounce *a priori* upon the complex. *Sensation* is one thing,
Perception another, *Scientific Knowledge* a third. There is more
in *Perception* than there is in *Sensation ;* more in *Scientific Knowledge* than there is in *Perception.* The radical error of modern
rationalistic psychology is, that it assumes Sensation to be the
origin and whole content of Knowledge. It ignores facts ; and
because it does not understand how *Perception* takes place,
it confounds it with *Sensation.* The two, however, are entirely
distinct. Scientific Knowledge does *not* start from Sensation,
but from Perception. Sensation is merely the consciousness
of an organic affection which tells us nothing but itself; it is
mere feeling : there is no element of objectivity in it. Knowledge begins with Perception, which, exactly the opposite of

Sensation, gives us ulterior information about the Sensation
which accompanies it, information which is something totally
different in kind from that Sensation. A dull organic feeling of
illness is an instance of Sensation; in a stomach-ache, Perception has begun, for we can to some slight extent locate the
feeling: in sight—as, for instance, the contemplation of Picca-
dilly Circus from the top of an omnibus—Perception rises to
its highest point.

No critical philosophy which ignores facts is worth the paper
it is printed on: of what value, then, are the lucubrations of the
idealistic or sensational schools, which to suit their theory lump
together Sensation and Perception, pay no attention to the latter,
and make Scientific Knowledge start from the former? The
truth is, that only from an Aristotelian and evolutionary point
of view is it possible to arrive at psychological truth. The
Cartesians, Berkleians, Humists, Kantians and Millites are
all statical and unevolutionary. They all attempt to identify the
last result of æons of evolution with the first dawn of consciousness: they all dogmatise upon *Knowledge* from their initial
assumption of *Sensation*, instead of analysing Knowledge and
its content as we have it, to find out what it contains, and going
backwards. Hence, starting from *Sensation*, it is impossible for
them ever to arrive at or explain *Knowledge*, for their premises
do not contain it. The evolutionary psychologist reverses all
this. However he may seek to explain *Knowledge* and *Perception*, he does not make the mistake of *denying the fact, because he
does not understand how it is done.* He does not fall into the
error of denying the complex, because it cannot be deduced
from some of its elements which do not contain it. He knows
that the fact that we are here, alive, proves that our Knowledge
and Perception are accurately responsive to the truth of things:
that our Perception is necessarily trustworthy, being the result
of untold millions of years of education and correction,—the
penalty of error being death: and that therefore it is the vainest
puerility to attempt to solve the mystery of Knowledge or
Perception with a superficial quibble based on the observation
of one or two men; it is only to be solved, not from the
individual, but the race; not from man, but all the long series
of lower forms out of which he has arisen. To attempt to
dogmatise on the *rationale* of Sight from one or two diseased
cases in an ophthalmic hospital; to attempt to understand

or explain Vision, beginning with the man when he is born, and
forgetting that he comes equipped with the inherited capacities
of incalculable ages of practise—is merely a mark of the utter
mental incapacity of the attempter, and a proof of his absolute
lack of appreciation of the problem. And the whole of
rationalistic psychology from Descartes to the last expounder
of the Kantian philosophy may be thrown with profit into the
fire, since its method of procedure is just this.

For the mere fact that we are here, proves beyond possibility
of refutation, that our normal and healthy perception of things
is true. Had it not been so, we should have disappeared long
ago. We cannot explain, we have not the dimmest idea,—and
no one ever had or will have—*how we perceive*. But the fact
remains. Perception is a relation between ourselves and its
object, giving us what we call an immediate intuitive knowledge
of that object (Scientific Knowledge differs from intuitive only
in its *chain* or *connection*); that is the fact; and no one will ever
succeed in explaining, still less in refuting it, by puerile rationalistic quibbles. We are *inside* the relation; we form one term
of it: nor will any one ever succeed in understanding how
it is done, in the abstract, just because he can never get outside
himself. Perception can only be understood by its exercise.
*That it shows us things as they really are is proved by the fact that
action or existence would be impossible, if it were not so. But they
are not impossible; they are actual; ergo, perception tells us the
truth of things. Were Perception false, we could not exist for five
minutes: we could do nothing:* LIFE IS POSSIBLE ONLY IF PER-
CEPTION IS TRUE. It is, however, quite wrong to call its teaching *inference*. This is an abuse of language. Inference is
a comparatively tardy, conscious, fallible drawing of conclusions
from preliminary knowledge: to call the automatic, spontaneous,
unconscious, inevitable and immediate, instantaneous, dictatorial
and necessary evidence of Perception, *inference*, disguises the
fact that the one is deep and real, the other shallow and rational;
the one is dictated by the necessities of things and reposes on
the accumulated verifications of whole geological epochs, the
other is simply the superficial process of one mind which as
often as not goes astray. In short, inference is merely logical,
rational, we might almost say exclusively human: whereas perception is vital, universal, the indispensable weapon and means
of self-preservation in every creature that lives and moves.

The only part of Kant's Transcendental Æsthetic which is true is a truism, and was clearly pointed out by Aristotle, out of whom comes all that modern philosophy has said worth saying. It is obvious that we cannot know *things-in-themselves*, and the world knew it and would have known it if Kant had never been born. As Aristotle says, when we are perceiving *e.g.* a tree, it is actually visible; when we are not perceiving it, it is potentially visible. Of course we cannot perceive the *thing-in-itself*—the *potentially visible*, because, in the act of vision, it becomes *actually visible*. We cannot perceive it, when it is not being perceived. There is also, in Kant's much overrated *dictum*, a reminiscence of Aristotle's remark, that matter is ἀγνωστὸς καθ' αὑτήν—matter is necessarily unknown, as it is in itself. But Kant has spoiled the profound *aperçu* of Aristotle by transferring it from its context, and confounding *matter* with *material objects*. And if we wished to imitate Kant, and put forth *Prolegomena to All Future Systems of Philosophy*, they would be contained in one line : *No philosophy is worth printing, which has not mastered the essential distinction between Sensation and Perception.*

APPENDIX, NO. II.

Note on the Bank Charter Act of 1844.

ACCORDING to Lord Beaconsfield, more people have been driven mad by the 'Currency Question' than even by the passion of love. And if this epigram is not without some justification, why is it so? Simply because the votaries of the Currency Question have had no method in their madness. It is true, that the question is one of the most intricate, and therefore the most difficult, that can be proposed. But this is not the true cause of the peculiar perplexity of this matter. Difficult it would always be, but it has been rendered unnaturally so, nay, insoluble, by the false theoretic dogmas with which everybody starts in the endeavour to unravel the mystery. No question however simple can be solved, if the principles on which the solution depends are directly opposed to the truth. Who could solve a mathematical problem, on the assumption that twice six were thirteen? Yet this is exactly what has been done here. Nothing can be more incomprehensible than the Bank Charter Act, approached from the point of view of theories that are palpably absurd : whereas in reality, when we closely investigate *the way in which its authors came to hold it*, and the cardinal assumptions on which it rests, its ludicrous fallacy emerges of itself into the clear light of day. And I take this opportunity of exposing it, because I have never met with any book dealing with the question in such a way as really lays bare the heart of the matter.

The primary object of the Bank Charter Act was to restrict the excessive issue, or 'over-issue,' of Bank Notes. Why? Because its author held the currency to be depreciated, owing to their excessive quantity; owing to a '*redundancy of currency.*' But what led them to suppose that this was the case? The drain, or export of gold, from this country to foreign parts. And why, again, did they suppose that this drain indicated a depreciation of the currency? Because Ricardo, Lord Overstone, and their disciples laid it down, that a drain of gold was an infallible sign of a depreciated currency : or in other words, that the only cause of a drain of gold was a depreciation of the currency.

I shall show presently that this opinion is a delusion, and stands in glaring contradiction to the most commonplace facts. But *how came they to hold it*? That is the really important thing; for a fallacy is not fully refuted till its psychological genesis is clearly explained.

Ricardo's fundamental financial dogma was this, that *commodities are purchased with commodities*. Buying and selling he identified with barter; or, as Lord Overstone put it, 'the normal 'and legitimate condition of trade is barter.' (It is, of course, nothing of the kind; the introduction of money is the abolition of barter, but let that pass.) Hence, the Ricardian dogma for International Trade was, that one nation buys the commodities of another nation with its own : *pays for commodities imported with commodities exported.* Now, obviously, the man who has to pay, will pay as little as he can. Hence Ricardo maintained, that *no nation would ever pay money*—send gold out of the country in payment for commodities—*unless* it was the cheapest commodity to send. But he said, that it never would be the cheapest commodity to send, unless the currency was depreciated; and as the coin was all right, this could only be due to an excessive issue of notes. From this it follows directly, that people only send gold out of the country, owing to a depreciated currency, a '*redundancy* of currency :' or in other words, whenever gold is observed to be leaving the country, the currency *must* be depreciated. It was to put a stop to this state of things that the Bank Charter Act was framed.

Now, parenthetically, nothing can be, according to our temper, more amusing, or more exasperating, than to see how, in their wilful and obstinate adherence to their preposterous dogma, these masters of financial legislation shut their eyes to facts that stare them in the face. Out of innumerable instances of this disposition, I shall content myself with one, but it is final. Of course, if there are *any other* causes of a drain of gold than the depreciation of the currency, the whole theory falls to the ground; for then it does not follow, because gold is leaving the country, that the currency *must* be depreciated. Accordingly, Lord Overstone was directly asked, by one of the Committee that sat upon the question in 1848, whether he was aware that the gold had gone to America, from which we had just then imported an abnormal quantity of wheat : *i.e.* whether the export of gold was not sufficiently explained by the extraordinary import of wheat.

And here is his Lordship's reply. '*I do not know, I do not know*' '*at all, where the gold goes to. If it goes, that is all I ever attend*' '*to.*' Is it conceivable? He actually confesses, not only without a blush, but even without a suspicion that anything is wrong, that he *never pays the slightest attention to the facts on which the settlement of the question essentially depends.* And this astounding person is a great financial expert! Why, how can we wonder that the Currency Question should be difficult of solution, when its 'authorities' are literally not ashamed to write themselves down like this?

The truth is, that the whole theory is a total delusion. The Theory of International Trade, on which foundation the Bank Charter Act reposes, is a pure absurdity. So far from it being true that a country *pays for commodities with commodities*, the exact converse is the case; a country *never* pays for commodities with commodities. The foreign trade of any country is simply the sum total of all its individual operations; and simple as it may appear, the truth which is completely overlooked by these superlative economists is just this, that people pay for commodities, *not* with commodities, but with money, which is not a commodity. It is perfectly true, that owing to the system of Bills of Exchange, and methods of cancelling what is common, that portion of a country's exports which balances the value of the imports may be regarded, *in result*, as paying for them. But though the *result* is the same, the *rationale* is totally different. The thing is *not* barter: it takes place through, and depends essentially on, money. People have not, as Ricardo asserted that they had, a *choice* in the matter. They cannot do, what he said they could do—pay in any commodity they choose, so that '*money is only sent when it is the cheapest*' '*exportable commodity.*' They must pay money, or by Bills of Exchange, which are a method of doing the same. If they cannot buy a Bill of Exchange, they must send money: they cannot send anything else that they choose. As if, forsooth, a man who owed a thousand pounds could send soap or candles! Further, on the theory that *commodities are paid for with commodities*, imports and exports ought exactly to balance one another. But as a matter of fact, they do not do so. Why, for example, are England's imports so enormously in excess of her exports? It is really heartrending to see the desperate shifts to which economists resort in their endeavours to solve this

mystery. I have heard people discussing the point, on economical premises, for hours, in a way that positively draws tears
to the eyes. And what, then, is the solution? Simply, that a
country (i.e. all the individuals engaged in mercantile pursuits in
that country) pays for its imports *in money:* not merely some,
but all : but its exports, owing to the cancelling agency of Bills
of Exchange and similar Credit Instruments, balance the imports up to the common point, where their value coincides : the
difference, of course, on whichever side it lies, cannot cancel,
and therefore must be directly discharged in bullion : *i.e.* bullion
must leave the country, NOT because the currency is depreciated,
but because debts must be paid. Hence, only a nation very
rich, in a pecuniary sense,—a nation, for example, that is the
great loan-monger of the world,— can buy more than she sells ;
i.e. by her imports exceeding her exports : whereas a very poor
nation, like a very poor man, cannot buy, if it has no money ; it
must produce commodities and exchange them for money. But
what, after this, becomes of the Ricardian dogma? Mark how
Ricardo puts the case : ' *we should not,*' he says, ' *import more*
' *goods than we export, unless we had a redundancy of currency ;*
' *which it therefore suits us to make part of our exports. The*
' *exportation of coin is caused by its cheapness, &c.*' *A redundancy*
of currency ! When a man has ten thousand a year over and
above his expenses, which he meets by producing; ten thousand
with which he can buy luxuries of all kinds, up comes Ricardo
and tells him his currency is *redundant*, and the best thing for
him to do is to *minimise it :* the poorer he grows, the better off,
says Ricardo, he will be. Why, was there ever such a miracle
of analytical acumen as Ricardo in any other age or country ?
A redundancy of currency, forsooth ! yes, there is a redundancy, but it is a redundancy of rubbish in Ricardian economics.
How that ever acquired ' currency ' is a mystery compared with
which the Currency Question is child's play.

And when, now, we realise the portentous absurdity of the
assumption on which the Bank Charter Act is founded, viz.
that *a drain of gold infallibly indicates a depreciation or redundancy of currency, and can arise from nothing else*, we are in
a position to understand it. We see, first, that the Bank
Charter Act was designed to cure an evil that never existed ;
and we see, secondly, that it is itself the cause of disasters that
without it would never arise. In times when Credit is good,

the Bank Act is useless; it is just as though it never existed; it exercises no restraints on commercial speculation, because people can buy commodities on Credit, whether they have Bank Notes or not. On the other hand, as soon as gold is observed leaving the country, the Bank Charter Act immediately tends to produce a panic. Because everybody knows that when the gold goes away, the Bank Charter Act compels notes to go too, and hence, as it goes away, the total amount of currency is reduced. This of itself gives a shock to confidence, because it is known that, should a panic occur, money, which is required when Credit collapses, and whose function notes will perform just as well as coin, will not be forthcoming. Thus the rate of interest rises, and that very drain of gold, which nobody would care two straws for, except for the Bank Charter Act, is turned by the Act into the initial cause of a panic that may, and often does, cause ruin to thousands of deserving persons and houses, whose progress is only arrested by the suspension of the Act.

The core of all these miserable sophistries is the Ricardian dogma that *money is a commodity:* a dogma analysed and exposed in my *Principle of Wealth Creation*, in my *Corner in Gold*, and in this book. Nor until the world will revise its cardinal economic assumptions, and throw Ricardo and all his inexpressible commentators into the fire, can it expect the Currency Question to be finally laid in its grave. Till that time, it will haunt us, bringing panic and disaster in its train, and, vampire like, feeding on the corpses of sound commercial houses. The day will come when we shall awake as from a horrid nightmare, induced by the indigestible nostrums of Ricardo, Lord Overstone, and Sir Robert Peel. Time will teach us to appreciate these economic doctors: as Lord Overstone himself said of Peel—and his Lordship's literary style is no less worthy of our admiration than his unique scientific methods—' *Sir Robert Peel had never been properly appreciated:* ' *but year by year the character of that man upon this subject will* ' *be appreciated.*' I will answer for it, that the prophecy of his Lordship was as accurate as it was unintentional and beautifully expressed.

And now, lastly, some one may ask, Why, if the Ricardian dogma, on which the whole thing hangs, is such nonsense, has it been accepted so long by the world? A most legitimate and pertinent query! There are two reasons why. In the first place, not one man in a thousand either knows or cares to know anything about Political Economy; partly because it is suspected, not without reason, of being a mere mass of theoretic absurdity: and here too the old maxim holds good, that *parmi les aveugles, borgne est roi.* And in the next place, the policy of *minimising the currency*, of which the Bank Charter Act is but a special case, plays directly into the hands of the most powerful interest in the world—the financial interest. Those who actually control the currency have the best of all possible reasons for applauding and maintaining any system, theoretic or legislative, which tends artificially to enhance the value of their ' commodity.' As our authority, Lord Overstone, said, once again, ' Sir Robert Peel's Acts of 1819 and 1844 obtained ample and ' efficient security that that *honest* foundation of our monetary ' system shall be effectually and permanently maintained ; and ' no inscription can be written upon his statue so honourable, as ' that he restored *our* money to its just value in 1819, and ' secured for us the means of maintaining that just value in 1844. ' Honour be to his name !' Lord Overstone appears, in this passage, to have been almost choking with financial emotion and hysterical gratitude to the man who had raised the value of his money : it needed only this, to make the grotesque amalgam of economic charlatanry and financial chicanery complete.

APPENDIX NO. III.

A Bird's-eye Review of the Substance of the Method.

IN order to assist the reader to grasp the exact purport of this book, I will here present a brief epitome of its inner tendency and essential economic upshot.

The whole essay is devoted to the working out in all directions of a single central idea, arrived at by the Analytic or Organic Method. This method, instead of attempting to deduce economic truths mathematically from abstract assumptions or 'laws,' plunges into the concrete complexity of things as they are, and argues analytically backward, contemplating every fact in its own peculiar constituent relations, *abstracted from which it does not and cannot exist.* It discovers principles by dissecting a particular specimen embodying those principles. Proceeding in this way, *pedetentim progredientes*, we discover the law, the universal law of all organic structure, to be this : that every structure is made what it is by its own action, or its function : briefly, that FUNCTION MAKES STRUCTURE.

I. *The first fundamental fallacy of all previous economic speculation is just this : that it has attempted to deduce structure, somehow or other, always unsuccessfully, from its* ELEMENTS, *instead of from its* FUNCTION.

Next, carefully examining structures in their totality, we find that there are four great kinds or classes of structure, viz. the *Species*, the *Commodity*, the *Work of Art*, the *Commonwealth ;* forming respectively the central conceptions of *Natural Economy*, *Political Economy* (or the *Science of Wealth*), *Æsthetics*, and *Ethics and Politics*. The universal principle, that Function makes Structure, appears differently clothed, manifests itself differently, in each sphere, owing to the essential difference of the functions of each central structure. For, as the laws of every structure, or as we might say, its *duties*, are derived from its function, where the functions differ, so must the laws. Therefore, *the laws of one kind of structure are not the laws of another*, as Aristotle saw and said long ago (οὐκ ἐστίν ἐξ ἄλλου γένους μεταβάντα δεῖξαι). The Work of Art cannot be subjected to the laws of the Commodity, nor the Commonwealth to the laws of the Species, without ceasing to be what it is; losing its essence in exact proportion to the degree in which it loses sight of its own peculiar laws.

II. *The second fundamental fallacy, then, of previous economic speculation is just this; that it wrongly and wilfully seeks to subordinate* ALL *kinds of structure to the* SAME *laws; which are either the laws of only one kind of structure, or else the laws of no kind of structure at all; and thus degrades or annihilates the various kinds.* Just so, for example, the Socialists would annihilate Wealth, the Commodity, by negating its laws, of which they are entirely ignorant.

And all this has come about, for want of training in the analytic method (δι' ἀπαιδευσίαν τῶν ἀναλυτικῶν) and consequent inability to distinguish between things that are distinct.

To give a single example, by neglecting the Commonwealth, and starting from the Individual, or in other words, by turning the individual from a member of a *Commonwealth* into a specimen of the *Species,* all his *obligations* or *duties* disappear, and morality is annihilated.

INDEX.

Monstrosities, significance of, 75, 95.
Moral action, analysed, 440.
Music, the function of, 331 *sqq.*: of the Spheres, 334.
Mysticism, social, 428 *sqq.*
Mythology, Aristotle and, 426.

Natural Selection, incompetent to explain the origin of species, 79 *sqq.*
Nature, what Aristotle meant by, 56 *n.*
Necessity, the two kinds of, material or absolute, and organic or conditional, 40, 48, 146, and *passim:* in history, 345: not contradictory of freedom, 286.
Newtonian theory, the, fatal to idealism, 18.
Nihilism, moral and political, origin of, 12, 23, 380.

Organic structure, the law of, 1, 40, 144 and *passim.*
Origin of Species, criticism of Darwin's, 79 *sqq.*: probable, 140.
Ornament, the artistic function of, 291.
Orthodox Political Economy, Philistinism of, 254: errors of, *see* Appendix III.

Painting, the function of, 307 *sqq.*
Perception, the basis of scientific knowledge, *see* Appendix I.
Political institutions, not rationally explicable, 420, 397.
Politics, the biological basis of, 391 *sqq.*: the errors of rationalistic, 377 *sqq.*
Potentiality, Darwin's variation corresponds to Aristotle's, 69.
Production, conditioned by action, 168: cost of, *see* Cost.
Protestantism, an antisocial religion, 434.

Rationalistic politics, errors of, 377 *sqq.*
Realism, in art, 320: in politics, 348: in literature, 368, 430, and *passim.*
Redundancy of Currency, *see* Appendix II.
Ricardian theory of value, refutation of, 173.
Ricardo, financial theories of, *see* Appendix II.
Roman Catholic Church, function of, 434.
Ruskin, critical error of, 282.

Schopenhauer, 13, 382.
Scholasticism, error of, 8.
Sculpture, the function of, 300 *sqq.*
Sensation, not the foundation of knowledge, *see* Appendix I.
Size, the problem of, 120.
Social Contract, Hobbes', 386.
Socialism, economic error of, 238.
Soul, Aristotle's definition of the, 41, 72, and *passim.*
Species, definition of a, 97: Origin of, criticised, 79 *sqq.*
State, definition of a, 395: has no theoretic existence, 420.
Structure, the law of organic, *see* Organic.

Teleology, in Darwin, 124: misunderstood, 76: the true meaning of, 40, 130, and *passim.*
Theory, inutility of political, 420.

H h

Printed by James Parker and Co., Crown Yard, Oxford.

By the same Author.

OCCAM'S RAZOR: THE APPLICATION OF A PRINCIPLE: TO POLITICAL ECONOMY: TO THE CONDITIONS OF PROGRESS: TO SOCIALISM: TO POLITICS. Crown 8vo., cloth, 179 pp., price 4s. 6d.

ANTICHRIST, A Short Examination of the Spirit of the Age. Crown 8vo., cloth, 252 pp., price 5s.

THE PRINCIPLE OF WEALTH CREATION: its Nature, Origin, Evolution, and Corollaries: being a Critical Reconstruction of Scientific Political Economy. Medium 8vo., cloth, 256 pp., price 10s. 6d.

THE CORNER IN GOLD: its History and Theory: being a Reply to Mr. Robert Giffen's 'Case against Bimettalism.' Fcap. 8vo., cloth, price 2s. 6d.

JAMES PARKER & Co., OXFORD AND LONDON.

DMITRI: A Tragi-Comedy. Cr. 8vo., cloth, 276 pp., price 6s.

TREACHERY: A Spanish Romance. Cr. 8vo., cloth, 280 pp., price 6s.

RIVINGTON, PERCIVAL & CO., LONDON.

CHRISTINA, Queen of Sweden. Cr. 8vo., cloth, 382 pp., price 7s. 6d.

W. H. ALLEN & CO., LONDON.